THE ODYSSEY OF HOMER

THE ODYSSEY

OF HOMER

Translated
with an introduction
by
RICHMOND
LATTIMORE

Harper & Row, Publishers
New York, Hagerstown, San Francisco, London

To Royal Nemiah

CONTENTS

CONTENTS

CONTENTS

CONTENTS

INTRODUCTION

THE OUTLINE OF THE ODYSSEY

The Odyssey as we have it is an epic of over twelve thousand lines. It has been divided, like the *Iliad* and probably at the same time, into twenty-four books. Book number and line number are the standard terms of reference.

The contents can be, very broadly, divided as follows:

> The Telemachy or Adventures of Telemachos, i–iv
> The Homecoming of Odysseus, v–viii and xiii.1–187
> The Great Wanderings, ix–xii
> Odysseus on Ithaka, xiii.187–xxiv.548.

We can also distinguish a Proem, Book i.1–10, and an End of the *Odyssey*, all of Book xxiv. This division is for convenience; it is arbitrary and not water-tight, but gives us terms to work with.[1]

I begin by summarizing the bare facts of the story. Odysseus spent ten years fighting at Troy, and another ten years getting home. During this time, none of his family knew what had happened to him, and he lost all his ships, all his men, and the spoils from Troy. After ten years, or in the tenth year, he was set down in his own country, alone and secretly, though with a new set of possessions, by the Phaiakians of Scheria, who were the last people he visited on his wanderings.

INTRODUCTION

When he took ship for Troy, Odysseus left behind his wife, Penelope, and his infant son, Telemachos. A few years before his return, the young bachelors of Odysseus' kingdom, Ithaka and the surrounding islands, began paying court to Penelope (ii.89–90). She was accomplished and clever, still beautiful, an heiress and presumably a widow; but she clung to the hope that Odysseus might come back, and held them off, without ever saying positively that she would never marry again.

The suitors made themselves at home as uninvited guests in the palace of Odysseus. Shortly before the return of Odysseus, Telemachos visited the mainland in search of news about his father. He heard from Menelaos that Odysseus was alive but detained without means of return on the island of Kalypso (iv.555–560). Telemachos returned to Ithaka. The suitors set an ambush, meaning to murder him, but he eluded them and reached Ithaka just after his father arrived.

The voyage of Telemachos, the arrival of Odysseus, and the recognition and reunion of father and son, were all supervised by Athene.

Father and son plotted the destruction of the suitors. Odysseus entered his own house unrecognized, mingled with the suitors and talked with Penelope. He and Telemachos contrived to catch them unarmed and with the help of two loyal serving men (and of course Athene) they slaughtered all 108 suitors. Penelope knew nothing of the plot; Odysseus revealed himself to her after the fighting was over. The relatives of the dead suitors attacked the heroes on the farm of Laertes, father of Odysseus, and a battle began, but it was ended by Zeus and Athene, who patched up a hasty reconciliation.

THE TELEMACHY

The *Odyssey*, like the *Iliad*, begins in the tenth year of the story's chief action, with events nearing their climax and final solution. We begin with a very rapid location of Odysseus in place, time, and stage in his career, but then (via the councils of the gods concerning his immediate fate) pass to Telemachos, with Athene's visit which sends him off on his journey. It is only after Telemachos has begun his visit in Sparta, and heard from Menelaos that his father is alive, and after the suitors have set their trap, that we return directly to Odysseus himself. We then follow Odysseus for the rest of the *Odyssey*. The poet now tells us of Odysseus' journey to Scheria and his sojourn there; and he makes Odysseus himself recount to the Phaiakians his previous wanderings (The Great Wanderings).

INTRODUCTION

They then convey him to Ithaka, and with his homecoming the tale of the wanderings of Odysseus joins on to the tale of Odysseus on Ithaka.

Thus in two respects the narrative order of the poem disagrees with the chronological order of the story. The early and chief wanderings of Odysseus are told by throwback narrative toward the middle of the poem; and the wanderings of Telemachos come first.

The joins or transitions from theme to theme are noteworthy. After the poet has located Odysseus in time and space, the gods consider the question. Athene urges the homecoming of Odysseus. Zeus proclaims that Athene shall have her way; Odysseus may now start for home. Athene answers (i.81–95)

> *Son of Kronos, our father, O lordliest of the mighty,*
> *if in truth this is pleasing to the blessed immortals,*
> *that Odysseus of the many designs shall return home, then*
> *let us dispatch Hermes, the guide, the slayer of Argos,*
> *to the island of Ogygia, so that with all speed*
> *he may announce to the lovely-haired nymph our absolute purpose,*
> *the homecoming of enduring Odysseus, that he shall come back.*
> *But I shall make my way to Ithaka, so that I may stir up*
> *his son a little, and put some confidence in him*
> *to summon into assembly the flowing-haired Achaians,*
> *and make a statement to all the suitors, who now forever*
> *slaughter his crowding sheep and lumbering horn-curved cattle;*
> *and I will convey him into Sparta and to sandy Pylos*
> *to ask after his dear father's homecoming, if he can hear something,*
> *and so that among people he may win a good reputation.*

This excellently motivates the Telemachy but it does perforce leave Odysseus stranded, and after the major part of the Telemachy, at the opening of Book v, the return to Odysseus shows more strain than the departure from him did. Athene has been to Ithaka, and to Pylos with Telemachos. She left the court of Nestor, presumably for Olympos (iii.371). Now she has to start all over again, almost as if the case of Odysseus had never come up, to complain of his sorrows; but ends with the perils of Telemachos; and Zeus seems to have to remind her that she herself planned everything that has just been happening (v.23). Hermes, who has been waiting for this for four books and five days, can at last get off (i.84; v.28) and the wanderings of Odysseus may be resumed.

The obviousness of the joins and the bulk of material not specifically related to Odysseus in Books iii–iv, his absence from Books i–ii, have

INTRODUCTION

suggested that the Telemachy was an independent poem which was, at some stage, incorporated more or less whole in the *Odyssey*.[2] This may be true, and there is no way to prove that it is not true. But it is also possible that the poet (or poets)[3] of the *Odyssey*, in the form in which we have it, deliberately developed this diversion, never meaning to take up Odysseus until he had first established Telemachos; that he so much desired to do this that he was willing to accept the necessary awkwardnesses of narrative joining in which it would involve him.

Why so? Let us consider the effects gained for the total poem from having the Telemachy with its present contents in its present place.

Odysseus in the *Iliad* was a great man, but his magnitude is increased by the flattering mentions of him by Nestor (iii.120–123), Menelaos (iv.333–346), and Athene herself (i.255–256 with 265–266). It is increased still more by the evident need for him felt by his family and friends, concisely stated by Athene (i.253–254): "How great your need is now of the absent Odysseus," and everywhere apparent.

Through Nestor and Menelaos, also, the *Odyssey* is secured in its place among the *Nostoi*,[4] the homecomings of the Achaians. The general character of the *Nostoi* is succinctly stated by Nestor (iii.130–135)

> *But after we had sacked the sheer citadel of Priam,*
> *and were going away in our ships, and the god scattered the Achaians,*
> *then Zeus in his mind devised a sorry homecoming*
> *for the Argives, since not all were considerate and righteous;*
> *therefore many of them found a bad way home, because of*
> *the ruinous anger of the Gray-eyed One, whose father is mighty.*

The sufferings of two great heroes, by long wandering away from home (Menelaos) and by treachery and disaster on arrival (Agamemnon), both well point up the case of Odysseus in two of its different aspects. For an audience well versed in the tale of Troy, or the *Iliad*, interest is added in a second viewing of some old favorites: Nestor, Helen, Menelaos, all very like themselves in the *Iliad*. Without planning some such excursus as the Telemachy, the poet could not have worked them in without a great deal more awkwardness than it has, in fact, cost him.

Another point gained through the Telemachy is the instigation to murder.

For Odysseus must end by murdering Penelope's suitors. So, it appears, the story demanded. Further, the story demanded, or the poet firmly in-

INTRODUCTION

tended, that Telemachos should assist his father in this business. The suitors are a bad lot and they have put themselves in the wrong, but we cannot assume that Homer's audience was so inured to bloodshed that they could take this altogether lightly (modern readers mostly cannot). In any case, there are numerous passages in the Telemachy which look as if they might be designed, which do in any case serve, to shore up the consciences of the avenging heroes and of their sympathizers in the story or in the audience.

Aigisthos seduced Agamemnon's wife while he was gone at Troy and murdered him on his return. Orestes murdered his father's murderer. The case may not seem quite parallel to the situation of the *Odyssey*, but Agamemnon's ghost used his story as a warning against the wife's-suitor danger (xi.441–446; 454–456); and when Athene tells Odysseus about Penelope and her suitors he immediately thinks of Agamemnon (xiii.383–385). Orestes' act seems to be taken as a precedent justifying murder when it means putting one's house in order. It is mentioned with approval by Zeus (i.35–43), and Athene specifically holds up Orestes as an example to Telemachos (i.298–300). Nestor tells Telemachos of Orestes' revenge, and immediately warns Telemachos not to stay too long away from home —once again, as if there were a specific connection (iii.306–316).

It is not only through her praise of Orestes that Athene shows, at the very outset of the *Odyssey*, that she favors, one might even say insists on, the slaughter of the suitors. She definitely tells Telemachos to do it (i.294–296). And in order that they may be the more guilty, she has apparently put the plot of ambushing Telemachos into their minds, while at the same time making sure that it must fail (v.23–24). The whole later action of the *Odyssey* is approved, authorized, encouraged by Athene.

She is carefully established in this role at the outset of the epic as we have it. This, I believe, is the chief reason why we start with the Telemachy. Here she can be cast as the fairy godmother, or guardian spirit. If the poet had begun at the beginning of the wanderings of Odysseus, he could not have cast her in this role, because the tradition was that at this time Athene was angry with all the Achaians, including even Odysseus. So, for instance, Phemios sang of (i.326–327)

the Achaians' bitter homecoming
from Troy, which Pallas Athene had inflicted upon them.

Nestor agrees, adding the wrath of Zeus (iii.130–135 quoted above).

INTRODUCTION

The wrath of Athene deserves special consideration, and I shall return to it when I discuss the wanderings of Odysseus. Here it may be sufficient to say that the poet has established the position of Athene, as guardian spirit of the family, by beginning with the Telemachy.

Last of all, and most obvious of all, the Telemachy gives us Telemachos. Once Odysseus is on the scene, our attention is mainly fixed on him, but his young helper quietly maintains the character that has been built up for him, without strain or hurry, in the first four books.

I think, then, that it can be said, as objectively as is possible in such cases, that the *Odyssey* gains much from its Telemachy. The cost is the delay in bringing us, first-hand, to Odysseus and his wanderings. But did Homer count such delay as cost?

In the *Odyssey*, the poet gives us a few indications of his views about storytelling. One should not be repetitive, xii.450–453:

> *Why tell the rest of*
> *this story again, since yesterday in your house I told it*
> *to you and your majestic wife? It is hateful to me*
> *to tell a story over again, when it has been well told.*

And well has Odysseus (Homer, that is) told his story. Thus Alkinoös, xi.366–368:

> *You have*
> *a grace upon your words, and there is sound sense within them,*
> *and expertly, as a singer would do, you have told the story.*

It is storytelling they like, and they are not impatient, xi.372–376:

> *Here is*
> *a night that is very long, it is endless. It is not time yet*
> *to sleep in the palace. But go on telling your wonderful story.*
> *I myself could hold out until the bright dawn, if only*
> *you could bear to tell me, here in the palace, of your sufferings.*

"If you could only hear him," says Eumaios to Penelope. "I had him for three nights, and he enchanted me" (xvii.512–521).

Delay, excursus, elaboration—whether by creative expansion or incorporation of by-material—is part of the technique of the epic, as opposed to chronicle. In the *Iliad,* the wrath of Achilleus is not hastened to its fulfill-

INTRODUCTION

ment; nor, in the *Odyssey*, the vengeance of Odysseus. Consider the day-dream of Telemachos, how he visualizes his father's homecoming, i.115–116:

> *imagining in his mind his great father, how he might come back*
> *and all throughout the house might cause the suitors to scatter.*

All he has to do is appear, armed, and the suitors will scatter in panic. So too Athene, i.255–256; 265–266:

> *I wish he could come now to stand in the outer doorway*
> *of his house, wearing a helmet and carrying shield and two spears. . . .*
> *I wish that such an Odysseus would come now among the suitors.*
> *They all would find death was quick, and marriage a painful matter.*[5]

Over too quickly, a tableau, not a story. How different is the actual return and slow-plotted slaying, directed by Athene herself. Delaying matter, if worthy, was, I think, welcome.

THE WANDERINGS OF ODYSSEUS

The wanderings themselves can be considered under four headings, as follows.

a. The Wanderings as part of the *Nostoi,* or general homecoming of the Achaians.
b. The Great Wanderings, from Troy to Kalypso's isle, recounted to the Phaiakians by Odysseus himself, Books ix–xii.
c. The Homecoming, from Kalypso's isle to Ithaka, including the stay with the Phaiakians. This is told by the poet as narrator, not by Odysseus, and occupies Books v–viii, and xiii.1–187, being interrupted by Odysseus' account of the Great Wanderings.
d. The lying stories told by Odysseus when he is disguised as a tramp pretending to be a fallen noble; together with some information which Odysseus as tramp claims to have heard about the true Odysseus.

a. The Wanderings of Odysseus are placed among the general home-comings, or *Nostoi* (the subject of a later epic) at the very outset, i.11–14:

INTRODUCTION

Then all the others, as many as fled sheer destruction,
were at home now, having escaped the sea and the fighting.
This one alone, longing for his wife and his homecoming,
was detained by the queenly nymph Kalypso, bright among goddesses.

Elsewhere in the first four books we have scattered allusions to the home-comings. They are generally characterized by Nestor's speech, iii.130–135:

But after we had sacked the sheer citadel of Priam,
and were going away in our ships, and the god scattered the Achaians,
then Zeus in his mind devised a sorry homecoming
for the Argives, since not all were considerate nor righteous;
therefore many of them found a bad way home, because of
the ruinous anger of the Gray-eyed One, whose father is mighty.

We are told of the murder of Agamemnon, the wreck and drowning of Aias Oïleus, the storm battering and wanderings of Menelaos. Yet there is sometimes an odd note of inconsistency. Nestor reports that he and Diomedes came home without mishap, and that he has heard that Neop-tolemos, Philoktetes, and Idomeneus did the same.[6] Proteus tells Menelaos that only two chiefs perished in the homecoming (iv.496–497). This does not square very well with the "sorry homecoming" spoken of by Nestor and mentioned elsewhere, nor does Nestor's account of the departure of Odysseus agree well with Odysseus' own account.[7] It is possible that there was an early variant version of the *Nostoi*.

b. and c. The Great Wanderings, starting from Troy, take Odysseus to the Kikonians, the Lotus-Eaters, the Cyclopes, Aiolos, the Laistrygones, Circe's isle, the Land of the Dead, the Sirens, Skylla and Charybdis, Thrinakia, and Kalypso's isle. From the Kikonians he is driven south, off the map, and his last certainly identifiable landmark is Kythera (ix.81). After that, except for a brief sight of Ithaka (x.28–55), he wanders among marvels, and though his seas and landfalls have often been identi-fied, all is hypothetical and nothing is secure.

Through these adventures, partly perhaps because Odysseus is telling them in his own person, the major gods appear very little. Athene does not appear at all. Responsibility for the troubled wanderings is pinned on Poseidon through the prayer of Polyphemos, his son, after his blinding (ix.528–536).

Here, as we have noted, the order in the epic narrative does not follow the chronological order. The invocation and the opening scene, before lead-

INTRODUCTION

ing to the Telemachy, establishes Poseidon as the persecutor of Odysseus, i.68–79 (Zeus speaking):

> *It is the earth encircler Poseidon who, ever relentless,*
> *nurses a grudge because of the Cyclops, whose eye he blinded;*
> *for Polyphemos like a god, whose power is greatest*
> *over all the Cyclopes. Thoösa, a nymph, was his mother,*
> *and she is daughter of Phorkys, lord of the barren salt water,*
> *who in the hollows of the caves had lain with Poseidon.*
> *For his sake Poseidon, shaker of the earth, although he does not*
> *kill Odysseus, yet drives him back from the land of his fathers.*
> *But come, let all of us who are here work out his homecoming,*
> *and see to it that he returns. Poseidon shall put away*
> *his anger; for all alone and against the will of the other*
> *immortal gods united he can accomplish nothing.*

Poseidon is Odysseus' persecutor, just as Athene is firmly established as his protector (i.48–62).

The Telemachy follows, and then the Homecoming, which as we have seen starts with Athene taking up the case of Odysseus. She helps him against Poseidon, who wrecks his raft and who proposes to take a final revenge on the Phaiakians for conveying him home. It looks like contrivance; at least, the result is to mitigate any tradition that the sufferings of Odysseus and the other Achaians were due to the wrath of Athene.

The hallmark of the wanderings, from Troy to home, is imaginative combination.

Except for the very beginning, known places do not figure; nor traditional characters, except in the Land of the Dead. The gods of Olympos, I have said, are not prominent. Rather, we see much of minor divinities, ill-attested outside of the *Odyssey* itself, such as Circe and Kalypso. We find monsters like Skylla and Charybdis, and the delightful but almost equally monstrous Sirens. We have mortals who are almost superhuman in one dimension or another. The Lotus-Eaters offer magic fruit (ix.92–97). The Phaiakians have their magic ships (viii.555–563), they may even have automatons (vii.91–94; 100–102),[8] their orchards bear fruit forever in season and out (vii.114–126), and the gods, who live near them, visit them openly without disguise (vii.201–206). The Laistrygones have supernatural strength and ferocity (x.116–124), and the normal seasons do not seem to apply in their country.

Consider also Aiolos. He lives a blissful life in a brazen tower with his six sons married to his six daughters (x.1–2) and, in flat contradiction to

---

INTRODUCTION

epic tradition elsewhere, he, a mortal, has been put by Zeus in charge of all the winds, whom he keeps tied up in a bag.

So, too, the Cyclopes of the *Odyssey* are quite different from the Cyclopes in Hesiod and elsewhere. Elsewhere they are gods; in the *Odyssey* they are mortals. Elsewhere there are three of them, and their names are Brontes, Steropes, and Arges; in the *Odyssey* they are apparently numerous, and one of them is named Polyphemos; this Polyphemos is the son of Poseidon, but elsewhere the Cyclopes are the sons of Ouranos and Gaia. Elsewhere they are smiths and builders, but in the *Odyssey* they are herdsmen, or at least Polyphemos is. Their chief and perhaps sole similarity is the single eye, and the name of Cyclops.[9]

Now Cyclops (Kyklops) means not "one-eyed" but "round-eyed." Thus Hesiod, not content with the name, describes them as being not merely round-eyed but one-eyed, *Theogony* 142–145:

> *These in all the rest of their shape were made like gods,*
> *but they had only one eye set in the middle of their foreheads.*
> *Kyklopes, Wheel-eyed, was the name given them, by reason*
> *of the single wheel-shaped eye that was set in their foreheads.*

Homer, on the other hand, while describing their nature and way of life, never tells us that they are one-eyed, but seems rather to assume that Polyphemos is one-eyed, or rather that we know he is. This comes up when Odysseus proposes to blind him, ix.331–333:

> *Next I told the rest of the men to cast lots, to find out*
> *which of them must endure with me to take up the great beam*
> *and spin it in Cyclops' eye when sweet sleep had come over him.*

The blinding scene which follows assumes throughout that there is only one eye to deal with.

This suggests to me that Homer "borrowed" the name and the notion of Cyclops for his story and that the name Cyclops by now "meant," that is implied, a one-eyed giant. The story itself may have been a previous folk tale, since it has many analogies;[10] or it may have been free invention. Be that as it may, the story of the blinding of Polyphemos the Cyclops as we have it brings Poseidon into the story. His prayer to his father (ix. 526–536) causes the troubled wanderings of Odysseus, as we were told at the start (i.68–75) and elsewhere. But Odysseus at the time of the blinding was *already* lost from home; his wanderings were begun before they were caused.

INTRODUCTION

The paradox seems most plausibly explained as a compromise. Homer knew and admitted the wrath of Athene (and Zeus and other gods)[11] which caused suffering to the Achaians, including Odysseus. But he alters it as far as he can to a situation where Athene merely acquiesces in the sufferings of Odysseus out of respect for Poseidon, whose wrath is thus emphasized.

On Ithaka, Odysseus gently complains to Athene that, while he enjoyed her patronage at Troy and among the Phaiakians, he did miss her company in between, that is, on the Great Wanderings (xiii.314–323). She ultimately answers this, xiii.339–343:

> *And I never did have any doubt, but in my heart always*
> *knew how you would come home, having lost all of your companions.*
> *But, you see, I did not want to fight with my father's*
> *brother, Poseidon, who was holding a grudge against you*
> *in his heart, and because you blinded his dear son, hated you.*

Perhaps this will stand as Athene's official version.

d. In addition to the authentic wanderings of Odysseus recounted by the hero himself or by the poet, there are five false stories told by the hero about himself. These are addressed respectively to Athene (xiii.256–286), Eumaios (xiv.191–359), the suitors (xvii.419–444), Penelope (xix. 165–202), and Laertes (xxiv.302–308). All the stories serve as answers to the standard question, spoken or unspoken, raised by the presence of a stranger (especially on an island) : "Who are you and where do you come from?" All the stories involve known and identifiable places. They are meant to be plausible, and the supernatural and the marvelous elements of the wanderings find no place here.

The longest and fullest account is the second, given to Eumaios. Here Odysseus represents himself as a Cretan, a veteran of the Trojan War, who subsequently led a disastrous raid on Egypt, was spared and befriended by the Egyptian King, survived the wreck of a Phoenician ship, and came to Ithaka by way of Thesprotia. The first, third, and fourth accounts vary or repeat these themes. All the first four necessarily represent Odysseus as a former nobleman down on his luck. By the time he talks to Laertes, however, he has recovered his property and status, and the story of the fallen noble is no longer necessary. He is from Alybas, wherever that may be, and has arrived from Sikania, presumably Sicily.

The story of the raid on Egypt has attracted special attention. It reads like an account of one of the great raids by the Peoples of the Sea, attested

INTRODUCTION

in the annals of Egypt, but told here from the invaders' point of view.[12] This would tie the Homeric poems to history, and suggest that the tradition of troubled homecomings for the Achaians might have originated in actual turbulence and wanderings after the Trojan War.

The presence of these stories in the final version of the *Odyssey* could perhaps be accounted for by the poet's desire to exploit and develop the talents of his hero, giving content to the general comment, xix.203:

He knew how to say many false things that were like true sayings.

But it is also possible that the lying stories, taken together, might represent a fragmentary outline of an original *Odyssey,* in which the wanderings were confined to known places in the Mediterranean: Crete, Cyprus, Egypt, Phoënicia, Thesprotia; and which the present *Odyssey* has replaced. One could thus make up a rough and imperfect series of analogies, such as, for instance:

Raid on Egypt	Great Wanderings
Egyptian counterattack	Laistrygones
King of Egypt	Circe or Kalypso
Phoenician wreck	Wreck of Odysseus' last ship or of the raft
Thesprotia	Scheria, the land of the Phaiakians:

Nothing like this can, of course, be pressed, but the lying stories in themselves emphasize the element of imagination in the *Odyssey* as we have it. By contrast to the Great Wanderings, the lying stories link rather to the *Nostoi.*

THE WORLD OF THE WANDERINGS

The world of the Wanderings has occasioned even more controversy. Briefly, there are two extreme views. On the one, the places in the Wanderings, such as the land of the Lotus-Eaters, Circe's Isle, Scheria, and so forth, represent real places in the Mediterranean, or even out of it; or at least some of them do. On the other view, they are imaginary. Both these views seem indeed to be extreme, but it is difficult to find a middle ground.

Many identifications have been made, and the whole subject is too large and complicated to treat in detail.[13] It may be useful to look at a few favorite identifications. The Lotus-Eaters are regularly located on the coast of Libya (Africa), because of the sailing log, though Homer, who knows

INTRODUCTION

of Libya, does not use the name here. There is a strong tradition that places Polyphemos and the Cyclopes in Sicily. Skylla and Charybdis have often, despite many objections, been located in the Straits of Messina. Korkyra (now often called Corfu) claimed to be Scheria, the land of the Phaiakians.

Some of these traditions are early. Thucydides, writing at the end of the fifth century B.C., refers to legends about Cyclopes, and also Laistrygones, in Sicily, and to the Korkyraians' pride in the ancient sea fame of the Phaiakians.[14] Also, the traditions have survived, or have been resuscitated, and to this day near Acireale the Sicilians will show you the rocks Polyphemos threw at the ship of Odysseus,[15] while at Corfu your guide will point out the little island which is the Phaiakian ship turned to stone, and the bay where Odysseus encountered Nausikaa.[16]

Yet there are serious difficulties. Nothing in the text of the *Odyssey* indicates that the Cyclopes lived in Sicily or, in fact, on an island at all. Phaiakian Scheria does seem to be an island, far out in the sea with no land near. Corfu is an island, but lies so close off the mainland that from the open sea, whence Odysseus approached it, and even from some places on the landward side, it is impossible to tell where the mainland ends and the island begins, or even that Corfu is an island at all. Yet as Odysseus first sees it (v.281)

it looked like a shield lying on the misty face of the water.

External evidence raises still greater difficulties. The *Odyssey* substantially as we have it could not have been completed much before the end of the eighth century B.C. The traditional foundation dates for many Greek cities in the West are earlier than that. Sicilian Naxos is said to have been settled in 735 B.C., Syracuse and Korkyra in 734, and half a dozen others before 700; Kyme (Cumae), near Naples, claims even greater age. These dates are generally accepted by modern scholars, and the pottery in some places even goes back to Mycenaean times.[17] Thus, by the time of the *Odyssey*'s completion, the western Mediterranean as far as Sicily was not only well explored, but pretty well settled with Greek colonies, colonies almost or quite as Hellenic as their mother cities in old Greece. How could such a place belong simultaneously to the known world and the wonder world of the Wanderings? How could Korkyra be both itself and Scheria? Only, one might say, by embedding features conceived very early in the process of accumulation, and ignoring later phases.

INTRODUCTION

This does not seem to be the normal process. Homer's Ithaka is Ithaka, not a wonderland. Sicily as Sikania is mentioned as if it were a real place (xxiv.307); the land of the Sikels (presumably Sicilians) is a source or market for slaves, not Cyclopes or other monsters (xx.383; xxiv.211; 365; 389). Menelaos speaks of Libya among other far but real places, iv.83–85:

> *I wandered to Cyprus and Phoenicia, to the Egyptians,*
> *I reached the Aithiopians, Eremboi, Sidonians,*
> *and Libya.*

The place is preternaturally prosperous, but it keeps company with Cyprus, Phoenicia, Egypt, and Ethiopia, not with the Lotus-Eaters, and a relatively workaday Phoenician ship was carrying Odysseus there to be sold as a slave (xiv.295–297).

Those who would find true points of reference for Aiolos, the Phaiakians, Laistrygones, and the rest frequently offer the support of topographical detail from the Homeric text. Sometimes this is too general for identification, but often it is plausible. The little island off the land of the Cyclopes is described in thoughtful detail, as if seen by the eye of a prospective settler (ix.116–169); but where is it? The land of the Laistrygones is vividly presented; we can still ask the same question. In these and other cases, the descriptions may well be based on authentic reports from mariners.

But they also may be put in the wrong place. That is, to say it another way, for this is important, it is possible to combine topographical accuracy with geographical incoherence.

This seems actually to have happened in the case of Ithaka. Topographical details are scattered through the poem. The scholar can review these and honestly say that Homer seems to know his Ithaka, and what it is like.[18] Only he does not seem to know where it is. Listen to Odysseus himself, who *ought* to know, ix.21–26:

> *I am at home in sunny Ithaka. There is a mountain*
> *there that stands tall, leaf-trembling Neritos, and there are islands*
> *settled around it, lying one very close to another.*
> *There is Doulichion and Same, wooded Zakynthos,*
> *but my island lies low and away, last of all on the water*
> *toward the dark, with the rest below facing east and sunshine.*

This simply will not do for Ithaka (Thiaki), though that has the landmarks, for it lies tucked close in against the *eastern* side of the far larger

---

INTRODUCTION

Kephallenia (Same?). Homer's description would in fact better suit Corfu (Korkyra), which all the world has already identified with Phaiakian Scheria.

I am thus forced back to the belief that the places of the Wanderings are combinations. They are made by the imagination. They are in part sheer fancy; and sailors' stories can involve monsters and enchanted places, as well as authentic report. But they probably contain bits and pieces of solid unassimilated fact. The lands of the Wanderings seem to stand on the same footing as their inhabitants. These too are of this world and stature, rather than that of Olympos and the Olympians. Yet they are not quite of this world either. They are people endowed like no people we shall ever meet, and live in places where no one, since Odysseus, will ever go.[19] And thus the Land of the Dead, where Odyssesus and his men (so soon to die) are the only living visitors, takes its natural place among the Wanderings. For it is described not as an underworld but as a far shore, with landmarks borrowed (perhaps) from some or several true places in the real world.

If the *Odyssey* is a work of the imagination, then, we must ask, are the Wanderings symbolic or allegorical? Do they represent the story not of a man but of Man? Many have thought so.[20] I think not. But the Wanderings do lend themselves to a morality, for it is easy to read the adventures as a series of trials. The Greek authors liked to dramatize the test (*peira*) by which a person established his quality. Odysseus passes or at least survives the trials by terror and force: the Kikonians, the Cyclops, the Laistrygones, the confrontation with the ghosts, Skylla, Charybdis, Zeus' storm, Poseidon's storm. And there is trial by temptation. His men fail disastrously against curiosity and hunger with the Bag of Winds and the Cattle of the Sun, but Odysseus endures, and he endures also against the temptations to stay with comfort and beauty and give up the hard voyage home: the charms of the Lotus-Eaters, Circe, the Sirens, Kalypso, Nausikaa.

But symbolism and allegory seem foreign to the biology of early Greek epic; it is hard for me to think that the moral proposition came first, with the story shaped to present it. Even in the case of Circe turning the men to swine, it is probably mistaken to read anything more meaningful than a fairy-tale transformation. There is plenty of morality in the *Odyssey,* but it is where it ought to be, inextricably implicit in the story itself. This is a brilliant series of adventures linked and fused by character. The tests (including the tests on Ithaka) are passed by the exercise of virtues, viz. (in ascending order) physical courage and strength; ingenuity where

INTRODUCTION

these might fail; restraint, patience, tact, and self-control; and the *will* for home.

These are the virtues not of Man, but of a particular valiant, resourceful, much-enduring hero, established as such in the *Iliad,* and developed in a development of the *Nostoi,* the sequel to the *Iliad.*

ODYSSEUS ON ITHAKA

In the middle of a line, xiii.187, we leave the Phaiakians forever, without even learning what finally happened to them, and henceforth we are concerned almost exclusively with Odysseus on Ithaka. He will not attack the suitors until Book xxii, and he will not reveal himself to Penelope until Book xxiii. Thus the length allotted to Odysseus on Ithaka is extraordinary. Nearly nine books, more than twice the text given to the Great Wanderings, are devoted to the time from Odysseus' arrival to his dropping of disguise and attack on the suitors, and for nearly nine books very little happens.

We can only guess at the purpose of this drawing-out. We may observe some of the effects. The revelations and recognitions, by Telemachos, Eumaios and Philoitios, Penelope, Laertes, are strung out bit by bit. We are teased by the abortive recognitions by Argos and Eurykleia, and by the times when the careful hero nearly gives himself and the game away (xviii.90–94; xx.28–30). There is the constant threat that Penelope will, at the very last moment, give in to the suitors (xix. 524–534; 576–581; xxi. 68–79). There arises that special irony where the audience or reader, in on the whole secret, can watch the victims being gulled by the hero, his merciless guarding divinity, and his equally merciless son.

The story of near-recognition is beautifully played out in the interview between the hero and his wife, where she confides in the stranger to whom she is so drawn that she can hardly let him go (xix.509). Here and elsewhere, the leisurely composition, in which talk is overwhelmingly predominant, gives opportunity to elaborate the characters. The epithets of the three leading persons—resourceful Odysseus, thoughtful Telemachos, and circumspect Penelope—gain depth and intensity through these slow books. Penelope, in particular, is done with great subtlety. Desperately pressed, with no power but her wits, charm, and heart, she plays a waiting game and never commits herself.

The leading suitors, Antinoös, Eurymachos, and Amphinomos, also

INTRODUCTION

gain some dimension. Both as a group and as individuals, in a few cases, the suitors could have been much simpler than they are. For the poet seems mostly to have seen the moral issue as just right against wrong.[21] The sin of the faithless maids and of the one faithless thrall is disloyalty. The sin of the suitors is perhaps this, too, but they also abuse hospitality. To Homer, perhaps because he was a wandering poet, this virtue is thematic, and again and again we are given object lessons on the right dealings between host and guest, through the conduct of Telemachos, Nestor and his family, Menelaos and a reformed Helen, the Phaiakians, Odysseus, Kalypso, Penelope. Horrid counter-examples are furnished by Polyphemos and the Laistrygones. The suitors are aware of the principle (xvii.481–487) but in action they are a living travesty of all proper custom. Thus they lose all divine favor. Not even an Olympian god is so prejudiced as to take their part.

Yet they are no indiscriminate group of villains, nor are they all villains. They are said to be plotting the murder of Telemachos but, once he has slipped past them, they seem irresolute about it (xvi.371–406). They appear to be more an intolerable nuisance than an actual menace. They have some moral notions and some sense of decency (xvi.400–406; xvii. 365–368; 481–487). While indirectly offending the gods by their treatment of people, they respect the gods and regularly observe the forms of religion. This, and their occasional kindnesses, do them no good (xvii. 363–364). Odysseus tries to warn the best of them, but Athene has no mercy (xviii.124–157).

Their doom seems excessive to me. I do not know how it seemed to Homer. But Penelope cried over her pet geese (xix.535–558), and Homer may have conceived some liking for his own creatures, and put off, as long as he could, their necessary slaughter.

THE END OF THE ODYSSEY

After the killing of the suitors and the reunion of Penelope and Odysseus, the end of the *Odyssey* reads like a hurried composition. The purpose of the second visit to the dead is not altogether clear. It does, however, in some sense dispose of the suitors, whose bodies were for some time lying about the palace (they are finally buried, xxiv.417); and it does link the Ithakan episode with the background of the Trojan War, in a manner not uncongenial to the poet of the eleventh book, if this is he.

INTRODUCTION

On the other hand, the previous narrative demands a reunion with Laertes, and it certainly demands some kind of patch-up of the chaotic situation in Ithaka, where "all the best young men" (i.245) are lying dead. A reconciliation is scrambled together by a hasty and inadequate *deus ex machina*, which ends the epic. The hand has lost its firmness,[22] but who can say for sure that the hand is not Homer's?

THE ODYSSEY AND THE ILIAD

This brings us to the question of unity, which cannot be solved but must be faced. For the *Odyssey*, as previously for the *Iliad*, I have been writing as if on the assumption of a single master hand or, in Kirk's phrase, monumental poet.[23] Only a study devoted to disintegration would proceed otherwise. Such unity cannot be proved, though the burden of proof is on the analysts rather than on the unitarians. Such unity also, if it exists, is qualified by the conditions of oral poetry, namely, the accumulation of saga material (less for the *Odyssey* than for the *Iliad*), and of formulaic language.

If there was such a monumental poet for the *Odyssey*, and a monumental poet for the *Iliad*, were they the same man? I can only say as I have said before: that this cannot be proved; but that, if someone not Homer composed the *Odyssey*, nobody had a name to give him; and that the burden of proof rests on those who would establish separate authorship.

Still, it is well to note some of the similarities and differences in the two poems. The *Odyssey*, like the *Iliad*, ignores historical developments between the time of the originating events and the time of composition. In the *Odyssey*, as in the *Iliad*, this principle is violated by occasional slips, the so-called anachronisms. The *Odyssey* adds a few of its own: Sicilians, Phoenicians in the western seas, Dorians in Crete, consultation of oracles. Little can be proved by this. The important anachronisms are deeper and harder to assess. How far, for instance, does the picture of Ithaka reflect life in a Mycenaean palace, and how much does it reflect life in a baronial house of the poet's own day, centuries later?

The *Odyssey* seems later than the *Iliad* principally because it assumes the existence of the *Iliad*, or at least of a fully told tale of Troy. That does not mean it must be so much later that we require a separate author. It is a coherent sequel to the *Iliad* and does not contradict it.

Consider the characters who are carried over from one epic to the other.

INTRODUCTION

Judgment of characterization is admittedly a subjective business. For what my opinion is worth, I would say that Odysseus, Nestor, Agamemnon, Menelaos, Helen, and Achilleus are the same "people" in both poems.[24] Those qualities which mark the Odysseus of the *Odyssey*—strength and courage, ingenuity, patience and self-control—all characterize the same hero in the *Iliad*. His friendship with the Atreidae and Nestor, suggested in the *Iliad*, is still more notable in the *Odyssey*. And in the *Iliad* his determination to win the war matches his determination to win the homecoming in the *Odyssey*. To achieve both ends, he is ruthless. Nestor in his garrulity, Agamemnon in his self-pity, Menelaos in his courtesy and strong moral sense, Achilleus in his devotion to the ideal of the warrior, all repeat striking characteristics of the persons in the *Iliad*. And Helen is as self-centered as ever; in neither epic can she make a speech without talking about herself.

All this, if it is allowed, does not of course prove a single poet for the two poems. It could mean no more than that whoever composed the *Odyssey* knew his *Iliad* well. But here we come upon a striking fact. When the *Odyssey* recounts episodes from the tale of Troy, these episodes are never a part of the *Iliad*, but seem to fall outside, either before or after, the action of the *Iliad*. Thus, apart from the Returns or *Nostoi,* we hear of the following:

The Trojan Horse and the final battle for Troy, iv.271–289; viii.499–520; xi.523–537.

Odysseus' spying expedition in Troy, iv.240–264 (rather than his spying expedition with Diomedes, *Iliad* X.254–578).

His wrestling match with Philomeleïdes of Lesbos, iv.341–344 (rather than with Aias, *Iliad* XXIII.707–737).

His fight in defense of the body of Achilleus, v.308–310 (rather than his fight alone against the Trojans when the other Achaians had fled, *Iliad* XI.401–488).

The quarrel of Odysseus and Achilleus, viii.75–82 (rather than that of Agamemnon and Achilleus, *Iliad* I.1–305).

The death and burial of Achilleus, xxiv.35–94 (rather than the death and burial of Patroklos).

INTRODUCTION

The quarrel of Odysseus and Aias over the armor of Achilleus, xi. 541–564.

The death of Antilochos, iv.187–188; 199–202.

The exploits or excellences of heroes who reached Troy after the action of the *Iliad* was over, such as Neoptolemos, Eurypylos, and Memnon, xi.505–537, and Philoktetes, viii.219.

The recruiting of the heroes, xxiv.114–119.

The exclusion of Iliadic episodes from the *Odyssey* can scarcely be accidental. We are left, as I see it, to choose between two conclusions. Either the poet of the *Odyssey* was ignorant of the *Iliad;*[25] or he deliberately avoided trespassing on the earlier poem. I cannot believe in the first alternative, and am forced to choose the second.

What are the other important *differences* between the two poems? Every Homeric scholar has his own list, and I must be brief. To me, the main differences are details of the whole general style of narrative. The *Odyssey* concentrates on relatively small groups. Without nations embattled, the Olympians of the *Iliad* are less needed, and the first-person narrative of the Great Wanderings virtually excludes them. There are also a few important and well-known differences in the concept of the divinities. Hermes, more of a magician than Iris, takes over her functions as messenger. Aphrodite, not Charis, is the wife of Hephaistos. Olympos turns into a never-never land (vi.41–47), strangely like the Elysian Field which is Menelaos' destination (iv.561–569), and well in accord with the *Odyssey*'s wander-world of monsters and fairyland people. Invention in the *Odyssey* extends to name making; a list of young Phaiakians shows a dozen and a half names, all meaning something to do with seamanship and shipbuilding (viii.111–115). The little thumbnail sketches of slaughtered warriors in the *Iliad* have a more traditional sound; such sketches are rare in the *Odyssey,* where we do not deal in large masses. The poet of the *Iliad* shows much lyric imagination in his similes. The *Odyssey* is far poorer here, and much of the same material is used differently. Storms in the *Iliad* are used imaginatively in similes; there is no weather in the *Iliad.*[26] Storms in the *Odyssey* are something Odysseus must contend with. The humble workingman enters the *Iliad* only through simile, but in the *Odyssey* he is there in the flesh.

When we come to language, rhythm, metrical phrasing, the overmaster-

INTRODUCTION

ing impression is one of unity. If there were two (or more) poets, they were trained in the same tradition of formula. Agamemnon is hailed in the *Iliad* (II.434, etc.) as

Son of Atreus, most lordly and king of men, Agamemnon,

and so he is in the *Odyssey* when the occasion arises (xi.397). His answering address (xi.405),

Son of Laertes and seed of Zeus, resourceful Odysseus,

is common to both epics. So is the summons to assembly (*Iliad* II.50–52; *Odyssey* ii.6–8), the introduction of a speaker (*Iliad* I.73, etc.; *Odyssey* ii.160, etc.), the course of ships through the water (*Iliad* I.481–483; *Odyssey* ii.427–429). In both epics, children are innocent, women are deep-girdled, iron is gray, ships are hollow, words are winged and go through the barrier of the teeth, the sea is wine-blue, barren, and salt, bronze is sharp and pitiless. The list is almost endless. Even the Ithakans are strong-greaved Achaians (*Odyssey* ii.72; xx.146), though they are not armed.

The *Odyssey* has many phrases, journey formulae for instance, which are not found in the *Iliad*.[27] Naturally, the *Iliad* has many combat formulae which are missing from the *Odyssey*. But when combat finally ensues between Odysseus and the suitors, the poet repeats brief formulae and even sizable sequences (compare *Iliad* XV.479–481 and *Odyssey* xxii.122–124). Adaptation may be necessary. Amphinomos goes down, *Odyssey* xxii.94:

He fell, thunderously, and took the earth full on his forehead.

We cannot quite have the standard *Iliad* line:

He fell, thunderously, and his armor clattered upon him.

Amphinomos has no armor. Occasionally, a few lines from a combat in the *Iliad* can fit a context in the *Odyssey* which is not military. The language for the Cyclops' throwing a stone is the same as that used for Aias (*Iliad* VII.268–269; *Odyssey* ix.537–538). The death of Odysseus' steersman (xii.412–414) is neatly adapted from the death of Epikles on the wall (*Iliad* XII.384–386).

INTRODUCTION

Can the formula in a changed setting ever mean parody? Sarpedon advances on the wall of the Achaians like a lion against a guarded sheepfold (*Iliad* XII.299–301), and that is appropriate; but the same language is adapted to Odysseus' embarrassed advance on a group of frightened girls (*Odyssey* vi.130; 133–134). When Telemachos sneezes, the sneeze "clashed horribly" (*Odyssey* xvii.542); the phrase was used of the helmet of Hektor in battle (*Iliad* XV.648) and other warlike noises. Eumaios is called *orchamos andron*, "leader of men" (xiv.121). This could mean "foreman (of swineherds)," which is what he is, but it suggests "commander of armies," which is what it means in the *Iliad*. It has been suggested that the arrangement that "noble swineherd" made for his sows reflected those made by Priam for his daughters (*Odyssey* xiv.13–15; *Iliad* VI.244–246). There are other such combinations which, with enough good will, can be seen as parodies. It is hard to be sure, but such amusements with formula would be in accord with the generally lighter tone of the *Odyssey*.[28]

Yet these very manipulations of metrical phrases attest a deep, intimate similarity of ear and verse building which can only be suggested here. We can illustrate by a short phrase taken almost at random: *peri chroï*, which means "next the skin" or "around the body," and having the metrical scheme ⌣–⌣⌣. It is used in a dozen *otherwise quite different* lines in the two poems. But it always comes in exactly the same place in the line, to form the line-end *peri chroï* –⌣⌣––. This shows not merely the reuse of materials, but a constant habit of metrical thought.

There is much that is obscure about the functions of a monumental poet. Within the limits of my ignorance, I can think of one Homer, composing, or completing, first the *Iliad*, then the *Odyssey*. Or I can think of an old master, called *Homer*, mainly responsible for the *Iliad;* and a young master, favored apprentice and poetic heir; perhaps a nephew or son-in-law; also going by the name, or assuming the name, of Homer; and mainly responsible for the *Odyssey*. I find the second combination more persuasive, but that is all I can say for it.

NOTE ON THE TRANSLATION

In my translation, I have followed the principles stated and followed in my translation of the *Iliad*. In particular, I have tried to follow, as far as the structure of English will allow, the formulaic practice of the original.

INTRODUCTION

Of course my memory has failed me at times and I have allowed myself some liberties.

NOTE ON THE TEXT

I have used the Oxford text of T. W. Allen, 2nd edition, and followed it except in a very few places. At iv.515–521 I have followed Bothe's suggestion and transposed the lines; the numbers show the original order. In x.117, I read the singular *nea*, "the (i.e., my) ship" instead of plural *neas*, "ships," which is in the manuscripts. The context shows that Odysseus, who sent the men, was separated from his main fleet. In xiii.158, I follow an ancient conjecture and read *mēde* instead of the manuscripts' *mega de*. In xvii.531, I read the plural *autōn* instead of the singular *autou*, which is in the manuscripts.

NOTES TO THE INTRODUCTION

[1] It may seem unreasonable to distinguish the Great Wanderings (Troy to Kalypso's island) from the Homecoming (Kalypso's island to Ithaka). The reason for the distinction is Homer's way of recounting these two stages. The Great Wanderings are told by Odysseus in the first person; the Homecoming by the poet in his own person. This makes a great difference. For instance, when Odysseus is made to report divine intervention unseen by him, he has to find a plausible explanation (xii.389–390); when the poet tells the story in his own person, he can do as he pleases. Thus the change of technique, if nothing else, puts the two stages of wandering on different levels.

[2] See D. L. Page, *The Homeric Odyssey* (Oxford, 1955), p. 53; for a contrary view, G. S. Kirk, *The Songs of Homer* (Cambridge, 1962), pp. 358–360.

[3] I believe in one poet. There may have been more. Having said so much, I shall henceforth speak of "the poet." There may, indeed there must, be interpolated lines and passages. I do not know which ones they are.

[4] By the *Nostoi* I mean, not the post-Homeric poem called *Nostoi* or returns, but the underlying material, traces of which are to be found in the *Odyssey* itself.

[5] Menelaos speaks in the same vein, iv.332–345.

[6] iii.180–192. It is interesting that for all these heroes, except Nestor, later variants had them either not reach home at all (Neoptolemos) or else wander after their homecomings. Both Diomedes and Idomeneus barely escaped the fate of Agamemnon. For Neoptolemos, see Pindar, *Sixth Paean;* for Idomeneus, see the late compilation of Apollodorus, edited and translated by J. A. Frazer (London and Cambridge, Mass., 1921), vol. ii, p. 249, and for Philoctetes, p. 257. For

NOTES

Diomedes, see the material in H. J. Rose, *A Handbook of Greek Mythology* (New York, 1959), p. 237.

[7] According to Nestor, Odysseus set off in his company, but then turned back with some others (who? how many?) to rejoin Agamemnon (iii.162–164). Odysseus says nothing about this; in his own story he simply sets off from Ilion by himself, with his own contingent. There is no outright contradiction; there is certainly a gap.

[8] Hephaistos in the *Iliad* also has automatons; see *Iliad* XVIII. 372–377; 417–420. But Hephaistos is a god, and the Phaiakians are mortal men.

[9] For the Cyclopes, see Hesiod, *Theogony*, 139–146; see further the brief and clear account of Rose, *op. cit.*, p. 22.

[10] Conveniently summarized by Frazer in an appendix to his translation of Apollodorus (cited above, note 6), vol. ii, pp. 404–455.

[11] We may instance the wraths, against Odysseus or other Achaian heroes, of Helios, i.9; xii.376; of Zeus and Helios, xix.276; of Zeus, iii.132, 152, 160, 288; ix.38, 552–555; xii.415; of Athene, i.327; iii.135; iv.502; v.108.

[12] See Kirk, *op. cit.*, pp. 41–43.

[13] See W. W. Hyde, *Ancient Greek Mariners* (New York, 1947), pp. 72–96. This is an excellent concise account of identifications, ancient and modern, made for sites and landmarks in the *Odyssey*. It needs, however, to be brought up to date.

[14] For Sicily, see Thucydides vi.2.1; for Korkyra, i.25.4.

[15] See Baedeker's *Southern Italy* (1912), p. 410.

[16] See Baedeker's *Greece* (1909), p. 262.

[17] See J. Boardman, *The Greeks Overseas* (London, 1964), pp. 179–181.

[18] See the chapter by F. H. Stubbings, in Wace and Stubbings, *Companion to Homer* (London and New York, 1962), pp. 398–421.

[19] "You will find where Odysseus wandered," said the Alexandrian geographer Eratosthenes, "when you find the cobbler who stitched the bag of the winds." See Strabo, *Geography* i.2.15.

[20] For a recent statement and defense of this view, see G. deF. Lord, *Homeric Renaissance* (New Haven, 1956).

[21] See, for one instance out of many, xxii.413–416.

[22] See Page, *op. cit.*, pp. 101–130 and, in particular pp. 112–114.

[23] See, for instance, Kirk, *op. cit.*, p. 96.

[24] For a contrary view see, for instance, D. B. Monro, *Homer's Odyssey* (Oxford, 1901), vol. 2, pp. 290–291. Monro comments on the "marked falling-off in the character of the chief actor."

[25] This is the view of Page, *op. cit.*, pp. 158–159.

[26] Contrast the story told by Odysseus to Eumaios about warriors on night picket duty before Troy, xiv.462–502. The chilliness of the task is emphasized.

[27] On this subject see Kirk, *op. cit.*, pp. 293–297.

[28] The words of Hektor to Andromache, *Iliad* VI.490–493 are repeated twice in the *Odyssey* (i.356–359; xxi. 350–353), and the last line and a half at xi.352–353; but the "fighting" of the *Iliad* passage is changed each time.

THE ODYSSEY OF HOMER

BOOK I

Tell me, Muse, of the man of many ways, who was driven
far journeys, after he had sacked Troy's sacred citadel.
Many were they whose cities he saw, whose minds he learned of,
many the pains he suffered in his spirit on the wide sea,
5 struggling for his own life and the homecoming of his companions.
Even so he could not save his companions, hard though
he strove to; they were destroyed by their own wild recklessness,
fools, who devoured the oxen of Helios, the Sun God,
and he took away the day of their homecoming. From some point
10 here, goddess, daughter of Zeus, speak, and begin our story.
   Then all the others, as many as fled sheer destruction,
were at home now, having escaped the sea and the fighting.
This one alone, longing for his wife and his homecoming,
was detained by the queenly nymph Kalypso, bright among goddesses,
15 in her hollowed caverns, desiring that he should be her husband.
But when in the circling of the years that very year came
in which the gods had spun for him his time of homecoming
to Ithaka, not even then was he free of his trials
nor among his own people. But all the gods pitied him
20 except Poseidon; he remained relentlessly angry
with godlike Odysseus, until his return to his own country.
   But Poseidon was gone now to visit the far Aithiopians,
Aithiopians, most distant of men, who live divided,
some at the setting of Hyperion, some at his rising,

25 to receive a hecatomb of bulls and rams. There
    he sat at the feast and took his pleasure. Meanwhile the other
    Olympian gods were gathered together in the halls of Zeus.
    First among them to speak was the father of gods and mortals,
    for he was thinking in his heart of stately Aigisthos,
30 whom Orestes, Agamemnon's far-famed son, had murdered.
    Remembering him he spoke now before the immortals:
        'Oh for shame, how the mortals put the blame upon us
    gods, for they say evils come from us, but it is they, rather,
    who by their own recklessness win sorrow beyond what is given,
35 as now lately, beyond what was given, Aigisthos married
    the wife of Atreus' son, and murdered him on his homecoming,
    though he knew it was sheer destruction, for we ourselves had told him,
    sending Hermes, the mighty watcher, Argeïphontes,
    not to kill the man, nor court his lady for marriage;
40 for vengeance would come on him from Orestes, son of Atreides,
    whenever he came of age and longed for his own country.
    So Hermes told him, but for all his kind intention he could not
    persuade the mind of Aigisthos. And now he has paid for everything.'
        Then in turn the goddess gray-eyed Athene answered him:
45 'Son of Kronos, our father, O lordliest of the mighty,
    Aigisthos indeed has been struck down in a death well merited.
    Let any other man who does thus perish as he did.
    But the heart in me is torn for the sake of wise Odysseus,
    unhappy man, who still, far from his friends, is suffering
50 griefs, on the sea-washed island, the navel of all the waters,
    a wooded island, and there a goddess has made her dwelling place;
    she is daughter of malignant Atlas, who has discovered
    all the depths of the sea, and himself sustains the towering
    columns which bracket earth and sky and hold them together.
55 This is his daughter; she detains the grieving, unhappy
    man, and ever with soft and flattering words she works to
    charm him to forget Ithaka; and yet Odysseus,
    straining to get sight of the very smoke uprising
    from his own country, longs to die. But you, Olympian,
60 the heart in you is heedless of him. Did not Odysseus
    do you grace by the ships of the Argives, making sacrifice
    in wide Troy? Why, Zeus, are you now so harsh with him?'
        Then in turn Zeus who gathers the clouds made answer:

and the wrath of Poseidon

'My child, what sort of word escaped your teeth's barrier?
65 How could I forget Odysseus the godlike, he who
is beyond all other men in mind, and who beyond others
has given sacrifice to the gods, who hold wide heaven?
It is the Earth Encircler Poseidon who, ever relentless,
nurses a grudge because of the Cyclops, whose eye he blinded;
70 for Polyphemos like a god, whose power is greatest
over all the Cyclopes. Thoösa, a nymph, was his mother,
and she was daughter of Phorkys, lord of the barren salt water.
She in the hollows of the caves had lain with Poseidon.
For his sake Poseidon, shaker of the earth, although he does not
75 kill Odysseus, yet drives him back from the land of his fathers.
But come, let all of us who are here work out his homecoming
and see to it that he returns. Poseidon shall put away
his anger; for all alone and against the will of the other
immortal gods united he can accomplish nothing.'
80   Then in turn the goddess gray-eyed Athene answered him:
'Son of Kronos, our father, O lordliest of the mighty,
if in truth this is pleasing to the blessed immortals
that Odysseus of the many designs shall return home, then
let us dispatch Hermes, the guide, the slayer of Argos,
85 to the island of Ogygia, so that with all speed
he may announce to the lovely-haired nymph our absolute purpose,
the homecoming of enduring Odysseus, that he shall come back.
But I shall make my way to Ithaka, so that I may
stir up his son a little, and put some confidence in him
90 to summon into assembly the flowing-haired Achaians
and make a statement to all the suitors, who now forever
slaughter his crowding sheep and lumbering horn-curved cattle;
and I will convey him into Sparta and to sandy Pylos
to ask after his dear father's homecoming, if he can hear something,
95 and so that among people he may win a good reputation.'
     Speaking so she bound upon her feet the fair sandals,
golden and immortal, that carried her over the water
as over the dry boundless earth abreast of the wind's blast.
Then she caught up a powerful spear, edged with sharp bronze,
100 heavy, huge, thick, wherewith she beats down the battalions of fighting
men, against whom she of the mighty father is angered,
and descended in a flash of speed from the peaks of Olympos,

and lighted in the land of Ithaka, at the doors of Odysseus
at the threshold of the court, and in her hand was the bronze spear.
105   She was disguised as a friend, leader of the Taphians, Mentes.
There she found the haughty suitors. They at the moment
in front of the doors were amusing their spirits with draughts games,
sitting about on skins of cattle whom they had slaughtered
themselves, and about them, of their heralds and hard-working henchmen,
110   some at the mixing bowls were combining wine and water,
while others again with porous sponges were wiping the tables
and setting them out, and others cutting meat in quantities.
        Now far the first to see Athene was godlike Telemachos,
as he sat among the suitors, his heart deep grieving within him,
115   imagining in his mind his great father, how he might come back
and all throughout the house might cause the suitors to scatter,
and hold his rightful place and be lord of his own possessions.
With such thoughts, sitting among the suitors, he saw Athene
and went straight to the forecourt, the heart within him scandalized
120   that a guest should still be standing at the doors. He stood beside her
and took her by the right hand, and relieved her of the bronze spear,
and spoke to her and addressed her in winged words: 'Welcome, stranger.
You shall be entertained as a guest among us. Afterward,
when you have tasted dinner, you shall tell us what your need is.'
125   So speaking he led the way, and Pallas Athene followed him.
Now, when the two of them were inside the lofty dwelling,
he took the spear he carried and set it against a tall column
in a rack for spears, of polished wood, where indeed there were other
spears of patient-hearted Odysseus standing in numbers,
130   and he led her and seated her in a chair, with a cloth to sit on,
the chair splendid and elaborate. For her feet there was a footstool.
For himself, he drew a painted bench next her, apart from the others,
the suitors, for fear the guest, made uneasy by the uproar,
might lose his appetite there among overbearing people,
135   and so he might also ask him about his absent father.
A maidservant brought water for them and poured it from a splendid
and golden pitcher, holding it above a silver basin
for them to wash, and she pulled a polished table before them.
A grave housekeeper brought in the bread and served it to them,
140   adding many good things to it, generous with her provisions,
while a carver lifted platters of all kinds of meat and set them

in front of them, and placed beside them the golden goblets,
and a herald, going back and forth, poured the wine for them.
 Then the haughty suitors came in, and all of them straightway

145 took their places in order on chairs and along the benches,
and their heralds poured water over their hands for them to wash with,
and the serving maids brought them bread heaped up in the baskets,
and the young men filled the mixing bowls with wine for their drinking.
They put their hands to the good things that lay ready before them.

150 But when they had put away their desire for eating and drinking,
the suitors found their attention turned to other matters,
the song and the dance; for these things come at the end of the feasting.
A herald put the beautifully wrought lyre in the hands
of Phemios, who sang for the suitors, because they made him.

155 He played his lyre and struck up a fine song. Meanwhile
Telemachos talked to Athene of the gray eyes, leaning
his head close to hers, so that none of the others might hear him:
'Dear stranger, would you be scandalized at what I say to you?
This is all they think of, the lyre and the singing. Easy

160 for them, since without penalty they eat up the substance
of a man whose white bones lie out in the rain and fester
somewhere on the mainland, or roll in the wash of the breakers.
If they were ever to see him coming back to Ithaka
all the prayer of them all would be to be lighter on their feet

165 instead of to be richer men for gold and clothing.
As it is, he has died by an evil fate, and there is no comfort
left for us, not even though some one among mortals
tells us he will come back. His day of homecoming has perished.
But come now, tell me this and give me an accurate answer.

170 What man are you, and whence? Where is your city? Your parents?
What kind of ship did you come here on? And how did the sailors
bring you to Ithaka? What men do they claim that they are?
For I do not think you could have traveled on foot to this country.
And tell me this too, tell me truly, so that I may know it.

175 Are you here for the first time, or are you a friend of my father's
from abroad? Since many other men too used to come and visit
our house, in the days when he used to go about among people.'
 Then in turn the goddess gray-eyed Athene answered him:
'See, I will accurately answer all that you ask me.

180 I announce myself as Mentes, son of Anchialos

Athene disapproves of the suitors

the wise, and my lordship is over the oar-loving Taphians.
Now I have come in as you see, with my ship and companions
sailing over the wine-blue water to men of alien language,
to Temese, after bronze, and my cargo is gleaming iron.
185 And my ship stands near by, at the country, away from the city,
at the harbor, Rheithron, underneath wooded Neion.
Your father and I claim to be guest-friends by heredity
from far back, as you would know if you went to the aged hero
Laertes, who, they say, no longer comes to the city
190 now, but away by himself on his own land leads a hard life
with an old woman to look after him, who serves him his victuals
and drink, at the times when the weariness has befallen his body
from making his toilsome way on the high ground of his vineyard.
Now I have come. They told me he was here in this country,
195 your father, I mean. But no. The gods are impeding his passage.
For no death on the land has befallen the great Odysseus,
but somewhere, alive on the wide sea, he is held captive,
on a sea-washed island, and savage men have him in their keeping,
rough men, who somehow keep him back, though he is unwilling.
200 Now, I will make you a prophecy, in the way the immortals
put it into my mind, and as I think it will come out,
though I am no prophet, nor do I know the ways of birds clearly.
He will not long be absent from the beloved land of his fathers,
even if the bonds that hold him are iron, but he will be thinking
205 of a way to come back, since he is a man of many resources.
But come now tell me this and give me an accurate answer.
Are you, big as you are, the very child of Odysseus?
Indeed, you are strangely like about the head, the fine eyes,
as I remember; we used to meet so often together
210 before he went away to Troy, where others beside him
and the greatest of the Argives went in their hollow vessels.
Since that time I have not seen Odysseus nor has he seen me.'
    Then the thoughtful Telemachos said to her in answer:
'See, I will accurately answer all that you ask me.
215 My mother says indeed I am his. I for my part
do not know. Nobody really knows his own father.
But how I wish I could have been rather son to some fortunate
man, whom old age overtook among his possessions.
But of mortal men, that man has proved the most ill-fated

220 whose son they say I am: since you question me on this matter.'
  Then in turn the goddess gray-eyed Athene answered him:
'The gods have not made yours a birth that will go nameless
hereafter, since Penelope bore such a son as you are.
But come now, tell me this and give me an accurate answer.
225 What feast is this, what gathering? How does it concern you?
A festival, or a wedding? Surely, no communal dinner.
How insolently they seem to swagger about in their feasting
all through the house. A serious man who came in among them
could well be scandalized, seeing much disgraceful behavior.'
230   Then the thoughtful Telemachos said to her in answer:
'My guest, since indeed you are asking me all these questions,
there was a time this house was one that might be prosperous
and above reproach, when a certain man was here in his country.
But now the gods, with evil intention, have willed it otherwise,
235 and they have caused him to disappear, in a way no other
man has done. I should not have sorrowed so over his dying
if he had gone down among his companions in the land of the Trojans,
or in the arms of his friends, after he had wound up the fighting.
So all the Achaians would have heaped a grave mound over him,
240 and he would have won great fame for himself and his son hereafter.
But now ingloriously the stormwinds have caught and carried him
away, out of sight, out of knowledge, and he left pain and lamentation
to me. Nor is it for him alone that I grieve in my pain now.
No longer. For the gods have inflicted other cares on me.
245 For all the greatest men who have the power in the islands,
in Doulichion and Same and in wooded Zakynthos,
and all who in rocky Ithaka are holders of lordships,
all these are after my mother for marriage, and wear my house out.
And she does not refuse the hateful marriage, nor is she able
250 to make an end of the matter; and these eating up my substance
waste it away; and soon they will break me myself to pieces.'
  Pallas Athene answered him in great indignation:
'Oh, for shame. How great your need is now of the absent
Odysseus, who would lay his hands on these shameless suitors.
255 I wish he could come now to stand in the outer doorway
of his house, wearing a helmet and carrying shield and two spears,
the way he was the first time that ever I saw him
in our own house, drinking his wine and taking his pleasure,

Telemachos is to search for news of his father

coming in from Ephyre and from Ilos son of Mermeros.
260 Odysseus, you see, had gone there also in his swift ship
in search of a poison to kill men, so he might have it
to smear on his bronze-headed arrows, but Ilos would not
give him any, since he feared the gods who endure forever.
But my father did give it to him, so terribly did he love him.
265 I wish that such an Odysseus would come now among the suitors.
They all would find death was quick, and marriage a painful matter.
Yet all these are things that are lying upon the gods' knees:
whether he will come home to his vengeance, here in his household,
or whether he will not. Rather I will urge you to consider
270 some means by which you can force the suitors out of your household.
Come now, pay close attention to me and do as I tell you.
Tomorrow, summon the Achaian warriors into assembly
and publish your word to all, let the gods be your witnesses.
Tell the suitors to scatter and go back to their own holdings,
275 and as for your mother, if the spirit urges her to be married,
let her go back to the palace of her powerful father,
and they shall appoint the marriage and arrange for the wedding presents
in great amount, as ought to go with a beloved daughter.
But for yourself, I will counsel you shrewdly, and hope you will listen.
280 Fit out a ship with twenty oars, the best you can come by,
and go out to ask about your father who is so long absent,
on the chance some mortal man can tell you, who has listened to Rumor
sent by Zeus. She more than others spreads news among people.
First go to Pylos, and there question the great Nestor,
285 and from there go over to Sparta to see fair-haired Menelaos,
since he came home last of all the bronze-armored Achaians.
Thus if you hear your father is alive and on his way home,
then, hard pressed though you are, you should still hold out for another
year. But if you hear he has died and lives no longer,
290 then make your way home to the beloved land of your fathers,
and pile up a tomb in his honor, and there make sacrifices
in great amount, as is fitting. And give your mother to a husband.
Then, after you have made an end of these matters, and done them,
next you must consider well in your heart and spirit
295 some means by which you can kill the suitors who are in your household,
by treachery or open attack. You should not go on
clinging to your childhood. You are no longer of an age to do that.

Enter Penelope

Or have you not heard what glory was won by great Orestes
among all mankind, when he killed the murderer of his father,
300   the treacherous Aigisthos, who had slain his famous father?
So you too, dear friend, since I can see you are big and splendid,
be bold also, so that in generations to come they will praise you.
But now it is time for me to go back down to my fast ship
and my companions, who must be very restless waiting
305   for me. Let all this be on your mind, and do as I tell you.'
     Then the thoughtful Telemachos said to her in answer:
'My guest, your words to me are very kind and considerate,
what any father would say to his son. I shall not forget them.
But come now, stay with me, eager though you are for your journey,
310   so that you may first bathe and take your ease and, well rested
and happy in your heart, then go back to your ship with a present,
something prized, altogether fine, which will be your keepsake
from me, what loving guests and hosts bestow on each other.'
     Then in turn the goddess gray-eyed Athene answered him:
315   'Do not detain me longer, eager as I am for my journey;
and that gift, whatever it is your dear heart bids you give me,
save it to give when I come next time, so I can take it
home; and choose a good one, and a fair exchange will befall you.'
     So spoke the goddess gray-eyed Athene, and there she departed
320   like a bird soaring high in the air, but she left in his spirit
determination and courage, and he remembered his father
even more than he had before, and he guessed the meaning,
and his heart was full of wonder, for he thought it was a divinity.
At once he went over, a godlike man, to sit with the suitors.
325   The famous singer was singing to them, and they in silence
sat listening. He sang of the Achaians' bitter homecoming
from Troy, which Pallas Athene had inflicted upon them.
     The daughter of Ikarios, circumspect Penelope,
heard and heeded the magical song from her upper chamber,
330   and descended the high staircase that was built in her palace,
not all alone, since two handmaidens went to attend her.
When she, shining among women, came near the suitors,
she stood by the pillar that supported the roof with its joinery,
holding her shining veil in front of her face, to shield it,
335   and a devoted attendant was stationed on either side of her.
All in tears she spoke then to the divine singer:

Penelope dismissed

'Phemios, since you know many other actions of mortals
and gods, which can charm men's hearts and which the singers celebrate,
sit beside them and sing one of these, and let them in silence
340 go on drinking their wine, but leave off singing this sad
song, which always afflicts the dear heart deep inside me,
since the unforgettable sorrow comes to me, beyond others,
so dear a head do I long for whenever I am reminded
of my husband, whose fame goes wide through Hellas and midmost
      Argos.'
345   Then the thoughtful Telemachos said to her in answer:
'Why, my mother, do you begrudge this excellent singer
his pleasing himself as the thought drives him? It is not the singers
who are to blame, it must be Zeus is to blame, who gives out
to men who eat bread, to each and all, the way he wills it.
350 There is nothing wrong in his singing the sad return of the Danaans.
People, surely, always give more applause to that song
which is the latest to circulate among the listeners.
So let your heart and let your spirit be hardened to listen.
Odysseus is not the only one who lost his homecoming
355 day at Troy. There were many others who perished, besides him.
Go therefore back in the house, and take up your own work,
the loom and the distaff, and see to it that your handmaidens
ply their work also; but the men must see to discussion,
all men, but I most of all. For mine is the power in this household.'
360   Penelope went back inside the house, in amazement,
for she laid the serious words of her son deep away in her spirit,
and she went back to the upper story with her attendant
women, and wept for Odysseus, her beloved husband, until
gray-eyed Athene cast sweet slumber over her eyelids.
365   But the suitors all through the shadowy halls were raising a tumult,
and all prayed for the privilege of lying beside her,
until the thoughtful Telemachos began speaking among them:
'You suitors of my mother, overbearing in your rapacity,
now let us dine and take our pleasure, and let there be no
370 shouting, since it is a splendid thing to listen to a singer
who is such a singer as this man is, with a voice such as gods have.
Then tomorrow let us all go to the place of assembly,
and hold a session, where I will give you my forthright statement,
that you go out of my palace and do your feasting elsewhere,

375 eating up your own possessions, taking turns, household by household.
But if you decide it is more profitable and better
to go on, eating up one man's livelihood, without payment,
then spoil my house. I will cry out to the gods everlasting
in the hope that Zeus might somehow grant a reversal of fortunes.
380 Then you may perish in this house, with no payment given.'
So he spoke, and all of them bit their lips, in amazement
at Telemachos and the daring way he had spoken to them.
It was Antinoös the son of Eupeithes who answered:
'Telemachos, surely it must be the very gods who prompt you
385 to take the imperious line and speak so daringly to us.
I hope the son of Kronos never makes you our king in seagirt
Ithaka. Though to be sure that is your right by inheritance.'
Then the thoughtful Telemachos said to him in answer:
'Antinoös, in case you wonder at what I am saying,
390 I would be willing to take that right, if Zeus should give it.
Do you think that is the worst thing that could happen to anyone?
It is not bad to be a king. Speedily the king's house
grows prosperous, and he himself has rank beyond others.
But in fact there are many other Achaian princes,
395 young and old, in seagirt Ithaka, any of whom might
hold this position, now that the great Odysseus has perished.
But I will be the absolute lord over my own household
and my servants, whom the great Odysseus won by force for me.'
Then in turn Eurymachos, son of Polybos, answered:
400 'Telemachos, these matters, and which of the Achaians will be king
in seagirt Ithaka, are questions that lie on the gods' knees.
But I hope you keep your possessions and stay lord in your own household.
May the man never come who against your will and by force shall drive
you
away from your holdings, while Ithaka is a place still lived in.
405 But, best of men, I wish to ask you about this stranger,
where he came from, what country he announces as being
his own, where lies his parent stock, and the fields of his fathers.
Has he brought some message from your father who is on his way here?
Or did he arrive pursuing some matter of his own business?
410 How suddenly he started away and vanished, and did not
wait to be made known. He was no mean man, by the look of him.'
Then the thoughtful Telemachos said to him in answer:

All retire

'Eurymachos, there is no more hope of my father's homecoming.
I believe no messages any more, even should there be one,
415 nor pay attention to any prophecy, those times my mother
calls some diviner into the house and asks him questions.
This stranger is a friend of my father's. He comes from Taphos
and announces himself as Mentes, the son of Anchialos
the wise. And he is lord of the lovers of the oar, the Taphians.'
420 So spoke Telemachos, but in his heart he knew the immortal
goddess. The others, turning to the dance and the delightful
song, took their pleasure and awaited the coming of evening,
and the black evening came on as they were taking their pleasure.
Then they went home to go to bed, each to his own house,
425 but Telemachos went where, off the splendid courtyard, a lofty
bedchamber had been built for him, in a sheltered corner.
There he went to go to bed, his heart full of problems,
and devoted Eurykleia went with him, and carried the flaring
torches. She was the daughter of Ops the son of Peisenor,
430 and Laertes had bought her long ago with his own possessions
when she was still in her first youth, and gave twenty oxen for her,
and he favored her in his house as much as his own devoted
wife, but never slept with her, for fear of his wife's anger.
She now carried the flaring torches for him. She loved him
435 more than the other maidservants, and had nursed him when he was
    little.
He opened the doors of the close-compacted bedchamber,
and sat down on the bed and took off his soft tunic
and put it into the hands of the sagacious old woman,
and she in turn folded the tunic, and took care of it for him,
440 and hung it up on a peg beside the corded bedstead.
Then she went out of the room, and pulled the door to behind her
with a silver hook, and with a strap drew home the door bolt.
There, all night long, wrapped in a soft sheepskin, he pondered
in his heart the journey that Pallas Athene had counseled.

BOOK II

Now when the young Dawn showed again with her rosy fingers,
the dear son of Odysseus stirred from where he was sleeping,
and put on his clothes, and slung a sharp sword over his shoulder.
Underneath his shining feet he bound the fair sandals
5   and went on his way from the chamber, like a god in presence.
He gave the word now to his clear-voiced heralds to summon
by proclamation to assembly the flowing-haired Achaians,
and the heralds made their cry, and the men were assembled swiftly.
Now when they were all assembled in one place together,
10 he went on his way to assembly, in his hands holding a bronze spear,
not all alone, but a pair of light-footed dogs went with him.
Athene drifted an enchantment of grace upon him,
and all the people had their eyes on him as he came forward.
He sat in his father's seat, and the elders made way before him.
15 The first now to speak to them was the hero Aigyptios,
who was bent over with age, and had seen things beyond number.
His own dear son, Antiphos the spearman, had gone off
with godlike Odysseus to Ilion, land of good horses,
in the hollow ships, and now the wild Cyclops had killed him
20 deep in his cave, and this was the last man he had eaten.
He had three other sons. One of them, Eurynomos,
went with the suitors; the other two kept the estates of their
        fathers.

Even so, he could not forget the lost one. He grieved and mourned
    for him,
and it was in tears for him, now, that he stood forth and
    addressed them:
25 'Hear me now, men of Ithaka, and the word I give you.
Never has there been an assembly of us or any session
since great Odysseus went away in the hollow vessels.
Now who has gathered us, in this way? What need has befallen
which of the younger men, or one of us who are older?
30 Has he been hearing some message about the return of the army
which, having heard it first, he could now explain to us?
Or has he some other public matter to set forth and argue?
I think he is a good man and useful. So may Zeus grant him
good accomplishment for whatever it is his mind desires.'
35   He spoke, and the dear son of Odysseus was glad for the omen,
nor did he remain seated long, his heart was for speaking,
and he stood in the middle of the assembly. The herald Peisenor,
a man of deep discretion, put into his hands the scepter.
First, in answer to the old man, he spoke and addressed him:
40 'Old sir, the man is not far, but here; you yourself shall know him.
It is I who assembled the people. To me this grief comes closest.
Not that I heard some message about the return of the army,
which, having heard it first, I could now explain to you;
nor have I some other public matter to set forth and argue,
45 but my own need, the evil that has befallen my household.
There are two evils. I have lost a noble father, one who
was king once over you here, and was kind to you like a father;
and now here is a greater evil, one which presently
will break up the whole house and destroy all my livelihood.
50 For my mother, against her will, is beset by suitors,
own sons to the men who are greatest hereabouts. These
shrink from making the journey to the house of her father
Ikarios, so that he might take bride gifts for his daughter
and bestow her on the one he wished, who came as his favorite;
55 rather, all their days, they come and loiter in our house
and sacrifice our oxen and our sheep and our fat goats
and make a holiday feast of it and drink the bright wine
recklessly. Most of our substance is wasted. We have no man here
such as Odysseus was, to drive this curse from the household.

60 We ourselves are not the men to do it; we must be
weaklings in such a case, not men well seasoned in battle.
I would defend myself if the power were in me. No longer
are the things endurable that have been done, and beyond all decency
my house has been destroyed. Even you must be scandalized
65 and ashamed before the neighboring men about us, the people
who live around our land; fear also the gods' anger,
lest they, astonished by evil actions, turn against you.
I supplicate you, by Zeus the Olympian and by Themis
who breaks up the assemblies of men and calls them in session:
70 let be, my friends, and leave me alone with my bitter sorrow
to waste away; unless my noble father Odysseus
at some time in anger did evil to the strong-greaved Achaians,
for which angry with me in revenge you do me evil
in setting these on me. But for me it would be far better
75 for you to eat away my treasures and eat my cattle.
If you were to eat them, there might be a recompense someday,
for we could go through all the settlement, with claims made public
asking for our goods again, until it was all regiven.
But now you are heaping me with troubles I cannot deal with.'
80   So he spoke in anger, and dashed to the ground the scepter
in a stormburst of tears; and pity held all the people.
Now all the rest were stricken to silence, none was so hardy
as to answer, angry word against word, the speech of Telemachos.
It was Antinoös alone spoke to him in answer:
85   'High-spoken intemperate Telemachos, what accusations
you have made to our shame, trying to turn opinion against us!
And yet you have no cause to blame the Achaian suitors,
but it is your own dear mother, and she is greatly resourceful.
And now it is the third year, and will be the fourth year presently,
90 since she has been denying the desires of the Achaians.
For she holds out hope to all, and makes promises to each man,
sending us messages, but her mind has other intentions.
And here is another stratagem of her heart's devising.
She set up a great loom in her palace, and set to weaving
95 a web of threads long and fine. Then she said to us:
"Young men, my suitors now that the great Odysseus has perished,
wait, though you are eager to marry me, until I finish
this web, so that my weaving will not be useless and wasted.

The charms and guile of Penelope

This is a shroud for the hero Laertes, for when the destructive
100 doom of death which lays men low shall take him, lest any
Achaian woman in this neighborhood hold it against me
that a man of many conquests lies with no sheet to wind him."
So she spoke, and the proud heart in us was persuaded.
Thereafter in the daytime she would weave at her great loom,
105 but in the night she would have torches set by, and undo it.
So for three years she was secret in her design, convincing
the Achaians, but when the fourth year came with the seasons returning,
one of her women, who knew the whole of the story, told us,
and we found her in the act of undoing her glorious weaving.
110 So, against her will and by force, she had to finish it.
Now the suitors answer you thus, so that you yourself
may know it in your mind, and all the Achaians may know it:
send your mother back, and instruct her to be married
to any man her father desires and who pleases her also.
115 But if she continues to torment the sons of the Achaians,
since she is so dowered with the wisdom bestowed by Athene,
to be expert in beautiful work, to have good character
and cleverness, such as we are not told of, even of the ancient
queens, the fair-tressed Achaian women of times before us,
120 Tyro and Alkmene and Mykene, wearer of garlands;
for none of these knew thoughts so wise as those Penelope
knew; yet in this single matter she did not think rightly;
so long, I say, will your livelihood and possessions be eaten
away, as long as she keeps this purpose, one which the very
125 gods, I think, put into her heart. She is winning a great name
for herself, but for you she is causing much loss of substance.
We will not go back to our own estates, nor will we go elsewhere
until she marries whichever Achaian man she fancies.'
Then the thoughtful Telemachos said to him in answer:
130 'Antinoös, I cannot thrust the mother who bore me,
who raised me, out of the house against her will. My father,
alive or dead, is elsewhere in the world. It will be hard
to pay back Ikarios, if willingly I dismiss my mother.
I will suffer some evil from her father, and the spirit will give me
135 more yet, for my mother will call down her furies upon me
as she goes out of the house, and I shall have the people's
resentment. I will not be the one to say that word to her.

Favorable portents

But as for you, if your feeling is scandalized by my answer,
go away from my palace and do your feasting elsewhere,
140 eating up your own possessions, taking turns, household by household.
But if you decide it is more profitable and better
to go on, eating up one man's livelihood, without payment,
then spoil my house. I will cry out to the gods everlasting
in the hope that Zeus might somehow grant a reversal of fortunes.
145 Then you may perish in this house with no payment given.'
     So spoke Telemachos, and for his sake Zeus of the wide brows
sent forth two eagles, soaring high from the peak of the mountain.
These for a while sailed on the stream of the wind together,
wing and wing, close together, wings spread wide. But when
150 they were over the middle of the vociferous assembly,
they turned on each other suddenly in a thick shudder
of wings, and swooped over the heads of all, with eyes glaring
and deadly, and tore each other by neck and cheek with their talons,
then sped away to the right across the houses and city.
155 Then all were astounded at the birds, when their eyes saw them,
and they pondered in their hearts over what might come of it,
and Halitherses, Mastor's son, an aged warrior,
spoke to them. He was far beyond the men of his generation
in understanding the meaning of birds and reading their portents.
160 Now, in kind intention toward all, he spoke and addressed them:
'Hear me now, men of Ithaka, what I have to tell you;
but what I say will be mostly a warning to the suitors,
for a great disaster is wheeling down on them. Surely Odysseus
will not be long away from his family, but now, already,
165 is somewhere close by, working out the death and destruction
of all these men, and it will be an evil for many others
of us who inhabit sunny Ithaka. So, well beforehand,
let us think how we can make them stop, or better let them
stop themselves. It will soon be better for them if they do so.
170 I who foretell this am not untried, I know what I am saying.
Concerning him, I say that everything was accomplished
in the way I said it would be at the time the Argives took ship
for Ilion, and with them went resourceful Odysseus.
I said that after much suffering, with all his companions
175 lost, in the twentieth year, not recognized by any,
he would come home. And now all this is being accomplished.'

The suitors refuse to leave

Then in turn Eurymachos, son of Polybos, answered:
'Old sir, better go home and prophesy to your children,
for fear they may suffer some evil to come. In these things
180 I can give a much better interpretation than you can.
Many are the birds who under the sun's rays wander
the sky; not all of them mean anything; Odysseus
is dead, far away, and how I wish that you had died with him
also. Then you would not be announcing all these predictions,
185 nor would you so stir up Telemachos, who is now angry,
looking for the gift for your own household, which he might give you.
But I will tell you straight out, and it will be a thing accomplished:
if you, who know much and have known it long, stir up a younger
man, and by talking him round with words encourage his anger,
190 then first of all, it will be the worse for him; he will not
on account of all these sayings be able to accomplish anything;
and on you, old sir, we shall lay a penalty, and it will grieve your
mind as you pay it, and that for you will be a great sorrow.
I myself, before you all, will advise Telemachos.
195 Let him urge his mother to go back to her father's,
and they shall appoint the marriage and arrange for the wedding presents
in great amount, as ought to go with a beloved daughter.
For I think the sons of the Achaians will not give over
their harsh courtship, for in any case we fear no one,
200 and surely not Telemachos, for all he is so eloquent.
Nor do we care for any prophecy, which you, old sir,
may tell us, which will not happen, and will make you even more hated;
and his possessions will wretchedly be eaten away, there will not
be compensation, ever, while she makes the Achaians put off
205 marriage with her, while we, awaiting this, all our days
quarrel for the sake of her excellence, nor ever go after
others, whom any one of us might properly marry.'
Then the thoughtful Telemachos said to him in answer:
'Eurymachos, and all you others who are haughty suitors,
210 I no longer entreat you in these matters, nor speak about them,
since by now the gods know about this, as do all the Achaians.
But come now, grant me a swift ship, and twenty companions
who can convey me on a course from one place to another.
For I am going to Sparta and going to sandy Pylos
215 to ask about the homecoming of my father, who is long absent,

on the chance of some mortal man telling me, or of hearing a Rumor
sent by Zeus. She more than others spreads news among people.
Then if I hear my father is alive and on his way home,
then, hard pressed though I be, I will still hold out for another
220 year. But if I hear he has died and lives no longer,
then I will make my way home to the beloved land of my fathers,
and pile up a tomb in his honor, and there make sacrifices
in great amount, as is fitting. And give my mother to a husband.'
   So he spoke, and sat down again, and among them rose up
225 Mentor, who once had been the companion of stately Odysseus,
and Odysseus, going on the ships, had turned over the household
to the old man, to keep it well, and so all should obey him.
He in kind intention now spoke forth and addressed them:
'Hear me now, men of Ithaka, what I have to tell you.
230 No longer now let one who is a sceptered king be eager
to be gentle and kind, be one whose thought is schooled in justice,
but let him always rather be harsh, and act severely,
seeing the way no one of the people he was lord over
remembers godlike Odysseus, and he was kind, like a father.
235 Now it is not so much the proud suitors I resent
for doing their violent acts by their minds' evil devising;
for they lay their heads on the line when violently they eat up
the house of Odysseus, who, they say to themselves, will not come back;
but now I hold it against you other people, how you all
240 sit there in silence, and never with an assault of words try
to check the suitors, though they are so few, and you so many.'
   Then Leokritos, son of Euenor, spoke forth against him:
'Mentor, reckless in words, wild in your wits, what a thing
you have said, urging them to stop us. It would be difficult
245 even with more men than these to fight us over our feasting.
For even if Odysseus of Ithaka himself were to
come back, and find the haughty suitors feasting in his house,
and be urgent in his mind to drive them out of his palace,
his wife would have no joy of his coming, though she longs for it
250 greatly, but rather he would meet an unworthy destiny
if he fought against too many. You have spoken to no purpose.
Come then, all people disperse now, each to his own holdings,
and Mentor and Halitherses will push forward this man's journey,
since these from the first have been his friends, as friends of his father.

End of assembly

255 But, I think, he will sit still for a long time, waiting for messages
here in Ithaka, and will never accomplish this voyage.'
So he spoke, and suddenly broke up the assembly,
and the people scattered and went their ways, each to his own house,
while the suitors went away into the house of godlike Odysseus.
260 But Telemachos, walking along the sea beach away from the others,
washed his hands in the gray salt water and prayed to Athene:
'Hear me, you who came yesterday, a god, into our house
and urged me on to go by ship out over the misty
face of the sea, to ask about the homecoming of my father
265 who is so long absent: now all this is delayed by the Achaians
and particularly the suitors in their evil overconfidence.'
So he spoke in prayer, and from nearby Athene came to him
likening herself to Mentor in voice and appearance.
Now she spoke aloud to him and addressed him in winged words:
270 'Telemachos, you are to be no thoughtless man, no coward,
if truly the strong force of your father is instilled in you;
such a man he was for accomplishing word and action.
Your journey then will be no vain thing nor go unaccomplished.
But if you are not the seed begotten of him and Penelope,
275 I have no hope that you will accomplish all that you strive for.
For few are the children who turn out to be equals of their fathers,
and the greater number are worse; few are better than their father is.
But since you are to be no thoughtless man, no coward,
and the mind of Odysseus has not altogether given out in you,
280 there is some hope that you can bring all these things to fulfillment.
So now, let be the purpose and the planning of these senseless
suitors, since they are neither thoughtful men nor just men,
and have not realized the death and black fatality
that stands close by, so that on a day they all must perish.
285 And that journey for which you are so urgent will not be long now,
such a companion am I to you, as of your father.
I will fit you out a fast ship, I myself will go with you.
But now you must go back to the house, and join the suitors,
and get ready provisions for the journey, pack all in containers,
290 have wine in handled jars, and barley meal, men's marrow,
in thick leather bags, and I, going round the town, will assemble
volunteer companions to go with you. There are ships in plenty
here in seagirt Ithaka, both old and new ones,

Athene as Mentor advises Telemachos

and I will look them over for you to find out the best one,
295 and soon we shall stow our gear and put out onto the wide sea.'
　　So spoke Athene, daughter of Zeus, nor did Telemachos
delay long after he had heard the voice of the goddess,
but went on his way to the house, the heart troubled within him.
He came upon the haughty suitors, there in his palace,
300 skinning goats and singeing fatted swine in the courtyard.
Antinoös, with a smile, came straight up to Telemachos,
and took him by the hand and spoke and named him, saying:
'High-spoken intemperate Telemachos, now let no other
evil be considered in your heart, neither action
305 nor word, but eat and drink with me, as you did in past time.
The Achaians will see to it that all these things are accomplished,
the ship, and chosen companions, so that you may the more quickly
reach sacred Pylos, after news about your proud father.'
　　Then the thoughtful Telemachos said to him in answer:
310 'Antinoös, there is no way for me to dine with you
against my will, and take my ease, when you are so insolent.
Is it not enough, you suitors, that in time past you ruined
my great and good possessions, when I was still in my childhood?
But now, when I am grown big, and by listening to others
315 can learn the truth, and the anger is steaming up inside me,
I will endeavor to visit evil destructions upon you,
either by going to Pylos, or remaining here in the district.
But I will go; that journey I speak of will not be made void;
but as a passenger; for I control no ship, not any
320 companions; this, I think, was the way you wished to have it.'
　　He spoke, and lightly drew away his hand from Antinoös'
hand, but the suitors about the house prepared their dinner,
and in their conversation they insulted him and mocked him,
and thus would go the word of one of the arrogant young men:
325 'Surely now Telemachos is devising our murder.
Either he will bring some supporters from sandy Pylos,
or even from Sparta, now he is so terribly eager;
or perhaps his purpose is to go to Ephyre, that rich
corn land, so that thence he can bring back poisonous medicines
330 and put them into our wine bowl, and so destroy all of us.'
　　And thus would speak another one of these arrogant young men:
'Who knows whether, when he goes in a hollow ship, he also

might perish straying far from his people, as did Odysseus?
Were this to happen, he would lighten all our work for us.
335   Then we could divide up his possessions, and give the house
to this man's mother to keep, and to the man who marries her.'
    So they spoke, but he went down into his father's high-roofed
and wide storeroom, where gold and bronze were lying piled up,
and abundant clothing in the bins, and fragrant olive oil,
340   and in it jars of wine, sweet to drink, aged,
were standing, keeping the unmixed divine drink inside them,
lined up in order close to the wall, for the day when Odysseus
might come home even after laboring through many hardships.
To close it there were double doors that fitted together
345   with two halves, and there by night and day was a woman
in charge who, with intelligent care, watched over all this,
Eurykleia the daughter of Ops the son of Peisenor.
Now Telemachos called her to the room, and spoke to her:
'Dear nurse, come, draw me some sweet wine in the handled
350   jars, choicest of all you have in your keeping, next after
what you are saving for the ill-fated man, the day when Zeus-sprung
Odysseus might come home, escaping death and its spirits.
Fill me twelve in all and fit them all with covers.
And pour me barley into bags stitched strongly, of leather.
355   Let me have twenty measures of the choice milled barley. You be
the only one that knows this. Let all be gathered together,
for I will pick it up in the evening, after my mother
climbs to her upper chamber and is ready for sleeping.
For I am going into Sparta and to sandy Pylos,
360   to ask after my dear father's homecoming, if I might hear something.'
    So he spoke, and the dear nurse Eurykleia cried out,
and bitterly lamenting she addressed him in winged words:
'Why, my beloved child, has this intention come into
your mind? Why do you wish to wander over much country,
365   you, an only and loved son? Illustrious Odysseus
has perished far from his country in some outlandish region.
And these men will devise evils against you, on your returning,
so you shall die by guile, and they divide all that is yours.
No, but stay here and guard your possessions. It is not right
370   for you to wander and suffer hardships on the barren wide sea.'
    Then the thoughtful Telemachos said to her in answer:

Preparations for sailing

'Do not fear, nurse. This plan was not made without a god's will.
But swear to tell my beloved mother nothing about this
until the eleventh day has come or the twelfth hereafter,
375 or until she misses me herself or hears I am absent,
so that she may not ruin her lovely skin with weeping.'
    So he spoke, and the old woman swore to the gods a great oath,
and after she had sworn to it and completed the oath taking,
she drew the wine in the handled jars at once thereafter
380 and poured his barley into bags stitched strongly of leather,
but Telemachos went back into the house and joined the suitors.
    Now the gray-eyed goddess Athene thought what to do next.
In the likeness of Telemachos she went all through the city
and, standing beside each man as she came to him, told them
385 all to assemble beside the fast ship in the evening.
Then she asked Noëmon, the glorious son of Phronios,
for a fast ship. And he with good will promised it to her.
    And the sun set, and all the journeying ways were darkened.
Now she drew the fast ship down to the sea, and in her
390 stowed all the running gear that strong-benched vessels carry.
She set it at the edge of the harbor, and around her the good companions
thronged and were assembled and the goddess urged on each man.
    Now the gray-eyed goddess Athene thought what to do next.
She went on her way, into the house of godlike Odysseus,
395 and there she drifted a sweet slumber over the suitors,
and struck them as they drank, and knocked the goblets out of
their hands, and they went to sleep in the city, nor did any one
sit long, after sleep was fallen upon his eyelids.
Afterward gray-eyed Athene spoke to Telemachos
400 when she had called him out from the well-established palace,
likening herself to Mentor in voice and appearance:
'Telemachos, already now your strong-greaved companions
are sitting at the oars, and waiting for you to set forth.
So let us go, and not delay our voyaging longer.'
405   So spoke Pallas Athene, and she led the way swiftly,
and the man followed behind her walking in the god's footsteps.
But when they had come down to the sea, and where the ship was,
they found the flowing-haired companions there by the seashore.
Now the hallowed prince, Telemachos, spoke his word to them:
410 'Here, friends, let us carry the provisions. They are all ready

and stacked in the hall. But my mother has been told nothing of this,
nor the rest of the serving women. Only one knows the story.'
    So he spoke and led the way, and the rest went with him.
They all carried the provisions down, and stowed them in the strong-
        benched
415   vessel, in the way the dear son of Odysseus directed them.
Telemachos went aboard the ship, but Athene went first
and took her place in the stern of the ship, and close beside her
Telemachos took his place. The men cast off the stern cables
and themselves also went aboard and sat to the oarlocks.
420   The goddess gray-eyed Athene sent them a favoring stern wind,
strong Zephyros, who murmured over the wine-blue water.
Telemachos then gave the sign and urged his companions
to lay hold of the tackle, and they listened to his urging
and, raising the mast pole made of fir, they set it upright
425   in the hollow hole in the box, and made it fast with forestays,
and with halyards strongly twisted of leather pulled up the white sails.
The wind blew into the middle of the sail, and at the cutwater
a blue wave rose and sang strongly as the ship went onward.
She ran swiftly, cutting across the swell her pathway.
430   When they had made fast the running gear all along the black ship,
then they set up mixing bowls, filling them brimful
with wine, and poured to the gods immortal and everlasting
but beyond all other gods they poured to Zeus' gray-eyed daughter.
All night long and into the dawn she ran on her journey.

BOOK III

Helios, leaving behind the lovely standing waters, rose up
into the brazen sky to shine upon the immortals
and also on mortal men across the grain-giving farmland.
They came to Pylos, Neleus' strong-founded citadel,
5   where the people on the shore of the sea were making sacrifice
of bulls who were all black to the dark-haired Earthshaker.
There were nine settlements of them, and in each five hundred
holdings, and from each of these nine bulls were provided.
Now as these tasted the entrails, and burned, for the god, the thigh bones,
10   these others put straight in, and on the balanced ship took off
the sails, and stowed them, and moored her in, and themselves landed.
Telemachos stepped out of the ship, but Athene went first,
and it was the gray-eyed goddess Athene who first spoke to him:
'Telemachos, here is no more need at all of modesty;
15   for this was why you sailed on the open sea, to find news
of your father, what soil covers him, what fate he has met with.
So come now, go straight up to Nestor, breaker of horses,
for we know what intelligence is hidden inside him.
You yourself must entreat him to speak the whole truth to you.
20   He will not tell you any falsehood; he is too thoughtful.'
     Then the thoughtful Telemachos said to her in answer:
'Mentor, how shall I go up to him, how close with him?
I have no experience in close discourse. There is
embarrassment for a young man who must question his elder.'

51

25   Then in turn the gray-eyed goddess Athene answered him:
'Telemachos, some of it you yourself will see in your own heart,
and some the divinity will put in your mind. I do not
think you could have been born and reared without the gods' will.'
    So spoke Pallas Athene, and she led the way swiftly,
30   and the man followed behind her walking in the god's footsteps.
They came to where the men of Pylos were gathered in session,
where Nestor was sitting with his sons, and companions about him
were arranging the feast, and roasting the meat, and spitting more
        portions.
These men, when they sighted the strangers, all came down together
35   and gave them greeting with their hands and offered them places.
First Peisistratos, son of Nestor, came close up to them
and took them both by the hands, and seated them at the feasting
on soft rugs of fleece there on the sand of the seashore
next to his brother Thrasymedes and next to his father.
40   He gave them portions of the vitals, and poured wine for them
in a golden cup, and spoke a word to both of them, pledging
Pallas Athene, who is daughter of Zeus of the aegis:
'My guest, make your prayer now to the lord Poseidon,
for his is the festival you have come to on your arrival;
45   but when you have poured to him and prayed, according to custom,
then give this man also a cup of the sweet wine, so that
he too can pour, for I think he also will make his prayer
to the immortals. All men need the gods. But this one
is a younger man than you, and of the same age as I am.
50   This is why I am first giving you the golden goblet.'
    So he spoke, and put in her hand the cup of sweet wine,
and Athene was happy at the thoughtfulness of a just man,
because it was to her he first gave the golden goblet.
Immediately she made her prayer to the lord Poseidon:
55   'Hear us, Poseidon, who circle the earth, and do not begrudge us
the accomplishment of all these actions for which we pray you.
First of all to Nestor and to his sons grant glory,
and then on all the rest of the Pylians besides confer
gracious recompense in return for this grand hecatomb,
60   and yet again grant that Telemachos and I go back
with that business done for which we came this way in our black ship.'
    She spoke in prayer, but herself was bringing it all to completion.

Telemachos asks after Odysseus

Next she gave Telemachos the fine two-handled goblet,
and the dear son of Odysseus prayed in the way that she had.
65 When they had roasted and taken off the spits the outer
meats, dividing shares they held their communal high feast.
But when they had put aside their desire for eating and drinking,
first to speak was the Gerenian horseman, Nestor:
'Now is a better time to interrogate our guests and ask
70 them who they are, now they have had the pleasure of eating.
Strangers, who are you? From where do you come sailing over the watery
ways? Is it on some business, or are you recklessly roving
as pirates do, when they sail on the salt sea and venture
their lives as they wander, bringing evil to alien people?'
75   Then the thoughtful Telemachos said to him in answer,
taking courage, for Athene herself had put that courage
in his heart, so that he might ask after his absent father,
and so that among people he might win a good reputation:
'O Nestor, Neleus' son, great glory of the Achaians,
80 you ask us where we come from. Therefore I will tell you.
We come from Ithaka under the mountain Neion. This is
a private matter, no public business, of which I tell you.
I follow the wide fame of my father, on the chance of hearing
of the great patient-hearted Odysseus, the man they say once
85 fought beside you and helped sack the city of the Trojans.
For we have been told about all the other men who once fought
the Trojans, how each one of them perished in sad destruction,
but the son of Kronos has made this man's death one that none knows.
There is no man who can plainly tell us when he perished,
90 whether he was killed on the mainland by men embattled
or on the open sea in the billows of Amphitrite.
That is why I come to your knees now, in case you might wish
to tell me of his dismal destruction, whether you saw it
perhaps with your own eyes, or heard the tale from another
95 who wandered too. His mother bore this man to be wretched.
Do not soften it because you pity me and are sorry
for me, but fairly tell me all that your eyes have witnessed.
I implore you, if ever noble Odysseus, my father,
ever undertook any word or work and fulfilled it
100 for you, in the land of the Trojans where you Achaians suffered,
tell me these things from your memory. And tell me the whole truth.'

Nestor remembers Troy

In turn Nestor the Gerenian horseman answered him:
'Dear friend, since you remind me of sorrows which in that country
we endured, we sons of the Achaians valiant forever,
105 or all we endured in our ships on the misty face of the water
cruising after plunder wherever Achilleus led us,
or all we endured about the great city of the lord Priam
fighting; and all who were our best were killed in that place;
there Aias lies, a man of battles, there lies Achilleus,
110 there lies Patroklos, one who was like the gods for counsel,
and there lies my own beloved son, both strong and stately,
Antilochos, surpassingly swift to run, and a fighter;
and many besides these were the evils we suffered; what man
who was one of the mortal people could ever tell the whole of it,
115 not if you were to sit beside me five years, and six years,
and asked me about the evils the great Achaians endured there;
sooner you would be tired of it and go back to your country.
For nine years we fabricated evils against them, trying them
with every kind of stratagem, and at last the son of Kronos
120 finished it. Then there was no man who wanted to be set up
for cunning against great Odysseus; he far surpassed them
in every kind of stratagem; your father; if truly
you are his son; and wonder seizes me when I look on you.
For surely your words are like his words, nor would anyone
125 ever have thought that a younger man could speak so like him.
For while I and the great Odysseus were there together,
we never spoke against one another, neither in council
nor assembly, but forever one in mind and in thoughtful
planning, we worked out how things would go best for the Argives.
130 But after we had sacked the sheer citadel of Priam,
and were going away in our ships, and the god scattered the Achaians,
then Zeus in his mind devised a sorry homecoming
for the Argives, since not all were considerate nor righteous;
therefore many of them found a bad way home, because of
135 the ruinous anger of the Gray-eyed One, whose father is mighty.
It was she who made a quarrel between the two sons of Atreus.
When these two called all the Achaians into assembly,
wildly, and in no kind of order, as the sun was setting,
and the sons of the Achaians came in, heavy with drinking
140 wine, these two spoke forth. It was why they assembled the people.

and the start of the homecoming

At this time Menelaos was urging all the Achaians
to think upon going home over the sea's wide ridges,
but this did not please Agamemnon at all; he wished rather
to hold the people there, and accomplish holy hecatombs
145   so as to soften Athene's deadly anger, poor fool
who had no thought in his mind of what he would have to suffer.
The will of the everlasting gods is not turned suddenly.
So these two, after making exchange with hard words, stood up
to go, and the rest of the strong-greaved Achaians rushed out
150   with inhuman clamor, and two opposed counsels pleased them.
That night we slept there, pondering in our minds hard thoughts
against each other; Zeus was contriving pain of hardship.
At dawn, some of us hauled our ships down into the divine sea,
and loaded our possessions aboard, and the deep-girdled women.
155   But half the people were held back because they remained there
with Agamemnon, Atreus' son, shepherd of the people.
We the other half went aboard and drove on, and the ships went
very fast, as a god flattened the sea full of monsters.
We came to Tenedos and made sacrifice to the immortals.
160   We were straining homeward; but Zeus, hard-hearted, was not yet
      devising
homecoming for us, but again inspired yet another quarrel.
Then some, who followed the lord Odysseus, the wise and resourceful,
turned about, and boarding once more their oarswept vessels
went back, bringing comfort to Atreus' son, Agamemnon.
165   But I, with all the ships that followed pulled together,
fled away, for I saw how the god was devising evils,
and the warlike son of Tydeus fled and urged his companions
on, and, late, fair-haired Menelaos came to join us
and caught us at Lesbos as we pondered our long sea-voyage,
170   whether we should sail over the top of rocky Chios
by the island Psyros, keeping it on our left hand, or else
to pass under Chios, by windy Mimas. We asked the god
to give us some portent for a sign, and the god gave us
one, and told us to cut across the middle main sea
175   for Euboia, and so most quickly escape the hovering evil.
A whistling wind rose up and began to blow and the ships ran
very fast across those ways full of fish, and at nighttime
brought us in at Geraistos. We sacrificed many thigh bones

The murder of Agamemnon

of bulls to Poseidon, having measured the great open water.
180 It was the fourth day when the companions of Diomedes
breaker of horses, Tydeus' son, made fast their balanced
ships at Argos. I held on for Pylos. Never once
did the wind fail, once the god had set it to blowing.
So, dear child, I came back, without news, and I knew nothing
185 of those other Achaians, which had survived, which ones had perished.
But all I have got by hearsay sitting here in my palace,
this you shall know; it is right you should; I will not conceal it.
They say that the Myrmidons, those furious spearmen led by
the glorious son of great-hearted Achilleus made a good voyage,
190 and Philoktetes, Poias' shining son, had fair sailing,
and Idomeneus brought back to Crete all of his companions
who had escaped from the fighting. The sea took none of these men.
You yourselves, though you live apart, have heard of Atreides,
how he came home, and how Aigisthos devised his wretched
195 death; but Aigisthos too paid for it, in a dismal fashion;
so it is good, when a man has perished, to have a son left
after him, since this one took vengeance on his father's killer,
the treacherous Aigisthos, who cut down his glorious father.
So you too, dear friend, for I see you are tall and splendid,
200 be brave too, so that men unborn may speak well of you.'
      Then the thoughtful Telemachos said to him in answer:
'O Nestor, son of Neleus, great glory of the Achaians,
it is all too true that he took revenge, and so the Achaians
will carry his glory far and wide, a theme for the singers
205 to come. If only the gods would give me such strength as he has
to take revenge on the suitors for their overbearing oppression.
They force their way upon me and recklessly plot against me.
No, the gods have spun out no such strand of prosperity
for me and my father. Now we must even have to endure it.'
210   Then in turn Nestor the Gerenian horseman answered him:
'Dear friend, since you have spoken about these things and reminded me,
they do say that many suitors for the sake of your mother
are in your palace against your will, and plot evil against you.
Tell me, are you willingly put down, or are the people
215 who live about you swayed by some divine voice, and hate you?
Who knows whether he will come someday and punish the violence
of these people, either by himself or all the Achaians with him?

If only gray-eyed Athene would deign to love you, as in
those days she used so to take care of glorious Odysseus
220 in the Trojan country, where we Achaians suffered miseries;
for I never saw the gods showing such open affection
as Pallas Athene, the way she stood beside him, openly;
if she would deign to love you as she did him, and care for you
in her heart, then some of those people might well forget about marrying.'
225   Then the thoughtful Telemachos said to him in answer:
'Old sir, I think that what you have said will not be accomplished.
What you mean is too big. It bewilders me. That which I hope for
could never happen to me, not even if the gods so willed it.'
   Now in turn the gray-eyed goddess Athene spoke to him:
230 'Telemachos, what sort of word escaped your teeth's barrier?
Lightly a god, if he wishes, can save a man, even from far off.
I myself would rather first have gone through many hardships
and then come home, and look upon my day of returning,
than come home and be killed at my own hearth, as Agamemnon
235 was killed, by the treacherous plot of his wife, and by Aigisthos.
But death is a thing that comes to all alike. Not even
the gods can fend it away from a man they love, when once
the destructive doom of leveling death has fastened upon him.'
   Then the thoughtful Telemachos said to her in answer:
240 'Mentor, though we sorrow let us speak no more of these things.
His homecoming is no longer a real thing, but already
the immortal gods must have contrived his death and black doom.
But now I would find out about another story, and question
Nestor, since the righteousness and thought in his mind outpass
245 others', and they say he has been lord over three generations
of men. He shapes as an immortal for me to look upon.
O Nestor, son of Neleus, tell me the true story.
How did Atreus' son, widely ruling Agamemnon,
die? And where was Menelaos? What scheme of death
250 did treacherous Aigisthos have, to kill one far better than he was?
Was Menelaos out of Achaia and Argos, wandering
elsewhere among men, that Aigisthos had courage to do it?'
   Then in turn Nestor the Gerenian horseman answered:
'So, my child, I will relate you the whole true story.
255 All would have happened just in the way you yourself have seen it,
if Atreus' son, fair-haired Menelaos, on his homecoming

from Troy had found Aigisthos still alive in his palace.
Even after his death none would have heaped any earth upon him,
but he would have lain in the field outside the city, and the dogs
260 and birds would have feasted on him, nor would any Achaian woman
have wailed over him. That was a monstrous plot he accomplished.
For we were sitting out there and accomplishing many hard tasks
while he, at ease deep in the corner of horse-pasturing Argos,
kept talking to Agamemnon's wife and trying to charm her.
265 Now in time before, beautiful Klytaimestra would not
consent to the act of shame, for her own nature was honest,
and also a man was there, a singer, whom Agamemnon,
when he went to Troy, had given many instructions to keep watch
on his wife; but when the doom of the gods had entangled the singer
270 in the need of death, Aigisthos took him away and left him
on a desert island for the birds of prey to spoil and feed on,
and took her back to his house, and she was willing as he was.
Then on the sacred altars of the gods he burned many thigh bones
and hung up many dedications, gold, and things woven,
275 for having accomplished this monstrous thing he never had hoped for.
Now we sailed back on our way from Troy together, Atreus'
son, Menelaos, and I, with friendly thoughts toward each other,
but when we came to holy Sounion, the cape of Athens,
there Phoibos Apollo, with a visitation of his painless
280 arrows, killed the steersman of Menelaos, the one who
held in his hands the steering oar of the running ship. This was
Phrontis, Onetor's son, who surpassed all the breed of mortals
in the steering of a ship whenever stormwinds were blowing.
So Menelaos, though straining for the journey, was detained
285 there, to bury his companion, and give him due rites.
But when he too had gone out on the wine-blue open water
in his hollow ships, and made his run as far as the steep rock
of Maleia, then Zeus of the wide brows devised that his journey
should be hateful, and poured out upon him the blast of shrilling
290 winds, and waves that bulged and grew monstrous, like mountains.
There he cut the fleet in two parts, and drove some on Crete
where the Kydonians lived around the streams of Iardanos.
There is the sheer of a cliff, a steep rock out in the water
at the other end of Gortys on the misty face of the main, where
295 the south wind piles up a huge surf on the left of the rock horn

toward Phaistos, and a little stone holds out the big water.
It was there they came, and by lively work the men avoided
destruction, but the waves smashed their ships on the splinters
of rock, but the wind and the water catching up the other

300 five dark-prowed ships bore them along and drove them on Egypt.
So Menelaos, gathering much gold and livelihood in those
parts, sailed with his ships to men of alien language,
and all the while at home Aigisthos worked out his grim plans.
Seven years he lived as lord over golden Mykene,

305 after he killed Atreides, with the people subject beneath him,
but in the eighth the evil came on him, great Orestes
come home from Athens, and he killed his father's murderer,
the treacherous Aigisthos, who had killed his glorious father.
When he had killed, he ordered among the Argives a grave mound

310 for his mother who was hateful and for unwarlike Aigisthos;
and on the same day Menelaos of the great war cry sailed in
bringing back many possessions, the burden his ships carried.
So, dear friend, do not you stay long and far wandering
away from home, leaving your possessions, and in your house men

315 so overbearing, for fear they divide up all your property
and eat it away, so all your journey will have no profit.
And yet I do encourage you and urge you to visit
Menelaos, for he is newly come from abroad, and people
who live where no man's mind would ever have hope of returning,

320 once the stormwinds had blundered him off his course and into
an open sea that is so great that not the birds even
cross it by their own strength, it is so big and terrible.
But go to him now, with your ship and with your companions,
or if you wish to go by land, here are horses and chariot,

325 and here are my own sons at your service, who will be your escorts
into shining Lakedaimon, the home of fair-haired Menelaos.
You yourself must entreat him to speak the whole truth to you.
He will not tell you any falsehood; he is too thoughtful.'
So he spoke, and the sun went down and the darkness came over,

330 and now the gray-eyed goddess Athene spoke forth before them:
'Old sir, all that you have said was fair and orderly.
But come now, cut out the tongues of the victims and mix the wine bowls,
so that when we have poured an offering to Poseidon
and the other immortals, we can think about sleep. It is that time.

Departure of Athene

335   For now the light has gone into the darkness, nor is it becoming
to sit about at the feast of the gods; but better to go home.'
So she spoke, the daughter of Zeus, and they listened to her.
The heralds poured water over their hands to wash with,
and the young men filled the mixing bowls with wine for their drinking,
340   and passed to all, after they had offered a drink in the goblets.
They threw the tongues in the fire and stood up and made a libation.
But when they had poured and drunk each as much as he wanted,
then Athene and godlike Telemachos started
up together to go away to their hollow vessel,
345   but Nestor detained them where they were, and made a speech to them:
'May Zeus and all the other immortals beside forfend
that you, in my domain, should go on back to your fast ship
as from some man altogether poor and without clothing,
who has not any abundance of blankets and rugs in his household
350   for his guests, or for himself to sleep in soft comfort.
But I do have abundance of fine rugs and blankets.
No, no, in my house the dear son of Odysseus shall not
have to go to sleep on the deck of a ship, as long as
I am alive, and my sons after me are left in my palace
355   to entertain our guests, whoever comes to my household.'
Then in turn the goddess gray-eyed Athene said to him:
'This was well said by you, dear old sir; it is fitting
that Telemachos should obey you, since it is much better that way.
So he shall go along with you now, so that he can sleep
360   in your palace, but I shall be going down to my black ship,
so that I can encourage my companions and tell them everything.
For I am the only man among them who can call myself
an elder; the rest, all of an age with the great-hearted
Telemachos, are younger men who out of love for him
365   went along. There I will lie down beside the black ship
now, but at dawn shall make for the great-hearted Kaukones,
where a debt owed me has been piling up, it is not a new thing
nor a small one. You, since this young man has come to your household,
give him conveyance with your son by chariot, and give him
370   those horses that are best for strength and the lightest runners.'
So speaking, gray-eyed Athene went away in the likeness
of a vulture, and amazement seized on all the Achaians,
and the old man was amazed at what his eyes saw. He took

Telemachos by the hand and spoke a word to him and named him:

375 'Dear friend, I have no thought that you will turn out mean and cowardly
if, when you are so young, the gods go with you and guide you
thus. Here was no other of those who have their homes on Olympos
but the very daughter of Zeus, most honored Tritogeneia,
who always among the Argives favored your noble father.

380 So now, O queen, be gracious, and grant me good reputation
for myself and for my children also and for my grave wife,
and I will sacrifice you a yearling cow, with wide forehead,
unbroken, one no man has ever led under the yoke yet.
I will gild both her horns with gold and offer her to you.'

385   So he spoke in prayer, and Pallas Athene heard him.
Now the Gerenian horseman Nestor led the way for
his sons and his sons-in-law back to his splendid dwelling.
But after they had reached the glorious dwelling of the king,
they took their places in order on chairs and along the benches,

390 and as they came in the old man mixed the wine bowl for them
with wine sweet to drink which the housekeeper had opened
in its eleventh year and loosed the sealing upon it.
The old man mixed the wine in the bowl and prayed much, pouring
a libation out to Athene daughter of Zeus of the aegis.

395   When they had poured and drunk, each man as much as he wanted,
they went away each one to sleep in his own dwelling,
but Nestor the Gerenian horseman gave Telemachos
the dear son of godlike Odysseus a place to sleep in
upon a corded bedstead in the echoing portico.

400 Next him was Peisistratos of the strong ash spear, leader
of men, who of his sons in the palace was still a bachelor.
But Nestor himself slept in the inner room of the high house,
and at his side the lady his wife served as bedfellow.
    But when the young Dawn showed again with her rosy fingers,

405 then Nestor the Gerenian horseman rose up from his bed,
and went outside and took his seat upon the polished stones
which were there in place for him in front of the towering doorway,
white stones, with a shine on them that glistened. On these before him
Neleus, a counselor like the gods, had held his sessions,

410 but he had been beaten down by his doom and gone down to Hades'
house, and now Gerenian Nestor, the Achaians' watcher,
sat there holding his staff, and his sons coming out of their chambers

Sacrifice to Athene

gathered in a cluster about him, Echephron and Stratios,
Perseus and Aretos and Thrasymedes the godlike,

415 and sixth was the hero Peisistratos who came to join them.
They brought out godlike Telemachos and seated him next them,
and Nestor the Gerenian horseman began speaking to them:
'Act quickly now, dear children, and do me this favor, so that
I may propitiate first of all the gods, Athene,

420 who came plainly to me at our happy feasting in the god's honor.
Come then, let one man go to the field for a cow, so that
she may come with all speed, and let one of the oxherds be driving her,
and one go down to the black ship of great-hearted Telemachos,
and bring back all his companions, leaving only two beside her,

425 and yet another go tell the worker in gold Laerkes
to come, so that he can cover the cow's horns with gold. You others
stay here all together in a group but tell the serving
women who are in the house to prepare a glorious dinner,
and set chairs and firewood in readiness, and fetch bright water.'

430 So he spoke, and they all bustled about. The cow came
in from the field, and the companions of great-hearted Telemachos
came from beside their fast black ship, and the smith came, holding
in his hands the tools for forging bronze, his handicraft's symbols,
the anvil and the sledgehammer and the well-wrought pincers

435 with which he used to work the gold, and Athene also
came to be at her rites. Now Nestor, the aged horseman,
gave the smith the gold, and he gilded the cow's horns with it
carefully, so the god might take pleasure seeing her offering.
Stratios and the noble Echephron led the cow by

440 the horns, and Aretos came from the inner chamber carrying
lustral water in a flowered bowl, and in the other hand
scattering barley in a basket. Steadfast Thrasymedes
stood by with the sharp ax in his hand, to strike down the heifer.
Perseus held the dish for the blood, and the aged horseman

445 Nestor began with the water and barley, making long prayers
to Athene, in dedication, and threw the head hairs in the fire.
Now when all had made prayer and flung down the scattering barley,
Thrasymedes, the high-hearted son of Nestor, standing
close up, struck, and the ax chopped its way through the tendons

450 of the neck and unstrung the strength of the cow, and now the daughters
and daughters-in-law of Nestor and his grave wife Eurydike,

eldest of the daughters of Klymenos, raised the outcry.
They lifted the cow from earth of the wide ways, and held her
fast in place, and Peisistratos, leader of men, slaughtered her.
455 Now when the black blood had run out, and the spirit went from
the bones, they divided her into parts, and cut out the thigh bones
all according to due order, and wrapped them in fat,
making a double fold, and laid shreds of flesh upon them.
The old man burned these on cleft sticks, and poured the gleaming
460 wine over, while the young men with forks in their hands stood about him.
But when they had burned the thigh pieces and tasted the vitals,
they cut all the remainder into pieces and spitted them,
and roasted all carefully and took off the pieces.
Meanwhile lovely Polykaste, who was the youngest
465 of the daughters of Nestor, son of Neleus, had bathed Telemachos.
But when she had bathed him and anointed him sleekly with olive oil,
she threw a splendid mantle and a tunic about him,
and he came out from the bath looking like an immortal
and came and sat down beside Nestor, shepherd of the people.
470 When they had roasted and taken off the spits the outer
meats, they dined where they were sitting, and men of quality
started up and poured them wine in the golden goblets.
But when they had put away their desire for eating and drinking,
Nestor the Gerenian horseman began speaking to them:
475 'Come now, my children, harness the bright-maned horses under
the yoke for Telemachos so that he can get on with his journey.'
So he spoke, and they listened well to him and obeyed him,
and quickly they harnessed the fast horses under the chariot,
and the woman who was housekeeper put bread and wine in,
480 and meats, such as kings whom the gods love feed on,
and Telemachos stepped up into the fair-wrought chariot,
and by him Peisistratos leader of men, the son of Nestor,
went up into the chariot, and in his hands took the reins
and whipped the horses to run, and they winged their way unreluctant
485 into the plain, and left behind the sheer city of Pylos.
All day long they shook the yoke they wore on their shoulders.
And the sun set, and all the journeying ways were darkened.
They came to Pherai and reached the house of Diokles, who was
son of Ortilochos, whom Alpheios once had childed.
490 There they slept the night and he gave them hospitality.

Arrival

But when the young Dawn showed again with her rosy fingers,
they yoked the horses again and mounted the chariots bright with
bronze, and drove them out the front door and the echoing portico,
and he whipped them into a run and they winged their way unreluctant.
495 They came into the plain full of wheat, and by that way
made good their journey as their fast horses took this by-way.
And the sun set, and all the journeying ways were darkened.

BOOK IV

They came into the cavernous hollow of Lakedaimon
and made their way to the house of glorious Menelaos.
They found him in his own house giving, for many townsmen,
a wedding feast for his son and his stately daughter. The girl
5 he was sending to the son of Achilleus, breaker of battalions,
for in Troy land first he had nodded his head to it and promised
to give her, and now the gods were bringing to pass their marriage;
so he was sending her on her way, with horses and chariots,
to the famous city of the Myrmidons, where Neoptolemos
10 was lord, and he brought Alektor's daughter from Sparta, to give
powerful Megapenthes, his young grown son born to him
by a slave woman; but the gods gave no more children to Helen
once she had borne her first and only child, the lovely
Hermione, with the beauty of Aphrodite the golden.
15   So these neighbors and townsmen of glorious Menelaos
were at their feasting all about the great house with the high roof,
and taking their ease, and among them stepped an inspired singer
playing his lyre, while among the dancers two acrobats
led the measures of song and dance, revolving among them.
20   These two now, the hero Telemachos and the shining
son of Nestor in the forecourt, themselves and their horses,
stood, while powerful Eteoneus, who was the active
henchman of glorious Menelaos, came forward and saw them
and went with his message through the house to the shepherd of the
         people.

Entertainment by Menelaos

25   He came and standing close beside him addressed him in winged words:
     'Menelaos, dear to Zeus, here are certain strangers,
     two men, and they look like the breed of great Zeus. Tell me
     then, whether we should unharness their fast horses,
     or send them on to somebody else, who can entertain them.'
30   Then, deeply vexed, fair-haired Menelaos answered him:
     'Eteoneus, son of Boëthoös, you were never
     a fool before, but now you are babbling nonsense, as a child
     would do. Surely we two have eaten much hospitality
     from other men before we came back here. May Zeus only
35   make an end of such misery hereafter. Unharness
     the strangers' horses then, and bring the men here to be feasted.'
      So he spoke, and the man hurried through the hall, bestirring
     the other active henchmen to come on the way along with him.
     They set free the sweating horses from under the harness,
40   and tethered them fast by the reins in front of the horse mangers,
     and put down fodder before them and mixed white millet into it,
     and leaned the chariots up against the glittering inner walls,
     and led the men inside the divine house. These marveled
     as they admired the palace of the king whom Zeus loved,
45   for as the shining of the sun or the moon was the shining
     all through this high-roofed house of glorious Menelaos.
     When with their eyes they had had their pleasure in admiration,
     they stepped into the bathtubs smooth-polished and bathed there.
     Then when the maids had bathed them and anointed them with oil,
50   and put cloaks of thick fleece and tunics upon them, they went
     and sat on chairs beside Menelaos the son of Atreus.
     A maidservant brought water for them and poured it from a splendid
     and golden pitcher, holding it above a silver basin
     for them to wash, and she pulled a polished table before them.
55   A grave housekeeper brought in the bread and served it to them,
     adding many good things to it, generous with her provisions,
     while a carver lifted platters of all kinds of meat and set them
     in front of them, and placed beside them the golden goblets.
     Then in greeting fair-haired Menelaos said to them:
60   'Help yourselves to the food and welcome, and then afterward,
     when you have tasted dinner, we shall ask you who among
     men you are, for the stock of your parents can be no lost one,
     but you are of the race of men who are kings, whom Zeus sustains,

who bear scepters; no mean men could have sons such as you are.'
65   So he spoke, and taking in his hands the fat beef loin
which had been given as his choice portion, he set it before them.
They put their hands to the good things that lay ready before them.
But when they had put away their desire for eating and drinking,
then Telemachos talked to the son of Nestor, leaning
70   his head close to his, so that none of the others might hear him:
'Son of Nestor, you who delight my heart, only look at
the gleaming of the bronze all through these echoing mansions,
and the gleaming of gold and amber, of silver and of ivory.
The court of Zeus on Olympos must be like this on the inside,
75   such abundance of everything. Wonder takes me as I look on it.'
      Menelaos of the fair hair overheard him speaking,
and now he spoke to both of them and addressed them in winged words:
'Dear children, there is no mortal who could rival Zeus, seeing
that his mansions are immortal and his possessions. There may be
80   some man who could rival me for property, or there may be
none. Much did I suffer and wandered much before bringing
all this home in my ships when I came back in the eighth year.
I wandered to Cyprus and Phoenicia, to the Egyptians,
I reached the Aithiopians, Eremboi, Sidonians,
85   and Libya where the rams grow their horns quickly. Three times
in the fulfillment of a year their sheepflocks give birth,
and there no lord would ever go wanting, nor would his shepherd,
for cheese or meat, nor for the sweet milk either, but always
the sheep yield a continuous supply for their sucklings.
90   But while I was wandering those parts and bringing together
much property, meanwhile another man killed my brother
secretly, by surprise and by his cursed wife's treachery.
So it is with no pleasure I am lord over all these possessions.
You will have heard all this from your fathers, whoever your fathers
95   are, for I have suffered much, and destroyed a household
that was very strongly settled and held many goods within it.
I wish I lived in my house with only a third part of all
these goods, and that the men were alive who died in those days
in wide Troy land far away from horse-pasturing Argos.
100   Still and again lamenting all these men and sorrowing
many a time when I am sitting here in our palace
I will indulge my heart in sorrow, and then another time

Enter Helen

give over, for surfeit of gloomy lamentation comes quickly.
But for none of all these, sorry as I am, do I grieve so much
105 as for one, who makes hateful for me my food and my sleep, when I
remember, since no one of the Achaians labored as much
as Odysseus labored and achieved, and for him the end was
grief for him, and for me a sorrow that is never forgotten
for his sake, how he is gone so long, and we knew nothing
110 of whether he is alive or dead. The aged Laertes
and temperate Penelope must surely be grieving for him,
with Telemachos whom he left behind in his house, a young child.'
He spoke, and stirred in the other the longing to weep for his father,
and the tears fell from his eyes to the ground when he heard his father's
115 name, holding with both hands the robe that was stained with purple
up before his eyes. And Menelaos perceived it,
and now he pondered two ways within, in mind and in spirit
whether he would leave it to him to name his father,
or whether he should speak first and ask and inquire about everything.
120   While he was pondering these things in his heart and his spirit,
Helen came out of her fragrant high-roofed bedchamber,
looking like Artemis of the golden distaff. Adreste
followed and set the well-made chair in place for her,
and the coverlet of soft wool was carried in by Alkippe,
125 and Phylo brought the silver workbasket which had been given
by Alkandre, the wife of Polybos, who lived in Egyptian
Thebes, where the greatest number of goods are stored in the houses.
Polybos himself gave Menelaos two silver bathtubs,
and a pair of tripods, and ten talents of gold, and apart from
130 these his wife gave her own beautiful gifts to Helen.
She gave her a golden distaff and a basket, silver,
with wheels underneath, and the edges were done in gold. Phylo,
her maidservant, now brought it in and set it beside her
full of yarn that had been prepared for spinning. The distaff
135 with the dark-colored wool was laid over the basket. Helen
seated herself on the chair, and under her feet was a footstool.
At once she spoke to her husband and questioned him about everything:
'Do we know, Menelaos beloved of Zeus, who these men
announce themselves as being, who have come into our house now?
140 Shall I be wrong, or am I speaking the truth? My heart tells me
to speak, for I think I never saw such a likeness, neither

in man nor woman, and wonder takes me as I look on him,
as this man has a likeness to the son of great-hearted Odysseus,
Telemachos, who was left behind in his house, a young child
145 by that man when, for the sake of shameless me, the Achaians
went beneath Troy, their hearts intent upon reckless warfare.'
    Then in answer fair-haired Menelaos said to her:
'I also see it thus, my wife, the way you compare them,
for Odysseus' feet were like this man's, his hands were like this,
150 and the glances of his eyes and his head and the hair growing.
Now too I was remembering things about Odysseus
and spoke of him, what misery he had in his hard work
for me, and he let fall a heavy tear from under his eyelids,
holding before his eyes the robe that was stained with purple.'
155   Now Peisistratos son of Nestor spoke up before him:
'Great Menelaos, son of Atreus, leader of the people,
this is in truth the son of that man, just as you are saying;
but he is modest, and his spirit would be shocked at the thought
of coming here and beginning a show of reckless language
160 in front of you, for we both delight in your voice, as if a god
were speaking. The Gerenian horseman Nestor sent me
to go along with him and escort him. He longed to see you
so that you could advise him somewhat, for word or action.
For a child endures many griefs in his house when his father
165 is gone away, and no others are there to help him, as now
Telemachos' father is gone away, and there are no others
who can defend him against the evil that is in his country.'
    Then in answer fair-haired Menelaos said to him:
'See now, this is the son of a man greatly beloved who has come now
170 into my house, one who for my sake endured many trials,
and I thought he would come, and I would love him beyond all other
Argives, if only Olympian Zeus of the wide brows granted
both of us to come home across the sea in our fast ships.
I would have settled a city in Argos for him, and made him
175 a home, bringing him from Ithaka with all his possessions,
his son, all his people. I would have emptied one city for him
out of those that are settled round about and under my lordship.
And, both here, we would have seen much of each other; nothing
would then have separated us two in our friendship and pleasure,
180 until the darkening cloud of death had shrouded us over.

All this must be what the very god himself begrudged him,
who made only him an unhappy man, without a homecoming.'
He spoke, and started in all of them the desire for weeping.
Helen of Argos, daughter of Zeus, wept, so too Telemachos
185   wept, as did Menelaos the son of Atreus, nor did
Nestor's son, Peisistratos, have eyes altogether tearless,
for he was thinking in his heart of stately Antilochos,
one whom the glorious son of the shining Dawn had cut down.
It was of him he thought as he addressed them in winged words:
190   'Son of Atreus, the aged Nestor used to say you were
thoughtful, surpassing other men, when we spoke about you
there in his own palace, and when we questioned each other.
So now, if it may be, would you do me a favor? For my part
I have no joy in tears after dinnertime. There will always
195   be a new dawn tomorrow. Yet I can have no objection
to tears for any mortal who dies and goes to his destiny.
And this is the only consolation we wretched mortals
can give, to cut our hair and let the tears roll down our faces.
For I myself had a brother who died, he was not the meanest
200   of the Argives, and you would have known him, but I for my part
never met nor saw him. They say he surpassed all others:
Antilochos: surpassingly swift of foot, and a fighter.'
Then in answer fair-haired Menelaos said to him:
'Dear friend, since you have said all that a man who is thoughtful
205   could say or do, even one who was older than you are—
why, this is the way your father is, so you too speak thoughtfully.
Easily recognized is the line of that man, for whom Kronos'
son weaves good fortune in his marrying and begetting,
as now he has given to Nestor, all his days, for himself
210   to grow old prosperously in his own palace, and also
that his sons should be clever and excellent in the spear's work.
Now we shall let the weeping be, that came to us just now,
and let us think again about dinner, let someone pour us
water for our hands, and there will be time for words tomorrow
215   at dawn, for Telemachos and me, to talk with each other.'
He spoke, and Asphalion, who was the active henchman
of glorious Menelaos, poured water for them to wash with.
They put their hands to the good things that lay ready before them.
Now Helen, who was descended of Zeus, thought of the next thing.

220   Into the wine of which they were drinking she cast a medicine
      of heartsease, free of gall, to make one forget all sorrows,
      and whoever had drunk it down once it had been mixed in the wine bowl,
      for the day that he drank it would have no tear roll down his face,
      not if his mother died and his father died, not if men
225   murdered a brother or a beloved son in his presence
      with the bronze, and he with his own eyes saw it. Such were
      the subtle medicines Zeus' daughter had in her possessions,
      good things, and given to her by the wife of Thon, Polydamna
      of Egypt, where the fertile earth produces the greatest number
230   of medicines, many good in mixture, many malignant,
      and every man is a doctor there and more understanding
      than men elsewhere. These people are of the race of Paiëon.
      Now when she had put the medicine in, and told them to pour it,
      taking up the story again she began to speak to them:
235   'Son of Atreus, dear to Zeus, Menelaos: and you who
      are here, children of noble fathers; yet divine Zeus sometimes
      gives out good, or sometimes evil; he can do anything.
      Sit here now in the palace and take your dinner and listen
      to me and be entertained. What I will tell you is plausible.
240   I could not tell you all the number nor could I name them,
      all that make up the exploits of enduring Odysseus,
      but here is a task such as that strong man endured and accomplished
      in the Trojan country where you Achaians suffered miseries.
      He flagellated himself with degrading strokes, then threw on
245   a worthless sheet about his shoulders. He looked like a servant.
      So he crept into the wide-wayed city of the men he was fighting,
      disguising himself in the likeness of somebody else, a beggar,
      one who was unlike himself beside the ships of the Achaians,
      but in his likeness crept into the Trojans' city, and they all
250   were taken in. I alone recognized him even in this form,
      and I questioned him, but he in his craftiness eluded me;
      but after I had bathed him and anointed him with olive oil
      and put some clothing upon him, after I had sworn a great oath
      not to disclose before the Trojans that this was Odysseus
255   until he had made his way back to the fast ships and the shelters,
      then at last he told me all the purpose of the Achaians,
      and after striking many Trojans down with the thin bronze
      edge, he went back to the Argives and brought back much information.

Memories of Odysseus

The rest of the Trojan women cried out shrill, but my heart
260 was happy, my heart had changed by now and was for going back
home again, and I grieved for the madness that Aphrodite
bestowed when she led me there away from my own dear country,
forsaking my own daughter, my bedchamber, and my husband,
a man who lacked no endowment either of brains or beauty.'
265   Then in answer fair-haired Menelaos said to her:
'Yes, my wife, all this that you said is fair and orderly.
In my time I have studied the wit and counsel of many
men who were heroes, and I have been over much of the world, yet
nowhere have I seen with my own eyes anyone like him,
270 nor known an inward heart like the heart of enduring Odysseus.
Here is the way that strong man acted and the way he endured
action, inside the wooden horse, where we who were greatest
of the Argives all were sitting and bringing death and destruction
to the Trojans. Then you came there, Helen; you will have been moved by
275 some divine spirit who wished to grant glory to the Trojans,
and Deïphobos, a godlike man, was with you when you came.
Three times you walked around the hollow ambush, feeling it,
and you called out, naming them by name, to the best of the Danaans,
and made your voice sound like the voice of the wife of each of the
    Argives.
280 Now I myself and the son of Tydeus and great Odysseus
were sitting there in the middle of them and we heard you crying
aloud, and Diomedes and I started up, both minded
to go outside, or else to answer your voice from inside,
but Odysseus pulled us back and held us, for all our eagerness.
285   Then all the other sons of the Achaians were silent:
there was only one, it was Antiklos, who was ready to answer,
but Odysseus, brutally squeezing his mouth in the clutch of his powerful
hands, held him, and so saved the lives of all the Achaians
until such time as Pallas Athene led you off from us.'
290   Then the thoughtful Telemachos said to him in answer:
'Great Menelaos, son of Atreus, leader of the people:
so much the worse; for none of all this kept dismal destruction
from him, not even if he had a heart of iron within him.
But come, take us away to our beds, so that at last now
295 we can go to bed and enjoy the pleasure of sweet sleep.'
    So he spoke, and Helen of Argos told her serving maids

Next morning, Telemachos asks about him

to make up beds in the porch's shelter and to lay upon them
fine underbedding of purple, and spread blankets above it
and fleecy robes to be an over-all covering. The maidservants
300 went forth from the main house, and in their hands held torches,
and they made the beds. The guests were led outside by a herald.
So the hero Telemachos and the glorious son of Nestor
slept in the place outside the house in the porch's shelter,
but the son of Atreus slept in the inner room of the high house,
305 and by him lay Helen of the light robes, shining among women.
     Now when the young Dawn showed again with her rosy fingers,
Menelaos of the great war cry rose from where he was sleeping
and put on his clothes, and slung a sharp sword over his shoulder.
Underneath his shining feet he bound the fair sandals
310 and went on his way from the chamber, like a god in presence,
and sat down by Telemachos and spoke to him and named him:
'What is the need that has brought you here, O hero Telemachos,
to shining Lakedaimon over the sea's wide ridges?
A public or a private matter? Tell me this truly.'
315   Then the thoughtful Telemachos said to him in answer:
'Great Menelaos, son of Atreus, leader of the people,
I have come to see if you could tell me some news of my father,
for my home is being eaten away, the rich fields are ruined,
and the house is full of hateful men, who now forever
320 slaughter my crowding sheep and lumbering horn-curved cattle,
these suitors of my mother, overbearing in their rapacity.
That is why I come to your knees now, in case you might wish
to tell me of his dismal destruction, whether you saw it
perhaps with your own eyes, or heard the tale from another
325 who wandered too. His mother bore this man to be wretched.
Do not soften it because you pity me and are sorry
for me, but fairly tell me all that your eyes have witnessed.
I implore you, if ever noble Odysseus, my father,
undertook any kind of word or work and fulfilled it
330 for you, in the land of the Trojans where all you Achaians suffered,
tell me these things from your memory. And tell me the whole truth.'
     Then deeply angered fair-haired Menelaos said to him:
'Oh, for shame, it was in the bed of a bold and strong man
they wished to lie, they themselves being all unwarlike.
335 As when a doe has brought her fawns to the lair of a lion

The wanderings of Menelaos,

and put them there to sleep, they are newborn and still suckling,
then wanders out into the foothills and the grassy corners,
grazing there, but now the lion comes back to his own lair
and visits a shameful destruction on both mother and children;
340 so Odysseus will visit shameful destruction on these men.
O father Zeus and Athene and Apollo, I wish that
as he was when upon a time in strong-founded Lesbos
he stood up and wrestled Philomeleides from a challenge
and threw him strongly, so delighting all the Achaians,
345 I wish that such an Odysseus would come now among the suitors.
They all would find death was quick and marriage a painful matter.
But for what you entreat me for and ask me about, I will not
turn away from the tale and speak idly, nor will I deceive you,
but of what the ever-truthful Old Man of the Sea told me
350 I will tell all without concealment, and hold back nothing.
      'The gods held me still in Egypt when I was eager to come back
here, for I had not rendered complete hecatombs to them.
The gods have always desired that their orders should be listened to.
There is an island there in the heavy wash of the open
355 sea, in front of Egypt, and they call it Pharos, as far out
as the distance a hollow ship can make in a whole day's sailing
when a sharp and following wind is blowing it onward.
And there is a harbor there with good anchorage, whence they put forth
their balanced ships to sea, after they have drawn dark water.
360 There the gods held me twenty days, nor did the sea winds
ever appear and blow across the salt water, such winds
as act to send ships sailing over the sea's wide ridges.
And now the food would all have been gone, and the men's strength with
      it,
if one of the gods had not been sorry for me, and shown mercy,
365 Eidothea, daughter to mighty Proteus, the Old Man
of the Sea, for it was her heart that I moved mostly
when she met me wandering by myself without my companions.
For always ranging about the island they would go fishing
with crooked fishhooks, and always the hunger oppressed their bellies.
370 She came and stood close beside me and spoke a word and addressed me:
"Are you so simple then, O stranger, and flimsy-minded,
or are you willingly giving up, and enjoying your hardships?
See, you are held so long on the island, and can find no way

out of it, while the heart in your companions diminishes."
375 So she spoke, and I in turn spoke up and made answer:
"So I will tell, whoever you may be of the goddesses,
that I am not detained of my own free will, but it must be
I have offended the immortals who hold wide heaven.
But do you then tell me, for the gods know everything, which one
380 of the immortals hampers me here and keeps me from my journey
and tell me how to make my way home on the sea where the fish swarm."
So I spoke, and she, shining among the goddesses, answered:
"See, I will accurately answer all that you ask me.
The ever truthful Old Man of the Sea ranges in these parts.
385 This is the Egyptian, immortal Proteus, and he knows
all the depths of the sea. He is Poseidon's underthegn.
And they say also he is my father, that he begot me.
If somehow you could lie in ambush and catch hold of him,
he could tell you the way to go, the stages of your journey,
390 and tell you how to make your way home on the sea where the fish swarm.
And he could tell you too, illustrious one, if you wish it,
what evil and what good has been done in your palace
while you have been gone away on your long and arduous voyage."
So she spoke, but then I answered her and said to her:
395 "Show me the way to lie in wait for this divine ancient,
for fear he may somehow see me first and be warned and avoid me.
A god is difficult for a mortal man to master."
So I spoke, and she, shining among goddesses, answered:
"See, I will accurately answer all that you ask me.
400 At the time when the sun has gone up to bestride the middle of heaven,
then the ever-truthful Old Man of the Sea will come out of the water
under the blast of the West Wind, circled in a shudder of darkening
water, and when he comes out he will sleep, under hollow caverns,
and around him seals, those darlings of the sea's lovely lady,
405 sleep in a huddle, after they have emerged from the gray sea,
giving off the sour smell that comes from the deep salt water.
There I will take you myself when dawn shows and arrange you
orderly in your ambush; you must choose from your companions
those three who are your best beside your strong-benched vessels.
410 Now I will tell you all the devious ways of this old man.
First of all he will go among his seals and count them,
but after he has reviewed them all and noted their number,

he will lie down in their midst, like a herdsman among his sheepflocks.
Next, as soon as you see that he is asleep, that will be
415   the time for all of you to use your strength and your vigor,
and hold him there while he strives and struggles hard to escape you.
And he will try you by taking the form of all creatures that come forth
and move on the earth, he will be water and magical fire.
You must hold stiffly on to him and squeeze him the harder.
420   But when at last he himself, speaking in words, questions you,
being now in the same form he was in when you saw him sleeping,
then, hero, you must give over your force and let the old man
go free, and ask him which one of the gods is angry with you,
and ask him how to make your way home on the sea where the fish
    swarm.''
425   So she spoke, and dived back into the surf of the water.
Then I went back again to our ships where they were stationed
along the sand, but my heart was a storm in me as I went. Now
when I had come back to where my ship lay by the seaside,
we made ready our dinner, and the immortal night came over,
430   and then we lay down to sleep along the break of the sea beach.
But when the young Dawn showed again with her rosy fingers,
then I made my way along the beach of the wide-wayed
sea, praying much to the gods, and I took along with me
those three companions I trusted most for any adventure.
435   'Meanwhile she had dived down into the sea's great cavern
and brought back the skins of four seals out of the water.
All were newly skinned. She was planning a trick on her father.
And hollowing out four beds in the sand of the sea, she sat there
waiting for us, and we came close up to her. Thereupon
440   she bedded us down in order, and spread a skin over each man.
That was a most awful ambush, for the pernicious
smell of those seals, bred in the salt water, oppressed us terribly.
Who would want to lie down to sleep by a sea-bred monster?
But she herself came to our rescue and devised a great help.
445   She brought ambrosia, and put it under the nose of each man,
and it smelled very sweet, and did away with the stench of the monster.
All that morning we waited there, with enduring spirit,
and the seals came crowding out of the sea, and when they came out
they lay down to sleep in order along the break of the sea beach.
450   At noon the Old Man came out of the sea and found his well-fed

seals, and went about to them all, and counted their number,
and we were among the first he counted; he had no idea
of any treachery. Then he too lay down among us.
We with a cry sprang up and rushed upon him, locking him
455 in our arms, but the Old Man did not forget the subtlety
of his arts. First he turned into a great bearded lion,
and then to a serpent, then to a leopard, then to a great boar,
and he turned into fluid water, to a tree with towering branches,
but we held stiffly on to him with enduring spirit.
460 But when the Old Man versed in devious ways grew weary
of all this, he spoke to me in words and questioned me:
"Which of the gods now, son of Atreus, has been advising you
to capture me from ambush against my will. What do you want?"
So he spoke, and I in turn spoke up and made answer:
465 "You know, Old Man. Why try to put me off with your answer?
See, I am held so long on the island, and can find no way
out of it, while the inward heart in me diminishes.
Do you then tell me, for the gods know everything, which one
of the immortals hampers me here and keeps me from my journey,
470 and tell me how to make my way home on the sea where the fish swarm."
So I spoke, and he in turn spoke up and made answer:
"But you should have made grand sacrifices to Zeus and the other
immortal gods, and so gone on board, so most quickly
to reach your own country, sailing over the wine-blue water.
475 It is not your destiny now to see your own people and come back
to your strong-founded house and to the land of your fathers,
until you have gone back once again to the water of Egypt,
the sky-fallen river, and there have accomplished holy hecatombs
in honor of all the immortal gods who hold wide heaven.
480 Then the gods will grant you that journey that you so long for."
So he spoke, and the inward heart in me was broken
because he ordered me to go back on the misty surface
of the water to Egypt again, a long way and a hard one,
but even so I answered him in words and said to him:
485 "All these things I will do, Old Man, in the way you tell me.
But come now, tell me this and give me an accurate answer.
Did all those Achaians Nestor and I left behind when we went
sailing from Troy come back in their ships, without injury,
or did any of them die by a dismal death on shipboard

The Old Man tells about Agamemnon

490   or in the arms of his friends after he had wound up the fighting?"
So I spoke, and he in turn spoke up and made answer:
"Son of Atreus, why did you ask me that? You should not
learn it, nor know what my mind knows, and I think you will not be
free of tears for long, once you have heard the whole story.
495   There were many of these men who were lost, and many left over,
but two alone who were leaders of the bronze-armored Achaians
died on the way home. You yourself were there at the fighting.
And there is one who is being held alive on the wide sea
somewhere. Aias was lost, and his long-oared vessels with him.
500   First of all Poseidon drove him against the great rocks
of Gyrai, and yet he saved him out of the water,
and Aias would have escaped his doom, though Athene hated him,
had he not gone wildly mad and tossed out a word of defiance;
for he said that in despite of the gods he escaped the great gulf
505   of the sea, and Poseidon heard him, loudly vaunting,
and at once with his ponderous hands catching up the trident
he drove it against the Gyrean rock, and split a piece off it,
and part of it stayed where it was, but a splinter crashed in the water,
and this was where Aias had been perched when he raved so madly.
510   It carried him down to the depths of the endless and tossing main sea.
So Aias died, when he had swallowed down the salt water.
Your brother somehow got away and escaped the death spirits
with his hollow ships. It was the lady Hera who saved him.
But now as he had come close to the point of making the sheer peak
515   Maleia, then the stormwinds caught him away and carried him,
516   groaning heavily, out on the open sea where the fish swarm.
519   But since even from out there an easy homecoming was manifest
520   for him, the gods twisted the wind back, and they made the homeland
517   at the uttermost edge of his estate, where before now Thyestes
518   had made his home, but now Aigisthos son of Thyestes
521   lived. Agamemnon stepped rejoicing on the soil of his country
and stroked the ground with his hand and kissed it, and his thronging
hot tears streamed down, so dear to him was the sight of his country.
But a watchman saw him from his lookout, a man whom Aigisthos
525   had treacherously taken and stationed there, and promised him
two talents of gold as pay. For a year he had been watching
so Agamemnon would not go by unnoticed and mindful
of his furious valor. The man ran to the house of the war lord

with his news, and at once Aigisthos devised a treacherous stratagem.
530 Choosing out the twenty best fighting men in the district,
he set an ambush, and beside it had them arrange a festival,
and went down to welcome Agamemnon, shepherd of the people,
with horses and chariots, and with shameful thoughts in his mind, then
led him in all unsuspicious of death, and feasted him
535 and killed him feasting, as one strikes down an ox at his manger.
Not one of Agamemnon's men who followed him was left
alive, nor one of Aigisthos' men. All were killed in the palace."
So he spoke, and the inward heart in me was broken,
and I sat down on the sand and cried, nor did the heart in me
540 wish to go on living any longer nor to look on the sunlight.
But when I had glutted myself with rolling on the sand and weeping,
then the ever-truthful Old Man of the Sea said to me:
"No longer now, son of Atreus, spend your time on these wasting
tears, for I know no good that will come of it. Rather with all speed
545 endeavor to make good your way back to the land of your fathers.
You might find Aigisthos still alive, or perhaps Orestes
has beaten you to the kill, but you might be there for the burying."
So he spoke, and the heart within me and the proud spirit
of the breast were softened, even though I was so sorrowful,
550 and now I spoke aloud to him and addressed him in winged words:
"These then I know. But do you tell me the name of the third man,
whoever it is who is being held alive on the wide sea,
or else he has died, but for all my sorrow, I would hear this."
So I spoke, and he in turn spoke up and made answer:
555 "That was Odysseus son of Laertes, who makes his home in
Ithaka, whom I saw on an island, weeping big tears
in the palace of the nymph Kalypso, and she detains him
by constraint, and he cannot make his way to his country,
for he has not any ships by him, nor any companions
560 who can convey him back across the sea's wide ridges.
But for you, Menelaos, O fostered of Zeus, it is not the gods' will
that you shall die and go to your end in horse-pasturing Argos,
but the immortals will convoy you to the Elysian
Field, and the limits of the earth, where fair-haired Rhadamanthys
565 is, and where there is made the easiest life for mortals,
for there is no snow, nor much winter there, nor is there ever
rain, but always the stream of the Ocean sends up breezes

of the West Wind blowing briskly for the refreshment of mortals.
This, because Helen is yours and you are son-in-law therefore
570 to Zeus." He spoke, and dived back into the tossing deep water.
But I went back again to my ships, and my godlike companions
went with me, but my heart was a storm in me as I went. Now
when we had come back to where our ship lay by the seaside,
we made ready our dinner, and the immortal night came over,
575 and then we lay down to sleep along the break of the sea beach.
But when the young Dawn showed again with her rosy fingers,
first of all we dragged the ship down into the bright water,
and in the balanced ships set the masts in place, and set sails,
and we ourselves also went aboard and sat to the oarlocks,
580 and sitting well in order we dashed the oars in the gray sea,
back to where Egypt is, the sky-fallen river, and there
I stranded my ships, and there I rendered complete hecatombs.
But when I had ended the anger of the gods, who are everlasting,
I piled a mound for Agamemnon, so that his memory
585 might never die. I did this, and set sail, and the immortals
gave me a wind, so brought me back to my own dear country
with all speed. Come, now, stay here with me in my palace
until it is the eleventh day and even the twelfth day,
and then I will send you well on your way, and give you glorious
590 gifts, three horses and a well-finished chariot; also
I will give you a fine goblet so that you can pour libations
to the immortals; and think of me, all your days, when you do so.'
     Then the thoughtful Telemachos said to him in answer:
'Son of Atreus, do not keep me with you here for a long time,
595 since I could well be satisfied to sit here beside you
for a year's time, without any longing for home or parents,
such strange pleasure do I take listening to your stories
and sayings, but by now my companions in sacred Pylos
are growing restless, yet for some time you would keep me with you.
600 And let the gift you give me be something that can be stored up.
I will not take the horses to Ithaka, but will leave them
here, for your own delight, since you are lord of a spreading
plain, there is plenty of clover here, there is galingale,
and there is wheat and millet here and white barley, wide grown.
605 There are no wide courses in Ithaka, there is no meadow;
a place to feed goats; but lovelier than a place to feed horses;

for there is no one of the islands that has meadows for driving horses;
they are all sea slopes; and Ithaka more than all the others.'
He spoke, and Menelaos of the great war cry smiled on him,
610 and stroked him with his hand and called him by name and spoke to him:
'You are of true blood, dear child, in the way you reason.
So I shall change all this for you, since I am able to,
and of all those gifts that lie stored away in my house I will give you
the one which is most splendid and esteemed at the highest value.
615 I will give you a fashioned mixing bowl. It is of silver
all but the edges, and these are finished in gold. This is
the work of Hephaistos. The hero Phaidimos, the Sidonians'
king, gave it to me, when his house took me in and sheltered me
there on my way home. I would give it to you for a present.'
620 So these two remained conversing this way together,
and the banqueters came now into the divine king's palace,
and they drove sheep and carried heartening wine, and with them
their wives, in handsome hoods, brought food along. In this way
they about the palace were busy preparing dinner;
625 but meanwhile before the palace of Odysseus the suitors
amused themselves with discs and with light spears for throwing
on a leveled floor, unruly men as they always had been,
but Antinoös and Eurymachos the godlike were seated
as lords of the suitors, out and away the best men among them,
630 and to them now came Phronios' son Noëmon, approaching
Antinoös, and spoke to him and asked him a question:
'Antinoös, do we have an idea in our minds or do we
not, when Telemachos will come back from sandy Pylos?
He has gone, and taken my ship, and now I find that I need her
635 for crossing over to spacious Elis, where I have a dozen
horses, mares, and suckling from them hard-working unbroken
mules; I would like to break one in, taking it from the others.'
So he spoke, and they were amazed at heart; they had not thought
he had gone to Pylos, the city of Neleus, but that he was somewhere
640 near, on his lands, among the flocks, or else with the swineherd.
It was Antinoös the son of Eupeithes that answered:
'Tell me the truth now, when did he go, and which of the young men
went with him? The choice men of Ithaka, or were they his own
following, henchmen and servants? Even he could accomplish so much.
645 And tell me this and tell me truly, so I can be certain,

did he take your black ship from you by force, when you were unwilling,
or did you willingly give it him, when he spoke to you for it?'
   Then the son of Noëmon, Phronios, gave him an answer:
'I gave it to him of my free will. What else could one do
650   when a man like this, with so many cares to trouble his spirit,
asked for it? It would be hard to deny him the giving.
And the young men who are going along with him are the noblest
in our neighborhood. Also, I saw going aboard as leader
Mentor, or it was a god, but he was in every way like him,
655   and yet I wonder, for yesterday early I saw the splendid
Mentor here; before, he was boarding a ship for Pylos.'
   So he spoke, and went away to the house of his father,
and the proud heart in both these suitors was filled with amazement.
They had the suitors sit down in a group and stopped their contests.
660   It was Antinoös the son of Eupeithes who spoke to them,
raging, the heart within filled black to the brim with anger
from beneath, but his two eyes showed like fire in their blazing:
'Here now is a monstrous thing, this voyage made by Telemachos,
and insolently put through. We thought he would never achieve it.
665   A young boy, in despite of so many of us, has hauled down
his ship, and gone away, choosing out the best men in the country.
The evil will begin to go further. May Zeus grant destruction
of the life in him, before he comes to full measure of manhood.
But come now, give me a fast ship and twenty companions,
670   so that I can watch his return and lie in wait for him
in the narrow strait between Ithaka and towering Samos,
and make him sorry for this sea-going in search of his father.'
   So he spoke, and they all approved what he said and urged it,
and at once they stood up and went inside the house of Odysseus.
675   Nor did Penelope go for a long time without knowing
of the counsels which the suitors had been secretly planning,
for Medon the herald told her, having overheard their counsels.
He had been standing outside the court while they plotted inside it,
and he went on his way with the message into the house of Penelope.
680   Penelope spoke to him as he stepped over the threshold:
'Herald, on what errand have the proud suitors sent you?
Is it to tell the serving maids of godlike Odysseus
to stop their work, so as to prepare the suitors a dinner?
Could this not be the last and the latest time of their dining

Penelope hears the news

685 here, whether coming to court me or meeting for some other reason?
You, who keep gathering here, and consuming away much livelihood,
the property of wise Telemachos, nor have you listened
to what you heard from your fathers before you, when you were children,
what kind of man Odysseus was among your own parents,
690 how he did no act and spoke no word in his own country
that was unfair; and that is a way divine kings have, one
will be hateful to a certain man, and favor another,
but Odysseus was never outrageous at all to any man.
But in you the spirit is plain to see, and your unjust actions,
695 how you have no gratitude thereafter for good things done you.'
Medon in turn, a man of thoughtful mind, said to her:
'If only, my queen, that could be the worst of the evil.
But the suitors now are devising another thing that is much worse
and harder to bear. May the son of Kronos not see it accomplished.
700 Now they are minded to kill Telemachos with the sharp bronze
on his way home. He went in quest of news of his father
to Pylos the sacrosanct and to glorious Lakedaimon.'
So he spoke, and her knees gave way and the heart in her.
She stayed a long time without a word, speechless, and her eyes
705 filled with tears, the springing voice was held still within her.
At long last she found words to speak to him and answer:
'Herald, why is my child gone from me? There was no reason
for him to board fast-running ships, which serve as horses
for men on the salt sea, and they cross the expanses of water.
710 Must it be so that even his name shall be gone from men's minds?'
Medon then, a thoughtful man, spoke to her in answer:
'I do not know whether some god moved him, or whether his own mind
had the impulse to go to Pylos, in order to find out
about his father's homecoming, or what fate he had met with.'
715 So speaking he went away back into the house of Odysseus,
and a cloud of heart-wasting sorrow was on her, she had no strength left
to sit down in a chair, though there were many there in the palace,
but sat down on the floor of her own well-wrought bedchamber
weeping pitifully, and about her her maids were wailing
720 all, who were there in the house with her, both young and old ones.
To them weeping constantly Penelope spoke now:
'Hear me, dear friends. The Olympian has given me sorrows
beyond all others who were born and brought up together

The sorrows of Penelope

with me, for first I lost a husband with the heart of a lion
725 and who among the Danaans surpassed in all virtues,
and great, whose fame goes wide through Hellas and midmost Argos;
and now again the stormwinds have caught away my beloved
son, without trace, from the halls, and I never heard when he left me.
Hard-hearted, not one out of all of you then remembered
730 to wake me out of my bed, though your minds knew all clearly,
when he went out and away to board the hollow black ship.
For if I had heard that he was considering this journey,
then he would have had to stay, though hastening to his voyage,
or he would have had to leave me dead in the halls. So now
735 let someone make her way quickly and summon the old man Dolios,
my own servant, whom my father gave me to have as I came here,
and he keeps an orchard full of trees for me, so that he may
go with speed to Laertes and sit beside him and tell him
all, and perhaps he, weaving out the design in his heart,
740 may go outside and complain to the people of those who are striving
to waste away his own seed and that of godlike Odysseus.'
      Then in turn Eurykleia her dear nurse said to her:
'Kill me then, dear girl, with the pitiless bronze, or else
let me be in the halls. I will not hide the story from you.
745 I did know all these things, and I gave him all that he asked for,
both bread and sweet wine, but he took a great oath from me
never to tell you of it until it came to the twelfth day,
or until you might miss him yourself or hear he was absent,
so that you might not ruin your lovely skin with weeping.
750 But go, wash with water and put clean clothing upon your body,
and going on to the upper story with your attendant
women, pray to Athene daughter of Zeus of the aegis,
for she would then be able to save him, even from dying.
But do not embitter the bitterness of the old man. I think
755 the seed of Arkeisios is not altogether hated
by the blessed gods, but there will still be one left to inherit
the high-roofed house and the rich fields that lie at a distance.'
      So she spoke, and stilled her grieving and stopped the weeping
of her eyes, and she washed and put clean clothing upon her body;
760 and went to the upper story with her attendant women,
and laid the barley grains in the basket and prayed to Athene:
'Hear me, Atrytone, child of Zeus of the aegis,

The ambush is set

if ever here in his own palace resourceful Odysseus
burned the rich thigh pieces of an ox or sheep in your honor,
765 remember it now for my sake and save for me my beloved
son, and fend off the suitors who are evilly overbearing.'
　　　She spoke, and raised the outcry, and the goddess listened to her
　　　　praying.
But the suitors all through the shadowy halls were raising a tumult,
and thus would go the word of one of the arrogant young men:
770 'Surely our much sought-after queen is consenting to marriage
with one of us, not knowing how the murder of her son is appointed.'
　　　Thus one of them would speak, not knowing what was appointed.
But it was Antinoös who now stood forth and addressed them:
'You are all mad. Keep clear of all this kind of disorderly
775 talk, for fear somebody may go inside and report us.
But come let us silently rise up now and put into action
that counsel which has been resolved in the hearts of all of us.'
　　　So he spoke, and chose out the twenty best men among them,
and they went along to the fast ship and the sand of the seashore,
780 and first of all they dragged the ship out to the deepening water,
and in the black hull set the mast in place, and set sails,
and made the oars fast in the leather slings of the oarlocks
all in good order, and hoisted the white sails and set them,
and their high-hearted henchmen carried their gear on for them.
785 They anchored her deep enough in the channel, and then disembarking
themselves, prepared their dinner and waited for the coming of evening.
　　　But she in the upper chamber, circumspect Penelope,
lay there fasting, she had tasted no food nor drink, only
pondering whether her stately son would escape from dying
790 or have to go down under the hands of the insolent suitors;
and as much as a lion caught in a crowd of men turns about
in fear, when they have made a treacherous circle about him,
so she was pondering, when the painless sleep came upon her
and all her joints were relaxed so that she slept there reclining.
795 　　Then the gray-eyed goddess Athene thought what to do next.
She made an image, and likened it to Penelope's sister
Iphthime, the daughter of great-hearted Ikarios,
whose husband was Eumelos, and he lived in his home at Pherai.
She sent her now into the house of godlike Odysseus
800 in order to stop Penelope, who was grieving, lamenting,

A dream from Athene

from her crying and tearful lamentation. The dream figure
went into the bedchamber passing beside the thong of the door bar,
and came and stood above her head and spoke a word to her:
'Penelope, are you sleeping so sorrowful in the inward
805 heart? But the gods who live at their ease do not suffer you
to weep and to be troubled, since your son will have his homecoming
even yet, since he has done no wrong in the gods' sight.'
    Circumspect Penelope said to her in answer,
sleeping very sweetly now in the dreams' gateway:
810 'Why have you come here, sister, now, when you were not used to
come before, since the home where you live is far away from us,
and now you tell me to give over from the grieving and sorrows
that are many upon me and trouble me in my heart and spirit,
since first I lost a husband with the heart of a lion,
815 and who among the Danaans surpassed in all virtues,
a great man, whose fame goes wide through Hellas and midmost Argos;
and now again a beloved son is gone on a hollow
ship, an innocent all unversed in fighting and speaking,
and it is for him I grieve even more than for that other one,
820 and tremble for him and fear, lest something should happen to him
either in the country where he has gone, or on the wide sea,
for he has many who hate him and are contriving against him
and striving to kill him before he comes back into his own country.'
    Then in turn the dark dream image spoke to her in answer:
825 'Take courage, let not your heart be too altogether frightened,
such an escort goes along with him, and one that other
men would have prayed to have standing beside them, for she has power,
Pallas Athene, and she has pity on you in your grieving,
and it is she who has sent me to you to tell you of these things.'
830 Circumspect Penelope said to her in answer:
'If then you are a god, and have heard the voice of the goddess,
come then, tell me of that other unfortunate, tell me
whether he still lives and looks upon the sun's shining,
or whether he has died and is now in the house of Hades.'
835 Then in turn the dark dream image spoke to her in answer:
'As for that other one, I will not tell you the whole story
whether he lives or has died. It is bad to babble emptily.'
    So she spoke, and drifted away by the bolt and the door post
and out and into the blowing winds. Ikarios' daughter

comforts Penelope

840 started up from her sleep, soothed in the inward heart, because
     this clear dream in the dim of the night had come to visit her.
          But the suitors went aboard and sailed out into the flowing
     ways, in their hearts devising sudden death for Telemachos.
     There is a rocky island there in the middle channel
845 halfway between Ithaka and towering Samos,
     called Asteris, not large, but it has a double anchorage
     where ships can be hidden. There the Achaians waited in ambush.

BOOK V

Now Dawn rose from her bed, where she lay by haughty Tithonos,
carrying light to the immortal gods and to mortals,
and the gods came and took their places in session, and among them
Zeus who thunders on high, and it is his power that is greatest,
5   and Athene spoke to them of the many cares of Odysseus,
remembering. Though he was in the nymph's house, she still thought of
     him:
'Father Zeus, and all other blessed gods everlasting,
no longer now let one who is a sceptered king be eager
to be gentle and kind, be one whose thought is schooled in justice,
10 but let him always rather be harsh, and act severely,
seeing the way no one of the people he was lord over
remembers godlike Odysseus, and he was kind, like a father.
But now he lies away on an island suffering strong pains
in the palace of the nymph Kalypso, and she detains him
15 by constraint, and he cannot make his way to his country,
for he has not any ships by him, nor any companions
who can convey him back across the sea's wide ridges.
And now there are those who are determined to murder his dear son
on his way home. He went in quest of news of his father
20 to Pylos the sacrosanct and to glorious Lakedaimon.'
     Then in turn Zeus who gathers the clouds made answer:
'My child, what sort of word has escaped your teeth's barrier?
For is not this your own intention, as you have counseled it,

how Odysseus shall make his way back, and punish those others?
25 Then bring Telemachos home skillfully, since you can do this,
so that all without harm he can come back to his own country
while the suitors in their ship come back with nothing accomplished.'
He spoke, and then spoke directly to his beloved son, Hermes:
'Hermes, since for other things also you are our messenger,
30 announce to the nymph with the lovely hair our absolute purpose:
the homecoming of enduring Odysseus, that he shall come back
by the convoy neither of the gods nor of mortal people,
but he shall sail on a jointed raft and, suffering hardships,
on the twentieth day make his landfall on fertile Scheria
35 at the country of the Phaiakians who are near the gods in origin,
and they will honor him in their hearts as a god, and send him
back, by ship, to the beloved land of his fathers,
bestowing bronze and gold in abundance upon him, and clothing,
more than Odysseus could ever have taken away from Troy, even
40 if he had escaped unharmed with his fair share of the plunder.
For so it is fated that he shall see his people and come back
to his house with the high roof and to the land of his fathers.'
He spoke, nor disobeyed him the courier Argeïphontes.
Immediately he bound upon his feet the fair sandals,
45 golden and immortal, that carried him over the water
as over the dry boundless earth abreast of the wind's blast.
He caught up the staff, with which he mazes the eyes of those mortals
whose eyes he would maze, or wakes again the sleepers. Holding
this in his hands, strong Argeïphontes winged his way onward.
50 He stood on Pieria and launched himself from the bright air
across the sea and sped the wave tops, like a shearwater
who along the deadly deep ways of the barren salt sea
goes hunting fish and sprays quick-beating wings in the salt brine.
In such a likeness Hermes rode over much tossing water.
55 But after he had made his way to the far-lying island,
he stepped then out of the dark blue sea, and walked on over
the dry land, till he came to the great cave, where the lovely-haired
nymph was at home, and he found that she was inside. There was
a great fire blazing on the hearth, and the smell of cedar
60 split in billets, and sweetwood burning, spread all over
the island. She was singing inside the cave with a sweet voice
as she went up and down the loom and wove with a golden shuttle.

Kalypso's island

There was a growth of grove around the cavern, flourishing,
alder was there, and the black poplar, and fragrant cypress,
65 and there were birds with spreading wings who made their nests in it,
little owls, and hawks, and birds of the sea with long beaks
who are like ravens, but all their work is on the sea water;
and right about the hollow cavern extended a flourishing
growth of vine that ripened with grape clusters. Next to it
70 there were four fountains, and each of them ran shining water,
each next to each, but turned to run in sundry directions;
and round about there were meadows growing soft with parsley
and violets, and even a god who came into that place
would have admired what he saw, the heart delighted within him.
75 There the courier Argeïphontes stood and admired it.
But after he had admired all in his heart, he went in
to the wide cave, nor did the shining goddess Kalypso
fail to recognize him when she saw him come into her presence;
for the immortal gods are not such as to go unrecognized
80 by one another, not even if one lives in a far home.
But Hermes did not find great-hearted Odysseus indoors,
but he was sitting out on the beach, crying, as before now
he had done, breaking his heart in tears, lamentation, and sorrow,
as weeping tears he looked out over the barren water.
85 But Kalypso, shining among goddesses, questioned Hermes
when she had seated him on a chair that shone and glittered:
'How is it, Hermes of the golden staff, you have come to me?
I honor you and love you; but you have not come much before this.
Speak what is in your mind. My heart is urgent to do it
90 if I can, and if it is a thing that can be accomplished.
But come in with me, so I can put entertainment before you.'
     So the goddess spoke, and she set before him a table
which she had filled with ambrosia, and mixed red nectar for him.
The courier, Hermes Argeïphontes, ate and drank then,
95 but when he had dined and satisfied his hunger with eating,
then he began to speak, answering what she had asked him:
'You, a goddess, ask me, a god, why I came, and therefore
I will tell you the whole truth of the tale. It is you who ask me.
It was Zeus who told me to come here. I did not wish to.
100 Who would willingly make the run across this endless
salt water? And there is no city of men nearby, nor people

who offer choice hecatombs to the gods, and perform sacrifice.
But there is no way for another god to elude the purpose
of aegis-bearing Zeus or bring it to nothing. He says

105 you have with you the man who is wretched beyond all the other
men of all those who fought around the city of Priam
for nine years, and in the tenth they sacked the city and set sail
for home, but on the voyage home they offended Athene,
who let loose an evil tempest and tall waves against them.

110 Then all the rest of his excellent companions perished,
but the wind and the current carried him here and here they drove him.
Now Zeus tells you to send him on his way with all speed.
It is not appointed for him to die here, away from his people.
It is still his fate that he shall see his people and come back

115 to his house with the high roof and to the land of his fathers.'
    So he spoke, and Kalypso, shining among divinities,
shuddered, and answered him in winged words and addressed him:
'You are hard-hearted, you gods, and jealous beyond all creatures
beside, when you are resentful toward the goddesses for sleeping

120 openly with such men as each has made her true husband.
So when Dawn of the rosy fingers chose out Orion,
all you gods who live at your ease were full of resentment,
until chaste Artemis of the golden throne in Ortygia
came with a visitation of painless arrows and killed him;

125 and so it was when Demeter of the lovely hair, yielding
to her desire, lay down with Iasion and loved him
in a thrice-turned field, it was not long before this was made known
to Zeus, who struck him down with a cast of the shining thunderbolt.
So now, you gods, you resent it in me that I keep beside me

130 a man, the one I saved when he clung astride of the keel board
all alone, since Zeus with a cast of the shining thunderbolt
had shattered his fast ship midway on the wine-blue water.
Then all the rest of his excellent companions perished,
but the wind and the current carried him here and here they drove him,

135 and I gave him my love and cherished him, and I had hopes also
that I could make him immortal and all his days to be endless.
But since there is no way for another god to elude the purpose
of aegis-bearing Zeus or bring it to nothing, let him go,
let him go, if he himself is asking for this and desires it,

140 out on the barren sea; but I will not give him conveyance,

for I have not any ships by me nor any companions
who can convey him back across the sea's wide ridges;
but I will freely give him my counsel and hold back nothing,
so that all without harm he can come back to his own country.'
145   Then in turn the courier Argeïphontes answered her:
'Then send him accordingly on his way, and beware of the anger
of Zeus, lest he hold a grudge hereafter and rage against you.'
     So spoke powerful Argeïphontes, and there he left her,
while she, the queenly nymph, when she had been given the message
150   from Zeus, set out searching after great-hearted Odysseus,
and found him sitting on the the seashore, and his eyes were never
wiped dry of tears, and the sweet lifetime was draining out of him,
as he wept for a way home, since the nymph was no longer pleasing
to him. By nights he would lie beside her, of necessity,
155   in the hollow caverns, against his will, by one who was willing,
but all the days he would sit upon the rocks, at the seaside,
breaking his heart in tears and lamentation and sorrow
as weeping tears he looked out over the barren water.
She, bright among divinities, stood near and spoke to him:
160   'Poor man, no longer mourn here beside me nor let your lifetime
fade away, since now I will send you on, with a good will.
So come, cut long timbers with a bronze ax and join them
to make a wide raft, and fashion decks that will be on the upper
side, to carry you over the misty face of the water.
165   Then I will stow aboard her bread and water and ruddy
wine, strength-giving goods that will keep the hunger from you,
and put clothing on you, and send a following stern wind after,
so that all without harm you can come back to your own country,
if only the gods consent. It is they who hold wide heaven.
170   And they are more powerful than I to devise and accomplish.'
     So she spoke to him, but long-suffering great Odysseus
shuddered to hear, and spoke again in turn and addressed her:
'Here is some other thing you devise, O goddess; it is not
conveyance, when you tell me to cross the sea's great open
175   space on a raft. That is dangerous and hard. Not even
balanced ships rejoicing in a wind from Zeus cross over.
I will not go aboard any raft without your good will,
nor unless, goddess, you can bring yourself to swear me a great oath
that this is not some painful trial you are planning against me.'

180   So he spoke, and Kalypso, shining among divinities,
smiled and stroked him with her hand and spoke to him and named him:
'You are so naughty, and you will have your own way in all things.
See how you have spoken to me and reason with me.
Earth be my witness in this, and the wide heaven above us,
185   and the dripping water of the Styx, which oath is the biggest
and most formidable oath among the blessed immortals,
that this is no other painful trial I am planning against you,
but I am thinking and planning for you just as I would do it
for my own self, if such needs as yours were to come upon me;
190   for the mind in me is reasonable, and I have no spirit
of iron anger inside my heart. It is full of pity.'
    So she spoke, a shining goddess, and led the way swiftly,
and the man followed behind her walking in the god's footsteps.
They made their way, the man and the god, to the hollow cavern,
195   and he seated himself upon the chair from which Hermes lately
had risen, while the nymph set all manner of food before him
to eat and drink, such things as mortal people feed upon.
She herself sat across the table from godlike Odysseus,
and her serving maids set nectar and ambrosia before her.
200   They put their hands to the good things that lay ready before them.
But after they had taken their pleasure in eating and drinking,
the talking was begun by the shining goddess Kalypso:
'Son of Laertes and seed of Zeus, resourceful Odysseus,
are you still all so eager to go on back to your own house
205   and the land of your fathers? I wish you well, however you do it,
but if you only knew in your own heart how many hardships
you were fated to undergo before getting back to your country,
you would stay here with me and be the lord of this household
and be an immortal, for all your longing once more to look on
210   that wife for whom you are pining all your days here. And yet
I think that I can claim that I am not her inferior
either in build or stature, since it is not likely that mortal
women can challenge the goddesses for build and beauty.'
    Then resourceful Odysseus spoke in turn and answered her:
215   'Goddess and queen, do not be angry with me. I myself know
that all you say is true and that circumspect Penelope
can never match the impression you make for beauty and stature.
She is mortal after all, and you are immortal and ageless.

Odysseus builds a raft

But even so, what I want and all my days I pine for
220 is to go back to my house and see my day of homecoming.
And if some god batters me far out on the wine-blue water,
I will endure it, keeping a stubborn spirit inside me,
for already I have suffered much and done much hard work
on the waves and in the fighting. So let this adventure follow.'
225 So he spoke, and the sun went down and the darkness came over.
These two, withdrawn in the inner recess of the hollowed cavern,
enjoyed themselves in love and stayed all night by each other,
But when the young Dawn showed again with her rosy fingers,
Odysseus wrapped himself in an outer cloak and a tunic,
230 while she, the nymph, mantled herself in a gleaming white robe
fine-woven and delightful, and around her waist she fastened
a handsome belt of gold, and on her head was a wimple.
She set about planning the journey for great-hearted Odysseus.
She gave him a great ax that was fitted to his palms and headed
235 with bronze, with a double edge each way, and fitted inside it
a very beautiful handle of olive wood, well hafted;
then she gave him a well-finished adze, and led the way onward
to the far end of the island where there were trees, tall grown,
alder and black poplar and fir that towered to the heaven,
240 but all gone dry long ago and dead, so they would float lightly.
But when she had shown him where the tall trees grew, Kalypso,
shining among divinities, went back to her own house
while he turned to cutting his timbers and quickly had his work finished.
He threw down twenty in all, and trimmed them well with his bronze ax,
245 and planed them expertly, and trued them straight to a chalkline.
Kalypso, the shining goddess, at that time came back, bringing him
an auger, and he bored through them all and pinned them together
with dowels, and then with cords he lashed his raft together.
And as great as is the bottom of a broad cargo-carrying
250 ship, when a man well skilled in carpentry fashions it, such was
the size of the broad raft made for himself by Odysseus.
Next, setting up the deck boards and fitting them to close uprights
he worked them on, and closed in the ends with sweeping gunwales.
Then he fashioned the mast, with an upper deck fitted to it,
255 and made in addition a steering oar by which to direct her,
and fenced her in down the whole length with wattles of osier
to keep the water out, and expended much timber upon this.

and Kalypso sends him off

Next Kalypso, the shining goddess, brought out the sail cloth
to make the sails with, and he carefully worked these also,
260   and attached the straps and halyards and sheets all in place aboard her,
and then with levers worked her down to the bright salt water.
    It was the fourth day and all his work was finished. Then on
the fifth day shining Kalypso saw him off from the island
when she had bathed him and put fragrant clothing upon him,
265   and the goddess put two skins aboard, one filled with dark wine
and the other, the big one, filled with water, and put on provisions
in a bag, and stored there many good things to keep a man's strength up,
and sent a following wind to carry him, warm and easy.
Glorious Odysseus, happy with the wind, spread sails
270   and taking his seat artfully with the steering oar he held her
on her course, nor did sleep ever descend on his eyelids
as he kept his eye on the Pleiades and late-setting Boötes,
and the Bear, to whom men give also the name of the Wagon,
who turns about in a fixed place and looks at Orion,
275   and she alone is never plunged in the wash of the Ocean.
For so Kalypso, bright among goddesses, had told him
to make his way over the sea, keeping the Bear on his left hand.
Seventeen days he sailed, making his way over the water,
and on the eighteenth day there showed the shadowy mountains
280   of the Phaiakian land where it stood out nearest to him,
and it looked like a shield lying on the misty face of the water.
    Coming back from the Aithiopians the strong Earthshaker
saw him from far on the mountains of the Solymoi. He was visible
sailing over the sea. Poseidon was the more angered
285   with him, and shook his head, and spoke to his own spirit:
'For shame, surely the gods have rashly changed their intentions
about Odysseus while I was away in the Aithiopians'
land, and he nears the Phaiakian country where it is appointed
that he shall escape this great trial of misery that is now his.
290   But I think I can still give him a good full portion of trouble.'
    He spoke, and pulled the clouds together, in both hands gripping
the trident, and staggered the sea, and let loose all the stormblasts
of all the winds together, and huddled under the cloud scuds
land alike and the great water. Night sprang from heaven.
295   East Wind and South Wind clashed together, and the bitter blown West
      Wind

Poseidon wrecks the raft

and the North Wind born in the bright air rolled up a heavy sea.
The knees of Odysseus gave way for fear, and the heart inside him,
and deeply troubled he spoke to his own great-hearted spirit:
'Ah me unhappy, what in the long outcome will befall me?
300 I fear the goddess might have spoken the truth in all ways
when she said that on the sea and before I came to my country
I would go through hardships; now all this is being accomplished,
such clouds are these, with which Zeus is cramming the wide sky
and has staggered the sea, and stormblasts of winds from every
305 direction are crowding in. My sheer destruction is certain.
Three times and four times happy those Danaans were who died then
in wide Troy land, bringing favor to the sons of Atreus,
as I wish I too had died at that time and met my destiny
on the day when the greatest number of Trojans threw their bronze-
    headed
310 weapons upon me, over the body of perished Achilleus,
and I would have had my rites and the Achaians given me glory.
Now it is by a dismal death that I must be taken.'
    As he spoke so, a great wave drove down from above him
with a horrible rush, and spun the raft in a circle,
315 and he was thrown clear far from the raft and let the steering oar
slip from his hands. A terrible gust of stormwinds whirling
together and blowing snapped the mast tree off in the middle,
and the sail and the upper deck were thrown far and fell in the water.
He himself was ducked for a long time, nor was he able
320 to come up quickly from under the great rush of the water,
for the clothing which divine Kalypso had given weighted him
down. At last he got to the surface, and spat the bitter
salt sea water that drained from his head, which was filled with it.
But he did not forget about his raft, for all his trouble,
325 but turned and swam back through the waves, and laid hold of it,
and huddled down in the middle of it, avoiding death's end.
Then the waves tossed her about the current now here, now there;
as the North Wind in autumn tumbles and tosses thistledown
along the plain, and the bunches hold fast one on another,
330 so the winds tossed her on the great sea, now here, now there,
and now it would be South Wind and North that pushed her between
    them,
and then again East Wind and West would burst in and follow.

but Leukothea rescues Odysseus

    The daughter of Kadmos, sweet-stepping Ino called Leukothea,
saw him. She had once been one who spoke as a mortal,
335   but now in the gulfs of the sea she holds degree as a goddess.
She took pity on Odysseus as he drifted and suffered hardship,
and likening herself to a winged gannet she came up
out of the water and perched on the raft and spoke a word to him:
'Poor man, why is Poseidon the shaker of the earth so bitterly
340   cankered against you, to give you such a harvest of evils?
And yet he will not do away with you, for all his anger.
But do as I say, since you seem to me not lacking in good sense.
Take off these clothes, and leave the raft to drift at the winds' will,
and then strike out and swim with your hands and make for a landfall
345   on the Phaiakian country, where your escape is destined.
And here, take this veil, it is immortal, and fasten it under
your chest; and there is no need for you to die, nor to suffer.
But when with both your hands you have taken hold of the mainland,
untie the veil and throw it out in the wine-blue water
350   far from the land; and turn your face away as you do so.'
    So spoke the goddess and handed him the veil, then herself
in the likeness of a gannet slipped back into the heaving
sea, and the dark and tossing water closed above her.
Now long-suffering great Odysseus pondered two courses,
355   and troubled he spoke then to his own great-hearted spirit:
'Ah me, which of the immortals is weaving deception
against me, and tells me to put off from the raft? But no,
I will not do it yet, since I have seen with my own eyes
that the shore, where she said I could escape, is still far from me.
360   But here is what I will do, and this seems to me the best way.
As long as the timbers hold together and the construction
remains, I will stay with it and endure though suffering hardships;
but once the heaving sea has shaken my raft to pieces,
then I will swim. There is nothing better that I can think of.'
365   Now as he was pondering these ways in his heart and spirit,
Poseidon, shaker of the earth, drove on a great wave,
that was terrible and rough, and it curled over and broke down
upon him, and as when the wind blows hard on a dry pile
of chaff, and scatters it abroad in every direction,
370   so the raft's long timbers were scattered, but now Odysseus
sat astride one beam, like a man riding on horseback,

Odysseus aided by Athene

and stripped off the clothing which the divine Kalypso had given him,
and rapidly tied the veil of Ino around his chest, then
threw himself head first in the water, and with his arms spread
375 stroked as hard as he could. The strong Earthshaker saw him
swimming, and shook his head and spoke to his own spirit:
'There, now, drift on the open sea, suffering much trouble,
until you come among certain people who are the gods' fosterlings.
Even so, I hope you will not complain that I stinted your hardships.'
380   So he spoke, and laid the lash on his fair-maned horses,
and made his way to Aigai, where he has his fabulous palace.
         But now Athene, daughter of Zeus, planned what was to follow.
She fastened down the courses of all the rest of the stormwinds,
and told them all to go to sleep now and to give over,
385 but stirred a hastening North Wind, and broke down the seas before him,
until Zeus-sprung Odysseus, escaping death and the spirits
of death, might join the company of oar-loving Phaiakians.
         Then he was driven two nights and two days on the heavy
seas, and many times his heart foresaw destruction,
390 but when Dawn with the lovely hair had brought the third morning,
then at last the gale went down and windless weather
came on, and now he saw the land lying very close to him
as he took a sharp look, lifted high on the top of a great wave.
And as welcome as the show of life again in a father
395 is to his children, when he has lain sick, suffering strong pains,
and wasting long away, and the hateful death spirit has brushed him,
but then, and it is welcome, the gods set him free of his sickness,
so welcome appeared land and forest now to Odysseus,
and he swam, pressing on, so as to set foot on the mainland.
400 But when he was as far away as a voice can carry
he heard the thumping of the sea on the jagged rock-teeth,
for a big surf, terribly sucked up from the main, was crashing
on the dry land, all was mantled in salt spray, and there were
no harbors to hold ships, no roadsteads for them to ride in,
405 but promontories out-thrust and ragged rock-teeth and boulders.
The knees of Odysseus gave way for fear, and the heart inside him,
and deeply troubled he spoke to his own great-hearted spirit:
'Ah me, now that Zeus has granted a sight of unhoped-for
land, and now I have made the crossing of this great distance,
410 I see no way for me to get out of the gray sea water,

for on the outer side are sharp rocks, and the surf about them
breaks and roars, and the sheer of the cliff runs up above them,
and the sea is deep close in shore so that there is no place
to stand bracing on both my feet and so avoid trouble.
415   I fear that as I climb out a great wave will catch and throw me
against the stony cliff. That will be a pitiful landing.
Yet if I try to swim on along in the hope of finding
beaches that slant against the waves or harbors for shelter
from the sea, I fear that once again the whirlwind will snatch me
420   and carry me out on the sea where the fish swarm, groaning heavily,
or else the divinity from the deep will let loose against me
a sea monster, of whom Amphitrite keeps so many;
for I know how bitterly the renowned Earthshaker hates me.'
    Now as he was pondering this in his heart and spirit,
425   meanwhile a great wave carried him against the rough rock face,
and there his skin would have been taken off, his bones crushed together,
had not the gray-eyed goddess Athene sent him an inkling,
and he frantically caught hold with both hands on the rock face
and clung to it, groaning, until the great wave went over. This one
430   he so escaped, but the backwash of the same wave caught him
where he clung and threw him far out in the open water.
As when an octopus is dragged away from its shelter
the thickly-clustered pebbles stick in the cups of the tentacles,
so in contact with the rock the skin from his bold hands
435   was torn away. Now the great sea covered him over,
and Odysseus would have perished, wretched, beyond his destiny,
had not the gray-eyed goddess Athene given him forethought.
He got clear of the surf, where it sucks against the land, and swam on
along, looking always toward the shore in the hope of finding
440   beaches that slanted against the waves or harbors for shelter
from the sea, but when he came, swimming along, to the mouth of
a sweet-running river, this at last seemed to him the best place,
being bare of rocks, and there was even shelter from the wind there.
He saw where the river came out and prayed to him in his spirit:
445   'Hear me, my lord, whoever you are. I come in great need
to you, a fugitive from the sea and the curse of Poseidon;
even for immortal gods that man has a claim on their mercy
who comes to them as a wandering man, in the way that I now
come to your current and to your knees after much suffering.

Odysseus comes ashore

450   Pity me then, my lord. I call myself your suppliant.'
     He spoke, and the river stayed his current, stopped the waves breaking,
     and made all quiet in front of him and let him get safely
     into the outlet of the river. Now he flexed both knees
     and his ponderous hands; his very heart was sick with salt water,
455   and all his flesh was swollen, and the sea water crusted stiffly
     in his mouth and nostrils, and with a terrible weariness fallen
     upon him he lay unable to breathe or speak in his weakness.
     But when he got his breath back and the spirit regathered into
     his heart, he at last unbound the veil of the goddess from him,
460   and let it go, to drift in the seaward course of the river,
     and the great wave carried it out on the current, and presently Ino
     took it back into her hands. Odysseus staggered from the river
     and lay down again in the rushes and kissed the grain-giving soil.
     Then deeply troubled he spoke to his own great-hearted spirit:
465   'What will happen now, and what in the long outcome will befall me?
     For if I wait out the uncomfortable night by the river,
     I fear that the female dew and the evil frost together
     will be too much for my damaged strength, I am so exhausted,
     and in the morning a chilly wind will blow from the river;
470   but if I go up the slope and into the shadowy forest,
     and lie down to sleep among the dense bushes, even if the chill
     and weariness let me be, and a sweet sleep comes upon me,
     I fear I may become spoil and prey to the wild animals.'
     In the division of his heart this last way seemed best,
475   and he went to look for the wood and found it close to the water
     in a conspicuous place, and stopped underneath two bushes
     that grew from the same place, one of shrub, and one of wild olive,
     and neither the force of wet-blowing winds could penetrate these
     nor could the shining sun ever strike through with his rays, nor yet
480   could the rain pass all the way through them, so close together
     were they grown, interlacing each other; and under these now Odysseus
     entered, and with his own hands heaped him a bed to sleep on,
     making it wide, since there was great store of fallen leaves there,
     enough for two men to take cover in or even three men
485   in the winter season, even in the very worst kind of weather.
     Seeing this, long-suffering great Odysseus was happy,
     and lay down in the middle, and made a pile of leaves over him.
     As when a man buries a burning log in a black ash heap

on the island of the Phaiakians

in a remote place in the country, where none live near as neighbors,
490   and saves the seed of fire, having no other place to get a light
from, so Odysseus buried himself in the leaves, and Athene
shed a sleep on his eyes so as most quickly to quit him,
by veiling his eyes, from the exhaustion of his hard labors.

BOOK VI

So long-suffering great Odysseus slept in that place
in an exhaustion of sleep and weariness, and now Athene
went her way to the district and city of the Phaiakian
men, who formerly lived in the spacious land, Hypereia,
5 next to the Cyclopes, who were men too overbearing,
and who had kept harrying them, being greater in strength. From here
godlike Nausithoös had removed and led a migration,
and settled in Scheria, far away from men who eat bread,
and driven a wall about the city, and built the houses,
10 and made the temples of the gods, and allotted the holdings.
But now he had submitted to his fate, and gone to Hades',
and Alkinoös, learned in designs from the gods, now ruled there.
It was to his house that the gray-eyed goddess Athene
went, devising the homecoming of great-hearted Odysseus,
15 and she went into the ornate chamber, in which a girl
was sleeping, like the immortal goddesses for stature and beauty,
Nausikaa, the daughter of great-hearted Alkinoös,
and beside her two handmaidens with beauty given from the Graces
slept on either side of the post with the shining doors closed.
20 She drifted in like a breath of wind to where the girl slept,
and came and stood above her head and spoke a word to her,
likening herself to the daughter of Dymas, famed for seafaring,
a girl of the same age, in whom her fancy delighted.
In this likeness the gray-eyed Athene spoke to her:

Nausikaa is inspired to go and wash the clothes

25   'Nausikaa, how could your mother have a child so careless?
     The shining clothes are lying away uncared for, while your
     marriage is not far off, when you should be in your glory
     for clothes to wear, and provide too for those who attend you.
     It is from such things that a good reputation among people
30   springs up, giving pleasure to your father and the lady your mother.
     So let us go on a washing tomorrow when dawn shows. I too
     will go along with you and help you, so you can have all
     done most quickly, since you will not long stay unmarried.
     For already you are being courted by all the best men
35   of the Phaiakians hereabouts, and you too are a Phaiakian.
     So come, urge your famous father early in the morning
     to harness the mules and wagon for you, and it shall carry
     the sashes and dresses and shining coverlets for you. In this way
     it will be so much more becoming than for you to go there
40   on foot, for the washing places are a long way from the city.'
         So the gray-eyed Athene spoke and went away from her
     to Olympos, where the abode of the gods stands firm and unmoving
     forever, they say, and is not shaken with winds nor spattered
     with rains, nor does snow pile ever there, but the shining bright air
45   stretches cloudless away, and the white light glances upon it.
     And there, and all their days, the blessed gods take their pleasure.
     There the Gray-eyed One went, when she had talked with the young girl.
         And the next the Dawn came, throned in splendor, and wakened the
             well-robed
     girl Nausikaa, and she wondered much at her dreaming,
50   and went through the house, so as to give the word to her parents,
     to her dear father and her mother. She found them within there;
     the queen was sitting by the fireside with her attendant
     women, turning sea-purple yarn on a distaff; her father
     she met as he was going out the door to the council
55   of famed barons, where the proud Phaiakians used to summon him.
     She stood very close up to her dear father and spoke to him:
     'Daddy dear, will you not have them harness me the wagon,
     the high one with the good wheels, so that I can take the clothing
     to the river and wash it? Now it is lying about, all dirty,
60   and you yourself, when you sit among the first men in council
     and share their counsels, ought to have clean clothing about you;
     and also, you have five dear sons who are grown in the palace,

Odysseus wakened by Nausikaa

two of them married, and the other three are sprightly bachelors,
and they are forever wanting clean fresh clothing, to wear it
65 when they go to dance, and it is my duty to think about all this.'
So she spoke, but she was ashamed to speak of her joyful
marriage to her dear father, but he understood all and answered:
'I do not begrudge you the mules, child, nor anything
else. So go, and the serving men will harness the wagon,
70 the high one with the good wheels that has the carrying basket.'
He spoke, and gave the order to the serving men. These obeyed,
and brought the mule wagon with good wheels outside and put it
together, and led the mules under the yoke and harnessed them,
and the girl brought the bright clothing out from the inner chamber
75 and laid it in the well-polished wagon. Meanwhile her mother
put in a box all manner of food, which would preserve strength,
and put many good things to eat with it, and poured out
wine in a goatskin bottle, and her daughter put that in the wagon.
She gave her limpid olive oil in a golden oil flask
80 for her and her attendant women to use for anointing.
Nausikaa took up the whip and the shining reins, then
whipped them into a start and the mules went noisily forward
and pulled without stint, carrying the girl and the clothing.
She was not alone. The rest, her handmaidens, walked on beside her.
85 Now when they had come to the delightful stream of the river,
where there was always a washing place, and plenty of glorious
water that ran through to wash what was ever so dirty,
there they unyoked the mules and set them free from the wagon,
and chased them out along the bank of the swirling river
90 to graze on the sweet river grass, while they from the wagon
lifted the wash in their hands and carried it to the black water,
and stamped on it in the basins, making a race and game of it
until they had washed and rinsed all dirt away, then spread it
out in line along the beach of the sea, where the water
95 of the sea had washed the most big pebbles up on the dry shore.
Then they themselves, after bathing and anointing themselves with olive
    oil,
ate their dinner all along by the banks of the river
and waited for the laundry to dry out in the sunshine.
But when she and her maids had taken their pleasure in eating,
100 they all threw off their veils for a game of ball, and among them

and the girls at play

it was Nausikaa of the white arms who led in the dancing;
and as Artemis, who showers arrows, moves on the mountains
either along Taÿgetos or on high-towering
Erymanthos, delighting in boars and deer in their running,
105 and along with her the nymphs, daughters of Zeus of the aegis,
range in the wilds and play, and the heart of Leto is gladdened,
for the head and the brows of Artemis are above all the others,
and she is easily marked among them, though all are lovely,
so this one shone among her handmaidens, a virgin unwedded.
110   But now, when she was about ready once more to harness
the mules, and fold the splendid clothing, and start on the way home,
then the gray-eyed goddess Athene thought what to do next;
how Odysseus should awake, and see the well-favored young girl,
and she should be his guide to the city of the Phaiakians.
115 Now the princess threw the ball toward one handmaiden,
and missed the girl, and the ball went into the swirling water,
and they all cried out aloud, and noble Odysseus wakened
and sat up and began pondering in his heart and his spirit:
'Ah me, what are the people whose land I have come to this time,
120 and are they violent and savage, and without justice,
or hospitable to strangers, with a godly mind? See now
how an outcry of young women echoes about me,
of nymphs, who keep the sudden and sheer high mountain places
and springs of the rivers and grass of the meadows, or am I truly
125 in the neighborhood of human people I can converse with?
But come now, I myself shall see what I can discover.'
         So speaking, great Odysseus came from under his thicket,
and from the dense foliage with his heavy hand he broke off
a leafy branch to cover his body and hide the male parts,
130 and went in the confidence of his strength, like some hill-kept lion,
who advances, though he is rained on and blown by the wind, and both
         eyes
kindle; he goes out after cattle or sheep, or it may be
deer in the wilderness, and his belly is urgent upon him
to get inside of a close steading and go for the sheepflocks.
135 So Odysseus was ready to face young girls with well-ordered
hair, naked though he was, for the need was on him; and yet
he appeared terrifying to them, all crusted with dry spray,
and they scattered one way and another down the jutting beaches.

Odysseus supplicates Nausikaa

Only the daughter of Alkinoös stood fast, for Athene
140   put courage into her heart, and took the fear from her body,
and she stood her ground and faced him, and now Odysseus debated
whether to supplicate the well-favored girl by clasping
her knees, or stand off where he was and in words of blandishment
ask if she would show him the city, and lend him clothing.
145   Then in the division of his heart this way seemed best to him,
to stand well off and supplicate in words of blandishment,
for fear that, if he clasped her knees, the girl might be angry.
So blandishingly and full of craft he began to address her:
'I am at your knees, O queen. But are you mortal or goddess?
150   If indeed you are one of the gods who hold wide heaven,
then I must find in you the nearest likeness to Artemis
the daughter of great Zeus, for beauty, figure, and stature.
But if you are one among those mortals who live in this country,
three times blessed are your father and the lady your mother,
155   and three times blessed your brothers too, and I know their spirits
are warmed forever with happiness at the thought of you, seeing
such a slip of beauty taking her place in the chorus of dancers;
but blessed at the heart, even beyond these others, is that one
who, after loading you down with gifts, leads you as his bride
160   home. I have never with these eyes seen anything like you,
neither man nor woman. Wonder takes me as I look on you.
Yet in Delos once I saw such a thing, by Apollo's altar.
I saw the stalk of a young palm shooting up. I had gone there
once, and with a following of a great many people,
165   on that journey which was to mean hard suffering for me.
And as, when I looked upon that tree, my heart admired it
long, since such a tree had never yet sprung from the earth, so
now, lady, I admire you and wonder, and am terribly
afraid to clasp you by the knees. The hard sorrow is on me.
170   Yesterday on the twentieth day I escaped the wine-blue
sea; until then the current and the tearing winds had swept me
along from the island Ogygia, and my fate has landed me
here; here too I must have evil to suffer; I do not
think it will stop; before then the gods have much to give me.
175   Then have pity, O queen. You are the first I have come to
after much suffering, there is no one else that I know of
here among the people who hold this land and this city.

who receives him kindly

Show me the way to the town and give me some rag to wrap me
in, if you had any kind of piece of cloth when you came here,
180   and then may the gods give you everything that your heart longs for;
may they grant you a husband and a house and sweet agreement
in all things, for nothing is better than this, more steadfast
than when two people, a man and his wife, keep a harmonious
household; a thing that brings much distress to the people who hate them
185   and pleasure to their well-wishers, and for them the best reputation.'
    Then in turn Nausikaa of the white arms answered him:
'My friend, since you seem not like a thoughtless man, nor a mean one,
it is Zeus himself, the Olympian, who gives people good fortune,
to each single man, to the good and the bad, just as he wishes;
190   and since he must have given you yours, you must even endure it.
But now, since it is our land and our city that you have come to,
you shall not lack for clothing nor anything else, of those gifts
which should befall the unhappy suppliant on his arrival;
and I will show you our town, and tell you the name of our people.
195   It is the Phaiakians who hold this territory and city,
and I myself am the daughter of great-hearted Alkinoös,
whose power and dominion are held by right, given from the Phaiakians.'
    She spoke, and to her attendants with well-ordered hair gave
      instruction:
'Stand fast, girls. Where are you flying, just because you have looked on
200   a man? Do you think this is some enemy coming against us?
There is no such man living nor can there ever be one
who can come into the land of the Phaiakians bringing
warlike attack; we are so very dear to the immortals,
and we live far apart by ourselves in the wash of the great sea
205   at the utter end, nor do any other people mix with us.
But, since this is some poor wanderer who has come to us,
we must now take care of him, since all strangers and wanderers
are sacred in the sight of Zeus, and the gift is a light and a dear one.
So, my attendants, give some food and drink to the stranger,
210   and bathe him, where there is shelter from the wind, in the river.'
    She spoke, and they stopped their flight, encouraging each other,
and led Odysseus down to the sheltered place, as Nausikaa
daughter of great-hearted Alkinoös had told them
to do, and laid out for him to wear a mantle and tunic,
215   and gave him limpid olive oil in a golden oil flask,

and told him he could bathe himself in the stream of the river.
Then the glorious Odysseus spoke to these serving maids:
'Stand as you are, girls, a little away from me, so that
I can wash the salt off my shoulders and use the olive oil
220   on them. It is long since my skin has known any ointment.
But I will not bathe in front of you, for I feel embarrassed
in the presence of lovely-haired girls to appear all naked.'
    He spoke, and they went away and told it to their young mistress.
But when great Odysseus had bathed in the river and washed from his
        body
225   the salt brine, which clung to his back and his broad shoulders,
he scraped from his head the scurf of brine from the barren salt sea.
But when he had bathed all, and anointed himself with olive oil,
and put on the clothing this unwedded girl had given him,
then Athene, daughter of Zeus, made him seem taller
230   for the eye to behold, and thicker, and on his head she arranged
the curling locks that hung down like hyacinthine petals.
And as when a master craftsman overlays gold on silver,
and he is one who was taught by Hephaistos and Pallas Athene
in art complete, and grace is on every work he finishes,
235   so Athene gilded with grace his head and his shoulders,
and he went a little aside and sat by himself on the seashore,
radiant in grace and good looks; and the girl admired him.
It was to her attendants with well-ordered hair that she now spoke:
'Hear me, my white-armed serving women; let me say something.
240   It is not against the will of all the gods on Olympos
that this man is here to be made known to the godlike Phaiakians.
A while ago he seemed an unpromising man to me. Now
he even resembles one of the gods, who hold high heaven.
If only the man to be called my husband could be like this one,
245   a man living here, if only this one were pleased to stay here.
But come, my attendants, give some food and drink to the stranger.'
    So she spoke, and they listened well to her and obeyed her,
and they set food and drink down beside Odysseus. He then,
noble and long-suffering Odysseus, eagerly
250   ate and drank, since he had not tasted food for a long time.
    Then Nausikaa of the white arms thought what to do next.
She folded the laundry and put it away in the fine mule wagon,
and yoked the mules with powerful hooves, and herself mounted,

and urged Odysseus and spoke a word and named him by title:
255 'Rise up now, stranger, to go to the city, so I can see you
to the house of my own prudent father, where I am confident
you will be made known to all the highest Phaiakians.
Or rather, do it this way; you seem to me not to be thoughtless.
While we are still among the fields and the lands that the people
260 work, for that time follow the mules and the wagon, walking
lightly along with the maids, and I will point the way to you.
But when we come to the city, and around this is a towering
wall, and a handsome harbor either side of the city,
and a narrow causeway, and along the road there are oarswept
265 ships drawn up, for they all have slips, one for each vessel;
and there is the place of assembly, put together with quarried
stone, and built around a fine precinct of Poseidon,
and there they tend to all that gear that goes with the black ships,
the hawsers and the sails, and there they fine down their oarblades;
270 for the Phaiakians have no concern with the bow or the quiver,
but it is all masts and the oars of ships and the balanced vessels
themselves, in which they delight in crossing over the gray sea;
and it is their graceless speech I shrink from, for fear one may mock us
hereafter, since there are insolent men in our community,
275 and see how one of the worse sort might say when he met us,
"Who is this large and handsome stranger whom Nausikaa
has with her, and where did she find him? Surely, he is
to be her husband, but is he a stray from some ship of alien
men she found for herself, since there are no such hereabouts?
280 Or did some god after much entreaty come down in answer
to her prayers, out of the sky, and all his days will he have her?
Better so, if she goes out herself and finds her a husband
from elsewhere, since she pays no heed to her own Phaiakian
neighbors, although many of these and the best ones court her."
285 So they will speak, and that would be a scandal against me,
and I myself would disapprove of a girl who acted
so, that is, without the good will of her dear father
and mother making friends with a man, before being formally
married. Then, stranger, understand what I say, in order
290 soon to win escort and a voyage home from my father.
You will find a glorious grove of poplars sacred to Athene
near the road, and a spring runs there, and there is a meadow

about it, and there is my father's estate and his flowering orchard,
as far from the city as the shout of a man will carry.
295 Sit down there and wait for time enough for the rest of us
to reach the town and make our way to my father's palace.
But when you estimate that we shall have reached the palace,
then go to the city of the Phaiakians and inquire for
the palace of my father, great-hearted Alkinoös. This is
300 easily distinguished, so an innocent child could guide you
there, for there are no other houses built for the other
Phaiakians anything like the house of the hero Alkinoös.
But when you have disappeared inside the house and the courtyard,
then go on quickly across the hall until you come to
305 my mother, and she will be sitting beside the hearth, in the firelight,
turning sea-purple yarn on a distaff, a wonder to look at,
and leaning against the pillar, and her maids are sitting behind her;
and there is my father's chair of state, drawn close beside her,
on which he sits when he drinks his wine like any immortal.
310 Go on past him and then with your arms embrace our mother's
knees; do this, so as to behold your day of homecoming
with happiness and speed, even if you live very far off.
For if she has thoughts in her mind that are friendly to you,
then there is hope that you can see your own people, and come back
315 to your strong-founded house, and to the land of your fathers.'
So Nausikaa spoke and with the shining lash whipped up
her mules, and swiftly they left the running river behind them,
and the mules, neatly twinkling their feet, ran very strongly,
but she drove them with care, so that those on foot, Odysseus
320 and the serving maids, could keep up, and used the whip with discretion.
And the sun went down and they came to the famous grove, sacred
to Athene; and there the great Odysseus sat down
and immediately thereafter prayed to the daughter of great Zeus:
'Hear me, Atrytone child of Zeus of the aegis,
325 and listen to me now, since before you did not listen
to my stricken voice as the famous shaker of the earth battered me.
Grant that I come, as one loved and pitied, among the Phaiakians.'
So he spoke in prayer, and Pallas Athene heard him,
but she did not yet show herself before him, for she respected
330 her father's brother, Poseidon, who still nursed a sore anger
at godlike Odysseus until his arrival in his own country.

BOOK VII

So long-suffering great Odysseus prayed, in that place,
but the strength of the mules carried the young girl on, to the city,
and when she had arrived at the glorious house of her father,
she stopped in the forecourt, and there her brothers around her
5 came and stood, men like immortal gods. They from
the mule wagon unyoked the mules and carried the laundry
inside, and she went into her chamber. There an old woman
of Apeire, Eurymedousa the chamber attendant, lighted
a fire for her. Oarswept ships once carried her over
10 from Apeire, and they chose her out as a prize for Alkinoös
because he ruled all the Phaiakians and the people listened, as to
a god. She had nursed white-armed Nausikaa in the palace.
Now she lit her a fire, and prepared her a supper, indoors.
    Then Odysseus rose to go to the city. Athene
15 with kind thought for Odysseus drifted a deep mist about him,
for fear some one of the great-hearted Phaiakians, meeting him,
might speak to him in a sneering way and ask where he came from.
But when he was about to enter the lovely city,
there the gray-eyed goddess Athene met him, in the likeness
20 of a young girl, a little maid, carrying a pitcher,
and she came and stood before him and great Odysseus questioned her:
'My child, would you not show me the way to the house of a certain
man, Alkinoös, who is lord over all these people?
For I am an unhappy stranger, and I have come here

Athene in disguise informs Odysseus

25   a long way from a distant land, and I know nobody
       here of the people who keep this city and the fields about it.'
          Then in turn the gray-eyed goddess Athene answered him:
       'Then, my friend and father, I will show you the house that you ask me
       to show, since the king lives close beside my own stately father.
30   But go on in silence the while I lead the way for you, and do not
       give any of these people your eye, neither ask them questions,
       for they do not have very much patience with men from the outlands,
       nor do they lovingly entertain the man come from elsewhere;
       they, confident in the speed of their running ships, cross over
35   the great open water, since this is the gift of the Earthshaker
       to them, whose ships move swift as thought, or as a winged creature.'
          So spoke Pallas Athene and she led the way swiftly,
       and the man followed behind her walking in the god's footsteps;
       but the Phaiakians famed for seafaring were not aware of him
40   as he walked among them through their city, because Athene
       of the ordered hair, a dread goddess, would not suffer them to, but drifted
       a magical mist about him, as she cared for him lovingly.
       But Odysseus now admired their balanced ships and their harbors,
       the meeting places of the heroes themselves and the long lofty
45   walls that were joined with palisades, a wonder to look at.
       But when they came to the king's glorious palace, then it was
       Pallas Athene, the gray-eyed goddess, who began speaking:
       'Here, my friend and father, you see the house which you asked me
       to tell you of. Here you will find the kings whom the gods love
50   busy feasting, but you go on in with a spirit that fears
       nothing. The bold man proves the better for every action
       in the end, even though he be a stranger coming from elsewhere.
       First of all you will find the mistress there in her palace.
       Arete is the name she is called, and she comes of the same
55   forebears as in fact produced the king Alkinoös.
       First of all Poseidon, shaker of the earth, and the fairest
       in form of women, Periboia, had a son Nausithoös.
       She was the youngest daughter of great-hearted Eurymedon,
       who in his time had been king over the high-hearted Giants.
60   But he lost his recklessly daring people and himself perished,
       but Poseidon lay in love with his daughter, and she engendered
       Nausithoös the great-hearted, who was lord over the Phaiakians.
       Nausithoös had children, Alkinoös and Rhexenor,

The palace of Alkinoös

but Apollo of the silver bow then struck down Rhexenor,
65 married but without sons in his hall, leaving only the one child
Arete, and Alkinoös made her his wife, and gave her
such pride of place as no other woman on earth is given
of such women as are now alive and keep house for husbands.
So she was held high in the heart and still she is so,
70 by her beloved children, by Alkinoös himself, and by
the people, who look toward her as to a god when they see her,
and speak in salutation as she walks about in her city.
For there is no good intelligence that she herself lacks.
She dissolves quarrels, even among men, when she favors them.
75 So if she has thoughts in her mind that are friendly to you,
then there is hope that you can see your own people, and come back
to your house with the high roof and to the land of your fathers.'
      So gray-eyed Athene spoke and went away from him
across the barren and open water, left lovely Scheria
80 and came to Marathon and to Athens of the wide ways,
and entered the close-built house of Erechtheus. But now Odysseus
came to the famous house of Alkinoös, but the heart pondered
much in him as he stood before coming to the bronze threshold.
For as from the sun the light goes or from the moon, such was
85 the glory on the high-roofed house of great-hearted Alkinoös.
Brazen were the walls run about it in either direction
from the inner room to the door, with a cobalt frieze encircling,
and golden were the doors that guarded the close of the palace,
and silver were the pillars set in the brazen threshold,
90 and there was a silver lintel above, and a golden handle,
and dogs made out of gold and silver were on each side of it,
fashioned by Hephaistos in his craftsmanship and cunning,
to watch over the palace of great-hearted Alkinoös,
being themselves immortal, and all their days they are ageless.
95 And within, thrones were backed against the wall on both sides
all the way from the inner room to the door, with fine-spun
delicate cloths, the work of women, spread out upon them.
There the leaders of the Phaiakians held their sessions
and drank and ate, since they held these forever, and there were
100 young men fashioned all of gold and in their hands holding
flaring torches who stood on the strong-compounded bases,
and shed a gleam through the house by night, to shine on the feasters.

The palace of Alkinoös

And in his house are fifty serving women, and of these
some grind the apple-colored grain at the turn of the hand mill,
105   and there are those who weave the webs and who turn the distaffs,
sitting restless as leaves of the tall black poplar, and from
the cloths where it is sieved oozes the limpid olive oil.
As much as Phaiakian men are expert beyond all others
for driving a fast ship on the open sea, so their women
110   are skilled in weaving and dowered with wisdom bestowed by Athene,
to be expert in beautiful work, to have good character.
On the outside of the courtyard and next the doors is his orchard,
a great one, four land measures, with a fence driven all around it,
and there is the place where his fruit trees are grown tall and
            flourishing,
115   pear trees and pomegranate trees and apple trees with their shining
fruit, and the sweet fig trees and the flourishing olive.
Never is the fruit spoiled on these, never does it give out,
neither in winter time nor summer, but always the West Wind
blowing on the fruits brings some to ripeness while he starts others.
120   Pear matures on pear in that place, apple upon apple,
grape cluster on grape cluster, fig upon fig. There also
he has a vineyard planted that gives abundant produce,
some of it a warm area on level ground where the grapes are
left to dry in the sun, but elsewhere they are gathering others
125   and trampling out yet others, and in front of these are unripe
grapes that have cast off their bloom while others are darkening.
And there at the bottom strip of the field are growing orderly
rows of greens, all kinds, and these are lush through the seasons;
and there two springs distribute water, one through all the garden
130   space, and one on the other side jets out by the courtyard
door, and the lofty house, where townspeople come for their water.
Such are the glorious gifts of the gods at the house of Alkinoös.
        And there long-suffering great Odysseus stopped still and admired it.
But when his mind was done with all admiration, lightly
135   he stepped over the threshold and went on into the palace,
and there found the leaders of the Phaiakians and men of counsel
pouring libation in cups to sharp-eyed Argeïphontes
to whom they always poured the last drink, when mindful of bedtime.
But now long-suffering great Odysseus went on through the house,
140   wearing still the deep mist that Athene had drifted about him,

until he came to Arete and to the king, Alkinoös.
Odysseus clasped Arete's knees in his arms, and at that time
the magical and surrounding mist was drifted from him,
and all fell silent through the house when they saw the man there,
145 and they wondered looking on him, and Odysseus made his entreaty:
'Arete, daughter of godlike Rhexenor, after much hardship
I have come to your knees as a suppliant, and to your husband
and to these feasters, on whom may the gods bestow prosperity
in their own lives, and grant to each to leave to his children
150 his property in his house and the rights the people have given him.
But for me, urge that conveyance be given quickly
to my country, since long now far from my people I suffer hardships.'
     So he spoke, and sat down beside the hearth in the ashes
next the fire, while all of them stayed stricken to silence.
155 But at long last the aged hero Echeneos spoke forth.
He was the most advanced in age of all the Phaiakians,
and surpassed all in words, knowing many things from time long past.
He in kind intention now spoke forth and addressed them:
'Alkinoös, this is not the better way, nor is it fitting
160 that the stranger should sit on the ground beside the hearth, in the ashes.
These others are holding back because they await your order.
But come, raise the stranger up and seat him on a silver-studded
chair, and tell your heralds to mix in more wine for us,
so we can pour a libation to Zeus who delights in the thunder,
165 and he goes together with suppliants, whose rights are sacred.
And let the housekeeper from her stores give the stranger a supper.'
     But when Alkinoös of the hallowed strength had heard this,
he took by the hand the wise and much-devising Odysseus,
and raised him up from the fireside, and set him in a shining chair,
170 displacing for this powerful Laodamas, his son,
who had been sitting next him and who was the one he loved most.
A maidservant brought water for him and poured it from a splendid
and golden pitcher, holding it above a silver basin
for him to wash, and she pulled a polished table before him.
175 A grave housekeeper brought in the bread and served it to him,
adding many good things to it, generous with her provisions.
Then long-suffering great Odysseus ate and drank. After
this, Alkinoös, the hallowed prince, spoke to his herald:
'Pontonoös, now mix a wine bowl and serve it to all here

Odysseus kindly received

180 in the hall, to make a libation to Zeus who delights in the thunder
and who goes together with suppliants, whose rights are sacred.'
   So he spoke, and Pontonoös mixed the kindly sweet wine,
and passed a portion to all, offering a drink in the goblets.
Then when they had made libation and drunk as much as each wanted,
185 Alkinoös made a public speech for them, and spoke thus:
'Hear me, leaders of the Phaiakians and men of counsel,
while I speak forth what the heart within my breast urges.
Now, having feasted, go home and take your rest, and tomorrow
at dawn we shall call the elders in, in greater numbers,
190 and entertain the guest in our halls, and to the immortals
accomplish fine sacrifices, and after that we shall think of
conveyance, and how our guest without annoyance or hardship
may come again, convoyed by us, to his own country,
in happiness and speed, even though it lies very far off,
195 and on the way between suffer no pain nor evil
until he sets foot on his own country; but there in the future
he shall endure all that his destiny and the heavy Spinners
spun for him with the thread at his birth, when his mother bore him.
But if he is one of the immortals come down from heaven,
200 then this is a new kind of thing the gods are devising;
for always in time past the gods have shown themselves clearly
to us, when we render them glorious grand sacrifices,
and they sit beside us and feast with us in the place where we do,
or if one comes alone and encounters us, as a wayfarer,
205 then they make no concealment, as we are very close to them,
as are the Cyclopes and the savage tribes of the Giants.'
   Then resourceful Odysseus spoke in turn and answered him:
'Alkinoös, let something else be in your mind; I am not
in any way like the immortals who hold wide heaven,
210 neither in build nor stature, but only to men who are mortal.
Whoever it is of people you know who wear the greatest
burden of misery, such are the ones whom I would equal
for pain endured, and I could tell of still more troubles
that are all mine and by the will of the gods I suffered.
215 But leave me now to eat my dinner, for all my sorrow,
for there is no other thing so shameless as to be set over
the belly, but she rather uses constraint and makes me think of her,
even when sadly worn, when in my heart I have sorrow

as now I have sorrow in my heart, yet still forever
220 she tells me to eat and drink and forces me to forgetfulness
of all I have suffered, and still she is urgent that I must fill her.
But you, when dawn tomorrow shows, see that you make speed
to set unhappy me once more on my own land, even
when I have much suffered; and let life leave me when I have once more
225 seen my property, my serving people, and my great high-roofed house.'
     So he spoke, and they all approved his word and encouraged
convoy for the stranger, for what he said was fair and orderly;
but when they had made libation and drunk, each as much as his heart
desired, they went away each to his house to rest, and now
230 he, the great Odysseus, remained still in the palace,
and along with him were Arete and the godlike Alkinoös,
who sat by him, and the servants cleared away the dinner things.
Now it was white-armed Arete who began their discourse,
for she recognized the mantle and tunic when she saw them, splendid
235 clothes which she herself had made, with her serving women.
Now she spoke aloud to him and addressed him in winged words:
'Stranger and friend, I myself first have a question to ask you.
What man are you, and whence? And who was it gave you this clothing?
Did you not say that you came here ranging over the water?'
240   Then resourceful Odysseus spoke in turn and answered her:
'It is a hard thing, O queen, to tell you without intermission,
all my troubles, since the gods of the sky have given me many.
But this now I will tell you in answer to the question you asked me.
There is an island, Ogygia. It lies in the water
245 far off. There the daughter of Atlas, subtle Kalypso,
lives, with ordered hair, a dread goddess, and there is no one,
neither a god nor mortal person, who keeps her company.
It was unhappy I alone whom my destiny brought there
to her hearth, when Zeus with a gathered cast of the shining lightning
250 shattered my fast ship midway on the wine-blue water.
There all the rest of my excellent companions perished,
but I, catching in my arms the keel of the oarswept vessel,
was carried for nine days, and on the tenth in the black night
the gods brought me to the island Ogygia, where Kalypso
255 lives, with ordered hair, a dread goddess, and she received me
and loved me excessively and cared for me, and she promised
to make me an immortal and all my days to be ageless,

but never so could she win over the heart within me.
There seven years I remained fast, but forever was drenching
260   with tears that clothing, immortal stuff, Kalypso had given.
But when in the turning of time the eighth year had befallen me,
she herself told me to go and urged me to do it, whether
by a message from Zeus or whether her own mind turned within her,
and she sent me on my way on a jointed raft, and gave me
265   much, bread and sweet wine, and put immortal clothing upon me,
and sent a following wind to carry me, warm and easy.
Seventeen days I sailed, making my way over the water,
and on the eighteenth day there showed the shadowy mountains
of your own country, and the dear heart was happy within me;
270   but I was unlucky, and had much misery left to live with
still, what was driven upon me by the Earthshaker, Poseidon,
who hampered me from my way, letting loose the winds upon me,
and stirred up an unspeakable sea, nor did the surf swell
let me sail along on my raft, though groaning constantly.
275   For now the stormwind scattered it far and wide, and I now
made my way across the great gulf by swimming, until
the wind and the water carried me and drove me to your shore;
but there, had I tried to set foot on the land, the rough wave
would have dashed me against tall rocks in a place that was cheerless,
280   so I backed away and swam again, until I came to
a river, and this at last seemed to me to be the best place,
being bare of rocks, and there was even shelter from the wind there.
I came out and dropped, nursing a hold on life, and immortal
night came on. I went out and away from the sky-fallen river,
285   and went to sleep there among the bushes, piled in a covering
of leaves, and the god drifted an infinite sleep about me.
And there among the leaves, my heart exhausted with sorrow,
I slept nightlong, and into the dawn, and on to the noonday,
and the sun was losing its light, and then the sweet sleep released me.
290   Then I was aware of your daughter's attendant women playing
on the beach, and she, looking like the goddesses, went there among them
I supplicated her, nor did she fail of the right decision;
it was as you could never have hoped for a young person, so confronted,
to act, for always the younger people are careless. Also
295   she gave me food in plenty to eat, she gave me gleaming
wine, and a bath in the river. She also gave me this clothing.

after suggesting a marriage with Nausikaa

Sorrowful as I am, all this is true I have told you.'
Then in turn Alkinoös spoke to him and answered:
'My friend, here is one proper thought that my daughter was not
300 aware of, when she failed to bring you, with her attendants,
here to our house. It was she to whom you first came as a suppliant.'
Then resourceful Odysseus spoke in turn and answered him:
'Hero, do not for my sake find fault with your blameless daughter.
She did urge me to follow along with her serving maidens,
305 but I for embarrassment and dread was not willing, for fear
that something in this might stir your spirit to anger seeing us.
For we who are people upon this earth are jealous in judgment.'
Then in turn Alkinoös spoke to him and answered:
'Stranger, the inward heart in my breast is not of such a kind
310 as to be recklessly angry. Always moderation is better.
O father Zeus, Athene and Apollo, how I wish
that, being the man you are and thinking the way that I do,
you could have my daughter and be called my son-in-law, staying
here with me. I would dower you with a house and properties,
315 if you stayed by your own good will. Against that, no Phaiakian
shall detain you. Never may such be to Zeus father's liking.
As for conveyance, so that you may be sure, I appoint it
for tomorrow, until which time giving way to slumber
you may rest, and they will sail in the calm, to bring you
320 back to your country and house and whatever else is dear to you,
even if this may be much further away than Euboia,
which those of our people who have seen it say is the farthest
away of all, at that time they carried fair-haired Rhadamanthys
on his way to visit Tityos the son of Gaia.
325 They went there, and without any strain they accomplished
the journey, and on the very same day they were back home with us.
You yourself will see and know in your mind how my ships
are best, and my young men for tossing up sea with the oarblade.'
So he spoke, and long-suffering great Odysseus was happy.
330 He spoke a word then in prayer and named him by name, saying:
'Father Zeus, may Alkinoös accomplish everything
of which he spoke, and so may he have imperishable glory
upon the grain-giving earth; and I come home to my country.'
So now these two were conversing thus with each other,
335 but Arete of the white arms told her attendant women

Odysseus rests

to make up a bed in the porch's shelter and to lay upon it
fine underbedding of purple and spread blankets above it,
and fleecy robes to be an over-all covering. The maidservants
went forth from the main house, and in their hands held torches.
340 When they had set to work and presently had a firm bed made,
they came and stood beside Odysseus, and with words roused him:
'Up, stranger, so you can go to rest. Your bed is made for you.'
So they spoke, and the thought of sleeping was welcome to him.
Then long-suffering great Odysseus lay down and slept there
345 upon a corded bedstead in the echoing portico,
but Alkinoös went to bed in the inner room of the high house,
and at his side the lady his wife served as bedfellow.

BOOK VIII

Then when the young Dawn showed again with her rosy fingers,
Alkinoös, the hallowed prince, rose up from his sleeping,
and the descendant of Zeus, Odysseus sacker of cities,
rose up, and Alkinoös, the hallowed prince, guided them
5   to the Phaiakians' place of assembly, which was built for them
by the ships. They went and took their seats on the polished
stones together, but Pallas Athene went through the city,
likening herself to the herald of wise Alkinoös,
as she was devising the return of great-hearted Odysseus.
10 She would go and stand beside each man and speak a word to him:
'Come with me, leaders of the Phaiakians and men of counsel,
to the place of assembly, there to find out about the stranger
who is new-come to the house of wise Alkinoös, after
wandering on the great sea, and in shape he is like the immortals.'
15   So she spoke, and stirred the spirit and strength in each man,
and quickly the place of assembly and seats were filled with people
who gathered there, and many wondered much as they looked on
the wise son of Laertes, and upon him Athene
drifted a magical grace about his head and his shoulders,
20 and made him taller for the eye to behold, and thicker,
so that he might be loved by all the Phaiakians, and to them
might be wonderful and respected, and might accomplish many
trials of strength by which the Phaiakians tested Odysseus.
But when they were assembled and all in one place together,

Feast in the palace

25   to them now Alkinoös spoke forth and addressed them:
      'Hear me, you leaders of the Phaiakians and men of counsel,
      while I speak forth what the heart within my breast urges.
      Here is this stranger, I do not know who he is, come wandering
      suppliant here to my house from the eastern or western people.
30   He urges conveyance, and entreats us for its assurance.
      So let us, as we have done before, hasten to convey him,
      for neither has any other man who has come to my house
      stayed here grieving a long time for the matter of convoy.
      Come then, let us drag a black ship down to the bright sea,
35   one sailing now for the first time, and have for it a selection
      from the district, fifty-two young men, who have been the finest
      before. Then, each man fastening his oar to the oarlock,
      disembark, then come to my house and make yourselves busy
      for a present feast, and I will make generous provision
40   for all. I say this to the young men, but also, you other
      sceptered kings, come to me in my splendid dwelling,
      so we can entertain the stranger guest in our palace.
      Let none refuse; and summon also the inspired singer
      Demodokos, for to him the god gave song surpassing
45   in power to please, whenever the spirit moves him to singing.'
        So he spoke, and led the way, and the others followed,
      as sceptered kings, but a herald went seeking the inspired singer,
      and also the fifty-two young men who had been selected
      went, as he told them, along the beach of the barren salt sea.
50   But when they had come down to the sea, and where the ship was,
      they dragged the black ship down to the deeper part of the water,
      and in the black hull set the mast in place, and set sails,
      and made the oars fast in the leather slings of the oarlocks
      all in good order, and hoisted the white sails and set them.
55   They anchored her deep enough in the channel, and then themselves
      made their way to the great house of wise Alkinoös,
      and the porticoes and enclosures and rooms were filled with people
      assembling, there were many men there, both old and young ones,
      and for them Alkinoös made a sacrifice, twelve sheep, eight
60   pigs with shining tusks, and two drag-footed oxen.
      These they skinned and prepared and made the lovely feast ready.
        The herald came near, bringing with him the excellent singer
      whom the Muse had loved greatly, and gave him both good and evil.

She reft him of his eyes, but she gave him the sweet singing
65   art. Pontonoös set a silver-studded chair out for him
in the middle of the feasters, propping it against a tall column,
and the herald hung the clear lyre on a peg placed over
his head, and showed him how to reach up with his hands and take it
down, and set beside him a table and a fine basket,
70   and beside him a cup to drink whenever his spirit desired it.
They put forth their hands to the good things that lay ready before them.
But when they had put away their desire for eating and drinking,
the Muse stirred the singer to sing the famous actions
of men on that venture, whose fame goes up into the wide heaven,
75   the quarrel between Odysseus and Peleus' son, Achilleus,
how these once contended, at the gods' generous festival,
with words of violence, so that the lord of men, Agamemnon,
was happy in his heart that the best of the Achaians were quarreling;
for so in prophecy Phoibos Apollo had spoken to him
80   in sacred Pytho, when he had stepped across the stone doorstep
to consult; for now the beginning of evil rolled on, descending
on Trojans, and on Danaans, through the designs of great Zeus.
    These things the famous singer sang for them, but Odysseus,
taking in his ponderous hands the great mantle dyed in
85   sea-purple, drew it over his head and veiled his fine features,
shamed for tears running down his face before the Phaiakians;
and every time the divine singer would pause in his singing,
he would take the mantle away from his head, and wipe the tears off,
and taking up a two-handled goblet would pour a libation
90   to the gods, but every time he began again, and the greatest
of the Phaiakians would urge him to sing, since they joyed in his stories,
Odysseus would cover his head again, and make lamentation.
There, shedding tears, he went unnoticed by all the others,
but Alkinoös alone understood what he did and noticed,
95   since he was sitting next him and heard him groaning heavily.
At once he spoke aloud to the oar-loving Phaiakians:
'Hear me, you leaders of the Phaiakians and men of counsel.
By this time we have filled our desire for the equal feasting
and for the lyre, which is the companion to the generous
100   feast. Now let us go outside and make our endeavor
in all contests, so that our stranger can tell his friends, after
he reaches his home, by how much we surpass all others

in boxing, wrestling, leaping and speed of our feet for running.'
So he spoke, and led the way, and the rest went with him,
105 and the herald hung up the clear lyre on its peg, and taking
Demodokos by the hand he led him out of the palace
and set him on the start of the way, where all the other
best men of the Phaiakians went, to gaze at the contests.
They went to the place of assembly, with an endless multitude
110 following, and many and excellent young men stood forth.
Akroneos stood up, and Okyalos and Elatreus,
Nauteus and Prymneus, Anchialos and Eretmeus,
Ponteus and Proreus, Thoön and Anabesineos,
Amphialos, son of Polyneos, the son of Tekton,
115 and Euryalos stood up, Naubolos' son, a man like murderous
Ares himself, and he was best of all the Phaiakians
in build and beauty, only except for stately Laodamas.
Also there stood forth three sons of stately Alkinoös,
Laodamas and Halios and godlike Klytoneos.
120 First of all they held a contest for speed in running.
The field strung out from the starting scratch, yet all at the same time
flew on together, turning up the dust of the plain. Of these
stately Klytoneos was far the best in the running,
and was out in front by the length of a furrow for mules plowing
125 a field, and came back first to the crowd, with the rest behind him.
Next these tried each other out in the painful wrestling,
and in this Euryalos surpassed all the best among them.
In the jump it was Amphialos who outdid all others,
while with the discus far the best of them was Elatreus,
130 and in boxing it was Alkinoös' fine son, Laodamas.
But after all had enjoyed their hearts with athletic contests,
Laodamas the son of Alkinoös spoke forth among them:
'Come, friends, let us ask the stranger if he has skill and knowledge
for any kind of contest. In his build he is no mean man,
135 for the lower legs and thighs he has, and both arms above them,
for the massive neck and the great strength, nor is it that he lacks
youth, but the crush of many misfortunes has used him hardly.
For I say there is no other thing that is worse than the sea is
for breaking a man, even though he may be a very strong one.'
140 Then in turn Euryalos spoke forth and answered:
'Laodamas, this word you spoke was fair and orderly.

He declines to compete

Go yourself then, and say it to him, and invite him to try it.'
Then when the excellent son of Alkinoös heard this answer,
he went and stood in the midst of them and spoke to Odysseus:
145 'Come you also now, father stranger, and try these contests,
if you have skill in any. It beseems you to know athletics,
for there is no greater glory that can befall a man living
than what he achieves by speed of his feet or strength of his hands. So
come then and try it, and scatter those cares that are on your spirit.
150 Your voyage will not be put off for long, but now already
your ship is hauled down to the sea, and your companions are ready.'
Then resourceful Odysseus spoke in turn and answered him:
'Laodamas, why do you all urge me on in mockery
to do these things? Cares are more in my mind than games are,
155 who before this have suffered much and had many hardships,
and sit here now in the middle of your assembly, longing
to go home, entreating your king for this, and all of his people.'
Euryalos answered him to his face and spoke to him roughly:
'No, stranger, for I do not see that you are like one versed
160 in contests, such as now are practiced much among people,
but rather to one who plies his ways in his many-locked vessel,
master over mariners who also are men of business,
a man who, careful of his cargo and grasping for profits,
goes carefully on his way. You do not resemble an athlete.'
165 Then looking at him darkly resourceful Odysseus answered:
'Friend, that was not well spoken; you seem like one who is reckless.
So it is that the gods do not bestow graces in all ways
on men, neither in stature nor yet in brains or eloquence;
for there is a certain kind of man, less noted for beauty,
170 but the god puts comeliness on his words, and they who look toward him
are filled with joy at the sight, and he speaks to them without faltering
in winning modesty, and shines among those who are gathered,
and people look on him as on a god when he walks in the city.
Another again in his appearance is like the immortals,
175 but upon his words there is no grace distilled, as in your case
the appearance is conspicuous, and not a god even
would make it otherwise, and yet the mind there is worthless.
Now you have stirred up anger deep in the breast within me
by this disorderly speaking, and I am not such a new hand
180 at games as you say, but always, as I think, I have been

But angered by the rude Euryalos

among the best when I still had trust in youth and hands' strength.
Now I am held in evil condition and pain; for I had much
to suffer: the wars of men; hard crossing of the big waters.
But even so for all my troubles I will try your contests,
185   for your word bit in the heart, and you have stirred me by speaking.'
    He spoke, and with mantle still on sprang up and laid hold of a discus
that was a bigger and thicker one, heavier not by a little
than the one the Phaiakians had used for their sport in throwing.
He spun, and let this fly from his ponderous hand. The stone
190   hummed in the air, and the Phaiakians, men of long oars
and famed for seafaring, shrank down against the ground, ducking
under the flight of the stone which, speeding from his hand lightly,
overflew the marks of all others, and Athene, likening
herself to a man, marked down the cast and spoke and addressed him:
195   'Even a blind man, friend, would be able to distinguish your mark
by feeling for it, since it is not mingled with the common
lot, but far before. Have no fear over this contest.
No one of the Phaiakians will come up to this mark or pass it.'
    She spoke, and much-enduring great Odysseus rejoiced, happy
200   to find one friendly companion in the assembled company.
Again he spoke to the Phaiakians, in language more blithe:
'Now reach me that mark, young men, and then I will make another
throw, as great as this, I think, or one even better.
Let any of the rest, whose heart and spirit are urgent for it,
205   come up and try me, since you have irritated me so, either
at boxing or wrestling or in a foot race, I begrudge nothing;
any of the Phaiakians, that is, except Laodamas
himself, for he is my host; who would fight with his friend? Surely
any man can be called insensate and good for nothing
210   who in an alien community offers to challenge
his friend and host in the games. He damages what is his. No,
but I refuse not one of the rest, nor do I scorn him,
but I am willing to look in his eyes and be tested against him.
I am not bad in any of the contests where men strive.
215   I know well how to handle the polished bow, and would be
first to strike my man with an arrow aimed at a company
of hostile men, even though many companions were standing
close beside me, and all shooting with bows at the enemies.
There was Philoktetes alone who surpassed me in archery

Odysseus excels in throwing the discus

220 when we Achaians shot with bows in the Trojan country.
But I will say that I stand far out ahead of all others
such as are living mortals now and feed on the earth. Only
I will not set myself against men of the generations
before, not with Herakles nor Eurytos of Oichalia,
225 who set themselves against the immortals with the bow, and therefore
great Eurytos died suddenly nor came to an old age
in his own mansions, since Apollo in anger against him
killed him, because he had challenged Apollo in archery. I can
throw with the spear as far as another casts with an arrow.
230 Only in a foot race I fear one of the Phaiakians
might outpass me; I have been through too much and shamefully battered
on many rough seas, since there could be no orderly training
on shipboard; because of this my legs have lost their condition.'
    So he spoke, and all of them stayed stricken to silence.
235 Only Alkinoös spoke up and gave him an answer:
'My friend, since it is not graceless for you to speak thus among us,
but you are willing to show that excellence you are endowed with,
angered because this man came up to you in our assembly
and belittled you, in a way no man would properly find fault
240 with your excellence, if he knew in his heart how to speak sensibly:
come then, attend to what I say, so that you can tell it
even to some other hero after this, when in your palace
you sit at the feasting with your own wife and children beside you,
remembering our excellence and what Zeus has established
245 as our activities, through time, from the days of our fathers.
For we are not perfect in our boxing, nor yet as wrestlers,
but we do run lightly on our feet, and are excellent seamen,
and always the feast is dear to us, and the lyre and dances
and changes of clothing and our hot baths and beds. Come then,
250 you who among all the Phaiakians are the best dancers,
do your dance, so that our guest, after he comes home
to his own people, can tell them how far we surpass all others
in our seamanship and the speed of our feet and dancing and singing.
Let someone go quickly and bring Demodokos his clear-voiced
255 lyre, which must have been set down somewhere in our palace.'
    So godlike Alkinoös spoke, and the herald rose up
to bring the hollowed lyre out of the king's house, and now
stewards of the course stood up, nine in all of them, chosen

out of the people, who on every occasion set in good order
260   the grounds for games, and they smoothed the dancing floor and set right
all the ground, and the herald came bringing with him the clear lyre
for Demodokos, who moved into the middle, and about him stood forth
young men in the first of their youth, well trained in dancing,
and beat the wonderful dancing floor with their feet. Odysseus
265   gazed on the twinkling of their feet, his heart full of wonder.
    Demodokos struck the lyre and began singing well the story
about the love of Ares and sweet-garlanded Aphrodite,
how they first lay together in the house of Hephaistos
secretly; he gave her much and fouled the marriage
270   and bed of the lord Hephaistos; to him there came as messenger
Helios, the sun, who had seen them lying in love together.
Hephaistos, when he had heard the heartsore story of it,
went on his way to his smithy, heart turbulent with hard sorrows,
and set the great anvil upon its stand, and hammered out fastenings
275   that could not be slipped or broken, to hold them fixed in position.
Now when, in his anger against Ares, he had made this treacherous
snare, he went to his chamber where his own dear bed lay,
and spun his fastenings around the posts from every direction,
while many more were suspended overhead, from the roof beams,
280   thin, like spider webs, which not even one of the blessed
gods could see. He had fashioned it to be very deceptive.
But when he had spun about the bedstead all of his treacherous
device, he started for Lemnos, the strong-founded citadel,
which, of all territories on earth, was far dearest to him.
285   Nor did Ares of the golden reins keep a blind watch on him,
as he saw Hephaistos the glorious smith go away, but he then
took his course so he entered the house of glorious Hephaistos,
lusting after the love of sweet-garlanded Kythereia.
She had lately come in from the house of her father, the powerful
290   son of Kronos, and sat there when Ares entered the house. Then
he took her by the hand and spoke to her and named her, saying:
'Come, my dear, let us take our way to the bed, and lie there,
for Hephaistos is no longer hereabouts, but by this time
he must have come to Lemnos and the wild-spoken Sintians.'
295   So he spoke, and she was well pleased to sleep with him. These two
went to bed, and slept there, and all about them were bending
the artful bonds that had been forged by subtle Hephaistos,

so neither of them could stir a limb or get up, and now
they saw the truth, and there was no longer a way out for them.
300   The glorious smith of the strong arms came and stood near. He had
turned back on his way, before ever reaching the Lemnian country,
for Helios had kept watch for him, and told him the story.
He took his way back to his own house, heart grieved within him,
and stood there in the forecourt, with the savage anger upon him,
305   and gave out a terrible cry and called to all the immortals:
'Father Zeus and all you other blessed immortal
gods, come here, to see a ridiculous sight, no seemly
matter, how Aphrodite daughter of Zeus forever
holds me in little favor, but she loves ruinous Ares
310   because he is handsome, and goes sound on his feet, while I am
misshapen from birth, and for this I hold no other responsible
but my own father and mother, and I wish they never had got me.
Now look and see, where these two have gone to bed and lie there
in love together. I am sickened when I look at them, and yet
315   I think they will not go on lying thus even for a little,
much though they are in love, I think they will have no wish
for sleeping, but then my fastenings and my snare will contain them
until her father pays back in full all my gifts of courtship
I paid out into his hand for the sake of his bitch-eyed daughter.
320   The girl is beautiful indeed, but she is intemperate.'
    So he spoke, and the gods gathered to the house with the brazen
floor. Poseidon came, the shaker of the earth, and the kindly
Hermes came, and the lord who works from afar, Apollo,
but the female gods remained each at her home, for modesty.
325   The gods, the givers of good things, stood there in the forecourt,
and among the blessed immortals uncontrollable laughter
went up as they saw the handiwork of subtle Hephaistos.
And thus they would speak to each other, each looking at the god next
      him:
'No virtue in bad dealings. See, the slow one has overtaken
330   the swift, as now slow Hephaistos has overtaken
Ares, swiftest of all the gods on Olympos, by artifice,
though he was lame, and Ares must pay the adulterer's damage.'
    This was the way of the gods as they conversed with each other,
but the lord Apollo son of Zeus said a word to Hermes:
335   'Hermes, son of Zeus, guide and giver of good things, tell me,

Ares and Aphrodite concluded

would you, caught tight in these strong fastenings, be willing
to sleep in bed by the side of Aphrodite the golden?'
    Then in turn the courier Argeïphontes answered:
'Lord who strike from afar, Apollo, I wish it could only
340   be, and there could be thrice this number of endless fastenings,
and all you gods could be looking on and all the goddesses,
and still I would sleep by the side of Aphrodite the golden.'
    He spoke, and there was laughter among the immortals, only
there was no laughter for Poseidon, but he kept entreating
345   Hephaistos, the famous craftsman, asking him to set Ares
free, and spoke aloud to him and addressed him in winged words:
'Let him go, and I guarantee he will pay whatever
you ask, all that is approved among the immortal deities.'
    Then in turn the renowned smith of the strong arms answered:
350   'Shaker of the earth, Poseidon, do not urge this on me.
The business of wretches is wretched even in guarantee giving.
To what could I hold you among the immortal gods, if Ares
were to go off, avoiding both his debt and his bondage?'
    Then in turn Poseidon, shaker of the earth, answered:
355   'Hephaistos, if Ares goes off and escapes, not paying
anything he may owe you, then I myself will pay it.'
    Then in turn the renowned smith of the strong arms answered:
'It cannot be, and it is not right, that I should deny you.'
    So mighty Hephaistos spoke and undid the fastenings. Straightway
360   the two of them, when they were set free of the fastening, though it
was so strong, sprang up, and Ares took his way Thraceward,
while she, Aphrodite lover of laughter, went back to Paphos
on Cyprus, where lies her sacred precinct and her smoky altar,
and there the Graces bathed her and anointed her with ambrosial
365   oil, such as abounds for the gods who are everlasting,
and put delightful clothing about her, a wonder to look on.
    So the famous singer sang his song, and Odysseus
enjoyed it in his heart as he listened, as did the others
there, Phaiakians, men of the long oar, famed for seafaring.
370   Then Alkinoös asked Halios and Laodamas to dance
all by themselves, since there was none to challenge them. These two,
after they had taken up in their hands the ball, a beautiful
thing, red, which Polybos the skillful craftsman had made them,
one of them, bending far back, would throw it up to the shadowy

375   clouds, and the other, going high off the ground, would easily
catch it again, before his feet came back to the ground. Then
after they had played their game with the ball thrown upward,
these two performed a dance on the generous earth, with rapid
interchange of position, and the rest of the young men standing
380   about the field stamped out the time, and a great sound rose up.
Then great Odysseus spoke a word to Alkinoös, saying:
'O great Alkinoös, pre-eminent among all people,
truly, as you boasted your people were the best dancers,
so it is done before me. Wonder takes me as I look on them.'
385   He spoke, and Alkinoös the hallowed king was pleased,
and at once he spoke aloud to the oar-loving Phaiakians:
'Hear me, leaders of the Phaiakians and men of counsel.
I think this stranger is a man of discretion. Therefore
come, let us give him a gift of friendship, as is becoming.
390   For here are twelve who are marked out as kings in our country
with power, and they act as leaders, and I myself am the thirteenth.
Then let each of you who are such contribute a well-washed
robe, and a tunic, and a talent of precious gold. Then
we shall assemble it all together, so that our stranger
395   may have it in his hands and be pleased as he goes in to supper.
But Euryalos shall make amends to him with a spoken
word and a gift, for having spoken out of due measure.'
     So he spoke, and they all approved what he said and urged it,
and each one sent his herald away to bring the gifts back.
400   Then Euryalos spoke in his turn and answered Alkinoös:
'O great Alkinoös, pre-eminent among all people,
certainly I will make amends to our guest, as you urge me.
I will give him this sword, which is all bronze, but the handle
on it is silver, and there is a scabbard of fresh-sawn ivory
405   cut in rings to hold it. He will find that it is of great value.'
     So he spoke, and put the sword with the nails of silver
into his hands, and spoke to him and addressed him in winged words:
'Farewell, father and stranger, and if any word was let slip
that was improper, may the stormwinds catch it away and carry it
410   off, and the gods grant you safe homecoming to your own country
and wife; since here, far from your own people, you must be suffering.'
     Then resourceful Odysseus spoke in turn and answered him:
'Farewell also to you, dear friend, and may the gods grant you

prosperity; may you never miss this sword you have given
415   me now, as a gift, and made amends to me with words spoken.'
    So he spoke, and slung the sword with the nails of silver
over his shoulder. The sun went down, and the glorious presents
came in, carried by the proud heralds of Alkinoös,
and these, surpassingly lovely gifts, the sons of Alkinoös
420   took over, and set them down beside their respected mother.
Now Alkinoös the hallowed king was their leader,
and all of them went into the house and sat on their high thrones.
Thereupon the king Alkinoös said to Arete:
'Come, wife, bring out a magnificent coffer, the best one you have,
425   and in it yourself lay a robe that is newly washed, and a tunic.
Then warm a brazen caldron over the fire, and heat water
for this man, so he may bathe and then see, all set out in order,
the presents which the stately Phaiakians brought here to give him,
and rejoice in the feast and in listening to the song of the singer.
430   I myself make him a present of this surpassingly lovely
golden cup, so that all his days he may remember me
as he makes libation at home to Zeus and the other immortals.'
    So he spoke, and Arete going to her maidservants told them
to set the great caldron over the fire, as quickly as might be,
435   and they set the tripod for the bathwater over the blazing
fire, and poured in the water and gathered kindling and lit it.
The fire worked on the belly of the caldron, the water heated.
Meanwhile Arete brought from out of her chamber the splendid
chest for the stranger, and in it laid the beautiful presents,
440   the clothing and the gold which the Phaiakians had given,
and she herself put in a robe, and a handsome tunic,
and spoke to the stranger and addressed him in winged words, saying:
'You yourself must see to the cover and nimbly fasten
a knot, so none may break in, while on your journey
445   you rest in a pleasant sleep as you go your ways in the black ship.'
    When long-suffering great Odysseus had heard this, straightway
he made the covering tight upon it and fastened it nimbly
with an intricate knot, whose knowledge the lady Circe had taught him.
Then the housekeeper told him without delay to enter
450   the tub for his bath, and he with joy in his heart looked on
the hot water, for he had not been used to be so looked after
in the time since he had left the house of fair-haired Kalypso,

though in that time he had been looked after as if he were truly
a god. When the maids had bathed him and anointed him with oil,
455   they put a lovely mantle and a tunic about him,
and he stepped from the bath and went to join the men at their wine
drinking. Then Nausikaa, with the gods' loveliness on her,
stood beside the pillar that supported the roof with its joinery,
and gazed upon Odysseus with all her eyes and admired him,
460   and spoke to him aloud and addressed him in winged words, saying:
'Goodbye, stranger, and think of me sometimes when you are
back at home, how I was the first you owed your life to.'
    Then resourceful Odysseus spoke in turn and answered her:
'Nausikaa, daughter of great-hearted Alkinoös,
465   even so may Zeus, high-thundering husband of Hera,
grant me to reach my house and see my day of homecoming.
So even when I am there I will pray to you, as to a goddess,
all the days of my life. For, maiden, my life was your gift.'
    He spoke, and went to sit on a chair by the king Alkinoös.
470   And now they were serving out the portions and mixing the wine, as
the herald came near, bringing with him the excellent singer
Demodokos, prized among the people, and set a chair for him
in the middle of the feasters, propping it against a tall column.
Resourceful Odysseus called the herald over and spoke to him,
475   but first he cut a piece from the loin of the pig with shining
teeth, with most of the meat left on, and edged with rich fat:
'Here, herald, take this piece of meat to Demodokos so that
he may eat, and I, though a sorry man, embrace him.
For with all peoples upon the earth singers are entitled
480   to be cherished and to their share of respect, since the Muse has taught
       them
her own way, and since she loves all the company of singers.'
    So he spoke, and the herald took the portion and placed it
in the hands of the hero Demodokos, who received it happily.
They put forth their hands to the good things that lay ready before them.
485   But when they had put away their desire for eating and drinking,
Odysseus the resourceful spoke to Demodokos, saying:
'Demodokos, above all mortals beside I prize you.
Surely the Muse, Zeus' daughter or else Apollo has taught you,
for all too right following the tale you sing the Achaians'
490   venture, all they did and had done to them, all the sufferings

of these Achaians, as if you had been there yourself or heard it
from one who was. Come to another part of the story, sing us
the wooden horse, which Epeios made with Athene helping,
the stratagem great Odysseus filled once with men and brought it
495   to the upper city, and it was these men who sacked Ilion.
If you can tell me the course of all these things as they happened,
I will speak of you before all mankind, and tell them
how freely the goddess gave you the magical gift of singing.'
     He spoke, and the singer, stirred by the goddess, began, and showed them
500   his song, beginning from where the Argives boarded their well-benched
ships, and sailed away, after setting fire to their shelters;
but already all these others who were with famous Odysseus
were sitting hidden in the horse, in the place where the Trojans assembled,
for the Trojans themselves had dragged it up to the height of the city,
505   and now it was standing there, and the Trojans seated around it
talked endlessly, and three ways of thought found favor, either
to take the pitiless bronze to it and hack open the hollow
horse, or drag it to the cliffs' edge and topple it over,
or let it stand where it was as a dedication to blandish
510   the gods, and this last way was to be the end of it, seeing
that the city was destined to be destroyed when it had inside it
the great horse made of wood, with all the best of Argives
sitting within and bearing death and doom for the Trojans.
He sang then how the sons of the Achaians left their hollow
515   hiding place and streamed from the horse and sacked the city,
and he sang how one and another fought through the steep citadel,
and how in particular Odysseus went, with godlike
Menelaos, like Ares, to find the house of Deïphobos,
and there, he said, he endured the grimmest fighting that ever
520   he had, but won it there too, with great-hearted Athene aiding.
     So the famous singer sang his tale, but Odysseus
melted, and from under his eyes the tears ran down, drenching
his cheeks. As a woman weeps, lying over the body
of her dear husband, who fell fighting for her city and people
525   as he tried to beat off the pitiless day from city and children;
she sees him dying and gasping for breath, and winding her body
about him she cries high and shrill, while the men behind her,
hitting her with their spear butts on the back and the shoulders,

force her up and lead her away into slavery, to have
530 hard work and sorrow, and her cheeks are wracked with pitiful weeping.
Such were the pitiful tears Odysseus shed from under
his brows, but they went unnoticed by all the others,
but Alkinoös alone understood what he did and noticed,
since he was sitting next him and heard him groaning heavily.
535 At once he spoke aloud to the oar-loving Phaiakians:
'Hear me, you leaders of the Phaiakians and men of counsel.
Let Demodokos now give over his loud lyre playing,
since it cannot be that he pleases all alike with this song.
Ever since we ate our supper and the divine singer
540 began, our guest has never ceased since then his sorry
lament. Great sorrow must have come on his heart, surely.
But let him hold now, so that all of us, guest receivers
and guest alike, may enjoy ourselves. This is the better way,
seeing that all this has been done for the sake of our honored
545 guest, this escort, these loving gifts we give him for friendship.
For any man whose wits have hold on the slightest achievement,
his suppliant and guest is as good as a brother to him.
So do not longer keep hiding now with crafty purposes
the truth of what I ask you. It is better to speak out.
550 Tell me the name by which your mother and father called you
in that place, and how the rest who live in the city about you
call you. No one among all the peoples, neither base man
nor noble, is altogether nameless, once he has been born,
but always his parents as soon as they bring him forth put upon him
555 a name. Tell me your land, your neighborhood and your city,
so that our ships, straining with their own purpose, can carry you
there, for there are no steersmen among the Phaiakians, neither
are there any steering oars for them, such as other ships have,
but the ships themselves understand men's thoughts and purposes,
560 and they know all the cities of men and all their fertile
fields, and with greatest speed they cross the gulf of the salt sea,
huddled under a mist and cloud, nor is there ever
any fear that they may suffer damage or come to destruction.
Yet this I have heard once on a time from my father, Nausithoös,
565 who said it, and told me how Poseidon would yet be angry
with us, because we are convoy without hurt to all men.
He said that one day, as a well-made ship of Phaiakian

Odysseus is invited to tell his life

men came back from a convoy on the misty face of the water,
he would stun it, and pile a great mountain over our city, to hide it.
570 So the old man spoke, and the god might either bring it
to pass, or it might be left undone, as the god's heart pleases.
So come now tell me this and give me an accurate answer:
Where you were driven off your course, what countries peopled
by men you came to, the men themselves and their strong-founded
575 cities, and which were savage and violent, and without justice,
and which were hospitable and with a godly mind for strangers.
And tell me why you weep in your heart and make lamentation
when you hear of the Argives' and the Danaans' venture, and hear
of Ilion. The gods did this, and spun the destruction
580 of peoples, for the sake of the singing of men hereafter.
Was there perhaps some kinsman by marriage, wife's father or brother,
a brave man who perished before Ilion? Such are the relatives
who next to a man's own blood and kin come closest to him?
Or could it then have been some companion, a brave man knowing
585 thoughts gracious toward you, since one who is your companion, and ha
     thoughts
honorable toward you, is of no less degree than a brother?'

BOOK IX

Then resourceful Odysseus spoke in turn and answered him:
'O great Alkinoös, pre-eminent among all people,
surely indeed it is a good thing to listen to a singer
such as this one before us, who is like the gods in his singing;
5   for I think there is no occasion accomplished that is more pleasant
than when festivity holds sway among all the populace,
and the feasters up and down the houses are sitting in order
and listening to the singer, and beside them the tables are loaded
with bread and meats, and from the mixing bowl the wine steward
10 draws the wine and carries it about and fills the cups. This
seems to my own mind to be the best of occasions.
But now your wish was inclined to ask me about my mournful
sufferings, so that I must mourn and grieve even more. What then
shall I recite to you first of all, what leave till later?
15 Many are the sorrows the gods of the sky have given me.
Now first I will tell you my name, so that all of you
may know me, and I hereafter, escaping the day without pity,
be your friend and guest, though the home where I live is far away from
     you.
I am Odysseus son of Laertes, known before all men
20 for the study of crafty designs, and my fame goes up to the heavens.
I am at home in sunny Ithaka. There is a mountain
there that stands tall, leaf-trembling Neritos, and there are islands
settled around it, lying one very close to another.

There is Doulichion and Same, wooded Zakynthos,
25   but my island lies low and away, last of all on the water
toward the dark, with the rest below facing east and sunshine,
a rugged place, but a good nurse of men; for my part
I cannot think of any place sweeter on earth to look at.
For in truth Kalypso, shining among divinities, kept me
30   with her in her hollow caverns, desiring me for her husband,
and so likewise Aiaian Circe the guileful detained me
beside her in her halls, desiring me for her husband,
but never could she persuade the heart within me. So it is
that nothing is more sweet in the end than country and parents
35   ever, even when far away one lives in a fertile
place, when it is in alien country, far from his parents.
But come, I will tell you of my voyage home with its many
troubles, which Zeus inflicted on me as I came from Troy land.
   'From Ilion the wind took me and drove me ashore at Ismaros
40   by the Kikonians. I sacked their city and killed their people,
and out of their city taking their wives and many possessions
we shared them out, so none might go cheated of his proper
portion. There I was for the light foot and escaping,
and urged it, but they were greatly foolish and would not listen,
45   and then and there much wine was being drunk, and they slaughtered
many sheep on the beach, and lumbering horn-curved cattle.
But meanwhile the Kikonians went and summoned the other
Kikonians, who were their neighbors living in the inland country,
more numerous and better men, well skilled in fighting
50   men with horses, but knowing too at need the battle
on foot. They came at early morning, like flowers in season
or leaves, and the luck that came our way from Zeus was evil,
to make us unfortunate, so we must have hard pains to suffer.
Both sides stood and fought their battle there by the running
55   ships, and with bronze-headed spears they cast at each other,
and as long as it was early and the sacred daylight increasing,
so long we stood fast and fought them off, though there were more
     them;
but when the sun had gone to the time for unyoking of cattle,
then at last the Kikonians turned the Achaians back and beat them,
60   and out of each ship six of my strong-greaved companions
were killed, but the rest of us fled away from death and destruction.

Departure from Troy—the Lotus-Eaters

'From there we sailed on further along, glad to have escaped death,
but grieving still at heart for the loss of our dear companions.
Even then I would not suffer the flight of my oarswept vessels
65   until a cry had been made three times for each of my wretched
companions, who died there in the plain, killed by the Kikonians.
Cloud-gathering Zeus drove the North Wind against our vessels
in a supernatural storm, and huddled under the cloud scuds
land alike and the great water. Night sprang from heaven.
70   The ships were swept along yawing down the current; the violence
of the wind ripped our sails into three and four pieces. These then,
in fear of destruction, we took down and stowed in the ships' hulls,
and rowed them on ourselves until we had made the mainland.
There for two nights and two days together we lay up,
75   for pain and weariness together eating our hearts out.
But when the fair-haired Dawn in her rounds brought on the third day,
we, setting the masts upright, and hoisting the white sails on them,
sat still, and let the wind and the steersmen hold them steady.
And now I would have come home unscathed to the land of my fathers,
80   but as I turned the hook of Maleia, the sea and current
and the North Wind beat me off course, and drove me on past Kythera.
'Nine days then I was swept along by the force of the hostile
winds on the fishy sea, but on the tenth day we landed
in the country of the Lotus-Eaters, who live on a flowering
85   food, and there we set foot on the mainland, and fetched water,
and my companions soon took their supper there by the fast ships.
But after we had tasted of food and drink, then I sent
some of my companions ahead, telling them to find out
what men, eaters of bread, might live here in this country.
90   I chose two men, and sent a third with them, as a herald.
My men went on and presently met the Lotus-Eaters,
nor did these Lotus-Eaters have any thoughts of destroying
our companions, but they only gave them lotus to taste of.
But any of them who ate the honey-sweet fruit of lotus
95   was unwilling to take any message back, or to go
away, but they wanted to stay there with the lotus-eating
people, feeding on lotus, and forget the way home. I myself
took these men back weeping, by force, to where the ships were,
and put them aboard under the rowing benches and tied them
100 fast, then gave the order to the rest of my eager

companions to embark on the ships in haste, for fear
someone else might taste of the lotus and forget the way home,
and the men quickly went aboard and sat to the oarlocks,
and sitting well in order dashed the oars in the gray sea.
105   'From there, grieving still at heart, we sailed on further
along, and reached the country of the lawless outrageous
Cyclopes who, putting all their trust in the immortal
gods, neither plow with their hands nor plant anything,
but all grows for them without seed planting, without cultivation,
110 wheat and barley and also the grapevines, which yield for them
wine of strength, and it is Zeus' rain that waters it for them.
These people have no institutions, no meetings for counsels;
rather they make their habitations in caverns hollowed
among the peaks of the high mountains, and each one is the law
115 for his own wives and children, and cares nothing about the others.
    'There is a wooded island that spreads, away from the harbor,
neither close in to the land of the Cyclopes nor far out
from it; forested; wild goats beyond number breed there,
for there is no coming and going of human kind to disturb them,
120 nor are they visited by hunters, who in the forest
suffer hardships as they haunt the peaks of the mountains,
neither again is it held by herded flocks, nor farmers,
but all its days, never plowed up and never planted,
it goes without people and supports the bleating wild goats.
125 For the Cyclopes have no ships with cheeks of vermilion,
nor have they builders of ships among them, who could have made them
strong-benched vessels, and these if made could have run them sailings
to all the various cities of men, in the way that people
cross the sea by means of ships and visit each other,
130 and they could have made this island a strong settlement for them.
For it is not a bad place at all, it could bear all crops
in season, and there are meadow lands near the shores of the gray sea,
well watered and soft; there could be grapes grown there endlessly,
and there is smooth land for plowing, men could reap a full harvest
135 always in season, since there is very rich subsoil. Also
there is an easy harbor, with no need for a hawser
nor anchor stones to be thrown ashore nor cables to make fast;
one could just run ashore and wait for the time when the sailors'
desire stirred them to go and the right winds were blowing.

140 Also at the head of the harbor there runs bright water,
spring beneath rock, and there are black poplars growing around it.
There we sailed ashore, and there was some god guiding
us in through the gloom of the night, nothing showed to look at,
for there was a deep mist around the ships, nor was there any moon

145 showing in the sky, but she was under the clouds and hidden.
There was none of us there whose eyes had spied out the island,
and we never saw any long waves rolling in and breaking
on the shore, but the first thing was when we beached the well-benched
vessels.
Then after we had beached the ships we took all the sails down,

150 and we ourselves stepped out onto the break of the sea beach,
and there we fell asleep and waited for the divine Dawn.
    'But when the young Dawn showed again with her rosy fingers,
we made a tour about the island, admiring everything
there, and the nymphs, daughters of Zeus of the aegis, started

155 the hill-roving goats our way for my companions to feast on.
At once we went and took from the ships curved bows and javelins
with long sockets, and arranging ourselves in three divisions
cast about, and the god granted us the game we longed for.
Now there were twelve ships that went with me, and for each one nine
goats

160 were portioned out, but I alone had ten for my portion.
So for the whole length of the day until the sun's setting,
we sat there feasting on unlimited meat and sweet wine;
for the red wine had not yet given out in the ships, there was
some still left, for we all had taken away a great deal

165 in storing jars when we stormed the Kikonians' sacred citadel.
We looked across at the land of the Cyclopes, and they were
near by, and we saw their smoke and heard sheep and goats bleating.
But when the sun went down and the sacred darkness came over,
then we lay down to sleep along the break of the seashore;

170 but when the young Dawn showed again with her rosy fingers,
then I held an assembly and spoke forth before all:
"The rest of you, who are my eager companions, wait here,
while I, with my own ship and companions that are in it,
go and find out about these people, and learn what they are,

175 whether they are savage and violent, and without justice,
or hospitable to strangers and with minds that are godly."

Odysseus and his companions

'So speaking I went aboard the ship and told my companions
also to go aboard, and to cast off the stern cables,
and quickly they went aboard the ship and sat to the oarlocks,
180 and sitting well in order dashed the oars in the gray sea.
But when we had arrived at the place, which was nearby, there
at the edge of the land we saw the cave, close to the water,
high, and overgrown with laurels, and in it were stabled
great flocks, sheep and goats alike, and there was a fenced yard
185 built around it with a high wall of grubbed-out boulders
and tall pines and oaks with lofty foliage. Inside
there lodged a monster of a man, who now was herding
the flocks at a distance away, alone, for he did not range with
others, but stayed away by himself; his mind was lawless,
190 and in truth he was a monstrous wonder made to behold, not
like a man, an eater of bread, but more like a wooded
peak of the high mountains seen standing away from the others.
'At that time I told the rest of my eager companions
to stay where they were beside the ship and guard it. Meanwhile
195 I, choosing out the twelve best men among my companions,
went on, but I had with me a goatskin bottle of black wine,
sweet wine, given me by Maron, son of Euanthes
and priest of Apollo, who bestrides Ismaros; he gave it
because, respecting him with his wife and child, we saved them
200 from harm. He made his dwelling among the trees of the sacred
grove of Phoibos Apollo, and he gave me glorious presents.
He gave me seven talents of well-wrought gold, and he gave me
a mixing bowl made all of silver, and gave along with it
wine, drawing it off in storing jars, twelve in all. This was
205 a sweet wine, unmixed, a divine drink. No one of his servants
or thralls that were in his household knew anything about it,
but only himself and his dear wife and a single housekeeper.
Whenever he drank this honey-sweet red wine, he would pour out
enough to fill one cup, then twenty measures of water
210 were added, and the mixing bowl gave off a sweet smell;
magical; then would be no pleasure in holding off. Of this
wine I filled a great wineskin full, and took too provisions
in a bag, for my proud heart had an idea that presently
I would encounter a man who was endowed with great strength,
215 and wild, with no true knowledge of laws or any good customs.

in the cave of Polyphemos

'Lightly we made our way to the cave, but we did not find him
there, he was off herding on the range with his fat flocks.
We went inside the cave and admired everything inside it.
Baskets were there, heavy with cheeses, and the pens crowded
220 with lambs and kids. They had all been divided into separate
groups, the firstlings in one place, and then the middle ones,
the babies again by themselves. And all his vessels, milk pails
and pans, that he used for milking into, were running over
with whey. From the start my companions spoke to me and begged me
225 to take some of the cheeses, come back again, and the next time
to drive the lambs and kids from their pens, and get back quickly
to the ship again, and go sailing off across the salt water;
but I would not listen to them, it would have been better their way,
not until I could see him, see if he would give me presents.
230 My friends were to find the sight of him in no way lovely.
      'There we built a fire and made sacrifice, and helping
ourselves to the cheeses we ate and sat waiting for him
inside, until he came home from his herding. He carried a heavy
load of dried-out wood, to make a fire for his dinner,
235 and threw it down inside the cave, making a terrible
crash, so in fear we scuttled away into the cave's corners.
Next he drove into the wide cavern all from the fat flocks
that he would milk, but he left all the male animals, billygoats
and rams, outside in his yard with the deep fences. Next thing,
240 he heaved up and set into position the huge door stop,
a massive thing; no twenty-two of the best four-wheeled
wagons could have taken that weight off the ground and carried it,
such a piece of sky-towering cliff that was he set over
his gateway. Next he sat down and milked his sheep and his bleating
245 goats, each of them in order, and put lamb or kid under each one
to suck, and then drew off half of the white milk and put it
by in baskets made of wickerwork, stored for cheeses,
but let the other half stand in the milk pails so as to have it
to help himself to and drink from, and it would serve for his supper.
250 But after he had briskly done all his chores and finished,
at last he lit the fire, and saw us, and asked us a question:
"Strangers, who are you? From where do you come sailing over the watery
ways? Is it on some business, or are you recklessly roving
as pirates do, when they sail on the salt sea and venture

255   their lives as they wander, bringing evil to alien people?"
     'So he spoke, and the inward heart in us was broken
     in terror of the deep voice and for seeing him so monstrous;
     but even so I had words for an answer, and I said to him:
     "We are Achaians coming from Troy, beaten off our true course
260   by winds from every direction across the great gulf of the open
     sea, making for home, by the wrong way, on the wrong courses.
     So we have come. So it has pleased Zeus to arrange it.
     We claim we are of the following of the son of Atreus,
     Agamemnon, whose fame now is the greatest thing under heaven,
265   such a city was that he sacked and destroyed so many
     people; but now in turn we come to you and are suppliants
     at your knees, if you might give us a guest present or otherwise
     some gift of grace, for such is the right of strangers. Therefore
     respect the gods, O best of men. We are your suppliants,
270   and Zeus the guest god, who stands behind all strangers with honors
     due them, avenges any wrong toward strangers and suppliants."
     'So I spoke, but he answered me in pitiless spirit:
     "Stranger, you are a simple fool, or come from far off,
     when you tell me to avoid the wrath of the gods or fear them.
275   The Cyclopes do not concern themselves over Zeus of the aegis,
     nor any of the rest of the blessed gods, since we are far better
     than they, and for fear of the hate of Zeus I would not spare
     you or your companions either, if the fancy took me
     otherwise. But tell me, so I may know: where did you
280   put your well-made ship when you came? Nearby or far off?"
     'So he spoke, trying me out, but I knew too much and was not
     deceived, but answered him in turn, and my words were crafty:
     "Poseidon, Shaker of the Earth, has shattered my vessel.
     He drove it against the rocks on the outer coast of your country,
285   cracked on a cliff, it is gone, the wind on the sea took it;
     but I, with these you see, got away from sudden destruction."
     'So I spoke, but he in pitiless spirit answered
     nothing, but sprang up and reached for my companions,
     caught up two together and slapped them, like killing puppies,
290   against the ground, and the brains ran all over the floor, soaking
     the ground. Then he cut them up limb by limb and got supper ready,
     and like a lion reared in the hills, without leaving anything,
     ate them, entrails, flesh and the marrowy bones alike. We

The men being eaten, two at a time

cried out aloud and held our hands up to Zeus, seeing
295 the cruelty of what he did, but our hearts were helpless.
But when the Cyclops had filled his enormous stomach, feeding
on human flesh and drinking down milk unmixed with water,
he lay down to sleep in the cave sprawled out through his sheep. Then I
took counsel with myself in my great-hearted spirit
300 to go up close, drawing from beside my thigh the sharp sword,
and stab him in the chest, where the midriff joins on the liver,
feeling for the place with my hand; but the second thought stayed me;
for there we too would have perished away in sheer destruction,
seeing that our hands could never have pushed from the lofty
305 gate of the cave the ponderous boulder he had propped there.
So mourning we waited, just as we were, for the divine Dawn.
'But when the young Dawn showed again with her rosy fingers,
he lit his fire, and then set about milking his glorious
flocks, each of them in order, and put lamb or kid under each one.
310 But after he had briskly done all his chores and finished,
again he snatched up two men, and prepared them for dinner,
and when he had dined, drove his fat flocks out of the cavern,
easily lifting off the great doorstone, but then he put it
back again, like a man closing the lid on a quiver.
315 And so the Cyclops, whistling loudly, guided his fat flocks
to the hills, leaving me there in the cave mumbling my black thoughts
of how I might punish him, how Athene might give me that glory.
And as I thought, this was the plan that seemed best to me.
The Cyclops had lying there beside the pen a great bludgeon
320 of olive wood, still green. He had cut it so that when it dried out
he could carry it about, and we looking at it considered
it to be about the size for the mast of a cargo-carrying
broad black ship of twenty oars which crosses the open
sea; such was the length of it, such the thickness, to judge by
325 looking. I went up and chopped a length of about a fathom,
and handed it over to my companions and told them to shave it
down, and they made it smooth, while I standing by them sharpened
the point, then put it over the blaze of the fire to harden.
Then I put it well away and hid it under the ordure
330 which was all over the floor of the cave, much stuff lying
about. Next I told the rest of the men to cast lots, to find out
which of them must endure with me to take up the great beam

and spin it in Cyclops' eye when sweet sleep had come over him.
The ones drew it whom I myself would have wanted chosen,
335 four men, and I myself was the fifth, and allotted with them.
With the evening he came back again, herding his fleecy
flocks, but drove all his fat flocks inside the wide cave
at once, and did not leave any outside in the yard with the deep fence,
whether he had some idea, or whether a god so urged him.
340 When he had heaved up and set in position the huge door stop,
next he sat down and started milking his sheep and his bleating
goats, each of them in order, and put lamb or kid under each one.
But after he had briskly done all his chores and finished,
again he snatched up two men and prepared them for dinner.
345 Then at last I, holding in my hands an ivy bowl
full of the black wine, stood close up to the Cyclops and spoke out:
"Here, Cyclops, have a drink of wine, now you have fed on
human flesh, and see what kind of drink our ship carried
inside her. I brought it for you, and it would have been your libation
350 had you taken pity and sent me home, but I cannot suffer
your rages. Cruel, how can any man come and visit
you ever again, now you have done what has no sanction?"
    'So I spoke, and he took it and drank it off, and was terribly
pleased with the wine he drank and questioned me again, saying:
355 "Give me still more, freely, and tell me your name straightway
now, so I can give you a guest present to make you happy.
For the grain-giving land of the Cyclopes also yields them
wine of strength, and it is Zeus' rain that waters it for them;
but this comes from where ambrosia and nectar flow in abundance."
360   'So he spoke, and I gave him the gleaming wine again. Three times
I brought it to him and gave it to him, three times he recklessly
drained it, but when the wine had got into the brains of the Cyclops,
then I spoke to him, and my words were full of beguilement:
"Cyclops, you ask me for my famous name. I will tell you
365 then, but you must give me a guest gift as you have promised.
Nobody is my name. My father and mother call me
Nobody, as do all the others who are my companions."
    'So I spoke, and he answered me in pitiless spirit:
"Then I will eat Nobody after his friends, and the others
370 I will eat first, and that shall be my guest present to you."
    'He spoke and slumped away and fell on his back, and lay there

with his thick neck crooked over on one side, and sleep who subdues all
came on and captured him, and the wine gurgled up from his gullet
with gobs of human meat. This was his drunken vomiting.

375   Then I shoved the beam underneath a deep bed of cinders,
waiting for it to heat, and I spoke to all my companions
in words of courage, so none should be in a panic, and back out;
but when the beam of olive, green as it was, was nearly
at the point of catching fire and glowed, terribly incandescent,

380   then I brought it close up from the fire and my friends about me
stood fast. Some great divinity breathed courage into us.
They seized the beam of olive, sharp at the end, and leaned on it
into the eye, while I from above leaning my weight on it
twirled it, like a man with a brace-and-bit who bores into

385   a ship timber, and his men from underneath, grasping
the strap on either side whirl it, and it bites resolutely deeper.
So seizing the fire-point-hardened timber we twirled it
in his eye, and the blood boiled around the hot point, so that
the blast and scorch of the burning ball singed all his eyebrows

390   and eyelids, and the fire made the roots of his eye crackle.
As when a man who works as a blacksmith plunges a screaming
great ax blade or plane into cold water, treating it
for temper, since this is the way steel is made strong, even
so Cyclops' eye sizzled about the beam of the olive.

395   He gave a giant horrible cry and the rocks rattled
to the sound, and we scuttled away in fear. He pulled the timber
out of his eye, and it blubbered with plenty of blood, then
when he had frantically taken it in his hands and thrown it
away, he cried aloud to the other Cyclopes, who live

400   around him in their own caves along the windy pinnacles.
They hearing him came swarming up from their various places,
and stood around the cave and asked him what was his trouble:
"Why, Polyphemos, what do you want with all this outcry
through the immortal night and have made us all thus sleepless?

405   Surely no mortal against your will can be driving your sheep off?
Surely none can be killing you by force or treachery?"
      'Then from inside the cave strong Polyphemos answered:
"Good friends, Nobody is killing me by force or treachery."
      'So then the others speaking in winged words gave him an answer:

410   "If alone as you are none uses violence on you,

why, there is no avoiding the sickness sent by great Zeus;
so you had better pray to your father, the lord Poseidon.''
    'So they spoke as they went away, and the heart within me
laughed over how my name and my perfect planning had fooled him.
415 But the Cyclops, groaning aloud and in the pain of his agony,
felt with his hands, and took the boulder out of the doorway,
and sat down in the entrance himself, spreading his arms wide,
to catch anyone who tried to get out with the sheep, hoping
that I would be so guileless in my heart as to try this;
420 but I was planning so that things would come out the best way,
and trying to find some release from death, for my companions
and myself too, combining all my resource and treacheries,
as with life at stake, for the great evil was very close to us.
And as I thought, this was the plan that seemed best to me.
425 There were some male sheep, rams, well nourished, thick and fleecy,
handsome and large, with a dark depth of of wool. Silently
I caught these and lashed them together with pliant willow
withes, where the monstrous Cyclops lawless of mind had used to
sleep. I had them in threes, and the one in the middle carried
430 a man, while the other two went on each side, so guarding
my friends. Three rams carried each man, but as for myself,
there was one ram, far the finest of all the flock. This one
I clasped around the back, snuggled under the wool of the belly,
and stayed there still, and with a firm twist of the hands and enduring
435 spirit clung fast to the glory of this fleece, unrelenting.
So we grieved for the time and waited for the divine Dawn.
    'But when the young Dawn showed again with her rosy fingers,
then the male sheep hastened out of the cave, toward pasture,
but the ewes were bleating all through the pens unmilked, their udders
440 ready to burst. Meanwhile their master, suffering and in
bitter pain, felt over the backs of all his sheep, standing
up as they were, but in his guilelessness did not notice
how my men were fastened under the breasts of his fleecy
sheep. Last of all the flock the ram went out of the doorway,
445 loaded with his own fleece, and with me, and my close counsels.
Then, feeling him, powerful Polyphemos spoke a word to him:
"My dear old ram, why are you thus leaving the cave last of
the sheep? Never in the old days were you left behind by
the flock, but long-striding, far ahead of the rest would pasture
450 on the tender bloom of the grass, be first at running rivers,

and be eager always to lead the way first back to the sheepfold
at evening. Now you are last of all. Perhaps you are grieving
for your master's eye, which a bad man with his wicked companions
put out, after he had made my brain helpless with wine, this

455 Nobody, who I think has not yet got clear of destruction.
If only you could think like us and only be given
a voice, to tell me where he is skulking away from my anger,
then surely he would be smashed against the floor and his brains go
spattering all over the cave to make my heart lighter

460 from the burden of all the evils this niddering Nobody gave me."
'So he spoke, and sent the ram along from him, outdoors,
and when we had got a little way from the yard and the cavern,
first I got myself loose from my ram, then set my companions
free, and rapidly then, and with many a backward glance, we

465 drove the long-striding sheep, rich with fat, until we reached
our ship, and the sight of us who had escaped death was welcome
to our companions, but they began to mourn for the others;
only I would not let them cry out, but with my brows nodded
to each man, and told them to be quick and to load the fleecy

470 sheep on board our vessel and sail out on the salt water.
Quickly they went aboard the ship and sat to the oarlocks,
and sitting well in order dashed the oars in the gray sea.
But when I was as far from the land as a voice shouting
carries, I called out aloud to the Cyclops, taunting him:

475 "Cyclops, in the end it was no weak man's companions
you were to eat by violence and force in your hollow
cave, and your evil deeds were to catch up with you, and be
too strong for you, hard one, who dared to eat your own guests
in your own house, so Zeus and the rest of the gods have punished you."

480 'So I spoke, and still more the heart in him was angered.
He broke away the peak of a great mountain and let it
fly, and threw it in front of the dark-prowed ship by only
a little, it just failed to graze the steering oar's edge,
but the sea washed up in the splash as the stone went under, the tidal

485 wave it made swept us suddenly back from the open
sea to the mainland again, and forced us on shore. Then I
caught up in my hands the very long pole and pushed her
clear again, and urged my companions with words, and nodding
with my head, to throw their weight on the oars and bring us

490 out of the threatening evil, and they leaned on and rowed hard.

The curse of Polyphemos

But when we had cut through the sea to twice the previous distance,
again I started to call to Cyclops, but my friends about me
checked me, first one then another speaking, trying to soothe me:
"Hard one, why are you trying once more to stir up this savage
495   man, who just now threw his missile in the sea, forcing
our ship to the land again, and we thought once more we were finished;
and if he had heard a voice or any one of us speaking,
he would have broken all our heads and our ship's timbers
with a cast of a great jagged stone, so strong is his throwing."
500   'So they spoke, but could not persuade the great heart in me,
but once again in the anger of my heart I cried to him:
"Cyclops, if any mortal man ever asks you who it was
that inflicted upon your eye this shameful blinding,
tell him that you were blinded by Odysseus, sacker of cities.
505   Laertes is his father, and he makes his home in Ithaka."
    'So I spoke, and he groaned aloud and answered me, saying:
"Ah now, a prophecy spoken of old is come to completion.
There used to be a man here, great and strong, and a prophet,
Telemos, Eurymos' son, who for prophecy was pre-eminent
510   and grew old as a prophet among the Cyclopes. This man told me
how all this that has happened now must someday be accomplished,
and how I must lose the sight of my eye at the hands of Odysseus.
But always I was on the lookout for a man handsome
and tall, with great endowment of strength on him, to come here;
515   but now the end of it is that a little man, niddering, feeble,
has taken away the sight of my eye, first making me helpless
with wine. So come here, Odysseus, let me give you a guest gift
and urge the glorious Shaker of the Earth to grant you conveyance
home. For I am his son, he announces himself as my father.
520   He himself will heal me, if he will, but not any other
one of the blessed gods, nor any man who is mortal."
    'So he spoke, but I answered him again and said to him:
"I only wish it were certain I could make you reft of spirit
and life, and send you to the house of Hades, as it is certain
525   that not even the Shaker of the Earth will ever heal your eye for you."
    'So I spoke, but he then called to the lord Poseidon
in prayer, reaching both arms up toward the starry heaven:
"Hear me, Poseidon who circle the earth, dark-haired. If truly
I am your son, and you acknowledge yourself as my father,

530   grant that Odysseus, sacker of cities, son of Laertes,
     who makes his home in Ithaka, may never reach that home;
     but if it is decided that he shall see his own people,
     and come home to his strong-founded house and to his own country,
     let him come late, in bad case, with the loss of all his companions,
535   in someone else's ship, and find troubles in his household."
       'So he spoke in prayer, and the dark-haired god heard him.
     Then for the second time lifting a stone far greater
     he whirled it and threw, leaning into the cast his strength beyond
          measure,
     and the stone fell behind the dark-prowed ship by only
540   a little, it just failed to graze the steering oar's edge,
     and the sea washed up in the splash as the stone went under; the tidal
     wave drove us along forward and forced us onto the island.
     But after we had so made the island, where all the rest of
     our strong-benched ships were waiting together, and our companions
545   were sitting about them grieving, having waited so long for us,
     making this point we ran our ship on the sand and beached her,
     and we ourselves stepped out onto the break of the sea beach,
     and from the hollow ships bringing out the flocks of the Cyclops
     we shared them out so none might go cheated of his proper
550   portion; but for me alone my strong-greaved companions
     excepted the ram when the sheep were shared, and I sacrificed him
     on the sands to Zeus, dark-clouded son of Kronos, lord over
     all, and burned him the thighs; but he was not moved by my offerings,
     but still was pondering on a way how all my strong-benched
555   ships should be destroyed and all my eager companions.
     So for the whole length of the day until the sun's setting,
     we sat there feasting on unlimited meat and sweet wine.
     But when the sun went down and the sacred darkness came over,
     then we lay down to sleep along the break of the seashore;
560   but when the young Dawn showed again with her rosy fingers,
     then I urged on the rest of my companions and told them
     to go aboard their ships and to cast off the stern cables,
     and quickly they went aboard the ships and sat to the oarlocks,
     and sitting well in order dashed their oars in the gray sea.
565   From there we sailed on further along, glad to have escaped death,
     but grieving still at heart for the loss of our dear companions.

BOOK X

'We came next to the Aiolian island, where Aiolos
lived, Hippotas' son, beloved by the immortal
gods, on a floating island, the whole enclosed by a rampart
of bronze, not to be broken, and the sheer of the cliff runs upward
5 to it; and twelve children were born to him in his palace,
six of them daughters, and six sons in the pride of their youth, so
he bestowed his daughters on his sons, to be their consorts.
And evermore, beside their dear father and gracious mother,
these feast, and good things beyond number are set before them;
10 and all their days the house fragrant with food echoes
in the courtyard, but their nights they sleep each one by his modest
wife, under coverlets, and on bedsteads corded for bedding.
We came to the city of these men and their handsome houses,
and a whole month he entertained me and asked me everything
15 of Ilion, and the ships of the Argives, and the Achaians'
homecoming, and I told him all the tale as it happened.
But when I asked him about the way back and requested
conveyance, again he did not refuse, but granted me passage.
He gave me a bag made of the skin taken off a nine-year
20 ox, stuffed full inside with the courses of all the blowing
winds, for the son of Kronos had set him in charge over
the winds, to hold them still or start them up at his pleasure.
He stowed it away in the hollow ship, tied fast with a silver
string, so there should be no wrong breath of wind, not even

The island of Aiolos and the bag of winds

25   a little, but set the West Wind free to blow me and carry
the ships and the men aboard them on their way; but it was not
so to be, for we were ruined by our own folly.
   'Nevertheless we sailed on, night and day, for nine days,
and on the tenth at last appeared the land of our fathers,
30   and we could see people tending fires, we were very close to them.
But then the sweet sleep came upon me, for I was worn out
with always handling the sheet myself, and I would not give it
to any other companion, so we could come home quicker
to our own country; but my companions talked with each other
35   and said that I was bringing silver and gold home with me,
given me by great-hearted Aiolos, son of Hippotas;
and thus they would speak to each other, each looking at the man next
       him:
"See now, this man is loved by everybody and favored
by all, whenever he visits anyone's land and city,
40   and is bringing home with him handsome treasures taken from the plunder
of Troy, while we, who have gone through everything he has
on the same venture, come home with our hands empty. Now too
Aiolos in favor of friendship has given him all these
goods. Let us quickly look inside and see what is in there,
45   and how much silver and gold this bag contains inside it."
   'So he spoke, and the evil counsel of my companions
prevailed, and they opened the bag and the winds all burst out. Suddenly
the storm caught them away and swept them over the water
weeping, away from their own country. Then I waking
50   pondered deeply in my own blameless spirit, whether
to throw myself over the side and die in the open water,
or wait it out in silence and still be one of the living;
and I endured it and waited, and hiding my face I lay down
in the ship, while all were carried on the evil blast of the stormwind
55   back to the Aiolian island, with my friends grieving.
   'There again we set foot on the mainland, and fetched water,
and my companions soon took their supper there by the fast ships.
But after we had tasted of food and drink, then I
took along one herald with me, and one companion,
60   and went up to the famous house of Aiolos. There I found him
sitting at dinner with his wife and with his own children.
We came to the house beside the pillars, and on the doorstone

All ships but one, with crews,

we sat down, and their minds wondered at us and they asked us:
"What brings you back, Odysseus? What evil spirit has vexed you?
65 We sent you properly on your way, so you could come back
to your own country and house and whatever else is dear to you."
     'So they spoke, and I though sorry at heart answered:
"My wretched companions brought me to ruin, helped by the pitiless
sleep. Then make it right, dear friends; for you have the power."
70   'So I spoke to them, plying them with words of endearment,
but they were all silent; only the father found words and answered:
"O least of living creatures, out of this island! Hurry!
I have no right to see on his way, none to give passage
to any man whom the blessed gods hate with such bitterness.
75 Out. This arrival means you are hateful to the immortals."
     'So speaking he sent me, groaning heavily, out of his palace,
and from there, grieving still at heart, we sailed on further,
but the men's spirit was worn away with the pain of rowing
and our own silliness, since homecoming seemed ours no longer.
80   'Nevertheless we sailed on, night and day, for six days,
and on the seventh came to the sheer citadel of Lamos,
Telepylos of the Laistrygones, where one herdsman, driving
his flocks in hails another, who answers as he drives
his flocks out; and there a man who could do without sleep could earn
     him
85 double wages, one for herding the cattle, one for the silvery
sheep. There the courses of night and day lie close together.
There as we entered the glorious harbor, which a sky-towering
cliff encloses on either side, with no break anywhere,
and two projecting promontories facing each other
90 run out toward the mouth, and there is a narrow entrance,
there all the rest of them had their oar-swept ships in the inward
part, they were tied up close together inside the hollow
  harbor, for there was never a swell of surf inside it,
neither great nor small, but there was a pale calm on it.
95 I myself, however, kept my black ship on the outside,
at the very end, making her fast to the cliff with a cable,
and climbed to a rocky point of observation and stood there.
From here no trace of cattle nor working of men was visible;
all we could see was the smoke going up from the country.
100 So I sent companions ahead telling them to find out

what men, eaters of bread, might live here in this country.
I chose two men, and sent a third with them, as a herald.
They left the ship and walked on a smooth road where the wagons
carried the timber down from the high hills to the city,
105 and there in front of the town they met a girl drawing water.
This was the powerful daughter of the Laistrygonian
Antiphates, who had gone down to the sweet-running wellspring,
Artakie, whence they would carry their water back to the city.
My men stood by her and talked with her, and asked her who was
110 king of these people and who was lord over them. She readily
pointed out to them the high-roofed house of her father.
But when they entered the glorious house, they found there a woman
as big as a mountain peak, and the sight of her filled them with horror.
At once she summoned famous Antiphates, her husband,
115 from their assembly, and he devised dismal death against them.
He snatched up one of my companions, and prepared him for dinner,
but the other two darted away in flight, and got back to my ship.
The king raised the cry through the city. Hearing him the powerful
Laistrygones came swarming up from every direction,
120 tens of thousands of them, and not like men, like giants.
These, standing along the cliffs, pelted my men with man-sized
boulders, and a horrid racket went up by the ships, of men
being killed and ships being smashed to pieces. They speared them
like fish, and carried them away for their joyless feasting.
125 But while they were destroying them in the deep-water harbor,
meanwhile I, drawing from beside my thigh the sharp sword,
chopped away the cable that tied the ship with the dark prow,
and called out to my companions, and urged them with all speed
to throw their weight on the oars and escape the threatening evil,
130 and they made the water fly, fearing destruction. Gladly
my ship, and only mine, fled out from the overhanging
cliffs to the open water, but the others were all destroyed there.
        'From there we sailed on further along, glad to have escaped death,
but grieving still at heart for the loss of our dear companions.
135 We came to Aiaia, which is an island. There lived Circe
of the lovely hair, the dread goddess who talks with mortals,
who is own sister to the malignant-minded Aietes;
for they both are children of Helios, who shines on mortals,
and their mother is Perse who in turn is daughter of Ocean.

Exploration of Circe's island

140 There we brought our ship in to the shore, in silence,
at a harbor fit for ships to lie, and some god guided us
in. There we disembarked, and for two days and two nights
we lay there, for sorrow and weariness eating our hearts out.
But when the fair-haired Dawn in her rounds brought on the third day,
145 then at last I took up my spear again, my sharp sword,
and went up quickly from beside the ship to find a lookout
place, to look for some trace of people, listen for some sound.
I climbed to a rocky point of observation and stood there,
and got a sight of smoke which came from the halls of Circe
150 going up from wide-wayed earth through undergrowth and forest.
Then I pondered deeply in my heart and my spirit,
whether, since I had seen the fire and smoke, to investigate;
but in the division of my heart this way seemed the best to me,
to go back first to the fast ship and the beach of the sea, and give
155 my companions some dinner, and then go forward and investigate.
But on my way, as I was close to the oar-swept vessel,
some god, because I was all alone, took pity upon me,
and sent a great stag with towering antlers right in my very
path; he had come from his range in the forest down to the river
160 to drink, for the fierce strength of the sun was upon him. As he
stepped out, I hit him in the middle of the back, next to
the spine, so that the brazen spearhead smashed its way clean through.
He screamed and dropped in the dust and the life spirit fluttered from
    him.
I set my foot on him and drew the bronze spear out of
the wound it had made, and rested it on the ground, while I
pulled growing twigs and willow withes and, braiding them into
a rope, about six feet in length, and looping them over
the feet of this great monster on both sides, lashed them together,
and with him loaded over my neck went toward the black ship,
170 propping myself on my spear, for there was no way to carry him
on the shoulder holding him with one hand, he was such a very
big beast. I threw him down by the ship and roused my companions,
standing beside each man and speaking to him in kind words:
"Dear friends, sorry as we are, we shall not yet go down into
175 the house of Hades. Not until our day is appointed.
Come then, while there is something to eat and drink by the fast ship,
let us think of our food and not be worn out with hunger."

Her enchanted beasts

'So I spoke, and they listened at once to me and obeyed me,
and unveiling their heads along the beach of the barren water
180 they admired the stag, and truly he was a very big beast.
But after they had looked at him and their eyes had enjoyed him,
they washed their hands and set to preparing a communal high feast.
So for the whole length of the day until the sun's setting
we sat there feasting on unlimited meat and sweet wine.
185 But when the sun went down and the sacred darkness came over,
then we lay down to sleep along the break of the seashore;
but when the young Dawn showed again with her rosy fingers,
then I held an assembly and spoke forth to all of them:
"Hear my words, my companions, in spite of your hearts' sufferings.
190 Dear friends, for we do not know where the darkness is nor the sunrise,
nor where the Sun who shines upon people rises, nor where
he sets, then let us hasten our minds and think, whether there is
any course left open to us. But I think there is none.
For I climbed to a rocky place of observation and looked at
195 the island, and the endless sea lies all in a circle
around it, but the island itself lies low, and my eyes saw
smoke rising in the middle through the undergrowth and the forest."
'So I spoke, and the inward heart in them was broken,
as they remembered Antiphates the Laistrygonian
200 and the violence of the great-hearted cannibal Cyclops,
and they wept loud and shrill, letting the big tears fall,
but there came no advantage to them for all their sorrowing.
'I counted off all my strong-greaved companions into two
divisions, and appointed a leader for each, I myself
205 taking one, while godlike Eurylochos had the other.
Promptly then we shook the lots in a brazen helmet,
and the lot of great-hearted Eurylochos sprang out. He then
went on his way, and with him two-and-twenty companions,
weeping, and we whom they left behind were mourning also.
210 In the forest glen they came on the house of Circe. It was
in an open place, and put together from stones, well polished,
and all about it there were lions, and wolves of the mountains,
whom the goddess had given evil drugs and enchanted,
and these made no attack on the men, but came up thronging
215 about them, waving their long tails and fawning, in the way
that dogs go fawning about their master, when he comes home

from dining out, for he always brings back something to please them;
so these wolves with great strong claws and lions came fawning
on my men, but they were afraid when they saw the terrible big beasts.
220 They stood there in the forecourt of the goddess with the glorious
hair, and heard Circe inside singing in a sweet voice
as she went up and down a great design on a loom, immortal
such as goddesses have, delicate and lovely and glorious
their work. Now Polites leader of men, who was
225 the best and dearest to me of my friends, began the discussion:
"Friends, someone inside going up and down a great piece
of weaving is singing sweetly, and the whole place murmurs to the echo
of it, whether she is woman or goddess. Come, let us call her."
    'So he spoke to them, and the rest gave voice, and called her,
230 and at once she opened the shining doors, and came out, and invited
them in, and all in their innocence entered; only
Eurylochos waited outside, for he suspected treachery.
She brought them inside and seated them on chairs and benches,
and mixed them a potion, with barley and cheese and pale honey
235 added to Pramneian wine, but put into the mixture
malignant drugs, to make them forgetful of their own country.
When she had given them this and they had drunk it down, next thing
she struck them with her wand and drove them into her pig pens,
and they took on the look of pigs, with the heads and voices
240 and bristles of pigs, but the minds within them stayed as they had been
before. So crying they went in, and before them Circe
threw down acorns for them to eat, and ilex and cornel
buds, such food as pigs who sleep on the ground always feed on.
    'Eurylochos came back again to the fast black ship,
245 to tell the story of our companions and of their dismal
fate, but he could not get a word out, though he was trying
to speak, but his heart was stunned by the great sorrow, and both eyes
filled with tears, he could think of nothing but lamentation.
But after we had wondered at him and asked him questions,
250 at last he told us about the loss of his other companions:
"We went, O glorious Odysseus, through the growth as you
told us, and found a fine house in the glen. It was
in an open place, and put together from stones, well polished.
Someone, goddess or woman, was singing inside in a clear voice
255 as she went up and down her loom, and they called her, and spoke to her,

and at once she opened the shining doors, and came out and invited
them in, and all in their innocence entered, only
I waited for them outside, for I suspected treachery.
Then the whole lot of them vanished away together, nor did one
260   single one come out, though I sat and watched for a long time."
      'So he spoke, and I slung my great bronze sword with the silver
nails across my shoulders, and hung my bow on also,
and told him to guide me back by the same way he had gone;
but he, clasping my knees in both hands, entreated me,
265   and in loud lamentation spoke to me and addressed me:
      "Illustrious, do not take me against my will there. Leave me
here, for I know you will never come back yourself, nor bring back
any of your companions. Let us rather make haste, and with these
who are left, escape, for we still may avoid the day of evil."
270   'So he spoke, and I answered again in turn and said to him:
      "Eurylochos, you may stay here eating and drinking, even
where you are and beside the hollow black ship; only
I shall go. For there is strong compulsion upon me."
      'So I spoke, and started up from the ship and the seashore.
275   But as I went up through the lonely glens, and was coming
near to the great house of Circe, skilled in medicines,
there as I came up to the house, Hermes, of the golden
staff, met me on my way, in the likeness of a young man
with beard new grown, which is the most graceful time of young
            manhood.
280   He took me by the hand and spoke to me and named me, saying:
      "Where are you going, unhappy man, all alone, through the hilltops,
ignorant of the land-lay, and your friends are here in Circe's
place, in the shape of pigs and holed up in the close pig pens.
Do you come here meaning to set them free? I do not think
285   you will get back yourself, but must stay here with the others.
But see, I will find you a way out of your troubles, and save you.
Here, this is a good medicine, take it, and go into Circe's
house; it will give you power against the day of trouble.
And I will tell you all the malevolent guiles of Circe.
290   She will make you a potion, and put drugs in the food, but she will not
even so be able to enchant you, for this good medicine
which I give you now will prevent her. I will tell you the details
of what to do. As soon as Circe with her long wand strikes you,

The herb moly saves Odysseus

then drawing from beside your thigh your sharp sword, rush
295   forward against Circe, as if you were raging to kill her,
and she will be afraid, and invite you to go to bed with her.
Do not then resist and refuse the bed of the goddess,
for so she will set free your companions, and care for you also;
but bid her swear the great oath of the blessed gods, that she
300   has no other evil hurt that she is devising against you,
so she will not make you weak and unmanned, once you are naked.''
   'So spoke Argeïphontes, and he gave me the medicine,
which he picked out of the ground, and he explained the nature
of it to me. It was black at the root, but with a milky
305   flower. The gods call it moly. It is hard for mortal
men to dig up, but the gods have power to do all things.
   'Then Hermes went away, passing over the wooded island,
toward tall Olympos, and I meanwhile made my way to the house
of Circe, but my heart was a storm in me as I went. Now
310   I stood outside at the doors of the goddess with the glorious
hair, and standing I shouted aloud; and the goddess heard me,
and at once she opened the shining doors and came out and invited
me in; and I, deeply troubled in my heart, went in with her.
She made me sit down in a chair that was wrought elaborately
315   and splendid with silver nails, and under my feet was a footstool.
She made a potion for me to drink and gave it in a golden
cup, and with evil thoughts in her heart added the drug to it.
Then when she had given it and I drank it off, without being
enchanted, she struck me with her wand and spoke and named me:
320   "Go to your sty now and lie down with your other friends there."
   'So she spoke, but I, drawing from beside my thigh the sharp sword,
rushed forward against Circe as if I were raging to kill her,
but she screamed aloud and ran under my guard, and clasping both knees
in loud lamentation spoke to me and addressed me in winged words:
325   "What man are you and whence? Where are your city and parents?
The wonder is on me that you drank my drugs and have not been
enchanted, for no other man beside could have stood up
under my drugs, once he drank and they passed the barrier
of his teeth. There is a mind in you no magic will work on.
330   You are then resourceful Odysseus. Argeïphontes
of the golden staff was forever telling me you would come
to me, on your way back from Troy with your fast black ship.

from Circe's spells

Come then, put away your sword in its sheath, and let us
two go up into my bed so that, lying together
335   in the bed of love, we may then have faith and trust in each other."
      'So she spoke, and I answered her again and said to her:
      "Circe, how can you ask me to be gentle with you, when it
      is you who turned my companions into pigs in your palace?
      And now you have me here myself, you treacherously
340   ask me to go into your chamber, and go to bed with you,
      so that when I am naked you can make me a weakling, unmanned.
      I would not be willing to go to bed with you unless
      you can bring yourself, O goddess, to swear me a great oath
      that there is no other evil hurt you devise against me."
345   'So I spoke, and she at once swore me the oath, as I asked her,
      But after she had sworn me the oath, and made an end of it,
      I mounted the surpassingly beautiful bed of Circe.
      'Meanwhile, the four maidservants, who wait on Circe
      in her house, were busy at their work, all through the palace.
350   These are daughters born of the springs and from the coppices
      and the sacred rivers which flow down to the sea. Of these
      one laid the coverlets, splendid and stained in purple, over
      the backs of the chairs, and spread on the seats the cloths to sit on.
      The second drew up the silver tables and placed them in front of
355   the chairs, and laid out the golden serving baskets upon them.
      The third mixed wine, kindly sweet and fragrant, in the silver
      mixing bowl, and set out the golden goblets. The fourth one
      brought in water, then set about building up an abundant
      fire, underneath the great caldron, and the water heated.
360   But when the water had come to a boil in the shining bronze, then
      she sat me down in the bathtub and washed me from the great caldron,
      mixing hot and cold just as I wanted, and pouring it
      over shoulders and head, to take the heart-wasting weariness
      from my limbs. When she had bathed me and anointed me with olive
            oil,
365   she put a splendid mantle and a tunic upon me,
      and made me sit down in a chair that was wrought elaborately
      and splendid with silver nails, and under my feet was a footstool.
      A maidservant brought water for us and poured it from a splendid
      and golden pitcher, holding it above a silver basin,
370   for us to wash, and she pulled a polished table before us.

The swine changed back to men

A grave housekeeper brought in the bread and served it to us,
adding many good things to it, generous with her provisions,
and told us to eat, but nothing pleased my mind, and I sat there
thinking of something else, mind full of evil imaginings.
375   'When Circe noticed how I sat there without ever putting
my hands out to the food, and with the strong sorrow upon me,
she came close, and stood beside me and addressed me in winged words:
"Why, Odysseus, do you sit so, like a man who has lost his
voice, eating your heart out, but touch neither food nor drink. Is it
380 that you suspect me of more treachery? But you have nothing
to fear, since I have already sworn my strong oath to you."
'So she spoke, but I answered her again and said to her:
"Oh, Circe, how could any man right in his mind ever
endure to taste of the food and drink that are set before him,
385 until with his eyes he saw his companions set free? So then,
if you are sincerely telling me to eat and drink, set them
free, so my eyes can again behold my eager companions."
'So I spoke, and Circe walked on out through the palace,
holding her wand in her hand, and opened the doors of the pigsty,
390 and drove them out. They looked like nine-year-old porkers. They stood
ranged and facing her, and she, making her way through their
ranks, anointed each of them with some other medicine,
and the bristles, grown upon them by the evil medicine Circe
had bestowed upon them before, now fell away from them,
395 and they turned back once more into men, younger than they had been
and taller for the eye to behold and handsomer by far.
They recognized me, and each of them clung to my hand. The lovely
longing for lamentation came over us, and the house echoed
terribly to the sound, and even the goddess took pity,
400 and she, shining among goddesses, came close and said to me:
"Son of Laertes and seed of Zeus, resourceful Odysseus,
go back down now to your fast ship and the sand of the seashore,
and first of all, drag your ship up on the land, stowing
your possessions and all the ship's running gear away in the sea caves,
405 and then come back, and bring with you your eager companions."
'So she spoke, and the proud heart in me was persuaded,
and I went back down to my fast ship and the sand of the seashore,
and there I found beside the fast ship my eager companions
pitiful in their lamentation and weeping big tears.

410   And as, in the country, the calves, around the cows returning
        from pasture back to the dung of the farmyard, well filled with grazing,
        come gamboling together to meet them, and the pens no longer
        can hold them in, but lowing incessantly they come running
        around their mothers, so these men, once their eyes saw me,
415   came streaming around me, in tears, and the spirit in them made them
        feel as if they were back in their own country, the very
        city of rugged Ithaka, where they were born and raised up.
        So they came in tears about me, and cried in winged words:
        "O great Odysseus, we are as happy to see you returning
420   as if we had come back to our own Ithakan country.
        But come, tell us about the death of our other companions."
              'So they spoke, but I answered in soft words and told them:
        "First of all, let us drag our ship up on the land, stowing
        our possessions and all the ship's running gear away in the sea caves,
425   and then make haste, all of you, to come along with me,
        so that you can see your companions, in the sacred dwelling
        of Circe, eating and drinking, for they have all in abundance."
              'So I spoke, and at once they did as I told them. Only
        Eurylochos was trying to hold back all my other
430   companions, and he spoke to them and addressed them in winged words:
        "Ah, poor wretches. Where are we going? Why do you long for
        the evils of going down into Circe's palace, for she will
        transform the lot of us into pigs or wolves or lions,
        and so we shall guard her great house for her, under compulsion.
435   So too it happened with the Cyclops, when our companions
        went into his yard, and the bold Odysseus was of their company;
        for it was by this man's recklessness that these too perished."
              'So he spoke, and I considered in my mind whether
        to draw out the long-edged sword from beside my big thigh,
440   and cut off his head and throw it on the ground, even though
        he was nearly related to me by marriage; but my companions
        checked me, first one then another speaking, trying to soothe me:
        "Zeus-sprung Odysseus, if you ask us to, we will leave
        this man here to stay where he is and keep watch over
445   the ship. You show us the way to the sacred dwelling of Circe."
              'So they spoke, and started up from the ship and the seashore;
        nor would Eurylochos be left alone by the hollow
        ship, but followed along in fear of my fierce reproaches.

Life with Circe

'Meanwhile, inside the house, Circe with loving care bathed
450   the rest of my companions, and anointed them well with olive oil,
and put about them mantles of fleece and tunics. We found them
all together, feasting well in the halls. When my men
looked each other in the face and knew one another,
they burst into an outcry of tears, and the whole house echoed,
455   But she, shining among goddesses, came close and said to us:
"Son of Laertes and seed of Zeus, resourceful Odysseus,
no longer raise the swell of your lamentation. I too
know all the pains you have suffered on the sea where the fish swarm,
and all the damage done you on the dry land by hostile
460   men. But come now, eat your food and drink your wine, until
you gather back again into your chests that kind of spirit
you had in you when first you left the land of your fathers
on rugged Ithaka. Now you are all dried out, dispirited
from the constant thought of your hard wandering, nor is there any
465   spirit in your festivity, because of so much suffering."
   'So she spoke, and the proud heart in us was persuaded.
There for all our days until a year was completed
we sat there feasting on unlimited meat and sweet wine.
But when it was the end of a year, and the months wasted
470   away, and the seasons changed, and the long days were accomplished,
then my eager companions called me aside and said to me:
"What ails you now? It is time to think about our own country,
if truly it is ordained that you shall survive and come back
to your strong-founded house and to the land of your fathers."
475   'So they spoke, and the proud heart in me was persuaded.
So for the whole length of the day until the sun's setting
we sat there feasting on unlimited meat and sweet wine.
But when the sun went down and the sacred darkness came over,
they lay down to sleep all about the shadowy chambers,
480   but I, mounting the surpassingly beautiful bed of Circe,
clasped her by the knees and entreated her, and the goddess
listened to me, and I spoke to her and addressed her in winged words:
"O Circe, accomplish now the promise you gave, that you
would see me on my way home. The spirit within me is urgent
485   now, as also in the rest of my friends, who are wasting
my heart away, lamenting around me, when you are elsewhere."
   'So I spoke, and she, shining among goddesses, answered:

Odysseus before going home must visit the land of the dead

"Son of Laertes and seed of Zeus, resourceful Odysseus,
you shall no longer stay in my house when none of you wish to;
490 but first there is another journey you must accomplish
and reach the house of Hades and of revered Persephone,
there to consult with the soul of Teiresias the Theban,
the blind prophet, whose senses stay unshaken within him,
to whom alone Persephone has granted intelligence
495 even after death, but the rest of them are flittering shadows."
'So she spoke, and the inward heart in me was broken,
and I sat down on the bed and cried, nor did the heart in me
wish to go on living any longer, nor to look on the sunlight.
But when I had glutted myself with rolling about and weeping,
500 then at last I spoke aloud and answered the goddess:
"Circe, who will be our guide on that journey? No one
has ever yet in a black ship gone all the way to Hades'."
'So I spoke, and she, shining among goddesses, answered:
"Son of Laertes and seed of Zeus, resourceful Odysseus,
505 let no need for a guide on your ship trouble you; only
set up your mast pole and spread the white sails upon it,
and sit still, and let the blast of the North Wind carry you.
But when you have crossed with your ship the stream of the Ocean, you
will
find there a thickly wooded shore, and the groves of Persephone,
510 and tall black poplars growing, and fruit-perishing willows;
then beach your ship on the shore of the deep-eddying Ocean
and yourself go forward into the moldering home of Hades.
There Pyriphlegethon and Kokytos, which is an off-break
from the water of the Styx, flow into Acheron. There is
515 a rock there, and the junction of two thunderous rivers.
There, hero, you must go close in and do as I tell you.
Dig a pit of about a cubit in each direction,
and pour it full of drink offerings for all the dead, first
honey mixed with mlk, then a second pouring of sweet wine,
520 and the third, water, and over all then sprinkle white barley,
and promise many times to the strengthless heads of the perished
dead that, returning to Ithaka, you will slaughter a barren
cow, your best, in your palace and pile the pyre with treasures,
and to Teiresias apart dedicate an all-black
525 ram, the one conspicuous in all your sheepflocks.

Sailing instructions—the men are told

But when with prayers you have entreated the glorious hordes
of the dead, then sacrifice one ram and one black female,
turning them toward Erebos, but yourself turn away from them
and make for where the river runs, and there the numerous
530 souls of the perished dead will come and gather about you.
Then encourage your companions and tell them, taking
the sheep that are lying by, slaughtered with the pitiless
bronze, to skin these, and burn them, and pray to the divinities,
to Hades the powerful, and to revered Persephone,
535 while you yourself, drawing from beside your thigh the sharp sword,
crouch there, and do not let the strengthless heads of the perished
dead draw nearer to the blood until you have questioned Teiresias.
Then, leader of the host, the prophet will soon come to you,
and he will tell you the way to go, the stages of your journey,
540 and tell you how to make your way home on the sea where the fish
          swarm.''
     'So she spoke, and Dawn of the golden throne came on us,
and she put clothing upon me, an outer cloak and a tunic,
while she, the nymph, mantled herself in a gleaming white robe
fine-woven and delightful, and around her waist she fastened
545 a handsome belt of gold, and on her head was a wimple;
while I walked all about the house and roused my companions,
standing beside each man and speaking to him in kind words:
"No longer lie abed and dreaming away in sweet sleep.
The queenly Circe has shown me the way. So let us go now.''
550   'So I spoke, and the proud heart in them was persuaded.
Yet I did not lead away my companions without some
loss. There was one, Elpenor, the youngest man, not terribly
powerful in fighting nor sound in his thoughts. This man,
apart from the rest of his friends, in search of cool air, had lain
555 down drunkenly to sleep on the roof of Circe's palace,
and when his companions stirred to go he, hearing their tumult
and noise of talking, started suddenly up, and never thought,
when he went down, to go by way of the long ladder,
but blundered straight off the edge of the roof, so that his neck bone
560 was broken out of its sockets, and his soul went down to Hades'.
     'Now as my men were on their way I said a word to them:
"You think you are on your way back now to your own beloved
country, but Circe has indicated another journey

Death of Elpenor

for us, to the house of Hades and of revered Persephone
565   there to consult with the soul of Teiresias the Theban."
    'So I spoke, and the inward heart in them was broken.
They sat down on the ground and lamented and tore their hair out,
but there came no advantage to them for all their sorrowing.
    'When we came down to our fast ship and the sand of the seashore,
570   we sat down, sorrowful, and weeping big tears. Circe
meanwhile had gone down herself to the side of the black ship,
and tethered aboard it a ram and one black female, easily
passing by us unseen. Whose eyes can follow the movement
of a god passing from place to place, unless the god wishes?

BOOK XI

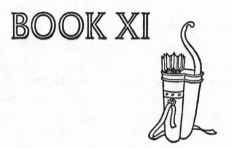

'Now when we had gone down again to the sea and our vessel,
first of all we dragged the ship down into the bright water,
and in the black hull set the mast in place, and set sails,
and took the sheep and walked them aboard, and ourselves also
5 embarked, but sorrowful, and weeping big tears. Circe
of the lovely hair, the dread goddess who talks with mortals,
sent us an excellent companion, a following wind, filling
the sails, to carry from astern the ship with the dark prow.
We ourselves, over all the ship making fast the running gear,
10 sat still, and let the wind and the steersman hold her steady.
All day long her sails were filled as she went through the water,
and the sun set, and all the journeying-ways were darkened.
   'She made the limit, which is of the deep-running Ocean.
There lie the community and city of Kimmerian people,
15 hidden in fog and cloud, nor does Helios, the radiant
sun, ever break through the dark, to illuminate them with his shining,
neither when he climbs up into the starry heaven,
nor when he wheels to return again from heaven to earth,
but always a glum night is spread over wretched mortals.
20 Making this point, we ran the ship ashore, and took out
the sheep, and ourselves walked along by the stream of the Ocean
until we came to that place of which Circe had spoken.
   'There Perimedes and Eurylochos held the victims
fast, and I, drawing from beside my thigh my sharp sword,

The land of the dead—the ghost of Elpenor

25   dug a pit, of about a cubit in each direction,
and poured it full of drink offerings for all the dead, first
honey mixed with milk, and the second pouring was sweet wine,
and the third, water, and over it all I sprinkled white barley.
I promised many times to the strengthless heads of the perished

30   dead that, returning to Ithaka, I would slaughter a barren
cow, my best, in my palace, and pile the pyre with treasures,
and to Teiresias apart would dedicate an all-black
ram, the one conspicuous in all our sheep flocks.
Now when, with sacrifices and prayers, I had so entreated

35   the hordes of the dead, I took the sheep and cut their throats
over the pit, and the dark-clouding blood ran in, and the souls
of the perished dead gathered to the place, up out of Erebos,
brides, and young unmarried men, and long-suffering elders,
virgins, tender and with the sorrows of young hearts upon them,

40   and many fighting men killed in battle, stabbed with brazen
spears, still carrying their bloody armor upon them.
These came swarming around my pit from every direction
with inhuman clamor, and green fear took hold of me.
Then I encouraged my companions and told them, taking

45   the sheep that were lying by, slaughtered with the pitiless
bronze, to skin these, and burn them, and pray to the divinities,
to Hades the powerful, and to revered Persephone,
while I myself, drawing from beside my thigh my sharp sword,
crouched there, and would not let the strengthless heads of the perished

50   dead draw nearer to the blood, until I had questioned Teiresias.
    'But first there came the soul of my companion, Elpenor,
for he had not yet been buried under earth of the wide ways,
since we had left his body behind in Circe's palace,
unburied and unwept, with this other errand before us.

55   I broke into tears at the sight of him, and my heart pitied him,
and so I spoke aloud to him and addressed him in winged words:
"Elpenor, how did you come here beneath the fog and the darkness?
You have come faster on foot than I could in my black ship."
    'So I spoke, and he groaned aloud and spoke and answered:

60   "Son of Laertes and seed of Zeus, resourceful Odysseus,
the evil will of the spirit and the wild wine bewildered me.
I lay down on the roof of Circe's palace, and never thought,
when I went down, to go by way of the long ladder,

but blundered straight off the edge of the roof, so that my neck bone
65   was broken out of its sockets, and my soul went down to Hades'.
But now I pray you, by those you have yet to see, who are not here,
by your wife, and by your father, who reared you when you were little,
and by Telemachos whom you left alone in your palace;
for I know that after you leave this place and the house of Hades
70   you will put back with your well-made ship to the island, Aiaia;
there at that time, my lord, I ask that you remember me,
and do not go and leave me behind unwept, unburied,
when you leave, for fear I might become the gods' curse upon you;
but burn me there with all my armor that belongs to me,
75   and heap up a grave mound beside the beach of the gray sea,
for an unhappy man, so that those to come will know of me.
Do this for me, and on top of the grave mound plant the oar
with which I rowed when I was alive and among my companions."
       'So he spoke, and I in turn spoke to him in answer:
80   "All this, my unhappy friend, I will do for you as you ask me."
       'So we two stayed there exchanging our sad words, I on
one side holding my sword over the blood, while opposite
me the phantom of my companion talked long with me.
       'Next there came to me the soul of my dead mother,
85   Antikleia, daughter of great-hearted Autolykos,
whom I had left alive when I went to sacred Ilion.
I broke into tears at the sight of her and my heart pitied her,
but even so, for all my thronging sorrow, I would not
let her draw near the blood until I had questioned Teiresias.
90   'Now came the soul of Teiresias the Theban, holding
a staff of gold, and he knew who I was, and spoke to me:
"Son of Laertes and seed of Zeus, resourceful Odysseus,
how is it then, unhappy man, you have left the sunlight
and come here, to look on dead men, and this place without pleasure?
95   Now draw back from the pit, and hold your sharp sword away from me,
so that I can drink of the blood and speak the truth to you."
       'So he spoke, and I, holding away the sword with the silver
nails, pushed it back in the sheath, and the flawless prophet,
after he had drunk the blood, began speaking to me.
100   "Glorious Odysseus, what you are after is sweet homecoming,
but the god will make it hard for you. I think you will not
escape the Shaker of the Earth, who holds a grudge against you

about the last voyage of Odysseus

in his heart, and because you blinded his dear son, hates you.
But even so and still you might come back, after much suffering,
105   if you can contain your own desire, and contain your companions',
at that time when you first put in your well-made vessel
at the island Thrinakia, escaping the sea's blue water,
and there discover pasturing the cattle and fat sheep
of Helios, who sees all things, and listens to all things.
110   Then, if you keep your mind on homecoming, and leave these unharmed,
you might all make your way to Ithaka, after much suffering;
but if you do harm them, then I testify to the destruction
of your ship and your companions, but if you yourself get clear,
you will come home in bad case, with the loss of all your companions,
115   in someone else's ship, and find troubles in your household,
insolent men, who are eating away your livelihood
and courting your godlike wife and offering gifts to win her.
You may punish the violences of these men, when you come home.
But after you have killed these suitors in your own palace,
120   either by treachery, or openly with the sharp bronze,
then you must take up your well-shaped oar and go on a journey
until you come where there are men living who know nothing
of the sea, and who eat food that is not mixed with salt, who never
have known ships whose cheeks are painted purple, who never
125   have known well-shaped oars, which act for ships as wings do.
And I will tell you a very clear proof, and you cannot miss it.
When, as you walk, some other wayfarer happens to meet you,
and says you carry a winnow-fan on your bright shoulder,
then you must plant your well-shaped oar in the ground, and render
130   ceremonies sacrifice to the lord Poseidon,
one ram and one bull, and a mounter of sows, a boar pig,
and make your way home again and render holy hecatombs
to the immortal gods who hold the wide heaven, all
of them in order. Death will come to you from the sea, in
135   some altogether unwarlike way, and it will end you
in the ebbing time of a sleek old age. Your people
about you will be prosperous. All this is true that I tell you."
    'So he spoke, but I in turn said to him in answer:
"All this, Teiresias, surely must be as the gods spun it.
140   But come now, tell me this and give me an accurate answer.
I see before me now the soul of my perished mother,

Antikleia his mother tells Odysseus

but she sits beside the blood in silence, and has not yet deigned
to look directly at her own son and speak a word to me.
Tell me, lord, what will make her know me, and know my presence?"
145   'So I spoke, and he at once said to me in answer:
"Easily I will tell you and put it in your understanding.
Any one of the perished dead you allow to come up
to the blood will give you a true answer, but if you begrudge this
to any one, he will return to the place where he came from."
150   'So speaking, the soul of the lord Teiresias went back into
the house of Hades, once he had uttered his prophecies, while I
waited steadily where I was standing, until my mother
came and drank the dark-clouding blood, and at once she knew me,
and full of lamentation she spoke to me in winged words:
155   "My child, how did you come here beneath the fog and the darkness
and still alive? All this is hard for the living to look on,
for in between lie the great rivers and terrible waters
that flow, Ocean first of all, which there is no means of crossing
on foot, not unless one has a well-made ship. Are you
160   come now to this place from Troy, with your ship and your companions,
after wandering a long time, and have you not yet come
to Ithaka, and there seen your wife in your palace?"
       'So she spoke, and I in turn said to her in answer:
"Mother, a duty brought me here to the house of Hades.
165   I had to consult the soul of Teiresias the Theban.
For I have not yet been near Achaian country, nor ever
set foot on our land, but always suffering I have wandered
since the time I first went along with great Agamemnon
to Ilion, land of good horses, and the battle against the Trojans.
170   But come now, tell me this, and give me an accurate answer.
What doom of death that lays men low has been your undoing?
Was it a long sickness, or did Artemis of the arrows
come upon you with her painless shafts, and destroy you?
And tell me of my father and son whom I left behind. Is
175   my inheritance still with them, or does some other
man hold them now, and thinks I will come no more? Tell me
about the wife I married, what she wants, what she is thinking,
and whether she stays fast by my son, and guards everything,
or if she has married the best man among the Achaians."
180   'So I spoke, and my queenly mother answered me quickly:

"All too much with enduring heart she does wait for you
there in your own palace, and always with her the wretched
nights and the days also waste her away with weeping.
No one yet holds your fine inheritance, but in freedom
185 Telemachos administers your allotted lands, and apportions
the equal feasts, work that befits a man with authority
to judge, for all call him in. Your father remains, on the estate
where he is, and does not go to the city. There is no bed there
nor is there bed clothing nor blankets nor shining coverlets,
190 but in the winter time he sleeps in the house, where the thralls do,
in the dirt next to the fire, and with foul clothing upon him;
but when the summer comes and the blossoming time of harvest,
everywhere he has places to sleep on the ground, on fallen
leaves in piles along the rising ground of his orchard,
195 and there he lies, grieving, and the sorrow grows big within him
as he longs for your homecoming, and harsh old age is on him.
And so it was with me also and that was the reason I perished,
nor in my palace did the lady of arrows, well-aiming,
come upon me with her painless shafts, and destroy me,
200 nor was I visited by sickness, which beyond other
things takes the life out of the body with hateful weakness,
but, shining Odysseus, it was my longing for you, your cleverness
and your gentle ways, that took the sweet spirit of life from me."
'So she spoke, but I, pondering it in my heart, yet wished
205 to take the soul of my dead mother in my arms. Three times
I started toward her, and my heart was urgent to hold her,
and three times she fluttered out of my hands like a shadow
or a dream, and the sorrow sharpened at the heart within me,
and so I spoke to her and addressed her in winged words, saying:
210 "Mother, why will you not wait for me, when I am trying
to hold you, so that even in Hades' with our arms embracing
we can both take the satisfaction of dismal mourning?
Or are you nothing but an image that proud Persephone
sent my way, to make me grieve all the more for sorrow?"
215   'So I spoke, and my queenly mother answered me quickly:
"Oh my child, ill-fated beyond all other mortals,
this is not Persephone, daughter of Zeus, beguiling you,
but it is only what happens, when they die, to all mortals.
The sinews no longer hold the flesh and the bones together,

220   and once the spirit has left the white bones, all the rest
of the body is made subject to the fire's strong fury,
but the soul flitters out like a dream and flies away. Therefore
you must strive back toward the light again with all speed; but remember
these things for your wife, so you may tell her hereafter.''

225   'So we two were conversing back and forth, and the women
came to me. They were sent my way by proud Persephone.
These were all who had been the wives and daughters of princes,
and now they gathered in swarms around the dark blood. I then
thought about a way to question them, each by herself,

230   and as I thought, this was the plan that seemed best to me;
drawing out the long-edged sword from beside my big thigh,
I would not let them all drink the dark blood at the same time.
So they waited and came to me in order, and each one
told me about her origin, and I questioned all of them.

235   'There first I saw Tyro, gloriously descended,
and she told me she was the daughter of stately Salmoneus,
but said she was the wife of Kretheus, the son of Aiolos,
and she was in love with a river, godlike Enipeus, by far
the handsomest of all those rivers whose streams cross over

240   the earth, and she used to haunt Enipeus' beautiful waters;
taking his likeness, the god who circles the earth and shakes it
lay with her where the swirling river finds its outlet,
and a sea-blue wave curved into a hill of water reared up
about the two, to hide the god and the mortal woman;

245   and he broke her virgin zone and drifted a sleep upon her.
But when the god had finished with the act of lovemaking,
he took her by the hand and spoke to her and named her, saying:
"Be happy, lady, in this love, and when the year passes
you will bear glorious children, for the couplings of the immortals

250   are not without issue. You must look after them, and raise them.
Go home now and hold your peace and tell nobody
my name, but I tell it to you; I am the Earthshaker Poseidon.''
     'So he spoke and dived back into the heaving water
of the sea, but she conceived and bore Pelias and Neleus,

255   and both of these grew up to be strong henchmen of mighty
Zeus; Pelias lived, rich in sheepflocks, in the wide spaces
of Iolkos, while the other was king in sandy Pylos;
but this queen among women bore the rest of her children to Kretheus,

Aison and Pheres and Amythaon delighting in horses.

260   'After her I saw Antiope, who was the daughter
of Asopos, who claimed she had also lain in the embraces
of Zeus, and borne two sons to him, Amphion and Zethos.
These first established the foundations of seven-gated
Thebes, and built the bulwarks, since without bulwarks they could not
265 have lived, for all their strength, in Thebes of the wide spaces.
    'After her I saw Amphitryon's wife, Alkmene,
who, after lying in love in the embraces of great Zeus,
brought forth Herakles, lion-hearted and bold of purpose.
And I saw Megara, daughter of high-spirited Kreion,
270 whom Amphitryon's bold and weariless son had married.
    'I saw the beautiful Epikaste, Oidipodes' mother,
who in the ignorance of her mind had done a monstrous
thing when she married her own son. He killed his father
and married her, but the gods soon made it all known to mortals.
275 But he, for all his sorrows, in beloved Thebes continued
to be lord over the Kadmeians, all through the bitter designing
of the gods; while she went down to Hades of the gates, the strong one,
knotting a noose and hanging sheer from the high ceiling,
in the constraint of her sorrow, but left to him who survived her
280 all the sorrows that are brought to pass by a mother's furies.
    'And I saw Chloris, surpassingly lovely, the one whom Neleus
married for her beauty, giving numberless gifts to win her.
She was the youngest daughter of Iasos' son Amphion,
who once ruled strongly over Orchomenos of the Minyai.
285 So she was queen of Pylos and she bore him glorious children,
Nestor and Chromios and proud Periklymenos. Also
she bore that marvel among mortals, majestic Pero,
whom all the heroes round about courted, but Neleus would not
give her to any, unless he could drive away the broad-faced
290 horn-curved cattle of strong Iphikles out of Phylake.
It was hard to do, and only the blameless seer Melampous
undertook it, but he was bound fast by the hard destiny
of the god, and the painful fetters on him, and the loutish oxherds.
But when the months and the days had come to an end, and the year
295 had gone full circle and come back with the seasons returning,
then strong Iphikles released him, when he had told him
all prophecies he knew; and the will of Zeus was accomplished.

'And I saw Leda, who had been the wife of Tyndareos,
and she had borne to Tyndareos two sons with strong hearts,
300   Kastor, breaker of horses, and the strong boxer, Polydeukes.
The life-giving earth holds both of them, yet they are still living,
and, even underneath the earth, enjoying the honor
of Zeus, they live still every other day; on the next day
they are dead, but they are given honor even as gods are.
305   'After her I saw Iphimedeia, wife of Aloeus,
but she told me how she had been joined in love with Poseidon
and borne two sons to him, but these in the end had not lived
long, Otos like a god, and the far-famed Ephialtes;
and these were the tallest men the grain-giving earth has brought forth
310   ever, and the handsomest by far, after famous Orion.
When they were only nine years old they measured nine cubits
across, but in height they grew to nine fathoms, and even made threats
against the immortal gods on Olympos, that they would carry
the turmoil of battle with all its many sorrows against them,
315   and were minded to pile Ossa on Olympos, and above Ossa
Pelion of the trembling leaves, to climb the sky. Surely
they would have carried it out if they had come to maturity,
but the son of Zeus whom Leto with ordered hair had borne him,
Apollo, killed them both, before ever the down gathered
320   below their temples, or on their chins the beards had blossomed.
      'I saw Phaidra and Prokris and Ariadne, the beautiful
daughter of malignant Minos. Theseus at one time
was bringing her from Crete to the high ground of sacred Athens,
but got no joy of her, since before that Artemis killed her
325   in sea-washed Dia, when Dionysos bore witness against her.
      'I saw Maira, Klymene, and Eriphyle the hateful,
who accepted precious gold for the life of her own dear husband.
But I could not tell over the whole number of them nor name all
the women I saw who were the wives and daughters of heroes,
330   for before that the divine night would give out. It is time now
for my sleep, either joining my companions on board the fast ship,
or here; but you, and the gods, will see to my homeward journey.'
      So he spoke, and all of them stayed stricken to silence,
held in thrall by the story all through the shadowy chambers.
335   Now it was white-armed Arete who began the discourse:
'Phaiakians, what do you think now of this man before you

for beauty and stature, and for the mind well balanced within him?
And again he is my own guest, but each one of you has some part
in honoring him. Do not hurry to send him off, nor cut short
340 his gifts, when he is in such need, for you all have many
possessions, by the grace of the gods, stored up in your palaces.'
　　Then in turn the aged hero Echeneos spoke forth,
who was the most advanced in age of all the Phaiakians:
'Friends, our circumspect queen is not off the mark in her speaking,
345 nor short of what we expect of her. Do then as she tells us.
From now on the word and the act belong to Alkinoös.'
　　Then in turn Alkinoös spoke to him and answered:
'Even so this word will be mine to say, as long as
I am alive and king over the oar-loving Phaiakians.
350 But let our guest, much though he longs for the homeward journey,
still endure to wait till tomorrow, until I have raised all
the contribution; but the men shall see to his convoy
home, and I most of all; for mine is the power in this district.'
　　Then resourceful Odysseus spoke in turn and answered him:
355 'O great Alkinoös, pre-eminent among all people,
if you urged me to stay here even for the length of a year,
and still sped my conveyance home and gave me glorious
presents, that would be what I wished, there would be much advantage
in coming back with a fuller hand to my own dear country,
360 and I would be more respected so and be more popular
with all people who saw me make my return to Ithaka.'
　　Then Alkinoös answered him in turn and said to him:
'Odysseus, we as we look upon you do not imagine
that you are a deceptive or thievish man, the sort that the black earth
365 breeds in great numbers, people who wander widely, making up
lying stories, from which no one could learn anything. You have
a grace upon your words, and there is sound sense within them,
and expertly, as a singer would do, you have told the story
of the dismal sorrows befallen yourself and all of the Argives.
370 But come now, tell me this and give me an accurate answer:
Did you see any of your godlike companions, who once with you
went to Ilion and there met their destiny? Here is
a night that is very long, it is endless. It is not time yet
to sleep in the palace. But go on telling your wonderful story.
375 I myself could hold out until the bright dawn, if only

you could bear to tell me, here in the palace, of your sufferings.'
    Then resourceful Odysseus spoke in turn and answered him:
'O great Alkinoös, pre-eminent among all people,
there is a time for many words, and a time for sleeping;
380   but if you insist on hearing me still, I would not begrudge you
the tale of these happenings and others yet more pitiful
to hear, the sorrows of my companions, who perished later,
who escaped onslaught and cry of battle, but perished
all for the sake of a vile woman, on the homeward journey.
385   'Now when chaste Persephone had scattered the female
souls of the women, driving them off in every direction,
there came the soul of Agamemnon, the son of Atreus,
grieving, and the souls of the other men, who died with him
and met their doom in the house of Aigisthos, were gathered around him.
390   He knew me at once, when he drank the dark blood, and fell to
lamentation loud and shrill, and the tears came springing,
and threw himself into my arms, meaning so to embrace me,
but there was no force there any longer, nor any juice left
now in his flexible limbs, as there had been in time past.
395   I broke into tears at the sight of him and my heart pitied him,
and so I spoke aloud to him and addressed him in winged words:
"Son of Atreus, most lordly and king of men, Agamemnon,
what doom of death that lays men low has been your undoing?
Was it with the ships, and did Poseidon, rousing a stormblast
400   of battering winds that none would wish for, prove your undoing?
Or was it on the dry land, did men embattled destroy you
as you tried to cut out cattle and fleecy sheep from their holdings,
or fighting against them for the sake of their city and women?"
    'So I spoke, and he in turn said to me in answer:
405   "Son of Laertes and seed of Zeus, resourceful Odysseus,
not in the ships, nor did Poseidon, rousing a stormblast
of battering winds that none would wish for, prove my destruction,
nor on dry land did enemy men destroy me in battle;
Aigisthos, working out my death and destruction, invited
410   me to his house, and feasted me, and killed me there, with the help
of my sluttish wife, as one cuts down an ox at his manger.
So I died a most pitiful death, and my other companions
were killed around me without mercy, like pigs with shining
tusks, in the house of a man rich and very powerful,

The ghost of Agamemnon

415   for a wedding, or a festival, or a communal dinner.
You have been present in your time at the slaughter of many
men, killed singly, or in the strong encounters of battle;
but beyond all others you would have been sorry at heart
for this scene, how we lay sprawled by the mixing bowl and the loaded

420   tables, all over the palace, and the whole floor was steaming
with blood; and most pitiful was the voice I heard of Priam's
daughter Kassandra, killed by treacherous Klytaimestra
over me; but I lifted my hands and with them beat on
the ground as I died upon the sword, but the sluttish woman

425   turned away from me and was so hard that her hands would not
press shut my eyes and mouth though I was going to Hades'.
So there is nothing more deadly or more vile than a woman
who stores her mind with acts that are of such sort, as this one
did when she thought of this act of dishonor, and plotted

430   the murder of her lawful husband. See, I had been thinking
that I would be welcome to my children and thralls of my household
when I came home, but she with thoughts surpassingly grisly
splashed the shame on herself and the rest of her sex, on women
still to come, even on the one whose acts are virtuous."

435   'So he spoke, and I again said to him in answer:
"Shame it is, how most terribly Zeus of the wide brows
from the beginning has been hateful to the seed of Atreus
through the schemes of women. Many of us died for the sake of Helen,
and when you were far, Klytaimestra plotted treason against you."

440   'So I spoke, and he in turn said to me in answer:
"So by this, do not be too easy even with your wife,
nor give her an entire account of all you are sure of.
Tell her part of it, but let the rest be hidden in silence.
And yet you, Odysseus, will never be murdered by your wife.

445   The daughter of Ikarios, circumspect Penelope,
is all too virtuous and her mind is stored with good thoughts.
Ah well. She was only a young wife when we left her
and went off to the fighting, and she had an infant child then
at her breast. That child now must sit with the men and be counted.

450   Happy he! For his dear father will come back, and see him,
and he will fold his father in his arms, as is right. My wife
never even let me feed my eyes with the sight of
my own son, but before that I myself was killed by her.

Interview with the ghost of Achilleus

And put away in your heart this other thing that I tell you.
455 When you bring your ship in to your own dear country, do it
secretly, not in the open. There is no trusting in women.
But come now, tell me this and give me an accurate answer;
tell me if you happened to hear that my son was still living,
whether perhaps in Orchomenos, or in sandy Pylos,
460 or perhaps with Menelaos in wide Sparta; for nowhere
upon the earth has there been any death of noble Orestes."
    'So he spoke, and I again said to him in answer:
"Son of Atreus, why do you ask me that? I do not know
if he is alive or dead. It is bad to babble emptily."
465   'So we two stood there exchanging our sad words, grieving
both together and shedding the big tears. After this,
there came to us the soul of Peleus' son, Achilleus,
and the soul of Patroklos and the soul of stately Antilochos,
and the soul of Aias, who for beauty and stature was greatest
470 of all the Danaans, next to the stately son of Peleus.
The soul of swift-footed Achilleus, scion of Aiakos, knew me,
and full of lamentation he spoke to me in winged words:
"Son of Laertes and seed of Zeus, resourceful Odysseus,
hard man, what made you think of this bigger endeavor, how could you
475 endure to come down here to Hades' place, where the senseless
dead men dwell, mere imitations of perished mortals?"
    'So he spoke, and I again said to him in answer:
"Son of Peleus, far the greatest of the Achaians, Achilleus,
I came for the need to consult Teiresias, if he might tell me
480 some plan by which I might come back to rocky Ithaka;
for I have not yet been near Achaian country, nor ever
set foot on my land, but always I have troubles. Achilleus,
no man before has been more blessed than you, nor ever
will be. Before, when you were alive, we Argives honored you
485 as we did the gods, and now in this place you have great authority
over the dead. Do not grieve, even in death, Achilleus."
    'So I spoke, and he in turn said to me in answer:
"O shining Odysseus, never try to console me for dying.
I would rather follow the plow as thrall to another
490 man, one with no land allotted him and not much to live on,
than be a king over all the perished dead. But come now,
tell me anything you have heard of my proud son, whether

or not he went along to war to fight as a champion;
and tell me anything you have heard about stately Peleus,
495 whether he still keeps his position among the Myrmidon
hordes, or whether in Hellas and Phthia they have diminished
his state, because old age constrains his hands and feet, and I
am no longer there under the light of the sun to help him,
not the man I used to be once, when in the wide Troad
500 I killed the best of their people, fighting for the Argives. If only
for a little while I could come like that to the house of my father,
my force and my invincible hands would terrify such men
as use force on him and keep him away from his rightful honors."
    'So he spoke, and I again said to him in answer:
505 "I have no report to give you of stately Peleus,
but as for your beloved son Neoptolemos, I will
tell you, since you ask me to do it, all the true story;
for I myself, in the hollow hull of a balanced ship, brought him
over from Skyros, to join the strong-greaved Achaians. Whenever
510 we, around the city of Troy, talked over our counsels,
he would always speak first, and never blunder. In speaking
only godlike Nestor and I were better than he was.
And when we Achaians fought in the Trojan plain, he never
would hang back where there were plenty of other men, nor stay with
515 the masses, but run far out in front, giving way to no man
for fury, and many were those he killed in the terrible fighting.
I could not tell over the number of all nor name all
the people he killed as he fought for the Argives, but what a great man
was one, the son of Telephos he slew with the brazen
520 spear, the hero Eurypylos, and many Keteian
companions were killed about him, by reason of womanish presents.
Next to great Memnon, this was the finest man I ever
saw. Again, when we who were best of the Argives entered
the horse that Epeios made, and all the command was given
525 to me, to keep close hidden inside, or sally out from it,
the other leaders of the Danaans and men of counsel
were wiping their tears away and the limbs were shaking under
each man of them; but never at any time did I see him
losing his handsome color and going pale, or wiping
530 the tears off his face, but rather he implored me to let him
sally out of the horse; he kept feeling for his sword hilt

and spear weighted with bronze, full of evil thoughts for the Trojans.
But after we had sacked the sheer citadel of Priam,
with his fair share and a princely prize of his own, he boarded
535 his ship, unscathed; he had not been hit by thrown and piercing
bronze, nor stabbed in close-up combat, as often happens
in fighting. The War God rages at all, and favors no man."
   'So I spoke, and the soul of the swift-footed scion of Aiakos
stalked away in long strides across the meadow of asphodel,
540 happy for what I had said of his son, and how he was famous.
   'Now the rest of the souls of the perished dead stood near me
grieving, and each one spoke to me and told of his sorrows.
Only the soul of Telamonian Aias stood off
at a distance from me, angry still over that decision
545 I won against him, when beside the ships we disputed
our cases for the arms of Achilleus. His queenly mother
set them as prize, and the sons of the Trojans, with Pallas Athene,
judged; and I wish I had never won in a contest like this,
so high a head has gone under the ground for the sake of that armor,
550 Aias, who for beauty and for achievement surpassed
all the Danaans next to the stately son of Peleus.
So I spoke to him now in words of conciliation:
"Aias, son of stately Telamon, could you then never
even in death forget your anger against me, because of
555 that cursed armor? The gods made it to pain the Achaians,
so great a bulwark were you, who were lost to them. We Achaians
grieved for your death as incessantly as for Achilleus
the son of Peleus at his death, and there is no other
to blame, but Zeus; he, in his terrible hate for the army
560 of Danaan spearmen, visited this destruction upon you.
Come nearer, my lord, so you can hear what I say and listen
to my story; suppress your anger and lordly spirit."
   'So I spoke. He gave no answer, but went off after
the other souls of the perished dead men, into the darkness.
565 There, despite his anger, he might have spoken, or I might
have spoken to him, but the heart in my inward breast wanted
still to see the souls of the other perished dead men.
   'There I saw Minos, the glorious son of Zeus, seated,
holding a golden scepter and issuing judgments among
570 the dead, who all around the great lord argued their cases,

some sitting and some standing, by the wide-gated house of Hades.
    'After him I was aware of gigantic Orion
in the meadow of asphodel, rounding up and driving together
wild animals he himself had killed in the lonely mountains,
575 holding in his hands a brazen club, forever unbroken.
    'And I saw Tityos, Earth's glorious son, lying
in the plain, and sprawled over nine acres. Two vultures,
sitting one on either side, were tearing his liver,
plunging inside the caul. With his hands he could not beat them
580 away. He had manhandled Leto, the honored consort
of Zeus, as she went through spacious Panopeus, toward Pytho.
    'And I saw Tantalos also, suffering hard pains, standing
in lake water that came up to his chin, and thirsty
as he was, he tried to drink, but could capture nothing;
585 for every time the old man, trying to drink, stooped over,
the water would drain away and disappear, and the black earth
showed at his feet, and the divinity dried it away. Over
his head trees with lofty branches had fruit like a shower descending,
pear trees and pomegranate trees and apple trees with fruit shining,
590 and figs that were sweet and olives ripened well, but each time
the old man would straighten up and reach with his hands for them,
the wind would toss them away toward the clouds overhanging.
    'Also I saw Sisyphos. He was suffering strong pains,
and with both arms embracing the monstrous stone, struggling
595 with hands and feet alike, he would try to push the stone upward
to the crest of the hill, but when it was on the point of going
over the top, the force of gravity turned it backward,
and the pitiless stone rolled back down to the level. He then
tried once more to push it up, straining hard, and sweat ran
600 all down his body, and over his head a cloud of dust rose. ,
    'After him I was aware of powerful Herakles;
his image, that is, but he himself among the immortal
gods enjoys their festivals, married to sweet-stepping
Hebe, child of great Zeus and Hera of the golden sandals.
605 All around him was a clamor of the dead as of birds scattering
scared in every direction; but he came on, like dark night,
holding his bow bare with an arrow laid on the bowstring,
and forever looking, as one who shot, with terrible glances.
There was a terrible belt crossed over his chest, and a golden

610 baldrick, with marvelous works of art that figured upon it,
   bears, and lions with glaring eyes, and boars of the forests,
   the battles and the quarrels, the murders and the manslaughters.
   May he who artfully designed them, and artfully put them
   upon that baldrick, never again do any designing.
615 He recognized me at once as soon as his eyes had seen me,
   and full of lamentation he spoke to me in winged words:
   "Son of Laertes and seed of Zeus, resourceful Odysseus,
   unhappy man, are you too leading some wretched destiny
   such as I too pursued when I went still in the sunlight?
620 For I was son of Kronian Zeus, but I had an endless
   spell of misery. I was made bondman to one who was far worse
   than I, and he loaded my difficult labors on me. One time
   he sent me here to fetch the dog back, and thought there could be
   no other labor to be devised more difficult than that
625 one, but I brought the dog up and led him from the realm of Hades,
   and Hermes saw me on my way, with Pallas Athene."
   'So he spoke, and went back into the realm of Hades,
   but I stayed fast in place where I was, to see if some other
   one of the generation of heroes who died before me
630 would come; and I might have seen men earlier still, whom I wanted
   to see, Perithoös and Theseus, gods' glorious children;
   but before that the hordes of the dead men gathered about me
   with inhuman clamor, and green fear took hold of me
   with the thought that proud Persephone might send up against me
635 some gorgonish head of a terrible monster up out of Hades'.
   So, going back on board my ship, I told my companions
   also to go aboard, and to cast off the stern cables;
   and quickly they went aboard the ship and sat to the oarlocks,
   and the swell of the current carried her down the Ocean river
640 with rowing at first, but after that on a fair wind following.

BOOK XII

'Now when our ship had left the stream of the Ocean river,
and come back to the wide crossing of the sea's waves, and to the island
of Aiaia, where lies the house of the early Dawn, her dancing
spaces, and where Helios, the sun, makes his uprising,
5 making this point we ran our ship on the sand and beached her,
and we ourselves stepped out onto the break of the sea beach,
and there we fell asleep and waited for the divine Dawn.
   'But when the young Dawn showed again with her rosy fingers,
then I sent my companions away to the house of Circe
10 to bring back the body of Elpenor, who had died there.
Then we cut logs, and where the extreme of the foreland jutted
out, we buried him, sorrowful, shedding warm tears for him.
But when the dead man had burned and the dead man's armor, piling
the grave mound and pulling the gravestone to stand above it,
15 we planted the well-shaped oar in the very top of the grave mound.
   'So we were busy each with our various work, nor was Circe
unaware that we had come back from Hades'. Presently
she came, attired, and her attendants following carried
bread at her will and many meats and the shining red wine.
20 Bright among goddesses she stood in our midst and addressed us:
"Unhappy men, who went alive to the house of Hades,
so dying twice, when all the rest of mankind die only
once, come then eat what is there and drink your wine, staying
here all the rest of the day, and then tomorrow, when dawn shows,

25   you shall sail, and I will show you the way and make plain
     all details, so that neither by land nor on the salt water
     you may suffer and come to grief by unhappy bad designing."
       'So she spoke, and the proud heart in us was persuaded.
     So for the whole length of the day until the sun's setting,
30   we sat there feasting on unlimited meat and sweet wine.
     But when the sun went down and the sacred darkness came over,
     the men lay down to sleep all by the ship's stern cables,
     but she, taking me by the hand, made me sit down away from
     my dear companions, and talked with me, and asked me the details
35   of everything, and I recited all, just as it had happened.
     Then the queenly Circe spoke in words and addressed me:
     "So all that has been duly done. Listen now, I will tell you
     all, but the very god himself will make you remember.
     You will come first of all to the Sirens, who are enchanters
40   of all mankind and whoever comes their way; and that man
     who unsuspecting approaches them, and listens to the Sirens
     singing, has no prospect of coming home and delighting
     his wife and little children as they stand about him in greeting,
     but the Sirens by the melody of their singing enchant him.
45   They sit in their meadow, but the beach before it is piled with boneheaps
     of men now rotted away, and the skins shrivel upon them.
     You must drive straight on past, but melt down sweet wax of honey
     and with it stop your companions' ears, so none can listen;
     the rest, that is, but if you yourself are wanting to hear them,
50   then have them tie you hand and foot on the fast ship, standing
     upright against the mast with the ropes' ends lashed around it,
     so that you can have joy in hearing the song of the Sirens;
     but if you supplicate your men and implore them to set you
     free, then they must tie you fast with even more lashings.
55   "Then, for the time when your companions have driven you past
        them,
     for that time I will no longer tell you in detail which way
     of the two your course must lie, but you yourself must consider
     this in your own mind. I will tell you the two ways of it.
     On one side there are overhanging rocks, and against them
60   crashes the heavy swell of dark-eyed Amphitrite.
     The blessed gods call these rocks the Rovers. By this way
     not even any flying thing, not even the tremulous

doves, which carry ambrosia to Zeus the father, can pass through,
but every time the sheer rock catches away one even
65   of these; but the Father then adds another to keep the number
right. No ship of men that came here ever has fled through,
but the waves of the sea and storms of ravening fire carry
away together the ship's timbers and the men's bodies.
That way the only seagoing ship to get through was Argo,
70   who is in all men's minds, on her way home from Aietes;
and even she would have been driven on the great rocks that time,
but Hera saw her through, out of her great love for Jason.
   ' "But of the two rocks, one reaches up into the wide heaven
with a pointed peak, and a dark cloud stands always around it,
75   and never at any time draws away from it, nor does the sunlight
ever hold that peak, either in the early or the late summer,
nor could any man who was mortal climb there, or stand mounted
on the summit, not if he had twenty hands and twenty
feet, for the rock goes sheerly up, as if it were polished.
80   Halfway up the cliff there is a cave, misty-looking
and turned toward Erebos and the dark, the very direction
from which, O shining Odysseus, you and your men will be steering
your hollow ship; and from the hollow ship no vigorous
young man with a bow could shoot to the hole in the cliffside.
85   In that cavern Skylla lives, whose howling is terror.
Her voice indeed is only as loud as a new-born puppy
could make, but she herself is an evil monster. No one,
not even a god encountering her, could be glad at that sight.
She has twelve feet, and all of them wave in the air. She has six
90   necks upon her, grown to great length, and upon each neck
there is a horrible head, with teeth in it, set in three rows
close together and stiff, full of black death. Her body
from the waist down is holed up inside the hollow cavern,
but she holds her heads poked out and away from the terrible hollow,
95   and there she fishes, peering all over the cliffside, looking
for dolphins or dogfish to catch or anything bigger,
some sea monster, of whom Amphitrite keeps so many;
never can sailors boast aloud that their ship has passed her
without any loss of men, for with each of her heads she snatches
100 one man away and carries him off from the dark-prowed vessel.
   ' "The other cliff is lower; you will see it, Odysseus,

Warning about the cattle of Helios

for they lie close together, you could even cast with an arrow
across. There is a great fig tree grows there, dense with foliage,
and under this shining Charybdis sucks down the black water.
105 For three times a day she flows it up, and three times she sucks it
terribly down; may you not be there when she sucks down water,
for not even the Earthshaker could rescue you out of that evil.
But sailing your ship swiftly drive her past and avoid her,
and make for Skylla's rock instead, since it is far better
110 to mourn six friends lost out of your ship than the whole company."
　'So she spoke, but I in turn said to her in answer:
"Come then, goddess, answer me truthfully this: is there
some way for me to escape away from deadly Charybdis,
but yet fight the other one off, when she attacks my companions?"
115 　'So I spoke, and she, shining among goddesses, answered:
"Hardy man, your mind is full forever of fighting
and battle work. Will you not give way even to the immortals?
She is no mortal thing but a mischief immortal, dangerous
difficult and bloodthirsty, and there is no fighting against her,
120 nor any force of defense. It is best to run away from her.
For if you arm for battle beside her rock and waste time
there, I fear she will make another outrush and catch you
with all her heads, and snatch away once more the same number
of men. Drive by as hard as you can, but invoke Krataiïs.
125 She is the mother of Skylla and bore this mischief for mortals,
and she will stay her from making another sally against you.
　' "Then you will reach the island Thrinakia, where are pastured
the cattle and the fat sheep of the sun god, Helios,
seven herds of oxen, and as many beautiful sheepflocks,
130 and fifty to each herd. There is no giving birth among them,
nor do they ever die away, and their shepherdesses
are gods, nymphs with sweet hair, Lampetia and Phaethousa,
whom shining Neaira bore to Hyperion the sun god.
These, when their queenly mother had given them birth and reared them,
135 she settled in the island Thrinakia, far away, to live
there and guard their father's sheep and his horn-curved cattle.
Then, if you keep your mind on homecoming and leave these unharmed,
you might all make your way to Ithaka, after much suffering;
but if you do harm them, then I testify to the destruction
140 of your ship and your companions, but if you yourself get clear,

you will come home in bad case with the loss of all your companions."
'So she spoke, and Dawn of the golden throne came on us.
She, shining among goddesses, went away, up the island.
Then, going back on board my ship, I told my companions
145   also to go aboard, and to cast off the stern cables,
and quickly they went aboard the ship and sat to the oarlocks,
and sitting well in order dashed the oars in the gray sea;
but fair-haired Circe, the dread goddess who talks with mortals,
sent us an excellent companion, a following wind, filling
150   the sails, to carry from astern the ship with the dark prow.
We ourselves, over all the ship making fast the running gear,
sat there, and let the wind and the steersman hold her steady.
Then, sorrowful as I was, I spoke and told my companions:
"Friends, since it is not right for one or two of us only
155   to know the divinations that Circe, bright among goddesses,
gave me, so I will tell you, and knowing all we may either
die, or turn aside from death and escape destruction.
First of all she tells us to keep away from the magical
Sirens and their singing and their flowery meadow, but only
160   I, she said, was to listen to them, but you must tie me
hard in hurtful bonds, to hold me fast in position
upright against the mast, with the ropes' ends fastened around it;
but if I supplicate you and implore you to set me
free, then you must tie me fast with even more lashings."
165   'So as I was telling all the details to my companions,
meanwhile the well-made ship was coming rapidly closer
to the Sirens' isle, for the harmless wind was driving her onward;
but immediately then the breeze dropped, and a windless
calm fell there, and some divinity stilled the tossing
170   waters. My companions stood up, and took the sails down,
and stowed them away in the hollow hull, and took their places
for rowing, and with their planed oarblades whitened the water.
Then I, taking a great wheel of wax, with the sharp bronze
cut a little piece off, and rubbed it together in my heavy
175   hands, and soon the wax grew softer, under the powerful
stress of the sun, and the heat and light of Hyperion's lordling.
One after another, I stopped the ears of all my companions,
and they then bound me hand and foot in the fast ship, standing
upright against the mast with the ropes' ends lashed around it,

180   and sitting then to row they dashed their oars in the gray sea.
But when we were as far from the land as a voice shouting
carries, lightly plying, the swift ship as it drew nearer
was seen by the Sirens, and they directed their sweet song toward us:
"Come this way, honored Odysseus, great glory of the Achaians,

185   and stay your ship, so that you can listen here to our singing;
for no one else has ever sailed past this place in his black ship
until he has listened to the honey-sweet voice that issues
from our lips; then goes on, well pleased, knowing more than ever
he did; for we know everything that the Argives and Trojans

190   did and suffered in wide Troy through the gods' despite.
Over all the generous earth we know everything that happens."
    'So they sang, in sweet utterance, and the heart within me
desired to listen, and I signaled my companions to set me
free, nodding with my brows, but they leaned on and rowed hard,

195   and Perimedes and Eurylochos, rising up, straightway
fastened me with even more lashings and squeezed me tighter.
But when they had rowed on past the Sirens, and we could no longer
hear their voices and lost the sound of their singing, presently
my eager companions took away from their ears the beeswax

200   with which I had stopped them. Then they set me free from my lashings.
    'But after we had left the island behind, the next thing
we saw was smoke, and a heavy surf, and we heard it thundering.
The men were terrified, and they let the oars fall out of
their hands, and these banged all about in the wash. The ship stopped

205   still, with the men no longer rowing to keep way on her.
Then I going up and down the ship urged on my companions,
standing beside each man and speaking to him in kind words:
"Dear friends, surely we are not unlearned in evils.
This is no greater evil now than it was when the Cyclops

210   had us cooped in his hollow cave by force and violence,
but even there, by my courage and counsel and my intelligence,
we escaped away. I think that all this will be remembered
some day too. Then do as I say, let us all be won over.
Sit well, all of you, to your oarlocks, and dash your oars deep

215   into the breaking surf of the water, so in that way Zeus
might grant that we get clear of this danger and flee away from it.
For you, steersman, I have this order; so store it deeply
in your mind, as you control the steering oar of this hollow

ship; you must keep her clear from where the smoke and the breakers
220 are, and make hard for the sea rock lest, without your knowing,
she might drift that way, and you bring all of us into disaster."
'So I spoke, and they quickly obeyed my words. I had not
spoken yet of Skylla, a plague that could not be dealt with,
for fear my companions might be terrified and give over
225 their rowing, and take cover inside the ship. For my part,
I let go from my mind the difficult instruction that Circe
had given me, for she told me not to be armed for combat;
but I put on my glorious armor and, taking up two long
spears in my hands, I stood bestriding the vessel's foredeck
230 at the prow, for I expected Skylla of the rocks to appear first
from that direction, she who brought pain to my companions.
I could not make her out anywhere, and my eyes grew weary
from looking everywhere on the misty face of the sea rock.
'So we sailed up the narrow strait lamenting. On one side
235 was Skylla, and on the other side was shining Charybdis,
who made her terrible ebb and flow of the sea's water.
When she vomited it up, like a caldron over a strong fire,
the whole sea would boil up in turbulence, and the foam flying
spattered the pinnacles of the rocks in either direction;
240 but when in turn again she sucked down the sea's salt water,
the turbulence showed all the inner sea, and the rock around it
groaned terribly, and the ground showed at the sea's bottom,
black with sand; and green fear seized upon my companions.
We in fear of destruction kept our eyes on Charybdis,
245 but meanwhile Skylla out of the hollow vessel snatched six
of my companions, the best of them for strength and hands' work,
and when I turned to look at the ship, with my other companions,
I saw their feet and hands from below, already lifted
high above me, and they cried out to me and called me
250 by name, the last time they ever did it, in heart's sorrow.
And as a fisherman with a very long rod, on a jutting
rock, will cast his treacherous bait for the little fishes,
and sinks the horn of a field-ranging ox into the water,
then hauls them up and throws them on the dry land, gasping
255 and struggling, so they gasped and struggled as they were hoisted
up the cliff. Right in her doorway she ate them up. They were screaming
and reaching out their hands to me in this horrid encounter.

That was the most pitiful scene that these eyes have looked on
in my sufferings as I explored the routes over the water.
260   'Now when we had fled away from the rocks and dreaded Charybdis
and Skylla, next we made our way to the excellent island
of the god, where ranged the handsome wide-browed oxen, and many
fat flocks of sheep, belonging to the Sun God, Hyperion.
While I was on the black ship, still out on the open water,
265   I heard the lowing of the cattle as they were driven
home, and the bleating of sheep, and my mind was struck by the saying
of the blind prophet, Teiresias the Theban, and also
Aiaian Circe. Both had told me many times over
to avoid the island of Helios who brings joy to mortals.
270   Then sorrowful as I was I spoke and told my companions:
"Listen to what I say, my companions, though you are suffering
evils, while I tell you the prophecies of Teiresias
and Aiaian Circe. Both have told me many times over
to avoid the island of Helios who brings joy to mortals,
275   for there they spoke of the most dreadful disaster that waited
for us. So drive the black ship onward, and pass the island."
    'So I spoke, and the inward heart in them was broken.
At once Eurylochos answered me with a bitter saying:
"You are a hard man, Odysseus. Your force is greater,
280   your limbs never wear out. You must be made all of iron,
when you will not let your companions, worn with hard work and
        wanting
sleep, set foot on this land, where if we did, on the seagirt
island we could once more make ready a greedy dinner;
but you force us to blunder along just as we are through the running
285   night, driven from the island over the misty face of the water.
In the nights the hard stormwinds arise, and they bring damage
to ships. How could any of us escape sheer destruction,
if suddenly there rises the blast of a storm from the bitter
blowing of the South Wind or the West Wind, who beyond others
290   hammer a ship apart, in despite of the gods, our masters?
But now let us give way to black night's persuasion; let us
make ready our evening meal, remaining close by our fast ship,
and at dawn we will go aboard and put forth onto the wide sea."
    'So spoke Eurylochos, and my other companions assented.
295   I saw then what evil the divinity had in mind for us,

and so I spoke aloud to him and addressed him in winged words:
"Eurylochos, I am only one man. You force me to it.
But come then all of you, swear a strong oath to me, that if
we come upon some herd of cattle or on some great flock
300   of sheep, no one of you in evil and reckless action
will slaughter any ox or sheep. No, rather than this, eat
at your pleasure of the food immortal Circe provided."
   'So I spoke, and they all swore me the oath that I asked them.
But after they had sworn me the oath and made an end of it,
305   we beached the well-made ship inside of the hollow harbor,
close to sweet water, and my companions disembarked also
from the ship, and expertly made the evening meal ready.
But when they had put away their desire for eating and drinking,
they remembered and they cried for their beloved companions
310   whom Skylla had caught out of the hollow ship and eaten,
and on their crying a quiet sleep descended; but after
the third part of the night had come, and the star changes,
Zeus the cloud gatherer let loose on us a gale that blustered
in a supernatural storm, and huddled under the cloud scuds
315   land alike and the great water. Night sprang from heaven.
But when the young Dawn showed again with her rosy fingers,
we berthed our ship, dragging her into a hollow sea cave
where the nymphs had their beautiful dancing places and sessions.
Then I held an assembly and spoke my opinion before them:
320   "Friends, since there is food and drink stored in the fast ship,
let us then keep our hands off the cattle, for fear that something
may befall us. These are the cattle and fat sheep of a dreaded
god, Helios, who sees all things and listens to all things."
   'So I spoke, and the proud heart in them was persuaded.
325   But the South Wind blew for a whole month long, nor did any other
wind befall after that, but only the South and the East Wind.
As long as they still had food to eat and red wine, the men kept
their hands off the cattle, striving as they were for sustenance. Then,
     when
all the provisions that had been in the ship had given
330   out, they turned to hunting, forced to it, and went ranging
after fish and birds, anything that they could lay hands on,
and with curved hooks, for the hunger was exhausting their stomachs.
Then I went away along the island in order

to pray to the gods, if any of them might show me some course
335   to sail on, but when, crossing the isle, I had left my companions
behind, I washed my hands, where there was a place sheltered
from the wind, and prayed to all the gods whose hold is Olympos;
but what they did was to shed a sweet sleep on my eyelids,
and Eurylochos put an evil counsel before his companions:
340   "Listen to what I say, my companions, though you are suffering
evils. All deaths are detestable for wretched mortals,
but hunger is the sorriest way to die and encounter
fate. Come then, let us cut out the best of Helios' cattle,
and sacrifice them to the immortals who hold wide heaven,
345   and if we ever come back to Ithaka, land of our fathers,
presently we will build a rich temple to the Sun God Helios
Hyperion, and store it with dedications, many
and good. But if, in anger over his high-horned cattle,
he wishes to wreck our ship, and the rest of the gods stand by him,
350   I would far rather gulp the waves and lose my life in them
once for all, than be pinched to death on this desolate island."
        'So spoke Eurylochos, and the other companions assented.
At once, cutting out from near at hand the best of Helios'
cattle; for the handsome broad-faced horn-curved oxen
355   were pasturing there, not far from the dark-prowed ship; driving
these, they stationed themselves around them, and made their prayers
to the gods, pulling tender leaves from a deep-leaved oak tree;
for they had no white barley left on the strong-benched vessel.
When they had made their prayer and slaughtered the oxen and skinned
        them,
360   they cut away the meat from the thighs and wrapped them in fat,
making a double fold, and laid shreds of flesh upon them;
and since they had no wine to pour on the burning offerings,
they made a libation of water, and roasted all of the entrails;
but when they had burned the thigh pieces and tasted the vitals,
365   they cut all the remainder into pieces and spitted them.
        'At that time the quiet sleep was lost from my eyelids,
and I went back down to my fast ship and the sand of the seashore,
but on my way, as I was close to the oar-swept vessel,
the pleasant savor of cooking meat came drifting around me,
370   and I cried out my grief aloud to the gods immortal:
"Father Zeus, and you other everlasting and blessed

gods, with a pitiless sleep you lulled me, to my confusion,
and my companions staying here dared a deed that was monstrous."
   'Lampetia of the light robes ran swift with the message

375 to Hyperion the Sun God, that we had killed his cattle,
and angered at the heart he spoke forth among the immortals:
"Father Zeus, and you other everlasting and blessed
gods, punish the companions of Odysseus, son of Laertes;
for they outrageously killed my cattle, in whom I always

380 delighted, on my way up into the starry heaven,
or when I turned back again from heaven toward earth. Unless
these are made to give me just recompense for my cattle,
I will go down to Hades' and give my light to the dead men."
   'Then in turn Zeus who gathers the clouds answered him:

385 "Helios, shine on as you do, among the immortals
and mortal men, all over the grain-giving earth. For my part
I will strike these men's fast ship midway on the open
wine-blue sea with a shining bolt and dash it to pieces."
   'All this I heard afterward from fair-haired Kalypso,

390 and she told me she herself had heard it from the guide, Hermes.
   'But when I came back again to the ship and the seashore,
they all stood about and blamed each other, but we were not able
to find any remedy, for the oxen were already dead. The next thing
was that the gods began to show forth portents before us.

395 The skins crawled, and the meat that was stuck on the spits bellowed,
both roast and raw, and the noise was like the lowing of cattle.
   'Six days thereafter my own eager companions feasted
on the cattle of Helios the Sun God, cutting the best ones
out; but when Zeus the son of Kronos established the seventh

400 day, then at last the wind ceased from its stormy blowing,
and presently we went aboard and put forth on the wide sea,
and set the mast upright and hoisted the white sails on it.
   'But after we had left the island and there was no more
land in sight, but only the sky and the sea, then Kronian

405 Zeus drew on a blue-black cloud, and settled it over
the hollow ship, and the open sea was darkened beneath it;
and she ran on, but not for a very long time, as suddenly
a screaming West Wind came upon us, stormily blowing,
and the blast of the stormwind snapped both the forestays that were
     holding

410   the mast, and the mast went over backwards, and all the running gear
      collapsed in the wash; and at the stern of the ship the mast pole
      crashed down on the steersman's head and pounded to pieces
      all the bones of his head, so that he like a diver
      dropped from the high deck, and the proud life left his bones there.
415   Zeus with thunder and lightning together crashed on our vessel,
      and, struck by the thunderbolt of Zeus, she spun in a circle,
      and all was full of brimstone. My men were thrown in the water,
      and bobbing like sea crows they were washed away on the running
      waves all around the black ship, and the god took away their
         homecoming.
420   'But I went on my way through the vessel, to where the high seas
      had worked the keel free out of the hull, and the bare keel floated
      on the swell, which had broken the mast off at the keel; yet
      still there was a backstay made out of oxhide fastened
      to it. With this I lashed together both keel and mast, then
425   rode the two of them, while the deadly stormwinds carried me.
         'After this the West Wind ceased from its stormy blowing,
      and the South Wind came swiftly on, bringing to my spirit
      grief that I must measure the whole way back to Charybdis.
      All that night I was carried along, and with the sun rising
430   I came to the sea rock of Skylla, and dreaded Charybdis.
      At this time Charybdis sucked down the sea's salt water,
      but I reached high in the air above me, to where the tall fig tree
      grew, and caught hold of it and clung like a bat; there was no
      place where I could firmly brace my feet, or climb up it,
435   for the roots of it were far from me, and the branches hung out
      far, big and long branches that overshadowed Charybdis.
      Inexorably I hung on, waiting for her to vomit
      the keel and mast back up again. I longed for them, and they came
      late; at the time when a man leaves the law court, for dinner,
440   after judging the many disputes brought him by litigious young men;
      that was the time it took the timbers to appear from Charybdis.
      Then I let go my hold with hands and feet, and dropped off,
      and came crashing down between and missing the two long timbers,
      but I mounted these, and with both hands I paddled my way out.
445   But the Father of Gods and men did not let Skylla see me
      again, or I could not have escaped from sheer destruction.
         'From there I was carried along nine days, and on the tenth night

Odysseus escapes to Kalypso's island

the gods brought me to the island Ogygia, home of Kalypso
with the lovely hair, a dreaded goddess who talks with mortals.
450   She befriended me and took care of me. Why tell the rest of
this story again, since yesterday in your house I told it
to you and your majestic wife? It is hateful to me
to tell a story over again, when it has been well told.'

BOOK XIII

So he spoke, and all of them stayed stricken to silence,
held in thrall by the story all through the shadowy chambers.
Then Alkinoös answered him in turn and said to him:
'Odysseus, now that you have come to my house, bronze-founded
5 with the high roof, I think you will not lose your homecoming,
nor be driven back from it again, for all your sufferings.
Now I lay this charge upon each man of you, such as
here in my palace drink the gleaming wine of the princes
always at my side, and hear the song of the singer.
10 Clothing for our guest is stored away in the polished
chest, and intricately wrought gold, and all those other
gifts the Phaiakian men of counsel brought here to give him.
Come, let us man by man each one of us give a great tripod
and a caldron, and we will make it good to us by a collection
15 among the people. It is hard for a single man to be generous.'
    So Alkinoös spoke, and his word pleased all the rest of them.
They all went home to go to bed, each one to his own house.
But when the young Dawn showed again with her rosy fingers,
they came in haste to the ship, and brought the lavish bronze with them,
20 and Alkinoös, the hallowed prince, himself going on board,
stowed it well away under the thwarts, so it would not hamper
any of the crew as they rowed with their oars and sent the ship speedily
on. Then all went to Alkinoös' house and made the feast ready.
    Alkinoös, the hallowed prince, sacrificed an ox for them

Preparations for Odysseus' departure

25   to Zeus, dark-clouded son of Kronos, lord over all men.
They burned the thigh pieces and enjoyed feasting on the glorious
banquet, and among them Demodokos, the divine singer,
sang his songs and was prized by the people. But now Odysseus
turned his head again and again to look at the shining

30   sun, to hasten its going down, since he was now eager
to go; and as a man makes for his dinner, when all day
long his wine-colored oxen have dragged the compact plow for him
across the field, and the sun's setting is welcome for bringing
the time to go to his dinner, and as he goes his knees fail him;

35   thus welcome to Odysseus now was the sun going under.
Now he spoke aloud to the oar-loving Phaiakians,
addressing his words to Alkinoös beyond all others:
'O great Alkinoös, pre-eminent among all people,
make libation and send me upon my way untroubled;

40   and yourselves fare well, for all my heart desired is now made
good, conveyance and loving gifts. May the sky gods make these
prosper for me. May I return to my house and find there
a blameless wife, and all who are dear to me unharmed. May you
in turn, remaining here, bring comfort and cheer to your wedded

45   wives and your children, and may the gods grant success in every
endeavor, and no unhappiness be found in your people.'
So he spoke, and they all approved his word and encouraged
convoy for the guest, for what he said was fair and orderly;
then the hallowed prince Alkinoös spoke to his herald:

50   'Pontonoös, now mix a bowl of wine and serve it
to all in the palace, so that, with a prayer to our father
Zeus, we may send our guest on his way, back to his own country.'
So he spoke, and Pontonoös mixed the sweet wine and served it
to all, standing beside each person. They poured a libation

55   to all the blessed immortal gods who hold wide heaven
from the chairs where they were sitting, but great Odysseus stood up
and put the handled goblet into the hand of Arete,
and spoke to her aloud and addressed her in winged words, saying:
'Farewell to you, O queen, and for all time, until old age

60   comes to you, and death, which befall all human creatures.
Now I am on my way; but have joy here in your household,
in your children and your people, and in your king, Alkinoös.'
So spoke great Odysseus, and strode out over the door sill,

and great Alkinoös sent his herald to go along with him
65 and show him the way to the fast ship and the sand of the seashore.
Also Arete sent her serving women with him. One
carried a mantle, washed and clean, and a tunic. Another
one she sent along with him to carry the well-made
chest, and a third went along with them bearing food and red wine.
70   But when they had come down to the sea, and where the ship was,
the proud escorts promptly took over the gifts, and stowed them
away in the hollow hull, and all the food and the drink, then
spread out a coverlet for Odysseus, and linen, out on
the deck, at the stern of the ship's hull, so that he could sleep there
75 undisturbed, and he himself went aboard and lay down
silently. They sat down each in his place at the oarlocks
in order, and slipped the cable free from its hole in the stone post.
They bent to their rowing, and with their oars tossed up the sea spray,
and upon the eyes of Odysseus there fell a sleep, gentle,
80 the sweetest kind of sleep with no awakening, most like
death; while the ship, as in a field four stallions drawing
a chariot all break together at the stroke of the whiplash,
and lifting high their feet lightly beat out their path, so
the stern of this ship would lift and the creaming wave behind her
85 boiled amain in the thunderous crash of the sea. She ran on
very steady and never wavering; even the falcon,
that hawk that flies lightest of winged creatures, could not have paced
        her,
so lightly did she run on her way and cut through the sea's waves.
She carried a man with a mind like the gods for counsel, one whose
90 spirit up to this time had endured much, suffering many
pains: the wars of men, hard crossing of the big waters;
but now he slept still, oblivious of all he had suffered.
    At the time when shines that brightest star, which beyond others
comes with announcement of the light of the young Dawn goddess,
95 then was the time the sea-faring ship put in to the island.
    There is a harbor of the Old Man of the Sea, Phorkys,
in the countryside of Ithaka. There two precipitous
promontories opposed jut out, to close in the harbor
and shelter it from the big waves made by the winds blowing
100 so hard on the outside; inside, the well-benched vessels
can lie without being tied up, once they have found their anchorage.

and leave him there asleep

At the head of the harbor, there is an olive tree with spreading
leaves, and nearby is a cave that is shaded, and pleasant,
and sacred to the nymphs who are called the Nymphs of the Wellsprings,
105 Naiads. There are mixing bowls and handled jars inside it,
all of stone, and there the bees deposit their honey.
And therein also are looms that are made of stone, very long, where
the nymphs weave their sea-purple webs, a wonder to look on;
and there is water forever flowing. It has two entrances,
110 one of them facing the North Wind, where people can enter,
but the one toward the South Wind has more divinity. That is
the way of the immortals, and no men enter by that way.
    It was into this bay they rowed their ship. They knew of it beforehand.
The ship, hard-driven, ran up onto the beach for as much as
115 half her length, such was the force the hands of the oarsmen
gave her. They stepped from the strong-benched ship out onto the dry
        land,
and first they lifted and carried Odysseus out of the hollow
hull, along with his bed linen and shining coverlet,
and set him down on the sand. He was still bound fast in sleep. Then
120 they lifted and carried out the possessions, those which the haughty
Phaiakians, urged by great-hearted Athene, had given him, as he
set out for home, and laid them next to the trunk of the olive,
all in a pile and away from the road, lest some wayfarer
might come before Odysseus awoke, and spoil his possessions.
125 Then they themselves turned back toward home. But the Earthshaker
had not forgotten those threats he had once uttered at godlike
Odysseus in the beginning, and he asked Zeus for counsel:
'Father Zeus, no longer among the gods immortal
shall I be honored, when there are mortals who do me no honor,
130 the Phaiakians, and yet these are of my own blood. See now,
I had said to myself Odysseus would come home only after
much suffering. I had not indeed taken his homecoming
altogether away, since first you nodded your head and assented
to it. But they carried him, asleep in the fast ship, over
135 the sea, and set him down in Ithaka, and gave him numberless
gifts, as bronze, and gold abundant, and woven clothing,
more than Odysseus could ever have taken from Troy, even
if he had come home ungrieved and with his fair share of the plunder.'
    Then in turn Zeus who gathers the clouds made answer:

140 'What a thing to have said, Earthshaker of the wide strength.
The gods do not hold you in dishonor. It would be a hard thing
if we were to put any slight on the eldest and best among us.
But if there is any man who, giving way to the violence
and force in him, slights you, it will be yours to punish him.
145 Now and always. Do as you will and as it pleases you.'
Then in turn Poseidon shaker of the earth made answer:
'I would act quickly, dark-clouded one, as you advise me,
but always I have respect for your anger, and keep out of
its way. This time, I wish to stun that beautiful vessel
150 of the Phaiakians out on the misty sea as it comes back
from its journey, so that they may stop, and give over conveying
people. And I would hide their city under a mountain.'
Then in turn Zeus who gathers the clouds made answer:
'Good brother, here is the way it seems to my mind best
155 to do. When all the people are watching her from the city
as she comes in, then turn her into a rock that looks like
a fast ship, close off shore, so that all people may wonder
at her. But do not hide their city under a mountain.'
When the shaker of the earth Poseidon heard him, he went off
160 striding to Scheria, where the Phaiakians are born and live. There
he waited, and the sea-going ship came close in, lightly
pursuing her way, and the Earthshaker came close up to her,
and turned her into stone and rooted her there to the bottom
with a flat stroke of his hand. And then he went away from her.
165 The Phaiakians of the long oars, the sea-famed people,
now began talking to each other and spoke in winged words;
and thus they would speak, each looking at the man next to him:
'Ah me, who was it fastened our swift ship in the water
as she came rowing in for home? Just now she could be seen plainly.'
170 Thus one or another spoke but they did not know what had happened.
To them now Alkinoös spoke forth and addressed them:
'Ah now, the prophecy of old is come to completion,
that my father spoke, when he said Poseidon someday would be angry
with us, because we are convoy without hurt to all men.
175 He said that one day, as a well-made ship of Phaiakian
men came back from a convoy on the misty face of the water,
he would stun it, and pile a great mountain over our city, to hide it.
So the old man spoke. Now all is being accomplished.

Odysseus' wakening

Come then, let us do as I say, let us all be won over.
180 Stop our conveying of every mortal who makes his arrival
here at our city. We must dedicate also to Poseidon
twelve bulls, chosen out of the herds. Then he might take pity
on us, and not pile up a high mountain over our city.'
   So he spoke, and they were afraid and made the bulls ready.
185 So these leaders of the Phaiakians and men of counsel
among their people made their prayer to the lord Poseidon,
standing around the altar. But now great Odysseus wakened
from sleep in his own fatherland, and he did not know it,
having been long away, for the goddess, Pallas Athene,
190 daughter of Zeus, poured a mist over all, so she could make him
unrecognizable and explain all the details to him,
to have his wife not recognize him, nor his townspeople
and friends, till he punished the suitors for their overbearing oppression.
Therefore to the lord Odysseus she made everything look otherwise
195 than it was, the penetrating roads, the harbors where all could
anchor, the rocks going straight up, and the trees tall growing.
He sprang and stood upright and looked about at his native
country, and groaned aloud and struck himself on both thighs
with the flats of his hands, and spoke a word of lamentation:
200 'Ah me, what are the people whose land I have come to this time,
and are they savage and violent, and without justice,
or hospitable to strangers and with minds that are godly?
And where shall I take all these many goods? Where shall I
myself be driven? I wish I had stayed among the Phaiakians,
205 just where I was, and I would have visited some other powerful
king, who then would have been my friend and seen to my journey.
Now I do not know where to put all this, and I cannot
leave it here, for fear it may become spoil for others.
Shame on the leaders of the Phaiakians and their men of counsel,
210 for they were not altogether thoughtful, nor were they righteous,
when they took me away here to another land; but they told me
they would bring me to sunny Ithaka, and they did not do it.
May Zeus of the suppliants punish them, for he oversees other
men besides, and punishes anyone who transgresses.
215 But come, let me count my goods and find out whether they might not
have gone taking some of it with them in the hollow vessel.'
   So speaking, he counted up the surpassingly beautiful tripods

and caldrons, and the gold and all the fine woven clothing.
There was nothing gone from all of this; but he in great sorrow
220 crept over the beach of his own country beside the resounding
sea, with much lamentation; but now Athene came near him,
likening herself in form to a young man, a herdsman
of sheep, a delicate boy, such as the children of kings are,
and wearing a well-wrought shawl in a double fold over her shoulders.
225 Under her shining feet she had sandals, and in her hand carried
a spear. Odysseus, in joy at the sight, came up to meet her,
and spoke aloud to her and addressed her in winged words, saying:
'Dear friend, since you are the first I have met with in this country,
I give you greeting. Do not cross me with evil purpose,
230 but rescue these possessions and me. I make my prayer to you
as to a god, and come to your dear knees as a suppliant.
And tell me this and tell me truly, so that I may know it.
What land is this, what neighborhood is it, what people live here?
Is it some one of the sunny islands, or is it some foreland
235 slanted out from the generous mainland into the salt sea?'
      Then in turn the gray-eyed goddess Athene answered:
'You are some innocent, O stranger, or else you have come from
far away, if you ask about this land, for it is not
so nameless as all that. There are indeed many who know it,
240 whether among those who live toward the east and the sunrise,
or those who live up and away toward the mist and darkness. See now,
this is a rugged country and not for the driving of horses,
but neither is it so unpleasant, though not widely shapen;
for there is abundant grain for bread grown here, it produces
245 wine, and there is always rain and the dew to make it
fertile; it is good to feed goats and cattle; and timber
is there of all sorts, and watering places good through the seasons;
so that, stranger, the name of Ithaka has gone even
to Troy, though they say that is very far from Achaian country.'
250   So she spoke, and resourceful great Odysseus was happy,
rejoicing in the land of his fathers when Pallas Athene
daughter of Zeus of the aegis told him the truth of it,
and so he answered her again and addressed her in winged words;
but he did not tell her the truth, but checked that word from the outset,
255 forever using to every advantage the mind that was in him:
'I heard the name of Ithaka when I was in wide Crete,

He lies to her

far away, across the sea; now I myself have come here
with these goods that you see, but leaving as much again to my children.
I have fled, an exile, because I killed the son of Idomeneus,
260 Orsilochos, a man swift of foot, who in wide Crete surpassed
all other mortal men for speed of his feet. I killed him
because he tried to deprive me of all my share of the plunder
from Troy, and for the sake of it my heart suffered many
pains: the wars of men; hard crossing of the big waters;
265 for I would not do his father favor, and serve as his henchman
in the land of Troy, but I led others, of my own following.
I lay in wait for him with a friend by the road, and struck him
with the bronze-headed spear as he came back from the fields. There was
a very dark night spread over all the sky, nor did anyone
270 see me, nor did anyone know of it when I stripped the life
from him. But then, when I had cut him down with the sharp bronze,
I went at once to a ship, and supplicated the lordly
Phoenician men, and gave them spoil, to stay their eagerness,
and asked them to carry me and to set me down in Pylos
275 or shining Elis where the Epeians are lords; but it happened
that the force of the wind beat them away from those places, greatly
against their will; it was not as if they wished to deceive me.
So, driven off those courses, we came in here, by night,
and rowed her hastily into the harbor, nor was there any
280 thought in us of the evening meal, much though we wanted it,
but all of us came off the ship as we were, and lay down;
then, weary as I was, the sweetness of sleep came upon me,
while they, taking all the possessions out of the hollow hull, set them
ashore on the sand, and close to the place where I was lying,
285 and they, embarking, went on their way to strongly settled
Sidon; but I, grieving at the heart, was left behind here.'
   So he spoke. The goddess, gray-eyed Athene, smiled on him,
and stroked him with her hand, and took on the shape of a woman
both beautiful and tall, and well versed in glorious handiworks,
290 and spoke aloud to him and addressed him in winged words, saying:
   'It would be a sharp one, and a stealthy one, who would ever get past you
in any contriving; even if it were a god against you.
You wretch, so devious, never weary of tricks, then you would not
even in your own country give over your ways of deceiving
295 and your thievish tales. They are near to you in your very nature.

Athene reveals herself

But come, let us talk no more of this, for you and I both know
sharp practice, since you are far the best of all mortal
men for counsel and stories, and I among all the divinities
am famous for wit and sharpness; and yet you never recognized
300   Pallas Athene, daughter of Zeus, the one who is always
standing beside you and guarding you in every endeavor.
And it was I who made you loved by all the Phaiakians.
And now again I am here, to help you in your devising
of schemes, and to hide the possessions which the haughty Phaiakians
305   bestowed—it was by my thought and counsel—on you, as you started
for home, and tell you all the troubles you are destined to suffer
in your well-wrought house; but you must, of necessity, endure
all, and tell no one out of all the men and the women
that you have come back from your wanderings, but you must endure
310   much grief in silence, standing and facing men in their violence.'
     Then in turn resourceful Odysseus spoke to her in answer:
'It is hard, O goddess, for even a man of good understanding
to recognize you on meeting, for you take every shape upon you.
But this I know well: there was a time when you were kind to me
315   in the days when we sons of the Achaians were fighting in Troy land.
But after we had sacked the sheer citadel of Priam,
and went away in our ships, and the god scattered the Achaians,
I never saw you, daughter of Zeus, after that, nor did I
know of your visiting my ship, to beat off some trouble
320   from me, but always with my heart torn inside its coverings
I wandered, until the gods set me free from unhappiness, until
in the rich territory of the Phaiakian men you cheered me
with words, then led me, yourself in person, into their city.
And now I entreat you in the name of your father; for I do not think
325   I have really come into sunny Ithaka, but have been driven
off course to another country, and I think you are teasing me
when you tell me I am, and saying it to beguile me; tell me
if it is true that I have come back to my own dear country.'
     Then in turn the goddess gray-eyed Athene answered him:
330   'Always you are the same, and such is the mind within you,
and so I cannot abandon you when you are unhappy,
because you are fluent, and reason closely, and keep your head always.
Anyone else come home from wandering would have run happily
off to see his children and wife in his halls; but it is not

335   your pleasure to investigate and ask questions, not till
     you have made trial of your wife; yet she, as always,
     sits there in your palace, and always with her the wretched
     nights, and the days also, waste her away with weeping.
     And I never did have any doubt, but in my heart always
340   knew how you would come home, having lost all of your companions.
     But, you see, I did not want to fight with my father's
     brother, Poseidon, who was holding a grudge against you
     in his heart, and because you blinded his dear son, hated you.
     Come, I will show you settled Ithaka, so you will believe me.
345   This is the harbor of the Old Man of the Sea, Phorkys,
     and here at the head of the harbor is the olive tree with spreading
     leaves, and nearby is the cave that is shaded, and pleasant,
     and sacred to the nymphs who are called the Nymphs of the
          Wellsprings,
     Naiads. That is the wide over-arching cave, where often
350   you used to accomplish for the nymphs their complete hecatombs;
     and there is the mountain, Neritos, all covered with forest.'
       So speaking the goddess scattered the mist, and the land was visible.
     Long-suffering great Odysseus was gladdened then, rejoicing
     in the sight of his country, and kissed the grain-giving ground, then
355   raised his hands in the air and spoke to the nymphs, praying:
     'Naiad nymphs, O daughters of Zeus, I never suspected
     that I would see you again. Be welcome now to my gentle
     prayers, but I will also give you gifts, as I used to
     before, if Athene the Spoiler, Zeus' daughter, freely grants me
360   to go on living here myself, and sustains my dear son.'
       Then in turn the goddess gray-eyed Athene said to him:
     'Never fear, let none of these matters trouble your mind. Rather
     let us hide these possessions without delay, deep in the inward
     part of the wonderful cave, so they will be kept safe for you.
365   Then we shall make our plans how all may come out best for us.'
       So the goddess spoke, and went inside the shadowy
     cave, looking through it for hiding places. Meanwhile, Odysseus
     brought everything close up, gold, tireless bronze, clothing
     that had been made with care, given him by the Phaiakians,
370   and stowed it well away inside; and Pallas Athene,
     daughter of Zeus of the aegis, set a stone against the doorway.
       The two sat down against the trunk of the hallowed olive,

and plotted out the destruction of the overmastering suitors.
Their discourse was begun by the goddess gray-eyed Athene:
375 'Son of Laertes and seed of Zeus, resourceful Odysseus,
consider how you can lay your hands on these shameless suitors,
who for three years now have been as lords in your palace,
and courting your godlike wife, and offering gifts to win her.
And she, though her heart forever grieves over your homecoming,
380 holds out some hope for all, and makes promises to each man,
sending them messages, but her mind has other intentions.'
    Then resourceful Odysseus spoke in turn and answered her:
'Surely I was on the point of perishing by an evil
fate in my palace, like Atreus' son Agamemnon, unless
385 you had told me, goddess, the very truth of all that has happened.
Come then, weave the design, the way I shall take my vengeance
upon them; stand beside me, inspire me with strength and courage,
as when together we brought down Troy's shining coronal.
For if in your fury, O gray-eyed goddess, you stood beside me,
390 I would fight, lady and goddess, with your help against three hundred
men if you, freely and in full heart, would help me.'
    Then in turn the goddess gray-eyed Athene answered:
'I will indeed be at your side, you will not be forgotten
at the time when we two go to this work, and I look for endless
395 ground to be spattered by the blood and brains of the suitors,
these men who are eating all your substance away. But come now,
let me make you so that no mortal can recognize you.
For I will wither the handsome flesh that is on your flexible
limbs, and ruin the brown hair on your head, and about you
400 put on such a clout of cloth any man will loathe when he sees you
wearing it; I will dim those eyes, that have been so handsome,
so you will be unprepossessing to all the suitors
and your wife and child, those whom you left behind in your palace.
First of all, you are to make your way to the swineherd
405 who is in charge of your pigs, but always his thoughts are kindly,
and he is a friend to your son and to circumspect Penelope.
You will find him posted beside his pigs, and these are herded
near the Rock of the Raven and beside the spring Arethousa,
to eat the acorns that stay their strength, and drink of the darkling
410 water, for these are nourishing for pigs, and fatten them.
There you shall wait, and stay with him, and ask him all questions,

Odysseus transformed into an old tramp

while I go over to Sparta, the country of lovely women,
and call back Telemachos, your own dear son, Odysseus,
who went into spacious Lakedaimon to see Menelaos

415 and ask him for news of you, and whether you were still living.'
    Then resourceful Odysseus spoke in turn and answered her:
'Why then did you not tell him, since in your mind you know all things?
Was it so that he too wandering over the barren
sea should suffer pains, while others ate up his substance?'

420   Then in turn the goddess gray-eyed Athene answered:
'Let him not be too much on your mind. It was I myself
who saw him along on that journey, so he would win reputation
by going there, and he has no hardship, but now is staying
at his ease with the son of Atreus, and all abundance is by him.

425 It is true that the young men with their black ship are lying
in wait for him to kill him before he reaches his country;
but I think this will not happen, but that sooner the earth will cover
some one of those suitors, who now are eating away your substance.'
    So spoke Athene, and with her wand she tapped Odysseus,

430 and withered the handsome flesh that was upon his flexible
limbs, and ruined the brown hair on his head, and about him,
to cover all his body, she put the skin of an ancient
old man, and then she dimmed those eyes that had been so handsome.
Then she put another vile rag on him, and a tunic,

435 tattered, squalid, blackened with the foul smoke, and over it
gave him the big hide of a fast-running deer, with the hairs rubbed
off, to wear, and she gave him a staff, and an ugly wallet
that was full of holes, with a twist of rope attached, to dangle it.
    So they two consulted and went their ways. The goddess

440 went to bright Lakedaimon to fetch the son of Odysseus.

BOOK XIV

But Odysseus himself left the harbor and ascended a rugged
path, through wooded country along the heights, where Athene
had indicated the noble swineherd, who beyond others
cared for the house properties acquired by noble Odysseus.
5   He found him sitting in front, on the porch, where the lofty
enclosure had been built, in a place with a view on all sides,
both large and handsome, cleared all about, and it was the swineherd
himself who had built it, to hold the pigs of his absent master,
far from his mistress and from aged Laertes. He made it
10   with stones from the field, and topped it off with shrubbery. Outside
he had driven posts in a full circle, to close it on all sides,
set close together and thick, the dark of the oak, split out
from the logs. Inside the enclosure he made twelve pig pens
next to each other, for his sows to sleep in, and in each of them
15   fifty pigs who sleep on the ground were confined. These were
the breeding females, but the males lay outside, and these were
fewer by far, for the godlike suitors kept diminishing
their numbers by eating them, since the swineherd kept having
to send them in the best of all the well-fattened porkers
20   at any time. Now, they numbered three hundred and sixty,
and four dogs, who were like wild beasts, forever were lying
by them. These the swineherd, leader of men, had raised up
himself. Now he was fitting sandals to his feet, cutting
out a well-colored piece of oxhide. Meanwhile, the other

25   swineherds were out with the herded pigs one place or another,
      three of them, but the fourth he had sent off to the city
      to take a pig to the insolent suitors, since they so forced him,
      so they could sacrifice it and glut their appetites on it.
         Suddenly the wild-baying dogs caught sight of Odysseus.
30   They ran at him with a great outcry, and Odysseus prudently
      sat down on the ground, and the staff fell out of his hand. But there,
      beside his own steading, he might have endured a shameful mauling,
      but the swineherd, quick and light on his feet, came hurrying to him
      across the porch, and let fall from his hand the shoe he was holding.
35   He shouted at the dogs and scared them in every direction
      with volleyed showers of stones, and spoke then to his own master:
      'Old sir, the dogs were suddenly on you and would have savaged you
      badly; so you would have covered me with shame, but already
      there are other pains and sorrows the gods have bestowed upon me.
40   For here I sit, mourning and grieving away for a godlike
      master, and carefully raise his fattened pigs for others
      to eat, while he, in need of finding some sustenance, wanders
      some city or countryside of alien-speaking people;
      if he still is alive somewhere and looks on the sunlight.
45   Come, old sir, along to my shelter, so that you also
      first may be filled to contentment with food and wine, then tell me
      where you come from, and about the sorrows you have been suffering.'
         So spoke the noble swineherd and led the way to the shelter,
      and brought him in, and seated him on brushwood piled up
50   beneath, and spread over this the hide of a hairy wild goat
      from his own bed. This was great and thick, and Odysseus was happy
      at how he received him, and spoke a word and named him, saying:
      'May Zeus, stranger, and the other gods everlasting grant you
      all you desire the most, for you have received me heartily.'
55   Then, O swineherd Eumaios, you said to him in answer:
      'Stranger, I have no right to deny the stranger, not even
      if one came to me who was meaner than you. All vagabonds
      and strangers are under Zeus, and the gift is a light and a dear one
      that comes from us, for that is the way of us who are servants
60   and forever filled with fear when they come under power of masters
      who are new. The gods have stopped the homeward voyage of that one
      who cared greatly for me, and granted me such possessions
      as a good-natured lord grants to the thrall of his house; a home

of his own, and a plot of land, and a wife much sought after,

65 when the man accomplishes much work and god speeds the labor
as he has sped for me this labor to which I am given.
So my lord would have done much for me if he had grown old here,
but he perished, as I wish Helen's seed could all have perished,
pitched away, for she has unstrung the knees of so many

70 men; for in Agamemnon's cause my master went also
to Ilion, land of good horses, there to fight with the Trojans.'
    He spoke, and pulled his tunic to with his belt, and went out
swiftly to his pig pens where his herds of swine were penned in,
and picked out a pair and brought them in and sacrificed them,

75 and singed them, and cut them into little pieces, and spitted them,
then roasted all and brought and set it before Odysseus
hot on the spits as it was, and sprinkled white barley over it,
and mixed the wine, as sweet as honey, in a bowl of ivy,
and himself sat down facing him, and urged him on, saying:

80 'Eat now, stranger, what we serving men are permitted
to eat: young pigs, but the fattened swine are devoured by the suitors,
who have no regard for anyone in their minds, no pity.
The blessed gods have no love for a pitiless action,
but rather they reward justice and what men do that is lawful;

85 and though those are hateful and lawless men who land on an alien
shore, and Zeus grants them spoil and plunder, when they have loaded
their ships with it they set sail away for home, for even
in the minds of these there is stored some fear, which is stronger than
       pity;
but these, you see, have heard some god-sent rumor, and they know

90 about the dismal death of our man, and they will not decently
make their suit, nor go home to their own houses, but at their
ease they forcibly eat up his property, and spare nothing.
For as many as are the nights and the days from Zeus, on not one
of these do they dedicate only a single victim, nor only

95 two, and they violently draw the wine and waste it. See now,
he had an endlessly abundant livelihood. Not one
of the heroes over on the black mainland had so much, no one
here on Ithaka, no twenty men together had such
quantity of substance as he. I will count it for you.

100 Twelve herds of cattle on the mainland. As many sheepflocks.
As many troops of pigs and again as many wide goatflocks,

and friends over there, and his own herdsmen, pasture them for him.
And here again, at the end of the island, eleven wide flocks
of goats in all are pastured, good men have these in their keeping.
105 And day by day each of these people brings in for the suitors
a sheep, and each brings in the fatted goat that seems finest,
and I myself keep watch on these pigs and guard them, and I too
choose with care the best of the pigs, and send it off to them.'
He spoke, and the other ate his meat and drank his wine, quietly,
110 greedily and without speaking, and devised evils for the suitors;
but when he had dined, and filled his desire with food, the other
filled the cup in which he was drinking and handed it to him,
all filled with wine, and he received it, and his heart was cheered
and he spoke to him then and addressed him in winged words, saying:
115 'Dear friend, who is the man who bought you with his possessions
and is so rich and powerful as you tell me? You say
he was one who perished in Agamemnon's cause. Then tell me,
and perhaps I might know him if he was such a man, for Zeus knows
as do the other immortal gods, if I might have seen him
120 and have some report to give you. I have wandered to many places.'
Then the swineherd, leader of men, said to him in answer:
'Old sir, there is none who could come here, bringing a report
of him, and persuade his wife and his dear son; and yet
there are vain and vagabond men in need of sustenance
125 who tell lies, and are unwilling to give a true story;
and any vagrant who makes his way to the land of Ithaka
goes to my mistress and babbles his lies to her, and she then
receives him well and entertains him and asks him everything,
and as she mourns him the tears run down from her eyes, since this is
130 the right way for a wife when her husband is far and perished.
So you too, old sir, might spin out a well-made story,
if someone would give you a cloak or tunic to wear for it. But, for
him, the dogs and the flying birds must by now have worried
the skin away from his bones, and the soul has left them; or else
135 the fish have eaten him, out in the great sea, and his bones lie
now on the mainland shore with the sand piled deeply upon them.
So he has perished there, and sorrows are made for his dear ones
all hereafter, and me most of all, for never again now
will I find again a lord as kind as he, wherever
140 I go; even if I could come back to my father and mother's

Asked who he is, Odysseus

house, where first I was born, and they raised me when I was little.
But I do not so much mourn for this, much though my longing
is to behold them with these eyes and in my own country,
but the longing is on me for Odysseus, and he is gone from me;
145 and even when he is not here, my friend, I feel some modesty
about naming him, for in his heart he cared for me greatly
and loved me. So I call him my master, though he is absent.'
    Then long-suffering great Odysseus spoke to him in answer:
'Dear friend, since you are altogether full of denial,
150 you do not think he will come, and your heart is ever untrusting;
but I will not speak in the same manner, but on my oath tell you
Odysseus is on his way home. Let me have my reward for good news
then, as soon as he is come back and enters his own house.
Give me fine clothing, a cloak and tunic to wear. Before that,
155 much as I stand in need of these, I will not accept them.
For as I detest the doorways of Death I detest that man who
under constraint of poverty babbles beguiling falsehoods.
Zeus be my witness, first of the gods, and the table of friendship,
and the hearth of blameless Odysseus, to which I come as a suppliant,
160 all these things are being accomplished in the way I tell them.
Sometime within this very year Odysseus will be here.
Either at the waning of the moon, or at its onset,
he will come home and take his vengeance here upon any
who deprives his wife and his glorious son of their due honor.'
165   Then, O swineherd Eumaios, you said to him in answer:
'Old sir, I will never pay you that gift for good news,
nor will Odysseus come to this house again. Be easy
and drink your wine. We will think of other matters. Do not then
keep on reminding me of this, for the heart within me
170 grieves whenever anyone speaks of my gracious master.
So we will let your oath alone, but I hope that Odysseus
will come back, as I wish, and as Penelope wishes,
and Laertes the old man too, and godlike Telemachos.
But now I grieve unforgettingly for Telemachos, the son
175 born to Odysseus. The gods made him grow like a young tree,
and I thought he would be among the men one not inferior
to his dear father, admirable for build and beauty;
but some immortal upset the balanced mind within him,
or else it was some man. He went after news of his father

180 to Pylos the sacrosanct, and the haughty suitors are lying
in wait for him as he comes home, to make Arkeisios'
stock and seed perish all away and be nameless in Ithaka.
Now we will let him be, however, whether they catch him
or whether he escapes and the son of Kronos protects him.

185 But come now, aged sir, recite me the tale of your sorrows,
and tell me this too, tell me truly, so that I may know it:
What man are you and whence? Where is your city? Your parents?
What kind of ship did you come here on? And how did the sailors
bring you to Ithaka? What men do they claim that they are?

190 For I do not think you could have traveled on foot to this country.'
        Then resourceful Odysseus spoke in turn and answered him:
'See, I will accurately answer all that you ask me.
I only wish there were food enough for the time, for us two,
and sweet wine for us here inside of the shelter, so that

195 we could feast quietly while others tended the work; then
easily I could go on for the whole of a year, and still not
finish the story of my heart's tribulations, all that
hard work I have done in my time, because the gods willed it.
I announce that my origin is from Crete, a spacious

200 land; I am son of a rich man, and there were many other
sons who were born to him and reared in his palace. These were
lawful sons by his wife, but a bought woman, a concubine,
was my mother, yet I was favored with the legitimate
sons by Kastor, Hylakos' son, whom I claim as father,

205 honored among the Cretans in the countryside as a god is,
in those days, for wealth and power and glorious children.
But then, you see, the death spirits caught and carried him from us
to the house of Hades, and his overbearing sons divided
the livelihood among them and cast lots for it. Little

210 enough, however, was what they gave me in goods and houses.
But I took for myself a wife from people with many possessions,
because of my courage, for I was no contemptible man, not
one who fled from the fighting; but now all that has gone from me,
but still, I think, if you look at the stubble you see what the corn was

215 like when it grew, but since then hardship enough has had me.
Ares and Athene endowed me with courage, that power
that breaks men in battle. Whenever I detailed the best fighters
to go into ambush, planning evil things for the enemy,

the proud heart in me had no image of death before it,
220 but far the first I would leap out and with my spear bring down
that enemy man whose speed of foot failed him against me.
Such was I in the fighting; but labor was never dear to me,
nor care for my house, though that is what raises glorious children;
but ships that are driven on by oars were dear to me always,
225 and the wars, and throwing spears with polished hafts, and the arrows,
gloomy things, which to other men are terrible, and yet
those things were dear to me which surely some god had put there
in my heart, for different men take joy in different actions.
Before the sons of the Achaians embarked for Troy, I was
230 nine times a leader of men and went in fast-faring vessels
against outland men, and much substance came my way, and of this
some I took out to stay my estate, but much I allotted
again, and soon my house grew greater, and from that time on
I went among the Cretans as one feared and respected.
235 But when Zeus of the wide brows devised for us that hateful
expedition, which unstrung the knees of so many
men, they were urgent upon me and renowned Idomeneus
to lead with the ships to Ilion, and there was no remedy,
nor any refusing, for the hard speech of the people constrained us.
240 Then for nine years we sons of the Achaians fought there,
and in the tenth we sacked the city of Priam, and went back
homeward with our ships, and the god scattered the Achaians.
But for wretched me Zeus of the counsels devised more hardships;
one month only I stayed, taking pleasure in my children
245 and my wedded wife and my possessions, but then the spirit
within me urged me to make an expedition to Egypt
with ships well appointed and with my godlike companions.
I appointed nine ships, and rapidly the people were gathered,
and for six days then my eager companions continued
250 feasting, but I provided them with abundant victims
for sacrifice to the gods, and for themselves to make ready
their feast. On the seventh day we went aboard and from wide Crete
sailed on a North Wind that was favorable and fair. It was
easy, like sailing downstream, so that never a single
255 one of my ships was hurt, and we, unharmed, without sickness,
sat still, and let the wind and the steersmen hold them steady.
On the fifth day we reached the abundant stream Aigyptos,

who came to grief in Egypt

and I stayed my oarswept ships inside the Aigyptos River.
Then I urged my eager companions to stay where they were, there
260 close to the fleet, and to guard the ships, and was urgent with them
to send look-outs to the watching places; but they, following
their own impulse, and giving way to marauding violence,
suddenly began plundering the Egyptians' beautiful
fields, and carried off the women and innocent children,
265 and killed the men, and soon the outcry came to the city.
They heard the shouting, and at the time when dawn shows, they came
on us, and all the plain was filled with horses and infantry
and the glare of bronze, and Zeus who delights in thunder flung down
a foul panic among my companions, and none was so hardy
270 as to stand and fight, for the evils stood in a circle around them.
There they killed many of us with the sharp bronze, and others
they led away alive, to work for them in forced labor;
but Zeus himself put this thought into my mind, as I will
tell you, but how I wish I had died and met my destiny
275 there in Egypt, for there was still more sorrow awaiting me.
At once I put the well-wrought helm from my head, the great shield
off my shoulders, and from my hand I let the spear drop,
and went out into the way of the king and up to his chariot,
and kissed his knees and clasped them; he rescued me and took pity
280 and seated me in his chariot and took me, weeping, homeward
with him; and indeed many swept in on me with ash spears
straining to kill me, for they were all too angered, but the king
held them off from me, and honored the anger of Zeus Protector
of Strangers, who beyond others is outraged at evil dealings.
285 There for seven years I stayed and gathered together
much substance from the men of Egypt, for all gave to me;
but when in the turning of time the eighth year had befallen me,
then there came a Phoenician man, well skilled in beguilements,
a gnawer at others' goods, and many were the hurts he inflicted
290 on men, and by his wits talked me over, so I went with him
to Phoenicia, where lay this man's house and possessions.
There for the fulfillment of a year I stayed with him,
but when the months and when the days had come to completion,
with the circling back of the year again, and the seasons came on,
295 then he took me on his seafaring ship to Libya,
with lying advices, that with him we could win a cargo, but in fact

so he could sell me there and take the immense price for me.
I went with him on his ship, forced to, although I suspected
all, on a North Wind that was favorable and fair, above
300 the middle of Crete, but Zeus was plotting these men's destruction.
But after we had left Crete behind us, and there was no more
land in sight, but only the sky and the sea, then Kronian
Zeus drew on a blue-black cloud, and settled it over
the hollow ship, and the open sea was darkened beneath it.
305 Zeus with thunder and lightning together crashed on our vessel,
and, struck by the thunderbolt of Zeus, she spun in a circle,
and all was full of brimstone. The men were thrown in the water,
and bobbing like sea crows they were washed away on the running
waves all around the black ship, and the god took away their homecoming.
310 But Zeus himself, though I had pain in my heart, then put
into my hands the giant mast of the ship with dark prows,
so that I still could escape the evil, and I embracing
this was swept along before the destructive stormwinds.
Nine days I was swept along, and on the tenth, in black night,
315 the great wave rolling washed me up on the shore of Thesprotia.
There the king of the Thesprotians, the hero Pheidon,
looked after me without price, for his own dear son had come on me
when I was beaten by weariness and cold air, and lifted me
up by the hands, and led me home to the house of his father,
320 and put a mantle and tunic about me to wear as clothing.
It was there I had word of Odysseus, for this king told me
he had feasted and friended him on his way back to his own country;
and he showed me all the possessions gathered in by Odysseus,
bronze and gold and difficultly wrought iron. Truly,
325 that would feed a succession of heirs to the tenth generation,
such are the treasures stored for him in the house of the great king.
But he said Odysseus had gone to Dodona, to listen
to the will of Zeus, out of the holy deep-leaved oak tree,
for how he could come back to the rich countryside of Ithaka,
330 in secret or openly, having been by now long absent.
And he swore to me in my presence, as he poured out a libation
in his house, that the ship was drawn down to the sea and the crew wer
  ready
to carry Odysseus back again to his own dear country;
but before that he sent me off, for a ship of Thesprotian

335 men happened then to be sailing for Doulichion, rich in wheatfields;
so he urged them to convey me there to the king Akastos,
in a proper way, but their hearts were taken with a bad counsel
concerning me, so I still should have the pain of affliction.
So when the seafaring ship had gone far out from the mainland,
340 they presently devised the day of slavery for me.
They took off me the mantle and tunic I wore as clothing,
and then they put another vile rag on me, and a tunic,
tattered, the one you yourself see with your eyes. At evening
time they made their way off the fields of sunny Ithaka,
345 and there they tied me fast in the strong-benched ship, with a rope's end
twisted and tightly about me, and themselves disembarking
speedily took their evening meal on the sand of the seashore.
But the very gods themselves untied the knots that were on me
easily, and I, wrapping my head in a rag, climbed down
350 the polished plank that was there for loading, and let my chest into
the sea, then struck out with both my arms, and thus swimming
I very soon was out of the water and close to where they were.
Then I went up, where there was a growth of flowering thicket,
and lay there, cowering; they with outcry great and sorrowful
355 came back to search, but then it seemed there was no more profit
in looking for me any longer, and so they went back, boarding
their hollow ship again; but it was the gods who concealed me
easily, and it was they who brought me here to the steading
of an understanding man. So now, life is still my portion.'
360   Then, O swineherd Eumaios, you said to him in answer:
'O sorrowful stranger, truly you troubled the spirit in me,
by telling me all these details, how you suffered and wandered;
yet I think some part is in no true order, and you will not persuade me
in your talk about Odysseus. Why should such a man as you are
365 lie recklessly to me? But I myself know the whole truth
of what my lord's homecoming is, how all the gods hated him
so much that they did not make him go down in the land of the Trojans,
nor in the arms of his friends, after he had wound up the fighting.
So all the Achaians would have heaped a grave mound over him,
370 and he would have won great fame for himself and his son hereafter.
But now ingloriously the stormwinds have caught and carried him.
But I keep away and with my pigs, and I do not go now
to the city, unless circumspect Penelope for some reason

asks me to go, when word comes in from one place or another;
375 and there are those who sit beside me and question me over
particulars, whether they are grieving for a lord long absent,
or are happy at eating up his substance without recompense.
But I have no liking for this inquiry and asking of questions,
since that time an Aitolian man beguiled me by telling
380 a story. This one had killed a man and wandered over
much country. He came to my house and I entertained him fondly.
He said he had seen him with Idomeneus, among the Cretan
men, repairing his ships, for the stormwinds had smashed them,
and he said he would be coming back, in the summer or autumn,
385 bringing in many possessions, and with his godlike companions.
You too, old man of many sorrows, since the spirit brought you
here to me, do not try to please me nor spell me with lying
words. It is not for that I will entertain and befriend you,
but for fear of Zeus, the god of guests, and for my own pity.'
390   Then resourceful Odysseus spoke in turn and answered him:
'Truly, the mind in you is something very suspicious.
Not even with an oath can I bring you round, nor persuade you.
Come now, we two shall make an agreement, and for the future
the gods who hold Olympos shall be witnesses to both sides.
395 As your lord makes his homecoming into his palace
here, you shall give me a tunic and mantle to wear, and send me
on my way to Doulichion, where my heart has been desiring
to go; but if your lord never comes in the way I tell you
he will, set your serving men on me, and throw me over a high cliff,
400 so the next vagabond will be careful, and not lie to you.'
        Then in turn the glorious swineherd spoke to him in answer:
'That would be virtuous of me, my friend, and good reputation
would be mine among men, for present time alike and hereafter,
if first I led you into my shelter, there entertained you
405 as guest, then murdered you and ravished the dear life from you.
Then cheerfully I could go and pray to Zeus, son of Kronos.
But now it is time for our dinner, and I hope my companions come in
soon, so we can prepare a good dinner here in my shelter.'
        So these two remained conversing this way together,
410 and the sows came up, and with them came the men who were
        swineherds,
and they penned the sows for the night inside their accustomed places,

and an endless clamor went up from the crowding swine. Thereafter
the glorious swineherd gave the word to his own companions:
'Bring in the best of the pigs, to sacrifice for our stranger
415   guest from afar, and we ourselves shall enjoy it, we who
long have endured this wretched work for the pigs with shining
teeth, while others at no cost eat up what we have worked on.'
     So he spoke, and with the pitiless bronze split kindling,
and the men brought in a pig, five years old and a very fat one,
420   and made it stand in front of the fireplace, nor did the swineherd
forget the immortal gods, for he had the uses of virtue;
but he cut off hairs from the head of the white-toothed pig, and threw
            them
into the fire as dedication, and prayed to all the gods
that Odysseus of the many designs should have his homecoming.
425   He hit the beast with a split of oak that he had lying by him.
The breath went out of the pig; then they slaughtered him and singed
            him,
then jointed the carcass, and the swineherd laid pieces of raw meat
with offerings from all over the body upon the thick fat,
and sprinkled these with meal of barley and threw them in the fire, then
430   they cut all the remainder into pieces and spitted them,
and roasted all carefully and took off the pieces,
and laid it all together on platters. The swineherd
stood up to divide the portions, for he was fair minded,
and separated all the meat into seven portions.
435   One he set aside, with a prayer, for the nymphs and Hermes,
the son of Maia, and the rest he distributed to each man,
but gave Odysseus in honor the long cuts of the chine's portion
of the white-toothed pig, and so exalted the heart of his master.
Then resourceful Odysseus spoke to him and addressed him:
440   'I wish, Eumaios, you could be as dear to our father
Zeus as to me, when I am so poor, but you grace me with good things.'
     Then, O swineherd Eumaios, you said to him in answer:
'Eat, my guest, strange man that you are, and take your pleasure
of what is here now; the god will give you such, or will let it
445   be, as in his own mind he may wish. He can do anything.'
     He spoke, and sacrificed first-offerings to the immortal
gods, then poured bright wine for Odysseus, sacker of cities,
and put the cup in his hands, and sat down to his own portion.

Odysseus hints for a mantle

Mesaulios served the bread to them, a man whom the swineherd
450 owned himself by himself and apart from his absent master,
and independently of his mistress and aged Laertes,
having bought him from the Taphians with his own possessions.
They put forth their hands to the good things that lay ready before them.
But when they had put away their desire for eating and drinking,
455 Mesaulios took the food away again, and they made haste
to go to bed, filled with bread and meat to repletion.
    A bad night came on, the dark of the moon, and Zeus rained
all night long, and the West Wind blew big, always watery.
Odysseus spoke among them. He was trying it out on the swineherd,
460 to see if he might take off his mantle and give it him, or tell
one of his men to do it, since he cared for him so greatly:
'Hear me now, Eumaios and all you other companions.
What I say will be a bit of boasting. The mad wine tells me
to do it. Wine sets even a thoughtful man to singing,
465 or sets him into softly laughing, sets him to dancing.
Sometimes it tosses out a word that was better unspoken.
But now I have broken into loud speech I will not suppress it.
I wish I were young again and the strength still steady within me,
as when, under Troy, we formed an ambush detail and led it.
470 The leaders were Odysseus and Atreus' son, Menelaos,
and I made a third leader with them, since they themselves asked me.
But when we had come underneath the city and the steep wall,
we, all about the city in marshy ground and the dense growth
of swamp grass and the reeds, and huddling under our armor,
475 lay there, and a bad night came on with a rush of the North Wind
freezing, and from above came a fall of snow, chilling
like frost, and on the shields' edges the ice formed, rimming them.
There all the other men were wearing both mantles and tunics,
and they slept at ease, pulling their great shields over their shoulders,
480 but I, in my carelessness when I started with my companions,
had left my mantle; I never thought I would be so cold,
but went along with only my shield and my shining waist guard.
But when it was the third time of the night and after the star change,
then I spoke to Odysseus, for he was lying next me,
485 nudging him with my elbow, and he listened at once. I said:
"Son of Laertes and seed of Zeus, resourceful Odysseus,
I shall no longer be left among the living. The weather

is too much for me. I have no mantle. The spirit made me
silly, to go half-dressed, and now there is no escape for me."
490 So I spoke, and he immediately had an idea
in his mind, such a man he was for counseling, as for fighting.
He spoke to me in a little voice and said a word to me:
"Be quiet now, let no other of the Achaians hear you."
Then he propped his head on his elbow and spoke a word, out loud:
495 "Hear me, friends. In my sleep a divine dream came to me.
We have come too far away from the ships. Now, would there be
someone
to tell Agamemnon, Atreus' son, shepherd of the people,
so he might send more of the men by the ships to come here to us?"
So he spoke, and Thoas sprang up, the son of Andraimon,
500 quickly, and took off and laid aside his red mantle,
and went on the run for the ships, and I lay down in his clothes,
happily, and rested until Dawn of the golden throne came.
I wish I were young like that and the strength still steady within me.
Some one of the swineherds in this house would give me a mantle,
505 both for love and out of respect for a strong warrior.
Now they slight me because I wear vile clothing upon me.'
     Then, O swineherd Eumaios, you said to him in answer:
'Old sir, that was a blameless fable the way you told it;
and you have made no unprofitable speech, nor one that
510 missed the point, so you shall not lack for clothes, nor anything
rightfully due the unhappy suppliant who approaches us.
For now, that is. You must flaunt your rags again in the morning.
There are not many extra mantles and extra tunics
here to change into. There is only one set for each man.
515 When, however, the dear son of Odysseus comes back,
he will give you a mantle and tunic to wear as clothing,
and send you wherever your heart and spirit desire to be sent.'
     So he spoke, and sprang up, and laid a bed for him next to
the fire, and threw the fleeces of sheep and goats over it.
520 There Odysseus lay down, and he threw over him a mantle
that was great and thick, which he kept by him as an extra covering
to wrap in when winter weather came on and was too rigorous.
     So there Odysseus went to bed and the young men beside him
lay down also to go to sleep. Only the swineherd
525 did not please to leave his pigs, and go to bed indoors,

but made preparations as he went out; and Odysseus was happy
that his livelihood was so well cared for while he was absent.
First the swineherd slung his sharp sword on his heavy shoulders,
and put a very thick mantle about him, to keep the wind out,
530   and took up also the hairy skin of a great, well-conditioned
goat, and took up a sharp javelin as a protection
against men and dogs, and went to sleep where his pigs, with shining
teeth, lay in the hollow of a rock, sheltered from the North Wind.

BOOK XV

At this time, Pallas Athene made her way into wide-spaced
Lakedaimon, to remind the shining son of great-hearted
Odysseus of his journey home, and speed his homecoming.
She found Telemachos there with the glorious son of Nestor,
5   sleeping in the forecourt of worshipful Menelaos.
Indeed, the son of Nestor was held fast in the softening
sleep, but the sweet sleep was not on Telemachos, wakeful
through the immortal night, with anxious thoughts of his father.
Gray-eyed Athene stood close by his head and addressed him:
10 'Telemachos, it no longer becomes you to stray off so far
from home, leaving your possessions behind and men in your palace
who are so overbearing. You must not let them divide up
and eat up all your substance, and make your journey a vain one.
So urge Menelaos of the great war cry with all speed to give you
15 conveyance, so you will find your stately mother is still there
at home, since now her father and her brothers are urgent with her
to marry Eurymachos. He is outdoing the rest of suitors
in the giving of gifts, and has been piling up presents to win her.
No property must go out of the house, unless you consent to it.
20 For you know what the mind is like in the breast of a woman.
She wants to build up the household of the man who marries her,
and of former children, and of her beloved and wedded husband,
she has no remembrance, when he is dead, nor does she think of him.
For yourself, when you come back, you should turn over everything

25   to whichever one of the serving women seems to be the best one,
until the gods show who is to be your honored wife. Also
you should put away in your heart this other thing that I tell you.
The best men of the suitors are lying in wait, on purpose,
for you in the passage between rocky Samos and Ithaka,

30   longing to kill you, before you come back to your own country.
But I think they will not achieve it. Sooner the earth will close over
some one of the suitors, they who are eating away your substance.
But you must keep your well-made ship away from the islands,
and sail with the night, and that one of the immortals who watches

35   over you and guards you will send a following stern wind.
But when you make land, at the first promontory on Ithaka,
then speed your ship and all your companions along to the city,
but you yourself go first of all to the swineherd, that man
who is in charge of the pigs, and whose thoughts toward you are kindly.

40   There spend the night, but speed the man along to the city
to take your message to circumspect Penelope, saying
that you are alive and safe, and you have come home from Pylos.'
    So she spoke, and then went away, back to tall Olympos,
and Telemachos wakened Nestor's son out of his sweet sleep,

45   stirring him with a nudge of his heel, and spoke a word to him:
'Wake, Peisistratos, son of Nestor, and bring your solid-hoofed
horses under the yoke to harness, so we can start back.'
    Peisistratos, the son of Nestor, said to him in answer:
'Telemachos, though we long for the journey, surely we cannot

50   drive through the dark of the night, but it will be daylight presently.
But wait until the hero, the son of Atreus, spear-famed
Menelaos, brings you his gifts to put in the chariot,
and speaks to us, and with kind words sends us away on our journey.
For a guest remembers all his days the man who received him

55   as a host receives a guest, and gave him the gifts of friendship.'
    So he spoke, and soon after Dawn of the golden throne came,
and, rising up from his bed where he lay by sweet-haired Helen,
Menelaos of the great war cry came and stood near them.
As soon then as the dear son of Odysseus noted him,

60   he made haste to slip the shimmering tunic over
his skin, and the hero threw a great mantle over his heavy
shoulders, and went to the door, and stood by his host and addressed
      him,

for permission to leave

he, Telemachos, the dear son of godlike Odysseus:
'Great Menelaos, son of Atreus, leader of the people,
65 now send me on my way at last to my own dear country,
for now the heart within me longs for the homeward journey.'
    Then in turn Menelaos of the great war cry answered:
'Telemachos, I for my part never will long detain you
here when you strain for home. I would disapprove of another
70 hospitable man who was excessive in friendship,
as of one excessive in hate. In all things balance is better.
It is equally bad when one speeds on the guest unwilling
to go, and when he holds back one who is hastening. Rather
one should befriend the guest who is there, but speed him when he
    wishes.
75 Yet stay, until I can bring you fine gifts to put in your chariot,
and you can look at them with your eyes, while I tell the women
to prepare a dinner out of what we have here in abundance.
For there is both honor and brilliance in it, and there also is profit,
to dine, then go a long way over the endless earth. Therefore,
80 if you wish to make a tour through Hellas and midmost Argos,
and have me go myself with you, I will harness my horses
and be your guide through the cities of men, and there will be no one
who will send us away just as we are, but each one will give us
one thing to carry away with us, some tripod or caldron
85 well wrought in bronze, or a pair of mules, or a golden goblet.'
    Then the thoughtful Telemachos said to him in answer:
'Great Menelaos, son of Atreus, leader of the people,
I wish now to go back to our country, for I left behind me
no one when I went, to look after my own possessions.
90 I must not, going in search of my godlike father, ruin
myself, or have some stored-up treasure lost from my palace.'
    But as soon as Menelaos of the great war cry had heard this,
immediately he told his wife and all the maidservants
to prepare a dinner out of what was there in abundance;
95 and, risen from his bed, Eteoneus the son of Boethoös
came to them, since he had his own dwelling not far from them.
Menelaos of the great war cry told him to kindle
the fire and roast the meat, nor did the man disobey him.
Meanwhile he himself went into the fragrant chamber,
100 not alone, but Megapenthes and Helen went with him.

But when they came to the place where they had their treasures stored,
the son of Atreus took up the goblet, handled on both sides,
and told Megapenthes to carry the mixing bowl, that was made
of silver; but Helen went to stand by the storing boxes,
105 where there were elaborately wrought robes. She herself had made them.
And Helen, shining among women, lifted out one of them,
that which was the loveliest in design and the largest
and shone like a star. It lay beneath the others. She went on
her way, further and out through the house, until she came to
110 Telemachos; then fair-haired Menelaos said to him:
'Telemachos, may Zeus, loud-thundering husband of Hera,
accomplish your homeward journey in the way that your heart desires it.
Of all those gifts that lie stored away in my house I will give you
the one which is most splendid and esteemed at the highest value.
115 I will give you a fashioned mixing bowl. It is of silver,
all but the edges, and these are finished in gold. This is
the work of Hephaistos. The hero Phaidimos, the Sidonians'
king, gave it to me, when his house took me in and sheltered me
there, on my way home. I would give it to you for a present.'
120 So speaking, the hero, Atreus' son, put the handled goblet
into his hands, and meanwhile strong Megapenthes carried
out the mixing bowl gleaming with silver and set it
before them. Helen of the fair cheeks stood by, holding
the robe in her hands, and spoke to him and named him, saying:
125 'I too give you this gift, dear child: something to remember
from Helen's hands, for your wife to wear at the lovely occasion
of your marriage. Until that time let it lie away in your palace,
in your dear mother's keeping; and I hope you come back rejoicing
to your own strong-founded house and to the land of your fathers.'
130 So speaking, she put it in his hands, and he gladly received it.
The hero Peisistratos took the presents and packed them into
the carrying basket, and in his own mind admired everything.
Fair-haired Menelaos led them back into his palace,
and the two young men seated themselves on chairs and benches.
135 A maidservant brought water for them and poured it from a splendid
and golden pitcher, holding it above a silver basin
for them to wash, and she pulled a polished table before them.
A grave housekeeper brought in the bread and served it to them,
adding many good things to it, generous with her provisions,

A portent read by Helen

140 and the son of Boethoös carved the meat and served out the portions,
while the son of glorious Menelaos poured the wine for them.
They put their hands to the good things that lay ready before them.
But when they had put away their desire for eating and drinking,
then Telemachos and the glorious son of Nestor
145 harnessed the horses and mounted up into the chariot bright with
bronze, and drove them out the front door and the echoing portico.
But fair-haired Menelaos the son of Atreus followed,
bearing in his right hand a golden cup that was filled with
wine as sweet as honey, so they could pour a libation
150 as they went. He stood before the chariot and spoke and pledged them:
'Farewell, young men; give my greeting to the shepherd of the people,
Nestor, for always he was kind to me like a father,
when we sons of the Achaians were fighting in Troy land.'
　　Then the thoughtful Telemachos said to him in answer:
155 'Surely, illustrious sir, when we arrive we shall tell him
all that you say, and I wish that even so I too, arriving
in Ithaka, could find Odysseus there in our palace,
and tell him I was returning from you, having had all loving
treatment, and bringing many excellent treasures given me.'
160 　　As he spoke a bird flew by on the right, an eagle
carrying in his talons a great white goose he had caught
tame from the yard, and all of them, men and women, with stopped
　　breath
followed his flight; but the eagle, as he approached them,
shot by on the right before the chariot, and they seeing
165 were filled with joy and the hearts in all of them were softened.
First of them to speak was Peisistratos, son of Nestor:
'Menelaos, illustrious, leader of the people, tell us
whether the god showed this sign for you, or was it for us two?'
　　So he spoke, and warlike Menelaos was pondering
170 how to speak his thoughts the right way and give them an answer;
but Helen of the light robes anticipated him, saying:
'Hear me! I shall be your prophet, the way the immortals
put it into my heart, and I think it will be accomplished.
As this eagle came down from the mountain, where was his origin
175 and parentage, and caught the goose that was nursed in the household,
so Odysseus, after wandering long and suffering
much, will come home and take revenge; or he is already

home, and making a plan of evil for all of the suitors.'
Then the thoughtful Telemachos said to her in answer:
180 'May Zeus, high thundering husband of Hera, so appoint it.
Then even at home I would make my prayers to you, as to a goddess.'
He spoke, and laid the lash on his horses, and they very quickly
and with eager spirit dashed away to the plain, through the city.
All day long they shook the yoke they wore on their shoulders.
185 And the sun set, and all the journeying ways were darkened.
They came to Pherai and reached the house of Diokles, who was
son of Ortilochos, whom Alpheios once had childed.
There they slept the night and he gave them hospitality.
But when the young Dawn showed again with her rosy fingers,
190 they yoked the horses again and mounted the chariots bright with
bronze, and drove them out the front door and the echoing portico,
and he whipped them into a run and they winged their way unreluctant.
Presently they approached the sheer citadel of Pylos,
and then Telemachos spoke a word to the son of Nestor:
195 'Son of Nestor, would you accept what I say and bring it
to pass? For you and I can avow ourselves friends forever
because of our fathers' love, and the two of us are the same age,
and this journey of ours will add to the feeling we have for each other.
Then do not take me, illustrious, past my ship, but leave me
200 there, for fear the old man in his affection will keep me
in his house longer than I wish. But I must make my way quickly.'
He spoke, and the son of Nestor pondered the thought within him,
how he could fairly undertake this and see it accomplished.
In the division of his heart this way seemed best to him.
205 He turned the horses toward the fast ship and the sand of the seashore,
and onto the stern of the ship unloaded the beautiful presents,
the clothing and the gold, which Menelaos had given,
and spoke, speeding him on his way, and addressed him in winged words:
'Go aboard now in haste, and urge on all your companions
210 to go, before I reach home and take the news to the old man.
For I know this thing well in my heart, and my mind knows it,
how overbearing his anger will be, and he will not let you
go, but will come himself to summon you, and I do not think
he will go away without you. As it is, he will be very angry.'
215 So he spoke, and drove away his bright-maned horses
back to the city of the Pylians, and reached his home quickly.

Encounter with a fugitive

Telemachos then gave the sign and urged his companions:
'Put all running gear in order, friends, on the black ship,
and let us ourselves go aboard, so we can get on with the journey.'
220   So he spoke, and they listened well to him and obeyed him,
and quickly they went aboard the ship and sat to the oarlocks.
So, while he was busy with prayer and sacrifice to Athene
beside the stern of the ship, there came to him an outlander
from Argos, where he had killed a man; now he was a fugitive.
225   He was a prophet, and by blood was of the stock of Melampous.
Melampous once had lived in Pylos, mother of sheepflocks,
a rich man among the Pylians, at home in his high house;
but then he came to the land of other men, fleeing his country
and great-hearted Neleus, the proudest of all men living,
230   who until a year was fulfilled kept much of his substance
by force, for Melampous meanwhile in the halls of Phylakos
was held in constraint of wearisome bondage, suffering strong pains
for the sake of Neleus' daughter, and the bitter infatuation
which the goddess Erinys, wrecker of houses, inflicted upon him.
235   Yet he escaped death, and drove away the loud-lowing cattle
from Phylake to Pylos, and achieved the unjust labor
godlike Neleus imposed on him, and led back the lady
to his brother's house; but he himself went to the land of others,
to horse-pasturing Argos, since now it was ordained for him
240   that he should live there and be lord over many Argives.
And there he too married a wife and established a high-roofed
house, and had children, Mantios and Antiphates, strong sons.
Antiphates had a son; this was great-hearted Oïkles.
His son was Amphiaraos, leader of storming armies,
245   whom Zeus of the aegis loved in his heart, as did Apollo,
with every favor, but he never came to the doorsill of old age,
but perished in Thebes, because his wife had been bribed with presents.
He in turn had sons, Amphilochos and Alkmaion.
The children born to Mantios were Polypheides and Kleitos,
250   but Dawn of the golden throne carried Kleitos away, because of
his beauty, so that he might dwell among the immortals;
but Apollo made high-hearted Polypheides a prophet,
and far the best among mortals, after Amphiaraos
had died. He, angered with his father, in Hyperesia
255   lived and was lord, and there he was a prophet for all men.

It was this man's son, by name Theoklymenos, who now
came to Telemachos and stood near, and there he found him
pouring libation and praying beside his fast black vessel.
He came and spoke to him aloud and addressed him in winged words:
260   'Dear friend, since I have found you in this place, making sacrifice,
I entreat you, first by these rites and spirit, then also
by your own head and by your companions, who travel with you,
tell me truly this thing that I ask you, and hold back nothing:
What man are you and whence? Where is your city? Your parents?'
265   Then the thoughtful Telemachos said to him in answer:
'Friend, I will accurately answer all that you ask me.
Ithaka is my country, and Odysseus is my father,
if ever he lived; but by now he must have died by a dismal
death. So, taking my black ship and with my companions,
270   I have come for news of my father who has been so long absent.'
Then godlike Theoklymenos said to him in answer:
'So I too am out of my country, because I have killed
a man of my tribe, but he had many brothers and relatives
in horse-pasturing Argos, with great power among the Achaians.
275   Avoiding death at the hands of these men and black doom, I am
a fugitive, since it is my fate to be a wanderer
among men. Give me a place in your ship, since I have come to you
as a suppliant, lest they kill me; for now I think they are after me.'
Then the thoughtful Telemachos said to him in answer:
280   'I will not willingly thrust you away from my balanced ship. Come, then,
with me. There you will be entertained, from what we have left.'
So Telemachos spoke, and took the bronze spear from him,
and laid it at length upon the deck of the oarswept vessel.
Then he himself mounted on board the seagoing vessel
285   and took his seat on the stern deck, and next him he seated
Theoklymenos, and now the men cast off the stern cables.
Telemachos then gave the sign and urged his companions
to lay hold of the tackle, and they listened to his urging,
and raising the mast pole made of fir they set it upright
290   in the hollow hole in the box, and made it fast with forestays,
and with halyards strongly twisted of leather pulled up the white sails.
The goddess gray-eyed Athene sent them a favoring stern wind
blustering stormily through the bright air, so that with all speed
the ship might run the whole of her course through the sea's salt water.

295 They ran past Krounoi, and past Chalkis on the fair waters.
And the sun set, and all the journeying ways were darkened.
Pressing on before the wind from Zeus, she ran past Pheai,
and on past shining Elis, where the Epeians are lords; then
Telemachos set her course over toward the Pointed Islands,
300 as he pondered whether he would escape death, or be captured.
But now in the shelter Odysseus and the noble swineherd
were eating their evening meal, and the rest of the men with them.
But when they had put away their desire for eating and drinking,
Odysseus spoke to them, making trial of the swineherd, to see
305 if he was truly his friend and would invite him to stay on
in his steading as he was, or would urge him to go to the city:
'Hear me now, Eumaios, and all you other companions.
I am very eager to make my way at dawn to the city
and beg there, so I will not wear you out, and your men. Only
310 advise me well, and send a good guide to go along with me
and see me there. Once in the town I must even go begging
in my need, for someone to hand me a bit of bread or a cupful.
Then I would go into the house of godlike Odysseus
with a message for circumspect Penelope, to tell her;
315 and I would mingle with the overbearing suitors, to see
if they, who have good things in great numbers, would give me a dinner.
Soon I would do good work for them, whatever they wanted.
For I tell you this, listen to me and understand me:
by grace of Hermes, the guide, who dispenses glory
320 and beauty upon the endeavors of all men, I am such a one
for work with my hands that no other man alive could compete
with me for building a good fire, for splitting up kindling,
for carving the meat or roasting the meat or filling the wine cups,
for all such work as meaner men bestow on their betters.'
325 Then, deeply troubled, you said to him, O swineherd Eumaios:
'O my guest, what is this idea that has come now into
your head? Are you utterly bent on achieving your own destruction
there, if you mean to lose yourself in that swarm of suitors
whose outrageous violence goes up into the iron
330 sky? For nothing like you are the serving men who work for them,
but young men, and well dressed in mantles and tunics, always
with neat oiled heads and handsome faces. These are the people
who serve under the suitors, and their well-polished tables

are heavily loaded with bread and meats and wine. No, rather
335   stay here. There is none here who is annoyed by your presence,
neither myself nor any companion whom I have with me.
When, however, the dear son of Odysseus comes back,
he will give you a mantle and tunic to wear as clothing,
and send you wherever your heart and spirit desire to be sent.'
340   Then much-enduring great Odysseus said to him in answer:
'I wish, Eumaios, you could be as dear to our father
Zeus as to me, since you stopped my wandering and my terrible
sorrow. There is nothing worse for mortal men than the vagrant
life, but still for the sake of the cursed stomach people
345   endure hard sorrows, when roving and pain and grief befall them.
But now, since you keep such a man as I am, and bid me stay here,
come then, tell me about the mother of godlike Odysseus,
and his father, whom when he went he left on the doorsill
of old age. Are they still alive in the beams of the sunlight,
350   or are they dead by now and gone to the house of Hades?'
    The swineherd, leader of men, then said to him in answer:
'So, my friend and guest, I will give you an accurate answer.
Laertes is still alive, but all the time he is praying
to Zeus that the spirit will leave his body in his own palace;
355   for terribly he mourns over the son who is absent,
and for his wedded virtuous wife, whose death has hurt him
more than all else, and gave him to a green untimely
old age. She died of grieving over her glorious son, by
a dismal death; I hope that no friend who lives here with me
360   dies such a death, nor any who does me the acts of friendship.
Now while she was still alive, in spite of her grieving,
it was my pleasure to try her out and to ask her questions,
because she brought me up along with her stately daughter,
Ktimene of the light robes, the youngest child. We two
365   grew up together, and I was only a little less favored.
But when we had both arrived at our lovely prime, they gave her
away for marriage, in Same, and for her were given numberless
gifts; but the lady gave me a mantle and tunic, excellent
clothing she put upon me, and giving me sandals for my feet
370   sent me to the estate. From the heart she loved me dearly.
Now I go lacking all these things, but the blessed immortals
prosper all the work that I myself do abiding

here, whence I eat and drink and give to people I honor;
but there is no sweet occasion now to hear from my mistress
375   in word or fact, since the evil has fallen upon our household,
these overbearing men, and greatly the serving people
miss the talk in their mistress' presence, the asking of questions
and eating and drinking there, then something to take home with them
to the country—which always warms the hearts of the serving people.'
380   Then resourceful Odysseus spoke in turn and answered him:
'You must have been very little then, O swineherd Eumaios,
when you wandered far away from your own country and your parents.
But come now, tell me this and give me an accurate answer.
Was there some storming of your wide-wayed city of people,
385   where your father and the lady your mother lived, or were you
caught alone beside your sheep and your cattle? And was it
enemy men who carried you in their ships and sold you
here in this man's house, being paid a fair price for you?'
     The swineherd, leader of men, then said to him in answer:
390   'My guest, since indeed you are asking me all these questions,
listen in silence and take your pleasure, and sit there drinking
your wine. These nights are endless, and a man can sleep through them,
or he can enjoy listening to stories, and you have no need
to go to bed before it is time. Too much sleep is only
395   a bore. And of the others, any one whose heart and spirit
urge him can go outside and sleep, and then, when the dawn shows,
breakfast first, then go out to tend the swine of our master.
But we two, sitting here in the shelter, eating and drinking,
shall entertain each other remembering and retelling
400   our sad sorrows. For afterwards a man who has suffered
much and wandered much has pleasure out of his sorrows.
So I will tell you now the answer to all your questions.
There is an island, called Syria, you may have heard of it,
lying above Ortygia, where the sun makes his turnings;
405   not so much a populous island, but a good one, good for
cattle and good for sheep, full of vineyards, and wheat raising.
No hunger ever comes on these people, nor any other
hateful sickness, of such as befall wretched humanity;
but when the generations of men grow old in the city,
410   Apollo of the silver bow, and Artemis with him,
comes with a visitation of painless arrows, and kills them.

There are two cities, and everything is divided between them,
and over both of these cities there was one king, my father,
Ktesios, Ormenos' son, in the likeness of the immortals.

415   'There came Phoenician men, famous seafarers, gnawers
at other men's goods, with countless pretty things stored in their black
      ship.
Now in my father's house there was a Phoenician woman,
both beautiful and tall, and skilled in glorious handiwork,
and yet these Phoenicians, subtle men in their talk, beguiled her.

420 First of all, when she went out washing, one of them lay with her
in love's embrace by the hollow ship, which for female women
is a heart's beguilement, even for the one who is a skilled worker.
Then he asked her who and whence she was. She readily
told them all about the high-roofed house of her father:

425 "I claim that I come from Sidon, rich in bronze; I am daughter
of Arybas, who has rivers of wealth, but men from Taphos,
pirates, caught me and carried me away as I came back
home from the fields, and carried me to this place and sold me
here in this man's house, being paid a fair price for me."

430   'Then the man who had lain with her secretly said to her:
"Would you then be willing to go back home again with us,
to see once more the high-roofed house of your father and mother
and themselves too? For they are still alive, and called wealthy."
    'Then in turn the woman answered them and said to them:

435 "That also could be done if you, sailors, were willing
to assure me by an oath that you would take me home safely."
    'So she spoke, and all of them swore to this, as she asked them.
But when they had sworn the oath, and made an end of their swearing,
then once again the woman spoke to them and said to them:

440 "Silence, now. None of your companions must say anything
to me, when he happens to meet me in the street, or else
perhaps at the spring; somebody might go to the house and tell it
to the old man, and he might be suspicious, and bind me
in painful bondage, and plan destruction against the rest of you.

445 But keep the word in your hearts, and get on with buying your homeward
cargo. But when your ship is loaded with goods, then let there
be someone sent to me at the house with word of it, quickly.
For I will bring you gold, whatever I can lay my hand on.
And there is another thing I would willingly give you, to pay for

and a treacherous nurse and sold

450 my way home. I am nurse to the man's son in his palace,
such a cunning child, as he runs around outside. If I
could take him aboard your ship, he would bring you a price beyond
    counting,
wherever you might sell him among alien-speaking people."
    'So she spoke, and went away back to the splendid palace,
455 and they, with their hollow ship, for the whole of a year remaining
in our country, traded and piled up much substance.
But when at last their hollow ship was loaded for sailing,
they sent their messenger, to bring the news to the woman.
There came a knowledgeable man to the house of my father,
460 with a golden necklace, and it was strung with pieces of amber.
Now in the hall the serving women with the lady my mother
were turning it in their hands and eying it and offering
to buy it, and the man nodded silently to the woman, then
after nodding to her he went away to the hollow
465 ship, and she took my hand and led me out of the palace.
There in the forecourt she came upon the cups and the tables
of men who had been feasting, associates of my father,
but these had gone to a session and debate of the people.
She snatched three goblets and hid them in the fold of her bosom,
470 and carried them off, and I in my innocence went with her.
And the sun set, and all the journeying ways were darkened.
Walking fast, we made our way to the glorious harbor,
where lay the fast-running ship of the men from Phoenicia.
They then putting out went over the ways of the water
475 after taking us aboard, and Zeus sent a wind to follow.
Thus it was that for six days, night and day, we sailed on,
but when Zeus, son of Kronos, had brought on the seventh
day, Artemis of the showering arrows struck down the woman,
and she dropped with a splash, like a diving tern, in the hull's bilge.
    They then
480 threw her overboard to be the spoil of the fishes
and seals, while I was left alone, heart full of sorrow;
and the wind and the current carried the men and brought them to Ithaka,
where Laertes bought me for himself with his own possessions.
Thus it was that I came to set eyes on this country.'
485   In turn illustrious Odysseus gave him an answer:
'Eumaios, you have deeply stirred the spirit within me

by telling me all these things, the sorrows your heart has suffered.
But beside the sorrow Zeus has placed some good for you, seeing
that after much suffering you came into the house of a kindly
490 man, who, as he ought to do, provides you with victuals
and drink, and the life you lead is a good one. But I come to you
only after much wandering in the cities of people.'
    So now these two were conversing thus with each other,
then slept, but not for very much time, only for a little,
495 since soon the glorious dawn came on. Ashore, Telemachos'
companions now loosened the sails, and took down the mast tree,
easily, and rowed her in with oars to the mooring.
They threw over the anchor stones and made fast the stern cables,
and themselves stepped out onto the break of the sea beach,
500 and then made ready their dinner, and mixed the bright wine with water.
But when they had put away their desire for eating and drinking,
then the thoughtful Telemachos began their discourse:
'The rest of you now take the black ship on to the city,
while I go out to visit the estate and the herdsmen.
505 In the evening, when I have looked at the holdings, I will come back
to town. I will set a good feast before you, meats and sweet-tasting
wine, to be my thanks for sharing the journey with me.'
    Then in turn godlike Theoklymenos said to him:
'Where shall I go then, dear child? Of the men who are lords here
510 in rocky Ithaka, who is there whose house I can visit?
Or shall I go straight to the house where you live, and to your mother?'
    Then the thoughtful Telemachos said to him in answer:
'Were things otherwise, indeed I would urge you to visit
our house; we lack no means as hosts, and yet for yourself
515 it would be worse, for I shall be absent, nor will my mother
see you; with suitors there in the house she does not often
appear, but stays in the upper room and works at her weaving.
But I will indicate another man you could go to,
Eurymachos, the glorious son of prudent Polybos,
520 whom now the people of Ithaka look on as on divinity,
since he is their best man by far, and is the most eager
to marry my mother and seize the rights and powers of Odysseus;
but Zeus the Olympian, dwelling in the high air, knows whether
the evil day will end him before he can make that marriage.'
525   As he spoke, a bird flew by on the right, a falcon,

swift messenger of Apollo, and in his claws he carried
a pigeon and tore at it so that a shower of feathers
drifted to the ground between the ship and Telemachos.
Theoklymenos called him away from his other companions
530 and took him by the hand and spoke and named him, saying:
'Telemachos, not without a god's will did this bird fly past you
on the right, for I knew when I saw it that it was a portent.
No other family shall be kinglier than yours in the country
of Ithaka, but you shall have lordly power forever.'
535 Then the thoughtful Telemachos said to him in answer:
'If only this word, stranger and guest, were brought to fulfillment,
soon you would be aware of my love and many gifts given
by me, so any man who met you would call you blessed.'
He spoke, and said a word to Peiraios, a faithful companion:
540 'Peiraios, son of Klytios, in other ways also you follow
my will, beyond the other friends who went with me to Pylos.
So now too take this guest home to your house and give him
his honor due and loving attention, until I come to you.'
So he spoke, and spear-famed Peiraios gave him an answer:
545 'Telemachos, even if you were to stay out there for a long time,
we shall lack no means as hosts to this man, and I shall look after him.'
So speaking he went aboard the ship and told his companions
also to go aboard, and to cast off the stern cables,
and quickly they went aboard the ships and sat to the oarlocks;
550 but under his feet Telemachos bound on his fair sandals,
and then caught up a powerful spear, edged with sharp bronze,
from the ship's deck, but the other men cast off the stern cables,
and pushed off and sailed away to the city, as they were asked to
by Telemachos, beloved son of godlike Odysseus.
555 He stepped out, and his feet took him swiftly, until he came to
the yard, where there were countless pigs, and near them always
slept the noble swineherd, with kind thoughts for his masters.

BOOK XVI

These two in the shelter, Odysseus and the noble
swineherd, stirred the fire at dawn, and arranged their breakfast,
and sent the herdsmen out with the pasturing pigs. At this time
the clamorous dogs came fawning around Telemachos, nor did
5   they bark at him as he came, and great Odysseus noticed
that the dogs were fawning; above them he heard the loud noise of
    footsteps.
Immediately he spoke in winged words to Eumaios:
'Eumaios, someone is on his way here who is truly
one of yours, or else well known, since the dogs are not barking
10 but fawning about him, and I can hear the thud of his footsteps.'
    His whole word had not been spoken when his beloved
son stood in the forecourt. Amazed, the swineherd started
up, and the vessels, where he had been busily mixing
the bright wine, fell from his hand. He came up to meet his master,
15 and kissed his head, and kissed too his beautiful shining
eyes, and both his hands, and the swelling tear fell from him.
And as a father, with heart full of love, welcomes his only
and grown son, for whose sake he has undergone many hardships
when he comes back in the tenth year from a distant country,
20 so now the noble swineherd, clinging fast to godlike
Telemachos, kissed him even as if he had escaped dying,
and in a burst of weeping he spoke to him in winged words:
'You have come, Telemachos, sweet light; I thought I would never

see you again, when you had gone in the ship to Pylos.

25   But come now into the house, dear child, so that I can pleasure
my heart with looking at you again when you are inside;
for you do not come very often to the estate and the herdsmen,
but you stay in town, since now it seems you are even minded
to face the deadly company of the lordly suitors.'

30   Then the thoughtful Telemachos said to him in answer:
'So it shall be, my father; but it was for your sake I came here,
to look upon you with my eyes, and to hear a word from you,
whether my mother endures still in the halls, or whether
some other man has married her, and the bed of Odysseus

35   lies forlorn of sleepers with spider webs grown upon it.'
Then in turn the swineherd, leader of men, said to him:
'All too much with enduring heart she does wait for him
there in your own palace, and always with her the wretched
nights and the days also waste her away with weeping.'

40   So he spoke, and took the bronze spear from him. Telemachos
then went inside and stepped over the sill of stone, and his father
Odysseus rose from his seat and yielded him place as he entered,
but Telemachos from the other side checked him and said to him:
'No, sit, my friend, and we shall find us another seat, here

45   in our own shelter; the man is here who will lay it for us.'
He spoke, and Odysseus went back again and sat down. The swineherd
strewed green brushwood and fleeces on the ground for him. There
the beloved son of Odysseus seated himself, and for them
the swineherd brought and set beside them platters of roasted

50   meat, which they had left over when they were eating earlier;
and hastily set bread by them, piling it in baskets,
and mixed the wine, as sweet as honey, in a bowl of ivy.
He himself sat down across from godlike Odysseus.
They put forth their hands to the good things that lay ready before them.

55   But when they had put away their desire for eating and drinking,
then at last Telemachos questioned the noble swineherd:
'Father, where did this stranger come from? How did the sailors
bring him to Ithaka? What men do they claim that they are?
For I do not think he could have traveled on foot to this country.'

60   Then, O swineherd Eumaios, you said to him in answer:
'So, my child, I will relate you the whole true story.
He announces himself by birth to be one from spacious

Crete, but his wanderings have wheeled him through many cities
of mortal men, for so the divinity spun his thread for him,
65 and now this time he has fled away off a ship of Thesprotian
men, and come to my steading. I put him into your hands now.
Do with him as you will. He names himself your suppliant.'
    Then the thoughtful Telemachos said to him in answer:
'Eumaios, this word you spoke hurt my heart deeply. For how
70 shall I take and entertain a stranger guest in my house?
I myself am young and have no faith in my hands' strength
to defend a man, if anyone else picks a quarrel with him;
and my mother's heart is divided in her, and ponders two ways,
whether to remain here with me, and look after the household,
75 keep faith with her husband's bed, and regard the voice of the people,
or go away at last with the best man of the Achaians
who pays her court in her palace, and brings her the most presents.
But as for this stranger, since it is your house he has come to,
I will give him a mantle and tunic to wear, fine clothing,
80 and give him sandals for his feet, a sword with two edges,
and send him wherever his heart and spirit desire to be sent.
Or if you will, keep him here in your steading and look after him,
and I will send the clothes out here, and all provisions
to eat, so he will not be hard on you, nor on your companions;
85 but I will not let him go down there and be where the suitors
are, for their outrageousness is too strong, and I fear
they may insult him, and that will be a hard sorrow upon me
and a difficult one for even a strong man to deal with
among too many of them, since they will be far the stronger.'
90   Then long-suffering great Odysseus spoke to him in answer:
'Dear friend, since in truth I am privileged to speak of this,
you eat away the dear heart in me, as I listen
to what you tell of the suitors and their reckless contrivings
inside your palace, against your will, when you are such a one
95 as you are. Tell me, are you willingly oppressed by them? Do the people
hate you throughout this place, swayed by some impulse given
from the gods? Do you find your brothers wanting? A man trusts
help from these in the fighting when a great quarrel arises.
I wish that I were truly as young as I am in spirit,
100 or a son of stately Odysseus were here, or he himself might
come in from his wandering. There is time still for hope. If such

things could be, another could strike my head from my shoulders
if I did not come as an evil thing to all those people
as I entered the palace of Odysseus, the son of Laertes.
105 And if I, fighting alone, were subdued by all their number,
then I would rather die, cut down in my own palace,
than have to go on watching forever these shameful activities,
guests being battered about, or to see them rudely mishandling
the serving women all about the beautiful palace,
110 to see them drawing the wine and eating up food in this utterly
reckless way, without end, forever and always at it.'
    Then the thoughtful Telemachos said to him in answer:
'So, my friend, I will tell you plainly the whole truth of it.
It is not that all the people hate me, nor are they angry,
115 nor is it that I find brothers wanting, whom a man trusts for
help in the fighting, whenever a great quarrel arises.
For so it is that the son of Kronos made ours a single
line. Arkeisios had only a single son, Laertes,
and Laertes had only one son, Odysseus; Odysseus in turn
120 left only one son, myself, in the halls, and got no profit
of me, and my enemies are here in my house, beyond numbering.
For all the greatest men who have the power in the islands,
in Doulichion and Same and in wooded Zakynthos,
and all who in rocky Ithaka are holders of lordships,
125 all these are after my mother for marriage, and wear my house out.
And she does not refuse the hateful marriage, nor is she able
to make an end of the matter; and these eating up my substance
waste it away; and soon they will break me myself to pieces.
Yet all these are things that are lying upon the gods' knees.
130 Father Eumaios, go quickly now, and tell the circumspect
Penelope that I am safe and have come from Pylos.
I myself will stay here. You go there quickly, and give this
message to her alone, and let no other Achaian
hear it; for there are many there who are plotting against me.'
135   Then, O swineherd Eumaios, you said to him in answer:
'I see, I understand; you speak to one who follows you.
But come now, tell me this and give me an accurate answer.
Shall I on the same errand go with the news to wretched
Laertes, who while he so greatly grieved for Odysseus
140 yet would look after his farm and with the thralls in his household

would eat and drink, whenever the spirit was urgent with him;
but now, since you went away in the ship to Pylos,
they say he has not eaten in this way, nor drunk anything,
nor looked to his farm, but always in lamentation and mourning
145 sits grieving, and the flesh on his bones is wasting from him.'
Then the thoughtful Telemachos said to him in answer:
'Though it hurts the more, we shall let him be, for all our sorrow.
For if it were somehow given to mortals to have their choosing
in all things, we should choose my father's day of homecoming.
150 But you, when you have given your message, come back and do not
go off to the estate to see him, but tell my mother
to tell the servant who is housekeeper to go there swiftly
and secretly, and she can give the news to the old man.'
He spoke, and started the swineherd, who in his hands took up
155 his sandals and tied them on his feet to start for the city.
Nor was Athene unaware that Eumaios the swineherd
had left the steading, but she came near, likened to a woman
beautiful and tall, and skilled in glorious handiwork,
and stood in the forecourt of the shelter, seen by Odysseus.
160 But Telemachos did not look her way nor did he perceive her;
for the gods do not show themselves in this way to everyone;
but Odysseus saw her and the dogs did; they were not barking,
but cowered away, whimpering, to the other side of the shelter.
She nodded to him with her brows, and noble Odysseus
165 saw her, and came from the house, outside the great wall of the courtyard,
and stood in her presence. Then Athene spoke to him, saying:
'Son of Laertes and seed of Zeus, resourceful Odysseus,
it is time now to tell your son the story; no longer
hide it, so that, contriving death and doom for the suitors,
170 you two may go to the glorious city. I myself shall not
be long absent from you in my eagerness for the fighting.'
So spoke Athene, and with her golden wand she tapped him.
First she made the mantle and the tunic that covered
his chest turn bright and clean; she increased his strength and stature.
175 His dark color came back to him again, his jaws firmed,
and the beard that grew about his chin turned black. Athene
went away once more, having done her work, but Odysseus
went back into the shelter. His beloved son was astonished
and turned his eyes in the other direction, fearing this must be

180 a god, and spoke aloud to him and addressed him in winged words:
'Suddenly you have changed, my friend, from what you were formerly;
your skin is no longer as it was, you have other clothing.
Surely you are one of the gods who hold the high heaven.
Be gracious, then: so we shall give you favored offerings

185 and golden gifts that have been well wrought. Only be merciful.'
    Then in turn long-suffering great Odysseus answered him:
'No, I am not a god. Why liken me to the immortals?
But I am your father, for whose sake you are always grieving
as you look for violence from others, and endure hardships.'

190   So he spoke, and kissed his son, and the tears running
down his cheeks splashed on the ground. Until now, he was always
      unyielding.
But Telemachos, for he did not yet believe that this was
his father, spoke to him once again in answer, saying:
'No, you are not Odysseus my father, but some divinity

195 beguiles me, so that I must grieve the more, and be sorry.
For no man who was mortal could ever have so contrived it
by his own mind alone, not unless some immortal, descending
on him in person, were lightly to make him a young or an old man.
For even now you were an old man in unseemly clothing,

200 but now you resemble one of the gods who hold wide heaven.'
    Then resourceful Odysseus spoke in turn and answered him:
'Telemachos, it does not become you to wonder too much
at your own father when he is here, nor doubt him. No other
Odysseus than I will ever come back to you. But here I am,

205 and I am as you see me, and after hardships and suffering
much I have come, in the twentieth year, back to my own country.
But here you see the work of Athene, the giver of plunder,
who turns me into whatever she pleases, since she can do this;
and now she will make me look like a beggar, but then the next time

210 like a young man, and wearing splendid clothes on my body;
and it is a light thing for the gods who hold wide heaven
to glorify any mortal man, or else to degrade him.'
    So he spoke, and sat down again, but now Telemachos
folded his great father in his arms and lamented,

215 shedding tears, and desire for mourning rose in both of them;
and they cried shrill in a pulsing voice, even more than the outcry
of birds, ospreys or vultures with hooked claws, whose children

were stolen away by the men of the fields, before their wings grew
strong; such was their pitiful cry and the tears their eyes wept.
220 And now the light of the sun would have set on their crying,
had not Telemachos spoken a quick word to his father:
'What kind of ship was it, father dear, in which the sailors
brought you to Ithaka? What men do they claim that they are?
For I do not think you could have traveled on foot to this country.'
225   Then long-suffering great Odysseus said to him in answer:
'So, my child, I will tell you all the truth. The Phaiakians
famed for seafaring brought me here, and they carry other
people as well, whoever may come into their country.
They brought me sleeping in their fast ship over the open
230 sea, and set me down in Ithaka, and gave me glorious
gifts, abundant bronze and gold and woven apparel.
All this, by the gods' grace, is lying stored in the caverns.
But now I have come to this place by the advice by Athene,
so we together can make our plans to slaughter our enemies.
235 Come then, tell me the number of suitors, and tell me about them,
so I can know how many there are, and which men are of them;
and then, when I have pondered it in my faultless mind, I can
decide whether we two alone will be able to face them
without any help, or whether we must go looking for others.'
240   Then the thoughtful Telemachos said to him in answer:
'Oh, father, I have always heard of your great fame, and how
you were a fighting man with your hands, and prudent in counsel;
but what you have spoken of is too big; I am awed; for it could not
be that two men could fight against strong men in these numbers.
245 The suitors are no simple number of ten, nor twice that,
but far more than that. Even now you shall hear the number
of those that are here. From Doulichion there are two and fifty
young men, choice men, and there are six thralls of their following;
the number of men come from Same is four and twenty,
250 and from Zakynthos there are twenty sons of the Achaians.
From Ithaka itself there are twelve, and all of their best men,
and Medon the herald is with them, and the divine singer,
and there are two henchmen with them, both skilled in carving. If we
set ourselves to fight against all who are in the palace,
255 I fear your revenge on their violence may be grim and bitter
for us. Then, if you can think of anyone to stand by us

and with forthright spirit be our protector, speak of him to me.'
    Then in turn long-suffering great Odysseus answered him:
'So, then, I will tell you. Hear me and understand me

260 and consider whether Athene with Zeus father helping will be
enough for us, or whether I must think of some other helper.'
    Then the thoughtful Telemachos said to him in answer:
'Those indeed are two excellent helpers you name to me, even
though they sit high away in the clouds, for they have power

265 over others besides, over mortal men and the gods immortal.'
    Then in turn long-suffering great Odysseus answered him:
'These are two who will not for a long time stay far off
from the strong battle, at that time when the War God's decision
is fought out in our halls between ourselves and the suitors.

270 But now, as for you, you must make your way, when dawn shows,
back to our house, and be with the group of insolent suitors.
At a later time the swineherd shall take me to the city,
and I shall look like a dismal vagabond, and an old man.
But if they maltreat me within the house, then let the dear heart

275 in you even endure it, though I suffer outrage, even
if they drag me by the feet through the palace to throw me out of it,
or pelt me with missiles; you must still look on and endure it;
though indeed you may speak to them with soft words and entreat them
to give over their mad behavior, but still they will never

280 listen to you, for the day of their destiny stands near them.
And put away in your heart this other thing that I tell you.
When Athene, lady of many counsels, puts it into
my mind, I will nod my head to you, and when you perceive it,
take all the warlike weapons which are stored in the great hall,

285 and carry them off and store them away in the inward corner
of the high chamber; and when the suitors miss them and ask you
about them, answer and beguile them with soft words, saying:
"I stored them away out of the smoke, since they are no longer
like what Odysseus left behind when he went to Troy land,

290 but are made foul, with all the smoke of the fire upon them.
Also, the son of Kronos put into my head this even
greater thought, that with the wine in you, you might stand up
and fight, and wound each other, and spoil the feast and the courting,
since iron all of itself works on a man and attracts him."

295 But leave behind, for you and me alone, a pair each

of swords and spears, and a pair of oxhide shields, to take up
in our hands, and wield them, and kill these men; and Zeus of the
    counsels
and Pallas Athene will be there to maze the wits in them.
And put away in your heart this other thing that I tell you.
300   If truly you are my own son, and born of our own blood,
then let nobody hear that Odysseus is in the palace;
let not Laertes hear of it, neither let the swineherd;
let no one in the household know, not even Penelope
herself; you and I alone will judge the faith of the women,
305   and, besides these, we can make trial of the serving men, to see
whether any of them is true to us and full of humility,
or whether one cares nothing for you, and denies your greatness.'
    Then in answer again his glorious son said to him:
'Father, I think you will learn what my spirit is like, when the time
    comes,
310   for the mood that is in my mind shows no slackening; only
I think in what you propose there will be no profit for either
of us, and I urge you to think well about it. You would
be going about our holdings, testing and learning the nature
of man after man, while they at their ease in the palace
315   overbearingly consume our goods, and spare nothing.
And yet I do urge you to find out about the women,
which of them care nothing for you, and which are innocent;
but I myself would not wish that we should go out to the steadings
to test the men, but this is a task to be left for later,
320   if truly you have been given some sign from Zeus of the aegis.'
    Now as these two were conversing thus with each other,
the well-made vessel which had carried Telemachos, together
with his companions, from Pylos, now came in to Ithaka.
They, when they were inside the many-hollowed harbor,
325   hauled the black-hulled ship onto the dry land, high up,
and their high-hearted henchmen carried their armor for them,
and took the beautiful presents to the house of Klytios.
But they sent a herald on his way to the house of Odysseus
to take a message to circumspect Penelope, saying
330   Telemachos was in the country now, but had told them to sail
the ship back to the city, so the magnificent queen would not
be terrified within her heart, and shed the soft tears.

from their futile ambush

The two of them met, the herald and noble swineherd, going
by reason of the same message, to report to the lady.
335 But when they had come to the house of the sacred king, the herald
stood in the midst of the serving maids and delivered his message:
'Now, O queen, your beloved son is back in this country.'
But the swineherd stood very close to Penelope and told her
all the message that her beloved son had entrusted
340 to him to tell, but when he had given her all the message,
he went back to his pigs, leaving the palace and courtyard.
      But the hearts of the suitors were disturbed and discouraged. They
            went
out of the palace and stood by the great wall of the courtyard,
and there in front of the palace gates they held an assembly.
345 First of them to speak was Eurymachos, son of Polybos:
'Friends, this is a monstrous thing, this voyage made by Telemachos
and insolently put through. We thought he would never achieve it.
But come, let us drag a black ship, our best one, down to the water,
and assemble sailors to row it, who can with all speed carry
350 the message to give to our others and tell them to come home quickly.'
      He had not yet said all before Amphinomos, turning
from his place, saw the ship inside the depths of the harbor,
and they had the oars now in their hands and were taking the sails down.
He laughed out sweetly and spoke a word then to his companions:
355 'We need send them no message now. Here they are, inside.
Either some god told it to them, or they themselves saw
the other ship pass by, and they were not able to catch her.'
      He spoke, and they stood up and went down to the sand of the
            seashore,
and others hauled their black-hulled ship up onto the dry land,
360 and their high-hearted henchmen carried their armor for them.
They went in a throng to the assembly, nor did they suffer
any of the young men or any of the elders to sit with them.
Thereupon Antinoös, son of Eupeithes, addressed them:
'It is shameful how the gods got this man clear of misfortune.
365 In the daytime we sat watchful along the windy headlands,
always succeeding each other, but when the sun set, we never
lay through the night on the dry land, but always on the open
water, cruising in a fast ship, we waited for the divine dawn,
watching to ambush Telemachos, so that we could cut him

370   off; but all the time some divinity brought him home. Therefore,
we who are here must make our plans for the grim destruction
of Telemachos, so he cannot escape us; since I have no thought
we can get our present purpose accomplished while he is living.
For he himself is understanding in thought and counsel,
375   and the people here no longer show us their entire favor.
But come now, before he can gather the Achaians and bring them
to assembly; for I think he will not let us go, but work out
his anger, and stand up before them all and tell them
how we designed his sudden murder, but we could not catch him;
380   and they will have no praise for us when they hear of our evil
deeds, and I fear they will work some evil on us, and drive us
from our own country, so we must make for another community;
then let us surprise him and kill him, in the fields away from the city,
or in the road, and ourselves seize his goods and possessions,
385   dividing them among ourselves fairly, but give his palace
to his mother to keep and to the man who marries her. Or else,
if what I say is not pleasing to you, but you are determined
to have him go on living and keep his father's inheritance,
then we must not go on gathering here and abundantly eating
390   away his fine substance, but from his own palace each man
must strive to win her with gifts of courtship; she will then marry
the man she is fated to have, and who brings her the greatest presents.'
      So he spoke, and all of them stayed stricken to silence.
Now Amphinomos spoke forth and addressed them. He was
395   the shining son of Nisos, son of the lord Aretiades,
and led those suitors who had come over from the abundant
grasslands and grainlands of Doulichion, and pleased Penelope
more than the others in talk, for he had good sense and discretion.
He in kind intention toward all spoke forth and addressed them:
400   'Dear friends, I for my part would not be willing to murder
Telemachos; it is terrible to kill one of royal
blood; we should first have to ask the gods for their counsel.
Then, if the ordinances of great Zeus approve of it,
I myself would kill him and tell all others to do so;
405   but I say we must give it up, if the gods deny us.'
      So Amphinomos spoke, and his word was acceptable to them.
Then they stood up at once and went into the house of Odysseus,
and entering they found their polished chairs, and were seated.

But now circumspect Penelope thought of her next move,
410   to show herself to her overbearingly violent suitors;
for she had heard how they had planned her son's death in the palace.
The herald, Medon, who overheard their planning, had told her.
She went with her attendant women into the great hall.
But when she, shining among women, came to the suitors,
415   she stood by the pillar that supported the roof with its joinery,
holding her shining veil in front of her face to shield it,
and spoke a word of reproach to Antinoös, naming him:
'Antinoös, violent man, deviser of evil: in Ithaka
the common account says you are the best man among your age mates
420   for speech and counsel. But you have never been such. Oh, boisterous
creature, why do you weave a design of death and destruction
for Telemachos, and take no heed of suppliants, over whom
Zeus stands witness? It is not right to plan harm for each other.
Do you not know how your father came here once, a fugitive
425   in fear of the people? These were terribly angered with him,
because he had thrown in his lot with the pirate Taphians
and harried the Thesprotians, and these were friends of our people.
They wanted to waste him away, to break the dear heart in him,
to eat up his substance and abundant livelihood. Only
430   Odysseus stayed their hand and held them, for all their fury.
Now you eat up his house without payment, pay court to his wedded
wife, try to murder his son, and do me great indignity.
I tell you to stop it, and ask the others to do so likewise.'
    Eurymachos the son of Polybos spoke then answering:
435   'Daughter of Ikarios, circumspect Penelope,
do not fear. Never let your heart be troubled for these things.
The man is not living, nor will there be one, nor can there ever
be one, who shall lay hands upon your son, Telemachos,
as long as I am alive on earth and look on the daylight.
440   For I tell you this straight out, and it will be a thing accomplished:
instantly his own black blood will stain my spear point.
My own spear; since often Odysseus, sacker of cities,
would seat me also upon his knees, and put pieces of roasted
meat in my hands, and hold the red wine out to me. Therefore,
445   of all men Telemachos is the dearest to me
by far, and I tell him to go in no fear of destruction
from the suitors. But if it comes from the gods, there is no escaping it.'

So he spoke, encouraging her, but himself was planning
the murder. She went back to the shining upper chamber
450 and wept for Odysseus, her dear husband, until the gray-eyed
goddess Athene drifted a sweet sleep over her eyelids.
   With the evening, the noble swineherd came back to Odysseus
and his son. Then they stood over the evening meal to prepare it,
and dedicated a year-old sow; but meanwhile Athene
455 had come and stood close by Odysseus, son of Laertes,
and tapped him with her wand and made him once more an old man,
and put foul clothing upon his skin, for fear the swineherd
might recognize him, face to face, and go with the message
to circumspect Penelope, and not keep fast the secret.
460   Now Telemachos was the first who spoke a word to him:
'So, noble Eumaios, you have come. And what was the rumor
in the town? Are the haughty suitors now back from their ambush,
or are they still lying in wait for me on my homeward journey?'
   Then, O swineherd Eumaios, you said to him in answer:
465 'It was not on my mind to go down through the city, nor to ask,
nor try to find out; rather the will was urgent within me
to speak my message with all speed and be on my way back here.
But one of your fellows as a swift messenger joined my company,
the herald; he was the first who told the word to your mother.
470 But here is another thing I know; with my eyes I saw it.
I was above the city, where the Hill of Hermes is, making
my way along, when I saw a fast vessel coming into
our harbor, making inshore, and many men were aboard her,
and she was loaded with shields and leaf-headed spears. Then I thought
475 that these would be the men we mean, but I do not know it.'
   So he spoke, and Telemachos, the hallowed prince, smiled
as he caught his father's eye, but avoided the eyes of the swineherd.
   They, when they had finished their work and got their feast ready,
feasted, nor was any man's hunger denied a fair portion.
480 But when they had put away their desire for eating and drinking,
they thought of going to bed, and accepted the gift of slumber.

BOOK XVII

But when the young Dawn showed again with her rosy fingers,
Telemachos, beloved son of godlike Odysseus,
  then bound underneath his feet the beautiful sandals,
  and took up a powerful spear which fitted his hand's grip,
5 on his way to the city, and going he spoke to his swineherd:
  'Father, I am going to the city, so that my mother
  will see me, since as I suppose she will never give over
  that bitter lamentation of hers and her tearful crying
  until she sees me myself. But here is what I will tell you
10 to do; take this unhappy stranger to the city, so that
  there he can beg his dinner, and any who will can give him
  his bit of bread and his cupful; it is not for me to put up with
  everybody, now when I have troubles on my mind. Therefore,
  even if the stranger is terribly angry, it will be only
15 the worse for him. Speaking the truth is the way I like best.'
    Then resourceful Odysseus spoke in turn and answered him:
  'Dear friend, neither do I desire that he should detain me
  here; a beggar is better begging his dinner in the city
  than in the country. Whoever wants to will give me something;
20 for I am no longer the right age to stay on the farms, the right age
  to carry out any task the foreman imposes on me.
  Go on then. This man, the one you have asked, will take me,
  as soon as I have warmed myself by the fire and there is some
  sunlight; these clothes are very poor, and I hope no morning

---

25 frost undoes me. They say it is very far to the city.'
  So he spoke, but Telemachos strode out through the steading,
  walking fast, and planning evil things for the suitors.
  But when he had arrived at the well-settled house, he carried
  his spear over to a tall column, and propped it against it,
30 and he himself went inside, stepping over the stone threshold.
  Far the first to see him was his nurse, Eurykleia,
  as she spread the fleeces on the elaborate chairs. She burst out
  in tears, and went straight to him, and around him the other
  serving maids of patient-hearted Odysseus clustered,
35 and made much of him, and kissed him on his head and his shoulders.
  But now circumspect Penelope came down from her chamber,
  looking like Artemis, or like golden Aphrodite,
  and burst into tears, and threw her arms around her beloved
  son, and kissed him on his head and both of his shining
40 eyes, and tearfully spoke winged words and addressed him:
  'You have come, Telemachos, sweet light, and I thought I would never
  see you again, when you had gone in the ship to Pylos
  secretly, and against my will, for news of the father
  you love. But come now, tell me what sights you have been seeing.'
45 Then the thoughtful Telemachos said to her in answer:
  'Mother, do not stir up a scene of sorrow, nor trouble
  my heart once more, now I have escaped from sheer destruction;
  but go, wash with water and put clean clothing upon your body,
  and going on to the upper story with your attendant
50 women, vow to all the gods the service of complete
  hecatombs, if Zeus grants requital for what is done to us.
  But I will go to the place of meeting, so I can summon
  my guest, who came along with me as I made my way here.
  I sent him on ahead of me with my godlike companions,
55 and told Peiraios to take him to his own house, and give him
  forthright honor and entertainment, until my arrival.'
  So he spoke, and she had no winged words for an answer,
  and she washed with water and put clean clothing upon her body,
  and vowed to all the gods the service of complete hecatombs,
60 if Zeus were to grant requital for what had been done to them.
  Telemachos then went striding out through the palace, and left it,
  holding his spear, and a pair of light-footed dogs went with him.
  Athene drifted an enchantment of grace upon him,

and all the people had their eyes on him as he came on.
65 Around him the haughty suitors clustered. They all were speaking
him fair, but in the deep of their hearts were devising evils.
Telemachos himself avoided their crowding numbers,
and where Mentor was sitting, and Antiphos and Halitherses,
the men who from the first had been his father's companions,
70 there he went and sat down, and they questioned him about everything.
Now Peiraios the famous spearman came near them, bringing
the guest through the city to the assembly, nor did Telemachos
stay for long far away from the guest, but came and stood by him.
First of the two to speak was Peiraios, who then said to him:
75 'Telemachos, have your women come to my house with all speed,
so I can send back the gifts which Menelaos has given you.'
    Then the thoughtful Telemachos said to him in answer:
'Peiraios, since we do not know how all this will come out,
or whether the haughty suitors will kill me here in my palace
80 treacherously, and divide up all my father's possessions,
I wish that you yourself, or one of these men, should keep them,
and have the profit. But if I can plot their death and destruction,
bring them to my house; and there will be gratitude shown on both sides.'
    So he spoke, and led the long-suffering stranger back to
85 his house. And when they had arrived at the well-settled palace,
they laid down their mantles along the chairs and the benches,
and stepped into the bathtubs, smooth-polished, and bathed there.
Then, when the maids had bathed them and anointed them with oil,
and put cloaks of thick fleece and tunics upon them, they went
90 forth from the bathing tubs, and took their places on settles.
A maidservant brought water for them and poured it from a splendid
and golden pitcher, holding it above a silver basin
for them to wash, and she pulled a polished table before them.
A grave housekeeper brought in the bread and served it to them,
95 adding many good things to it, generous with her provisions.
His mother sat opposite beside the pillar supporting
the hall, sitting back on a chair and turning fine yarn on a distaff.
They put forth their hands to the good things that lay ready before them.
But when they had put away their desire for eating and drinking,
100 it was circumspect Penelope who began their discourse:
'Telemachos, I will go back now to my upper chamber,
and lie down on my bed, which is made sorrowful, always

disordered with the tears I have wept, ever since Odysseus
went with the sons of Odysseus to Troy; and you had no patience
105 to tell me—before the haughty suitors arrive at our palace—
any news you may have heard of your father's homecoming.'
Then the thoughtful Telemachos said to her in answer:
'Then, my mother, I will tell you the whole true story.
We went to Pylos, and to Nestor, shepherd of the people,
110 and he, in his high house, gave me hospitality, and loving
free attention, as a father would to his own beloved
son, who was newly arrived from a long voyage elsewhere. So he
freely took care of me, with his own glorious children.
But he said he had heard nothing about enduring Odysseus,
115 nor whether he was alive or dead, from any of the peoples
of earth. He sent me to Atreus' son, spear-famed Menelaos,
giving me passage with his own horses and compact chariot.
There I saw Helen of Argos, for whose sake Argives and Trojans
had undergone much hardship by the gods' will. Menelaos
120 of the great war cry questioned me, when I came to him,
and asked what need had brought me to glorious Lakedaimon;
whereupon I told him the whole truth of my story,
and he in turn spoke to me then and gave me an answer:
"Oh, for shame, it was in the bed of a bold and strong man
125 they wished to lie, they themselves being all unwarlike.
As when a doe has brought her fawns to the lair of a lion,
and put them there to sleep, they are newborn and still suckling,
then wanders out into the foothills and the grassy corners,
grazing there, but now the lion comes back to his own lair
130 and visits a shameful destruction on both mother and children;
so now Odysseus will visit shameful destruction on these men.
O father Zeus and Athene and Apollo, I wish that
as he was when, upon a time, in strong-founded Lesbos
he stood up and wrestled Philomeleides from a challenge,
135 and threw him strongly, so delighting all the Achaians;
I wish that such an Odysseus would come now among the suitors.
They all would find death was quick and marriage a painful matter.
But for what you entreat me for and ask me about, I will not
turn away from the tale and speak idly, nor will I deceive you,
140 but of what the ever-truthful Old Man of the Sea told me,
I will tell you all without concealment, and hold back nothing.

He said he had seen him on an island, suffering strong pains
in the palace of the nymph Kalypso, and she detains him,
by constraint, and he cannot make his way to his country;
145   for he has not any ships by him, nor any companions
who can convey him back across the sea's wide ridges."
So spoke Atreus' son, spear-famed Menelaos. After
I had done all this I came back. The immortals gave me a following
wind, and brought me quickly to the dear land of my fathers.'
150   So he spoke, and stirred the spirit within her. And now
Theoklymenos, a godlike man, spoke to both of them:
'O respected wife of Odysseus, son of Laertes,
attend my word, because he does not understand clearly,
but I shall prophesy truly to you, and hold back nothing.
155   Zeus be my witness, first of the gods, and the table of friendship,
and the hearth of blameless Odysseus, to which I come as a suppliant,
that Odysseus is already here in the land of his fathers,
sitting still or advancing, learning of all these evil
actions, and devising evils for all of the suitors.
160   Such was the bird sign I interpreted, and I told it
to Telemachos, as I sat aboard the strong-benched vessel.'
       Then in turn circumspect Penelope answered him:
'If only this word, stranger and guest, were brought to fulfillment,
soon you would be aware of my love and many gifts given
165   by me, so any man who met you would call you blessed.'
       So now these three were conversing thus with each other,
but meanwhile before the palace of Odysseus the suitors
amused themselves with discs and with light spears for throwing,
on a leveled floor, unruly men, as they always had been.
170   But when it was time for dinner, and the sheep from the fields had been
          coming
in from all sides, and the same men as usual drove them,
then Medon spoke to the suitors. It was he among all the heralds
whom they liked best, and he used to wait on them at their feasting:
'Young men, since you have all taken your pleasure in exercise,
175   go on into the house so we can make dinner ready.
Nothing is any the worse when meals are taken in season.'
       He spoke, and they stood up and went, and did as he told them;
and they, when they had gone into the well-settled palace,
laid their mantles down along the chairs and the benches,

180 and set about sacrificing great-sized sheep, and fat goats,
and sacrificing an ox of the herd, and fattened porkers,
as they prepared their feast. But Odysseus now and the noble
swineherd were stirring themselves to go to town from the country.
First of the two to speak was the swineherd, leader of people:

185 'Stranger, since then you are eager to go to the city
today, as my master told you to do, though I could have wanted
you rather to stay here and guard the steading—even so
I go in awe of him and fear him, and any reproaches
he might give me; a scolding comes hard from a master—so then,

190 let us be on our way, for most of the day is already
gone. The evening is coming on. You may find it colder.'
Then resourceful Odysseus spoke in turn and answered him:
'I see, I understand. You speak to one who follows you.
But let us be on our way. You be my guide on the journey.

195 Only give me some kind of cudgel, if you have any
cut, to lean on. They say the road is very slippery.'
    He spoke, and over his shoulder slung the ugly wallet
that was full of holes, with a twist of rope attached to dangle it.
Eumaios gave him a walking stick that suited his fancy,

200 and the two of them went on, with the dogs and the herdsman staying
behind to guard the farm. He led his lord to the city,
looking as he did like a dismal vagabond and an old man,
propping on a stick, and wore wretched clothing upon his body.
    Now as they went down over the stony road, and were coming

205 close to the city, and had arrived at the fountain, sweet-running
and made of stone; and there the townspeople went for their water;
Ithakos had made this, and Neritos, and Polyktor;
and around it was a grove of black poplars, trees that grow by
water, all in a circle, and there was cold water pouring

210 down from the rock above; over it had been built an altar
of the nymphs, and there all the wayfarers made their sacrifice;
there Melanthios, son of Dolios, came upon them
as he drove his goats, the ones that were finest among his goatflocks,
for the suitors' dinner, and two other herdsmen went along with him.

215 Seeing the two he spoke and named them, giving them curses
overbearing and shameful, and stirred the heart of Odysseus:
'See now how the rascal comes on leading a rascal
about; like guides what is like itself, just as a god does.

on their way to town

Where, you detestable swineherd, are you taking this wretched
220 man, this bothersome beggar who spoils the fun of the feasting,
the kind who stands and rubs his shoulders on many doorposts,
begging only for handouts, never for swords or caldrons.
If you would turn him over to me to keep my steading,
then he could drink whey and build up a big leg muscle,
225 sweeping my pens, and carrying green stuff in to the young goats.
But since he has learned nothing but mischief, he will not be willing
to go to work, but would rather go begging all through the district,
asking for handouts and feeding up his bottomless belly.
But I tell you this straight out and it will be a thing accomplished.
230 If he ever comes near the house of godlike Odysseus,
his ribs and head will feel the weight of plenty of footstools
flung at him all over the house by the hands of heroes.'
   So he spoke, and as he went by recklessly lashed out
with his heel to the hip, but failed to knock him out of the pathway,
235 for Odysseus stood it, unshaken, while he pondered within him
whether to go for him with his cudgel, and take the life from him,
or pick him up like a jug and break his head on the ground. Yet
still he stood it, and kept it all inside him. The swineherd
stared, and cursed him, and prayed aloud with his hands uplifted:
240 'Nymphs of the fountain, daughters of Zeus, if ever Odysseus
burned for you the thigh pieces of lambs or goats, wrapping them
in the rich fat, then grant me this favor I ask for, namely
that the man himself will come home, with the divinity guiding him;
so, Melanthios, he would send flying all those glories
245 you wear now in your insolence, forever loitering
here in the town, while useless herdsmen ruin the sheepflocks.'
   Then in turn Melanthios the goatherd answered him:
'Shame on the speaking of this nasty-minded dog. Some day
I will get him aboard a strong-benched ship, and take him
250 far from Ithaka, where he could win me a good livelihood.
If only Apollo, silver-bowed, would strike down Telemachos
today in his halls, or he were killed by the suitors, as surely
as Odysseus, far away, has lost his day of homecoming.'
   So he spoke, and left them there, as they went on easily;
255 but he went forward, and quickly came to the house of his master.
He went straight on inside, and sat down next to the suitors,
opposite Eurymachos, whom he was fondest of. The servants

doing the dinner placed a portion of meat before him.
A grave housekeeper brought the bread and set it down for him
260 to eat. Odysseus, on his way with the noble swineherd,
stood close in front of the house, and around them came the clamor
of the hollow lyre, for Phemios had struck up the music
to sing. Odysseus took the swineherd's hand, and said to him:
'Eumaios, surely this is the handsome house of Odysseus.
265 Easily it is singled out and seen among many,
for one part is joined on to another, and the courtyard is worked on
with wall and copings, and the doors have been well made, with double
panels. Nobody could belittle this house. And also
I realize that many men are holding a feast there,
270 for the smell of the food comes to me, and there is the clamor
of the lyre, which the gods made to be companion of feasting.'
        Then, O swineherd Eumaios, you said to him in answer:
'Easily you perceived it, nor are you otherwise without
sense; but come, let us think out how we will act in these matters.
275 Either you go on first into the well-settled palace,
and go among the suitors, and leave me here on the outside;
or if you will, stay here, while I go on ahead of you.
But do not be slow, or someone here outside, seeing you,
might strike you, or throw something. Here, I bid you be careful.'
280   Then much-enduring great Odysseus said to him in answer:
'I see, I understand; you speak to one who follows you.
But you go on ahead, and I will stay here on the outside.
I am not unfamiliar with blows, and things thrown at me.
The spirit in me is enduring, since I have suffered much hardship
285 on the waves and in the fighting; so let this adventure follow.
Even so, there is no suppressing the ravenous belly,
a cursed thing, which bestows many evils on men, seeing
that even for its sake the strong-built ships are handled
across the barren great sea, bringing misfortune to enemies.'
290   Now as these two were conversing thus with each other,
a dog who was lying there raised his head and ears. This was
Argos, patient-hearted Odysseus' dog, whom he himself
raised, but got no joy of him, since before that he went to sacred
Ilion. In the days before, the young men had taken him
295 out to follow goats of the wild, and deer, and rabbits;
but now he had been put aside, with his master absent,

and lay on the deep pile of dung, from the mules and oxen,
which lay abundant before the gates, so that the servants
of Odysseus could take it to his great estate, for manuring.
300 There the dog Argos lay in the dung, all covered with dog ticks.
Now, as he perceived that Odysseus had come close to him,
he wagged his tail, and laid both his ears back; only
he now no longer had the strength to move any closer
to his master, who, watching him from a distance, without Eumaios
305 noticing, secretly wiped a tear away, and said to him:
'Eumaios, this is amazing, this dog that lies on the dunghill.
The shape of him is splendid, and yet I cannot be certain
whether he had the running speed to go with this beauty,
or is just one of the kind of table dog that gentlemen
310 keep, and it is only for show that their masters care for them.'
    Then, O swineherd Eumaios, you said to him in answer:
'This, it is too true, is the dog of a man who perished
far away. If he were such, in build and performance,
as when Odysseus left him behind, when he went to Ilion,
315 soon you could see his speed and his strength for yourself. Never
could any wild animal, in the profound depths of the forest,
escape, once he pursued. He was very clever at tracking.
But now he is in bad times. His master, far from his country,
has perished, and the women are careless, and do not look after him;
320 and serving men, when their masters are no longer about, to make them
work, are no longer willing to do their rightful duties.
For Zeus of the wide brows takes away one half of the virtue
from a man, once the day of slavery closes upon him.'
    So he spoke, and went into the strongly-settled palace,
325 and strode straight on, to the great hall and the haughty suitors,
But the doom of dark death now closed over the dog, Argos,
when, after nineteen years had gone by, he had seen Odysseus.
    Godlike Telemachos was the first by far to notice
the swineherd as he came into the house, and quickly he nodded
330 to summon him over. The swineherd, looking about him, picked up
a chair that was lying near where the carver sat, cutting
much meat for the suitors, as these feasted all through the palace.
This he took and placed it by Telemachos' table
facing him, then sat down there himself, and the herald
335 took a portion, and served him, and passed him bread from the basket.

Close after him Odysseus now came into the palace,
looking as he did like a dismal vagabond and an old man,
propping on a stick, and wore foul clothing upon his body.
He sat down then on the ashwood threshold, inside the doorway,
340   leaning against the doorpost of cypress wood, which the carpenter
once had expertly planed, and drawn it true to a chalkline;
but Telemachos spoke a word to the swineherd, calling him over,
taking and giving him a whole loaf from the beautiful basket,
with meat, as much food as both arms could hold in their compass:
345   'Take all this and give it to the stranger, but also tell him
to go about among the suitors, and beg from all of them.
Modesty, for a man in need, is not a good quality.'
So he spoke, and the swineherd went, when he heard his order.
He came and stood close by Odysseus, and spoke in winged words:
350   'Stranger, Telemachos gives you this, and also he tells you
to go about among the suitors, and beg from all of them.
He said that modesty, for a poor man, is no good quality.'
Then resourceful Odysseus spoke in turn and answered him:
'Lord Zeus, let Telemachos be one of the prosperous
355   men; let everything befall him that his heart longs for.'
He spoke, and with both hands accepting everything, laid it
there in front of his feet, on top of the ugly wallet,
and ate it, all the while the singer sang in the halls. Then,
when he had eaten his dinner, and the divine singer was finished,
360   the suitors raised their tumult along the halls; but Athene
came then and stood close by Odysseus, son of Laertes,
and stirred him to go collect his bits of bread from the suitors,
and so learn which of them were fair, which unfair; but even
so, she would not deliver any of them from disaster.
365   He went on his way, from left to right, so to beg from each man,
reaching his hand out always, as if for a long time he had been
a beggar, and they took pity and gave, and they wondered at him;
they asked each other what man he was, and where he came from.
But now Melanthios, the goat-herding man, said to them:
370   'Hear me now, you suitors of our glorious queen, concerning
this stranger; for I have seen him before; know then
that it was the swineherd who guided him here, but I do not know
    clearly
who the man is himself, or what race he claims to come of.'

So he spoke. Antinoös spoke then and scolded the swineherd:
375 'O most distinguished swineherd, why did you bring this fellow
to the city? Do we not already have enough other
vagabonds, and bothersome beggars to ruin our feasting?
Or, now that men gather here to eat up your master's substance,
is that not enough, but you had to invite this one in also?'
380   Then, O swineherd Eumaios, you said to him in answer:
'Antinoös, though you are noble, this was not well spoken.
For who goes visiting elsewhere so as to call in another
stranger, unless he is one who works for the people, either
a prophet, or a healer of sickness, or a skilled workman,
385 or inspired singer, one who can give delight by his singing?
These are the men who all over the endless earth are invited.
But nobody would ask in a beggar, one who would feed on
himself. You, though, beyond all the other suitors, are heavy
on the servants of Odysseus, and me most of all, but I
390 for my part do not care, while still circumspect Penelope
lives in the palace, together with godlike Telemachos.'
    Then the thoughtful Telemachos said to him in answer:
'Silence. Do not answer him at such length. Antinoös
has made it his habit always to irritate others with hurtful
395 words, and stir them up, and encourages others to do so.'
    So he spoke, and then addressed his words to Antinoös:
'Antinoös, as a father for his son you take good care
of me, when you tell our stranger guest to get out of the palace,
with a strict word. May this not be the end god makes of it.
400 Take and give. I do not begrudge you. I even urge you.
And do not have any respect for my mother, nor yet for any
thrall beside, who lives in the house of godlike Odysseus.
But such is not the kind of intention you keep within you.
You are more eager to eat, yourself, than to give to another.'
405   Then in turn Antinoös said to him in answer:
'High-spoken intemperate Telemachos, what accusations
you have made. If all the suitors would hand him this kind of present,
the house would then do without him for the space of three months.'
    So he spoke, and picked up a footstool that lay by the table
410 and showed it. He had his shining feet on it as he feasted.
But all the others gave to him, and they filled his wallet
with bread and meat, and Odysseus was on the point of finishing

his test of the Achaians, and getting back free to his doorsill;
but now he stood by Antinoös, and spoke a word to him:
415 'Give, dear friend. You seem to me, of all the Achaians,
not the worst, but the best. You look like a king. Therefore,
you ought to give me a better present of food than the others
have done, and I will sing your fame all over the endless
earth, for I too once lived in my own house among people,
420 prospering in wealth, and often I gave to a wanderer
according to what he was and wanted when he came to me;
and I had serving men by thousands, and many another
good thing, by which men live well and are called prosperous. Only
Zeus, son of Kronos, spoiled it all—somehow he wished to—
425 when he put it into my head to go with the roving pirates
to Egypt, a long voyage, so that I must be ruined.
I stayed my oarswept ships inside the Aigyptos River.
Then I urged my eager companions to stay where they were, there
close to the fleet, and to guard the ships, and was urgent with them
430 to send lookouts to the watching places, but they following
their own impulse, and giving way to marauding violence,
suddenly began plundering the Egyptians' beautiful
fields, and carried off the women and innocent children,
and killed the men, and soon the outcry came to the city.
435 They heard the shouting, and at the time when dawn shows, they came
on us, and all the plain was filled with horses and infantry
and the glare of bronze; and Zeus who delights in the thunder flung
     down
a foul panic among my companions, and none was so hardy
as to stand and fight, for the evils stood in a circle around them.
440 There they killed many of us with the sharp bronze, and others
they led away alive, to work for them in forced labor;
but they gave me away, into Cyprus, to a stranger arriving,
Dmetor, Iasos' son, who was the strong king in Cyprus.
From there I came here, where I am now, suffering hardships.'
445   Then Antinoös answered him in turn, and said to him:
'What spirit brought this pain upon us, to spoil our feasting?
Stand off, so, in the middle, and keep away from my table,
or otherwise you may find yourself in a sorry Cyprus
or Egypt, you are so bold a one, and a shameless beggar.
450 You went the whole circle and stood by all, and they all gave to you

recklessly, for there is no holding back nor sparing
of favors from another man's goods, since each has plenty.'
    Now resourceful Odysseus spoke, as he drew back from him:
'Shame; the wits in you, it is clear, do not match your outward

455 beauty. You would not give a bit of salt to a servant
in your own house, since now, sitting at another's, you could not
take a bit of bread and give it to me. It is there in abundance.'
    He spoke, and Antinoös in his heart grew still more angry.
Looking at him from under his brows, he addressed him in winged
        words:

460 'Now I think that you can no longer make a respectable
retreat out of the palace, since what you say is scurrilous.'
    He spoke, and threw the footstool and hit him in the right shoulder
near the base, in the back, but he stood up to it, steady
as a rock, nor did the missile thrown by Antinoös shake him,

465 but he shook his head in silence, deeply devising evils.
He went back to the sill and sat there, and spread out before him
the wallet that was well filled, and spoke a word to the suitors:
'You who are suitors of this most glorious queen, hear me
while I speak out what the heart within my breast urges:

470 there is no grief that comes to the heart, nor yet any sorrow,
when a man is hit, fighting in battle for the sake of his own
possessions, either to guard his shining sheep or his cattle;
but Antinoös struck me all because of my wretched belly,
that cursed thing, who bestows many evils on men. Therefore,

475 if there are any gods or any furies for beggars,
Antinoös may find his death before he is married.'
    Then Antinoös, son of Eupeithes, gave him an answer:
'Go in peace, stranger, and sit down, or go away elsewhere,
or else, for the way you talk, the young men might take you and drag you

480 by hand or foot through the house, and tear the skin on your body.'
    So he spoke, but all the rest were wildly indignant,
and this is the way one of these haughty young men would speak to him:
'Antinoös, you did badly to hit the unhappy vagabond:
a curse on you, if he turns out to be some god from heaven.

485 For the gods do take on all sorts of transformations, appearing
as strangers from elsewhere, and thus they range at large through the
        cities,
watching to see which men keep the laws, and which are violent.'

So spoke the suitors, but he paid no attention to what they were
saying.
But Telemachos sustained in his heart a great sorrow over
490   the blow, but he did not let fall from his eyes any groundward
tear, but shook his head in silence, deeply devising
evils. But when circumspect Penelope heard that the stranger
had been struck in her halls, she spoke to her serving women:
'Thus, I pray, may the archer Apollo strike at the striker.'
495   Then the housekeeper, Eurynome, spoke and answered:
'If only some fulfillment befell our prayers. Then not one
of these men would be alive to meet the Dawn in her splendor.'
Circumspect Penelope said to her in answer:
'Mother, they are all hateful, since all are devising evils,
500   but Antinoös, beyond the rest, is like black death. Here is
a stranger, some unfortunate man, who goes through our palace
asking alms of the men, for his helplessness forces him to it.
Then all the others gave and filled his bag, but this man
struck him with a footstool at the base of the right shoulder.'
505   So Penelope, sitting up in her chamber, conversed
with her serving women, while great Odysseus was eating his dinner.
But now she summoned the noble swineherd to her, saying:
'Go on your way now, noble Eumaios, and tell the stranger
to come, so I can befriend him, and so I can ask him
510   if he has somewhere heard any news of steadfast Odysseus
or seen him in person. He seems like a man who has wandered widely.'
Then, O swineherd Eumaios, you said to her in answer:
'If only these Achaians, my queen, would let you have silence!
Such stories he tells, he would charm out the dear heart within you.
515   Three nights I had him with me, and for three days I detained him
in my shelter, for he came first to me. He had fled from a vessel;
but he has not yet told the story of all his suffering.
But as when a man looks to a singer, who has been given
from the gods the skill with which he sings for delight of mortals,
520   and they are impassioned and strain to hear it when he sings to them,
so he enchanted me in the halls as he sat beside me.
He says that he is a friend by family of Odysseus,
with his home in Crete, where lives the generation of Minos,
and from there he made his way to this place, suffering hardships,
525   driven helpless along. He claims he has heard that Odysseus

is near, in the rich country of the men of Thesprotia,
and alive, and bringing many treasures back to his household.'
    Then in turn circumspect Penelope said to him:
'Go now, call him here, so he can tell me directly,
530 and let these people sit by the doors and play their games, or else
go and do it at home, whenever the spirit favors.
For their own properties are stored, unspoiled, in their houses,
bread, and sweet wine, but this their own house-people eat. Meanwhile,
they, day by day visiting our house, and always
535 dedicating our oxen, and our sheep and fat goats,
hold their festival and recklessly drink up our shining
wine; and most of it is used up, for there is no man here
such as Odysseus was, to keep the plague from his household.
But if Odysseus could come, and return to the land of his fathers,
540 soon, with his son, he could punish the violence of these people.'
    She spoke, and Telemachos sneezed amain, and around him the palace
re-echoed terribly to the sound. Penelope, laughing,
spoke presently to Eumaios and addressed him in winged words:
'Go, please, and summon the stranger into my presence. Do you
545 not see how my son sneezed for everything I have spoken?
May it mean that death, accomplished in full, befall the suitors
each and all, not one avoiding death and destruction.
And put away in your heart this other thing that I tell you.
If I learn that everything he says is truthfully spoken,
550 I will give him beautiful clothing to wear, a tunic and mantle.'
    So she spoke, and the swineherd went, when he heard what she told
      him,
and he came and stood close by Odysseus and spoke in winged words:
'Father and friend, circumspect Penelope, mother
of Telemachos, summons you, for her heart is urgent to find out
555 from you about her husband, though she is suffering troubles.
And if she learns that all you say is truthfully spoken,
she will give you a tunic and mantle to wear, what you have need of
most of all; and you, by begging your bread through the city,
can keep your belly sustained; and he who will can give to you.'
560   Then in turn much-enduring great Odysseus answered him:
'Eumaios, by and by I will tell everything truly
to the daughter of Ikarios, circumspect Penelope.
For I know well about him, we have suffered the same sad story.

Eumaios goes back

Only now I am afraid of this swarm of rough suitors,
565   whose outrageous violence goes up into the iron
sky. For even now, as I went through the house, doing
no harm, and this man struck me and gave me over to suffering,
Telemachos could not save me from this, nor could any other.
Tell Penelope, therefore, for all her eagerness, to wait
570   for me in the palace until the sun has set. Let her
then question me about her husband's day of homecoming,
giving me a seat close to the fire, since these are wretched
clothes I have. You know this yourself; you are my first patron.'
     So he spoke, and the swineherd went, when he heard what he told him.
575   But Penelope said to him as he stepped over the threshold:
'You do not bring him, Eumaios? What is this vagabond thinking?
Does he fear some indignity, or is he otherwise bashful
about the house? A bashful vagabond makes a bad beggar.'
     Then, O swineherd Eumaios, you said to her in answer:
580   'He speaks within reason, as another man might think also,
in keeping away from the violence of these insolent men. Therefore
he tells you to wait until after the sun has gone down. For you
yourself also, my queen, this way it will be much better:
to talk in private to the stranger, and hear his story.'
585   Then in turn circumspect Penelope answered him:
'So it shall be. The stranger's thought is not without good sense,
since never yet among mortal mankind have there been any
men who have been so violent in their wild endeavors.'
     So she instructed him, and the noble swineherd went back
590   into the crowd of the suitors, when he had understood all of it.
At once he spoke his winged words to Telemachos, leaning
his head close to him, so that none of the others might hear him:
'Dear child, I am going back to guard the pigs and that other
livelihood that is yours and mine. Let all be in your charge
595   here. First of all take care of yourself, and be very watchful
against harm to you. There are many Achaians who wish you evil.
May Zeus destroy them before they can make any harm befall us.'
     Then the thoughtful Telemachos said to him in answer:
'So it shall be, my father. Go, when you have had your supper;
600   but come again in the morning, and bring us beautiful victims.
I myself will see to things here, as will the immortals.'
     So he spoke, and the other sat down again on a polished

---

chair. But when he had had his fill of eating and drinking,
he went on back to the pigs, and left the courts and the palace
605   full of banqueters, who took their pleasure in singing
and dancing. By now the later part of the day had come on.

BOOK XVIII

And now there arrived a public beggar, who used to go begging
through the town of Ithaka, known to fame for his ravenous belly
and appetite for eating and drinking. There was no real strength
in him, nor any force, but his build was big to look at.
5 He had the name Arnaios, for thus the lady his mother
called him from birth, but all the young men used to call him Iros,
because he would run and give messages when anyone told him.
This man had come to chase Odysseus out of his own house
and now he spoke, insulting him, and addressed him in winged words:
10 'Give way, old sir, from the forecourt, before you are taken and dragged
        out
by the foot. Do you see how all of them are giving the signal
and telling me to drag you. Still, I am ashamed to do it.
So up, before it comes to a battle of hands between us.'
    Then looking at him darkly resourceful Odysseus answered:
15 'Strange man, I am doing you no harm, nor speaking any,
nor am I jealous, if someone takes plenty and gives it to you.
This doorsill is big enough for both of us, nor have you any
need to be jealous of others. I think you are a vagabond
as I am too. Prosperity is in the gods' giving.
20 Leave blows alone, do not press me too hard, or you may make me
angry so that, old as I am, I may give you a bloody
chest and mouth. Then I could have peace, and still more of it
tomorrow, for I do not think you will make your way back here

a second time to the house of Odysseus, son of Laertes.'
25 Then in anger Iros the vagabond said to him:
'Shame on how the old hulk rolls along in his speech, like
an old woman at the oven. I have some bad plans for him:
hit him with both hands, and spatter all of the teeth out
from his jaws on the ground, as if he were a wild pig rooting
30 the crops. Come, tuck up, so all these people can see us
do battle. But how can you fight against a man who is younger?'
So, in front of the towering doors, and upon the threshold
polished smooth, these two hurled jagged words at each other;
and Antinoös, the sacred prince, stirred them on to battle,
35 and laughing sweetly he spoke aloud to the rest of the suitors:
'Friends, in the past nothing has ever happened to match
this entertainment that the god has now brought to the palace;
for the stranger and Iros are now making ready for battle
with their fists. Come, let the rest of us speed the encounter.'
40 So he spoke, and the rest of them all sprang up, laughing,
and gathered all in a group around the two ragged beggars.
It was Antinoös the son of Eupeithes who spoke to them:
'Listen to me, you haughty suitors, while I say something.
Here are some goat paunches set on the fire; we filled them
45 with blood and fat, and set them there, to eat after supper.
Whichever of these men wins the contest, and is proved better,
let him come up, and help himself to whichever he likes best;
and he shall always have dinner with us, nor shall we ever
admit any other beggar to join us inside, and beg from us.'
50 So Antinoös spoke, and what he had said was pleasing.
But now resourceful Odysseus, with crafty thoughts, said to him:
'Friends, it is not possible for a man who is older
and worn with sorrow to fight with a younger man, but my villainous
belly drives me to do it, and fall to his fists. Therefore,
55 come, swear me a strong oath all of you, that no one
will take the side of Iros and lightheartedly strike me
down with a heavy hand, and make me fall to his onset.'
So he spoke, and they all swore him the oath as he asked it.
But when all had sworn the oath and made an end of their swearing,
60 the hallowed prince Telemachos now spoke out among them:
'Stranger, if your heart and spirit are urgent with you
to defend yourself against this man, then fear no other

Achaian. The man who strikes you shall have to fight against numbers.
I myself am your host, with the assent of the two kings
65 Antinoös and Eurymachos, both men of prudence.'
　　So he spoke, and they all applauded him. But Odysseus
girded up his rags about his body, displaying
his thighs, splendid and large, and one could see the wide shoulders;
his chest showed, and his ponderous arms; and also Athene
70 standing close beside the shepherd of the people magnified
his limbs, and the suitors all in their insolence were astonished,
and thus would one of them speak, looking over at his next neighbor:
'Iros will soon be Iros no more, with himself to thank for
the evil. See what limbs the old man's rags have uncovered.'
75 　　So he spoke, and the heart in Iros was stirred with trouble,
but even so the thralls girt him forcibly up, and dragged him
there. He was frightened, and the flesh shook all over his body.
Antinoös scolded him with a word and spoke out and named him:
'I do not care if you live or die, you great ox, nor what happens
80 to you, when you are afraid of this man, and tremble before him,
an old man, and worn with the sorrows that have come upon him.
But I tell you this straight out, and it will be a thing accomplished.
If this man wins the fight with you, and is proved the better,
I will throw you into a black ship, and send you across to the mainland,
85 to Echetos, who preys on all men, and who is king there,
and he with the pitiless bronze will cut off your nose and ears,
and tear off your privates and give them raw for the dogs to feed on.'
　　So he spoke, and the trembling even more took hold of
his limbs, but they pulled him on, and both men put their hands up.
90 At that time, much-enduring great Odysseus pondered
whether to hit him so that the life would go out of him, as he
went down, or only to stretch him out by hitting him lightly.
And in the division of his heart this way seemed best to him,
to hit him lightly, so the Achaians would not be suspicious.
95 They put up their hands, and Iros hit him on the right shoulder,
but Odysseus struck the neck underneath the ear, and shattered
the bones within, and the red blood came in his mouth, filling it.
He dropped, bleating, in the dust, with teeth set in a grimace,
and kicking at the ground with his feet, and the haughty suitors
100 held up their hands and died with laughing. Meanwhile, Odysseus
dragged him by the foot through the porch, till he came to the courtyard

and the portico doors, and propped him against the courtyard
wall, sitting up, and stuck the staff in his hand, to hold it.
Then he spoke to him aloud and addressed him in winged words:
105 'Sit there now, and scare away the dogs and the stray pigs.
But you must no longer try to be king of the strangers and beggars,
being such a wretch, or you may win yourself still more evil.'
    He spoke, and threw across his shoulders his ugly wallet
that was full of holes, with a twist of rope attached to dangle it.
110 He went back to the sill again and sat down, but the others
went inside again, laughing sweetly, and drank to him, saying:
'May Zeus, stranger, and all the other immortals give you
what you want most of all and what is dear to your spirit,
for having stopped the wandering of this greedy creature
115 in our neighborhood. Soon we will take him across to the mainland,
to Echetos, who preys on all men, and who is king there.'
    So they spoke, and great Odysseus was pleased at the omen.
Now Antinoös set before him the great paunch pudding
that was all filled with fat and blood. Amphinomos, taking
120 two loaves of bread out of the basket, set them before him,
and drank his health in a golden cup and spoke to him, saying:
'Your health, father and stranger; may prosperous days befall you
hereafter; but now you are held in the grip of many misfortunes.'
    Then resourceful Odysseus spoke in turn and answered him:
125 'Amphinomos, you seem to me very prudent, being
the son of such a father, whose excellent fame I have heard of,
Nisos, that is, of Doulichion, both strong and prosperous;
they say you are his son, and you seem like a man well-spoken.
So I will tell you, and you in turn understand and listen.
130 Of all creatures that breathe and walk on the earth there is nothing
more helpless than a man is, of all that the earth fosters;
for he thinks that he will never suffer misfortune in future
days, while the gods grant him courage, and his knees have spring
in them. But when the blessed gods bring sad days upon him,
135 against his will he must suffer it with enduring spirit.
For the mind in men upon earth goes according to the fortunes
the Father of Gods and Men, day by day, bestows upon them.
For I myself once promised to be a man of prosperity,
but, giving way to force and violence, did many reckless
140 things, because I relied on my father and brothers. Therefore,

let no man be altogether without the sense of righteousness,
but take in silence the gifts of the gods, whatever they give him.
Even so, now, I see the suitors, their reckless devisings,
how they show no respect to the wife, and despoil the possessions
145 of a man who, I think, will not for long be far from
his country and friends. He is very close by. But I hope your destiny
takes you home, out of his way. I hope you never will face him,
at the time he comes back to the beloved land of his fathers.
For I believe that, once he enters his halls, there will be
150 a reckoning, not without blood, between that man and the suitors.'
        So he spoke, and poured, and drank the honey-sweet wine, then
put the cup back into the hands of the lord of the people;
but the other went back across the room, heart saddened within him,
shaking his head, for in his spirit he saw the evil,
155 but still could not escape his doom, for Athene had bound him
fast, to be strongly killed by the hands and spear of Telemachos.
He went back and sat down on the chair from which he had risen.
        But now the goddess, gray-eyed Athene, put it in the mind
of the daughter of Ikarios, circumspect Penelope,
160 to show herself to the suitors, so that she might all the more
open their hearts, and so that she might seem all the more precious
in the eyes of her husband and son even than she had been before this.
She laughed, in an idle way, and spoke to her nurse and named her:
'Eurynome, my heart desires, though before it did not,
165 to show myself to the suitors, although I still hate them. Also,
I would speak a word to my son, and that would be for the better,
that he should not always go among the insolent suitors,
who speak him well, but are plotting evil things for the future.'
        Eurynome the housekeeper said to her in answer:
170 'Now all this you have said, my child, was fair and orderly.
Go then, and speak a word to your son, hide nothing. Only
first you should wash your body and anoint your face. Do not
go down with a face so ravaged all over by tears, as it now is,
since nothing is gained by indiscriminate sorrowing always.
175 For now your son is come of age, and you know you always
prayed the immortals, beyond all else, to see him bearded.'
        Circumspect Penelope said to her in answer:
'Eurynome, though you care for me, do not speak of such matters
as washing my body and anointing myself with unguents,

to appear before the suitors

180   seeing that the gods, they who possess Olympos, ruined
    my glory, from that time when he went away in the hollow
    ships. But tell Autonoë and Hippodameia
    to come, so that they can stand at my side in the great hall.
    I will not go alone among men. I think that immodest.'
185   So she spoke, and the old woman went away through the palace,
    and brought the word to the women, and urged them to go to their
        mistress.
      Then the goddess gray-eyed Athene thought what to do next.
    She drifted a sweet sleep over Ikarios' daughter,
    and all her joints were relaxed so that she slumbered, reclining
190   there on the couch. Meanwhile she, shining among goddesses,
    endowed her with gifts immortal, to make the Achaians admire her.
    First, for her beauty's sake, she freshened all her fine features
    with ambrosia, such as fair-garlanded Kythereia uses
    for salve, whenever she joins the lovely dance of the Graces.
195   She made her taller for the eye to behold, and thicker,
    and she made her whiter than sawn ivory. After so doing,
    she, Athene, shining among goddesses, departed,
    and the white-armed handmaidens came running in from the great hall,
    with clamor, about Penelope, and the sweet sleep released her.
200   She rubbed her cheeks with both her hands and spoke aloud, saying:
    'That was a strange thing, that soft sleep that shrouded me.
    How I wish chaste Artemis would give me a death so
    soft, and now, so I would not go on in my heart grieving
    all my life, and longing for love of a husband excellent
205   in every virtue, since he stood out among the Achaians.'
      So she spoke, and made her descent from her shining chamber,
    not all alone, since two handmaidens went to attend her.
    When she, shining among women, came near the suitors,
    she stood by the pillar that supported the roof with its joinery,
210   holding her shining veil in front of her face, to shield it,
    and a devoted attendant was stationed on either side of her.
    Their knees gave way, and the hearts in them were bemused with passion,
    and each one prayed for the privilege of lying beside her;
    but she spoke rather to her beloved son, Telemachos:
215   'Telemachos, your mind and thoughts are no longer steadfast.
    When you were a child still, you had better thoughts in mind. Now,
    when you are big, and come to the measure of maturity, and one

Penelope hints at marriage

who saw you, some outsider, viewing your size and beauty,
would say you were the son born of a prosperous man;
220 your thoughts are no longer righteous, nor your perception;
such a thing has been done now, here in our palace, and you
permitted our stranger guest to be so outrageously handled.
How must it be now, if the stranger who sits in our household
is to be made to suffer so from bitter brutality?
225 That must be your outrage and shame as people see it.'
     Then the thoughtful Telemachos said to her in answer:
'My mother, I cannot complain of your anger. I myself
notice all these things in my heart and know of them, better
and worse alike, but before now I was only an infant;
230 but still I cannot see my way to the wise course always,
for these men come from one place or another, and sit beside me
with their evil thoughts, and distract me, and there are none here to help
     me.
Yet it was not by the will of the suitors that this struggle took place
between Iros and the stranger, and he was stronger than Iros
235 in battle. O father Zeus, and Athene, and Apollo,
if only in our house, in such a manner, the suitors
could be defeated and bow their heads, some in the courtyard
and some inside of the house, and the limbs be unstrung in each of them;
as now for Iros, as he sits over there by the courtyard
240 gates, lolling his head like a drunken man, and unable
to stand upright on his feet again and make his way homeward
to wherever he makes his home, since there is no strength in his body.'
     So these two were conversing in this way with each other;
but Eurymachos now spoke out and addressed Penelope:
245 'Daughter of Ikarios, circumspect Penelope,
if only all the Achaians in Iad Argos could see you,
at dawn of day tomorrow there would be even more suitors
come to feast in your house, since you surpass all women
for beauty and stature and for the mind well balanced within you.'
250   Circumspect Penelope said to him in answer:
'Eurymachos, all my excellence, my beauty and figure,
were ruined by the immortals at that time when the Argives took ship
for Ilion, and with them went my husband, Odysseus.
If he were to come back to me and take care of my life, then
255 my reputation would be more great and splendid. As it is

now, I grieve; such evils the god has let loose upon me.
When he went and left me behind in the land of his fathers,
he took me by the right hand at the wrist, and then said to me:
"Dear wife, since I do not think the strong-greaved Achaians
260   will all come safely home from Troy without hurt, seeing
that people say the Trojans are men who can fight in battle,
that they are throwers of the spear, and shooters of arrows,
and riders with fast-footed horses, who with the greatest
speed settle the great and hateful issue of common battle,
265   I do not know if the god will spare me, or if I must be lost
there in Troy; here let everything be in your charge.
You must take thought for my father and mother here in our palace,
as you do now, or even more, since I shall be absent.
But when you see our son grown up and bearded, then you may
270   marry whatever man you please, forsaking your household."
So he spoke then; and now all this is being accomplished.
And there will come that night when a hateful marriage is given
to wretched me, for Zeus has taken my happiness from me.
But this thing comes as a bitter distress to my heart and spirit:
275   the behavior of these suitors is not as it was in time past
when suitors desired to pay their court to a noble woman
and daughter of a rich man, and rival each other. Such men
themselves bring in their own cattle and fat sheep, to feast
the family of the bride, and offer glorious presents.
280   They do not eat up another's livelihood, without payment.'
      She spoke, and much-enduring great Odysseus was happy
because she beguiled gifts out of them, and enchanted their spirits
with blandishing words, while her own mind had other intentions.
      Then Antinoös the son of Eupeithes answered:
285   'Daughter of Ikarios, circumspect Penelope,
whatever gift any Achaian wishes to bring here,
take it; it is not honorable to refuse the giving.
We will not go back to our own estates, nor will we go elsewhere,
until you marry whichever Achaian you fancy.'
290   So spoke Antinoös, and his word pleased the rest of them.
Each man sent his herald off to bring back the presents.
Antinoös' herald brought in a great robe, beautiful
and elaborate, and in it were twelve double pins, golden
all through, and fitted with bars that opened and closed easily.

Odysseus is scolded by Melantho

295 Eurymachos' man came back with an elaborate necklace
  of gold, strung with bits of amber, and bright as sunshine.
  Eurydamas' servants came back bringing a pair of earrings
  with triple drops in mulberry clusters, and there was radiant
  charm in them. From the house of the lord Peisandros, Polyktor's
300 son, his servant brought a necklace, a wonderful offering.
  Each of the Achaians brought a different beautiful
  present; and she, shining among women, went back to her upper
  room, and her maidservants carried the beautiful presents for her.
   But now the suitors, turning to the dance and delightful
305 song, took their pleasure and awaited the coming of evening,
  and the black night came on as they were taking their pleasure.
  Accordingly, they set up three cressets about the palace,
  to give them light, and about them they laid piles of firewood
  pieces, long dried and seasoned, but lately split with the brazen
310 ax; and put kindling in with it, and the maids of enduring
  Odysseus were ready to take turns keeping them burning,
  when illustrious resourceful Odysseus himself spoke to them:
  'You maids of Odysseus, whose master has long been absent,
  go back into the house where the respected queen is,
315 and in her presence turn your distaffs, and sit beside her
  in the halls, and comfort her, or comb your wool in your hands there.
  But I myself will provide the light for all of these people.
  And even if they wish to keep at it until the high-throned
  dawn, they will not wear me out. I am very enduring.'
320 So he spoke, and they burst out laughing and looked at each other;
  but Melantho of the lovely face shamefully scolded him.
  Dolios was her father, but Penelope had taken
  her in, and cared for her like a daughter, and cheered her with presents;
  but even so her heart had no sorrow for Penelope,
325 but she used to sleep with Eurymachos, and she was his sweetheart.
  Now she spoke to Odysseus and gave him a scolding:
  'Wretched stranger, you must be one whose wits are distracted,
  when you will not go where the smith is at work, and sleep there,
  or to some public gathering place, but staying here speak out
330 boldly and at length among many men, and your spirit
  knows no fear. The wine must have your brains; or else always
  you are such a man in your mind, a babbler of nonsense.
  Are you so brave because you beat the vagabond Iros?

Take care lest a better man than Iros stand up against you,
335 one who can pummel you about the head with his heavy
hands, beat you, draw blood, and chase you out of the palace.'
　　　Then looking at her darkly resourceful Odysseus answered:
'I think I will go to Telemachos, you bitch, and tell him
how you are talking, so that he will cut you to pieces.'
340　　Speaking in words like this he fluttered the women. They went
on their way back into the house, and the knees of each one
went loose with fear. They thought he was speaking the truth. He then
took his place by the burning cressets, and kept them lighted,
looking after them all himself, but the heart within him
345 was pondering other thoughts, which were not to go unaccomplished.
　　　But Athene did not altogether permit the haughty
suitors to forgo their hard insolence, so that still more
grief would invade the heart of Odysseus, son of Laertes.
Eurymachos, son of Polybos, began speaking among them,
350 taunting Odysseus, and started up laughter among his companions:
'Hear me, all you suitors of the glorious queen, hear me
while I speak out what the heart within my breast urges.
This man comes as gift of the gods to the house of Odysseus.
It is my thought that he can give us illumination
355 from his bald head, which has no hair, not even a little.'
　　　So he spoke, and addressed Odysseus, sacker of cities:
'Stranger, if I were to take you up, would you be willing
to work for me on my outer estate—I would give you adequate
pay—assembling stones for fences, and growing the tall trees?
360 There I would provide you with an allowance of victuals,
and give you shoes to wear on your feet, and clothing to put on.
But since all the work you have learned is bad, you will not be willing
to go off and work hard; no, you would rather beg where the people
are, and so be able to feed that ravenous belly.'
365　　Then resourceful Odysseus spoke in turn and answered him:
'Eurymachos, I wish there could be a working contest
between us, in the spring season when the days are lengthening,
out in the meadow, with myself holding a well-curved sickle,
and you one like it, so to test our endurance for labor,
370 without food, from dawn till dark, with plenty of grass for our mowing.
Or if it were oxen to be driven, those of the best sort,
large ones and ruddy, both well fed with grass, of an equal

Eurymachos throws a footstool at Odysseus

age and carrying power, and their strength is not contemptible,
and there were four acres to plow, with the glebe giving to the plowshare.

375 There you would see if I could carve a continuous furrow.
Or again, if this day the son of Kronos should bring on
a battle, and I were given a great shield and two spears,
and a helmet all of bronze well fitted over my temples,
so you would see me taking my place as one of the foremost

380 fighters, and you could not speak so in scorn of my belly.
But now you are very insulting, and think to be short with me; also,
as I suppose, you think you are a tall man and powerful,
because you have dealings with few men and no brave ones; surely,
if Odysseus were to come back to the land of his fathers,

385 the gates of the house, although they are very wide, would suddenly
be too narrow as you took flight to escape from the forecourt.'
   He spoke, and the anger mounted in the heart of Eurymachos,
and looking darkly at him he addressed him in winged words:
'Wretch, I will do you an injury for the way you are talking,

390 boldly and at length among many men, and your spirit
knows no fear. The wine must have your brains; or else always
you are such a man in your mind, a babbler of nonsense.
Are you so brave because you defeated the vagabond Iros?'
   So he spoke, and caught up a footstool; but Odysseus

395 crouched against the knees of Doulichian Amphinomos
in fear of Eurymachos, who threw, and hit the cupbearer
in the right hand. The pitcher fell to the ground, clashing,
but the cupbearer fell on his back in the dust, groaning.
But the suitors all through the shadowy halls were raising a tumult,

400 and thus they would speak, each man looking at the man next him:
'How I wish this stranger could have gone to perdition
somewhere else, before he came here; he has raised such a tumult,
and now we are fighting over beggars; there will be no pleasure
in the stately feast at all, since vile things will be uppermost.'

405   Now the hallowed prince Telemachos spoke a word to them:
'Fools, you are out of your minds and no longer conceal inside you
what you have eaten and drunk. It must be some god who troubles you.
You have feasted well; go to your homes and sleep, whenever,
that is, anyone desires to go home; I drive away no man.'

410   So he spoke, and all of them bit their lips in amazement
at Telemachos, and the daring way he had spoken to them.

The suitors go home

Now they were addressed and spoken to by Amphinomos,
the glorious son of Nisos, son of the lord Aretios:
'Dear friends, no man must be angry, nor yet with violent
415   answers attack what has been spoken in justice. And do not
strike the stranger, as you have done, nor yet any other
serving man who is in the house of godlike Odysseus.
Come now, let the cupbearer pour wine in our goblets,
so we can pour a libation and then retire to our houses;
420   and in the halls of Odysseus we shall let Telemachos
look after the stranger, since it is his house that he came to.'
    So he spoke, and the word he spoke was pleasing to all of them.
The hero Moulios, the Doulichian herald, mixed them
wine in the bowl. He was the henchman of Amphinomos.
425   He passed it around to all in order, and they, pouring
a libation to the blessed gods, drank the honey-sweet wine.
But when they had made libation and drunk as much as they wanted,
then they went home to go to bed, each man to his own house.

BOOK XIX

Now great Odysseus still remained in the hall, pondering
how, with the help of Athene, he would murder the suitors.
Presently he spoke in winged words to Telemachos:
'Telemachos, we must have the weapons stored away inside

5 the high chamber; and when the suitors miss them and ask you
about them, answer and beguile them with soft words, saying:
"I stored them away out of the smoke, since they are no longer
like what Odysseus left behind when he went to Troy land,
but are made foul, with all the smoke of the fire upon them.

10 Also, the son of Kronos put into my head this even
greater thought, that with the wine in you, you might stand up
and fight, and wound each other, and spoil the feast and the courting;
since iron all of itself works on a man and attracts him." '
So he spoke, and Telemachos obeyed his dear father,

15 and summoned out Eurykleia his nurse, and said to her:
'Come, nurse, please detain the women inside the palace,
while I put away my father's beautiful armor
in the inner room; it is carelessly laid in the house, and darkened
with smoke, in my father's absence, and I was a child all that time.

20 Now I would put it away, where smoke from the fire will not reach it.'
Then in turn Eurykleia his dear nurse said to him:
'I only hope, my child, that you will assume such foresight
in taking care of the house and protecting all our possessions.
But tell me, who is it will go with you and hold the light for you?

Odysseus and Telemachos remove the armor

25   The maids were tending the light, but you would not let them come out.'
      Then the thoughtful Telemachos said to her in answer:
    'This stranger will. I will not suffer a man who feeds from
    our stores, and does not work, even though he comes from far off.'
      So he spoke, and she had no winged words for an answer.
30   Eurykleia barred the doors of the strong-built great hall.
    The two men, Odysseus and his glorious son, sprang up
    and began carrying helmets, shields massive in the middle,
    and pointed spears, and before them Pallas Athene, holding
    a golden lamp, gave them splendid illumination.
35   Suddenly Telemachos spoke a word to his father:
    'Father, here is a great wonder that my eyes look on.
    Always it seems that the chamber walls, the handsome bases
    and roof timbers of fir and tall columns sustaining them,
    shine in my eyes as if a fire were blazing. There must be
40   surely a god here, one of those who hold the high heaven.'
      Then resourceful Odysseus spoke in turn and answered him:
    'Hush, and keep it in your own mind, and do not ask questions.
    For this is the very way of the gods, who hold Olympos.
    You should now go to bed, and I shall remain behind here,
45   so that I can continue to stir up the maids, and also
    your mother; and she in her sorrow will question me about everything.'
      So he spoke, and Telemachos went out of the great hall
    to his own chamber to go to bed, with torches to light him
    to his bed, where he always lay when sweet sleep came on him.
50   There he lay this time also and waited for the divine Dawn,
    while great Odysseus still remained in the hall, pondering
    how, with the help of Athene, he would murder the suitors.
      But now circumspect Penelope came down from her chamber,
    looking like Artemis or like golden Aphrodite.
55   They set a chair for her to sit on close by the fireplace.
    The chair was inlaid with ivory and silver; the craftsman
    Ikmalios had made it, and for the feet he had joined on
    a footstool, all of one piece with it; a great fleece was spread out
    over the chair, and upon it circumspect Penelope
60   took her place. Her white-armed handmaidens came from the palace.
    They cleared and carried away a great deal of food, with the tables
    and goblets, where the men in high spirits had been drinking,
    and shook the ash from the cressets onto the ground, then piled them

again with pieces of wood, to give them light, and to warm them.
65 Again for the second time Melantho scolded Odysseus:
'Stranger, do you mean to stay here all night and bother us
by poking all over the house and spying upon the women?
Take yourself out of the door, you wretch, and be well satisfied
with your feast, or you may be forced to get out, with a torch thrown
  at you.'
70   Then looking darkly at her resourceful Odysseus said to her:
'I wonder, why do you hold such an angry grudge against me?
Is it because I am dirty, and wear foul clothing upon me,
and go about as a public beggar? The need is on me,
for such is the lot of vagabonds and men who are homeless.
75 I too was one who lived in my own house among people,
prospering in wealth, and often I gave to a wanderer
according to what he was and wanted when he came to me;
and I had serving men by thousands, and many another
good thing, by which men live well and are called prosperous, only
80 Zeus, son of Kronos, spoiled it all—somehow he wished to.
So, woman, you should now beware lest you lose all of
that glorious look with which you shine among the handmaidens.
Beware of your mistress, who may grow angry with you and hate you.
Or Odysseus may come back. There is still time for hope there.
85 And even if he has perished and will no longer come back,
here is Telemachos, his son, by grace of Apollo
grown such a man, and in his palace none of the women
will be sinful and escape, since he is a child no longer.'
  So he spoke, and circumspect Penelope heard him,
90 and spoke to her maidservant by name and gave her a scolding:
'Always I know well what monstrous thing you are doing,
you bold and shameless bitch; you will wipe it off on your own head.
You understood all this very well, because you had heard it
from me, how in my halls I intended to question the stranger
95 about my husband; since I am troubled for him incessantly.'
  So she spoke and addressed her housekeeper, Eurynome:
'Eurynome, bring up a chair and put a fleece on it,
so that the stranger can be seated, and tell me his story,
and listen also to what I say. I wish to question him.'
100 So she spoke, and the servant quickly brought up and set down
a well-polished chair, and laid a fleece across to cover it.

who tells her story

On this, much-enduring great Odysseus was seated,
and their discourse was begun by circumspect Penelope:
'Stranger, I myself first have a question to ask you.
105 What man are you and whence? Where is your city? Your parents?'
    Then resourceful Odysseus spoke in turn and answered her:
'Lady, no mortal man on the endless earth could have cause
to find fault with you; your fame goes up into the wide heaven,
as of some king who, as a blameless man and god-fearing,
110 and ruling as lord over many powerful people,
upholds the way of good government, and the black earth yields him
barley and wheat, his trees are heavy with fruit, his sheepflocks
continue to bear young, the sea gives him fish, because of
his good leadership, and his people prosper under him.
115 Question me now here in your house about all other
matters, but do not ask who I am, the name of my country,
for fear you may increase in my heart its burden of sorrow
as I think back; I am very full of grief, and I should not
sit in the house of somebody else with my lamentation
120 and wailing. It is not good to go on mourning forever.
Some one of your maids, or you yourself, might find fault with me
and say I swam in tears because my brain drowned in liquor.'
    Circumspect Penelope said to him in answer:
'Stranger, all of my excellence, my beauty and figure,
125 were ruined by the immortals at that time when the Argives took ship
for Ilion, and with them went my husband, Odysseus.
If he were to come back to me and take care of my life, then
my reputation would be more great and splendid. As it is
now, I grieve; such evils the god has let loose upon me.
130 For all the greatest men who have the power in the islands,
in Doulichion and Same and in wooded Zakynthos,
and all who in rocky Ithaka are holders of lordships,
all these are my suitors against my will, and they wear my house out.
Therefore, I pay no attention to strangers, nor to suppliants,
135 nor yet to heralds, who are in the public service, but always
I waste away at the inward heart, longing for Odysseus.
These men try to hasten the marriage. I weave my own wiles.
First the divinity put the idea of the web in my mind,
to set up a great loom in my palace, and set to weaving
140 a web of threads, long and fine. Then I said to them:

Odysseus pretends

"Young men, my suitors now that the great Odysseus has perished,
wait, though you are eager to marry me, until I finish
this web, so that my weaving will not be useless and wasted.
This is a shroud for the hero Laertes, for when the destructive

145 doom of death which lays men low shall take him, lest any
Achaian woman in this neighborhood hold it against me
that a man of many conquests lies with no sheet to wind him."
So I spoke, and the proud heart in them was persuaded.
Thereafter in the daytime I would weave at my great loom,

150 but in the night I would have torches set by, and undo it.
So for three years I was secret in my designs, convincing
the Achaians, but when the fourth year came with the seasons returning,
and the months faded, and many days had been brought to completion,
then at last through my maidservants, those careless hussies,

155 they learned, and came upon me and caught me, and gave me a scolding.
So, against my will and by force, I had to finish it.
Now I cannot escape from this marriage; I can no longer
think of another plan; my parents are urgent with me
to marry; my son is vexed as they eat away our livelihood;

160 he sees it all; he is a grown man now, most able
to care for the house, and it is to him Zeus grants this honor.
But even so, tell me who you are, and the place where you come from.
You were not born from any fabulous oak, or a boulder.'
    Then resourceful Odysseus spoke in turn and answered her:

165 'O respected wife of Odysseus, son of Laertes,
you will not stop asking me about my origin?
Then I will tell you; but you will give me over to sorrows
even more than I have; but such is the way of it, when one
strays away from his own country as long as I have,

170 wandering many cities of men and suffering hardships.
Even so, I will tell you what you ask me and seek for.
There is a land called Crete in the middle of the wine-blue water,
a handsome country and fertile, seagirt, and there are many
peoples in it, innumerable; there are ninety cities.

175 Language with language mix there together. There are Achaians,
there are great-hearted Eteokretans, there are Kydonians,
and Dorians in three divisions, and noble Pelasgians;
and there is Knossos, the great city, the place where Minos
was king for nine-year periods, and conversed with great Zeus.

---

to have entertained Odysseus in Crete

180   He was the father of my father, great-hearted Deukalion.
      Deukalion had two sons, myself and the lord Idomeneus,
      but Idomeneus had gone with the curved ships to Ilion
      along with the sons of Atreus. My glorious name was Aithon,
      and I was the younger born, but he was the elder and better.
185   It was there that I knew Odysseus and entertained him,
      for the force of the wind had caught him, as he was making for Ilion,
      and brought him to Crete, driving him off course past Maleia.
      He stopped at Amnisos, where there is a cave of Eileithyia,
      in difficult harbors, and barely he had escaped from the stormwind.
190   He went up to the town at once, and asked for Idomeneus,
      for he said he was his hereditary friend, and respected;
      but it was now the tenth or eleventh day since Idomeneus
      had gone away along with his curved ships for Ilion.
      But I took him back to my own house, and well entertained him
195   with proper hospitality, since there was abundance
      in the house, and for his other companions, who were his followers,
      I collected from the public and gave them barley, and shining
      wine, and cattle to dedicate, to content their spirits.
      There the noble Achaians stayed twelve days, for a mighty
200   North Wind contained them, such that a man could not stand upright
      and walk the earth. Some harsh divinity must have roused it.
      But on the thirteenth day the wind fell, and they put forth.'
          He knew how to say many false things that were like true sayings.
      As she listened her tears ran and her body was melted,
205   as the snow melts along the high places of the mountains
      when the West Wind has piled it there, but the South Wind melts it,
      and as it melts the rivers run full flood. It was even
      so that her beautiful cheeks were streaming tears, as Penelope
      wept for her man, who was sitting there by her side. But Odysseus
210   in his heart had pity for his wife as she mourned him,
      but his eyes stayed, as if they were made of horn or iron,
      steady under his lids. He hid his tears and deceived her.
      But when she had taken her pleasure of tearful lamentation,
      then she answered him once again and spoke and addressed him:
215   'Now, my friend, I think I will give you a test, to see if
      it is true that there, and with his godlike companions,
      you entertained my husband, as you say you did, in your palace.
      Tell me what sort of clothing he wore on his body, and what sort

He claims Odysseus is in Thesprotia

of man he was himself, and his companions, who followed him.'
220   Then resourceful Odysseus spoke in turn and answered her:
'Lady, it is difficult to tell you, with so much
time between, for now it is the twentieth year since
he was in that place and went away from my country.
Still, I will tell you, in the way my heart imagines him.
225 Great Odysseus was wearing a woolen mantle of purple,
with two folds, but the pin to it was golden and fashioned
with double sheaths, and the front part of it was artfully
done: a hound held in his forepaws a dappled
fawn, preying on it as it struggled; and all admired it,
230 how, though they were golden, it preyed on the fawn and strangled it
and the fawn struggled with his feet as he tried to escape him.
I noticed also the shining tunic that he was wearing
on his body. It was like the dried-out skin of an onion,
so sheer it was and soft, and shining bright as the sun shines.
235 Many of the women were looking at it in admiration.
But put away in your heart this other thing that I tell you.
I do not know if this clothing Odysseus wore had come from
his home, or if some companion gave it to him as he boarded
his fast ship; or some friend abroad, since Odysseus had friendship
240 with many men. Indeed, there were few Achaians like him.
I myself gave him a brazen sword and a double
cloak of purple, a handsome thing, and a fringed tunic,
and saw him off in the proper way on his strong-benched vessel.
Also there was a herald, a little older than he was,
245 who went with him. I will describe to you what he looked like.
He was round in the shoulders, black-complexioned, wooly-haired,
and had the name Eurybates. Odysseus prized him
above his other companions, for their thoughts were in harmony.'
He spoke, and still more aroused in her the passion for weeping,
250 as she recognized the certain proofs Odysseus had given.
But when she had taken her pleasure of tearful lamentation,
then once again she spoke to him and gave him an answer:
'Stranger, while before this you had my pity, you now shall
be my friend and be respected here in my palace.
255 For I myself gave him this clothing, as you describe it.
I folded it in my chamber, and I too attached the shining
pin, to be his adornment; but I shall never welcome him

home, come back again to the beloved land of his fathers.
It was on a bad day for him that Odysseus boarded
260   his hollow ship for that evil, not-to-be-mentioned Ilion.'
    Then resourceful Odysseus spoke in turn and answered her:
'O respected wife of Odysseus, son of Laertes,
no longer waste your beautiful skin nor eat your heart out
in lamentation for your husband. Yet I do not blame you.
265   For any woman mourns when she loses her wedded husband,
with whom she has lain in love and borne children, even a lesser
man than Odysseus. They say that he was like the immortals.
But now give over your lamentation, and mark what I tell you,
for I say to you without deception, without concealment,
270   that I have heard of the present homecoming of Odysseus.
He is near, in the rich land of the men of Thesprotia,
and alive, and bringing many treasures back to his household.
He collects this about the district. His eager companions
were lost to him, with his hollow ship, on the wine-blue water
275   as he left the island of Thrinakia, for Zeus and Helios
hated him, since his companions killed the cattle of Helios.
So they all perished in the wash of the great sea; only
Odysseus, riding the keel, was cast ashore by the sea swell
on the land of the Phaiakians, who are near the immortals;
280   and they honored him in their hearts as if he had been a divinity,
and gave him much, and they themselves were willing to carry him
home without harm. So Odysseus would have been home a long time
before this, but in his mind he thought it more profitable
to go about and visit much country, collecting possessions.
285   For Odysseus knew profitable ways beyond all other
men who are mortal, no other man could rival him at it.
So Pheidon, king of the Thesprotians, told me the story;
and he swore to me in my presence, as he poured out a libation
in his house, that the ship was drawn down to the sea, and the crew were
        ready
290   to carry Odysseus back again to his own dear country;
but before that he sent me off, for a ship of Thesprotian
men happened then to be sailing for Doulichion, rich in wheatfields.
And he showed me all the possessions gathered in by Odysseus;
these would feed a succession of heirs to the tenth generation,
295   so many treasures are stored for him in the house of the great king.

But he said Odysseus had gone to Dodona, to listen
to the will of Zeus, out of the holy deep-leaved oak tree,
for how he could come back to the rich countryside of Ithaka,
in secret or openly, having been by now long absent.
300 So he is safe, as you see, and is now coming back. He is very
close at hand, and will not for long be far from his country
and his own people. I will swear you a firm oath to this.
Zeus be my witness, first of the gods, and the table of friendship,
and the hearth of blameless Odysseus, to which I come as a suppliant,
305 all these things are being accomplished in the way I tell them.
Some time within this very year Odysseus will be here,
either at the waning of the moon or at its onset.'
    Circumspect Penelope said to him in answer:
'If only this word, stranger and guest, were brought to fulfillment,
310 soon you would be aware of my love and many gifts given
by me, so any man who met you would call you blessed.
But here is the way I think in my mind, and the way it will happen.
Odysseus will never come home again, nor will you be given
conveyance, for there are none to give orders left in the household
315 such as Odysseus was among men—if he ever existed—
for receiving respected strangers and sending them off on their journeys.
But come, handmaidens, give him a wash and spread a couch for him
here, with bedding and coverlets and with shining blankets,
so that he can keep warm as he waits for Dawn of the golden
320 throne, and early tomorrow you shall give him a bath, anoint him,
so that he can sit in the hall beside Telemachos
and expect to dine there; and it will be the worse for any
of those men who inflicts heart-wasting annoyance on him;
he will accomplish nothing here for all his terrible
325 spite; for how, my friend, will you learn if I in any way
surpass the rest of women, in mind and thoughtful good sense,
if you must attend, badly dressed and unwashed, the feasting
in the palace? Human beings live for only a short time,
and when a man is harsh himself, and his mind knows harsh thoughts,
330 all men pray that sufferings will befall him hereafter
while he lives; and when he is dead all men make fun of him.
But when a man is blameless himself, and his thoughts are blameless,
the friends he has entertained carry his fame widely
to all mankind, and many are they who call him excellent.'

to wash Odysseus' feet

335   Then resourceful Odysseus spoke in turn and answered her:
'O respected wife of Odysseus, son of Laertes,
coverlets and shining rugs have been hateful to me
ever since that time when I left the snowy mountains
of Crete behind me, and went away on my long-oared vessel.
340   I will lie now as I have lain before through the sleepless
nights; for many have been the nights when on an unpleasant
couch I lay and awaited the throned Dawn in her splendor.
Nor is there any desire in my heart for foot basins, to wash
my feet, nor shall any woman lay hold of my feet, not one
345   of those such as do your work for you in your palace;
not unless there is some aged and virtuous woman
whose heart has had to endure as many troubles as mine has.
If such a one were to touch my feet, I should not be angry.'
    Then in turn circumspect Penelope answered:
350   'Dear friend, never before has there been any man so thoughtful,
among those friends from far places who have come to my palace
as guests, so thoughtful and so well-considered is everything
you say. I do have one old woman, whose thoughts are prudent,
who was nurse to that unhappy man, and took good care of him.
355   She took him up in her hands when first his mother had borne him,
and she shall wash your feet, though she has little strength for it.
Come then, circumspect Eurykleia, rise up and wash
the feet of one who is the same age as your master. Odysseus
must by this time have just such hands and feet as you do,
360   for in misfortune mortal men grow old more suddenly.'
    So he spoke, and the old woman covered her face in her hands,
and shed hot tears, and spoke to him in words of compassion:
'How helpless I am to help you, my child. Surely Zeus hated you
beyond all other men, though you had a godly spirit;
365   for no man among mortals ever has burned so many
thigh pieces to Zeus who delights in the thunder, nor given so many
choice and grand sacrifices, as you prayed you might come to
a sleek old age, and raise your glorious son to manhood.
Now for you alone he took away your day of homecoming.
370   So it must be for him also that in the houses of far-off
friends, whose famous homes he enters, the women tease him,
as now these sluts are all teasing you, stranger, and it is
to avoid their abuse and shameful speaking you will not let them

wash your feet. But circumspect Penelope, daughter
375   of Ikarios told me to do it, nor am I unwilling.
So I shall wash your feet, both for the sake of Penelope
but also for yourself, since the heart is stirred within me
by sorrows; but come, attend to me and the word I tell you.
There have been many hard-traveling strangers who have come here,
380   but I say I have never seen one as like as you are
to Odysseus, both as to your feet, and voice and appearance.'
        Then resourceful Odysseus spoke in turn and answered her:
'So all say, old dame, who with their eyes have looked on
the two of us. They say we two are very similar
385   each to each, as you yourself have noticed and tell me.'
        So he spoke, and the old woman took up the shining basin
she used for foot washing, and poured in a great deal of water, the cold
first, and then she added the hot to it. Now Odysseus
was sitting close to the fire, but suddenly turned to the dark side;
390   for presently he thought in his heart that, as she handled him,
she might be aware of his scar, and all his story might come out.
She came up close and washed her lord, and at once she recognized
that scar, which once the boar with his white tusk had inflicted
on him, when he went to Parnassos, to Autolykos and his children.
395   This was his mother's noble father, who surpassed all men
in thievery and the art of the oath, and the god Hermes
himself had endowed him, for he had pleased him by burning the thigh
        bones
of lambs and kids, and the god freely gave him his favor.
Autolykos came once to the rich country of Ithaka,
400   and found that a child there was newly born to his daughter;
and, as he finished his evening meal, Eurykleia laid him
upon his very knees, and spoke him a word and named him:
'Autolykos, now find yourself that name you will bestow
on your own child's dear child, for you have prayed much to have him.'
405   Then Autolykos spoke to her and gave her an answer:
'My son-in-law and daughter, give him the name I tell you;
since I have come to this place distasteful to many, women
and men alike on the prospering earth, so let him be given
the name Odysseus, that is distasteful. Then when he grows up,
410   and comes to the great house of his mother's line, and Parnassos,
where there are possessions that are called mine, I will give him

freely of these to make him happy, and send him back to you.'
This was why Odysseus came, so that he would give him
glorious presents. Autolykos and the sons of Autolykos
415　greeted him with clasping of hands and words of endearment,
and Amphithea, his mother's mother, embraced Odysseus,
and kissed his head and kissed too his beautiful shining
eyes. Autolykos gave his glorious sons the order
to make ready the dinner, and they listened to his urging.
420　Presently they brought in an ox, a male, five years old.
They skinned the victim and put it in order, and butchered the carcass,
and cut the meat expertly into small pieces, and spitted the morsels,
and roasted all carefully, and shared out the portions.
So, for the whole length of the day until the sun's setting,
425　they feasted, nor was any man's hunger denied a fair portion;
but when the sun went down and the sacred darkness came over,
then they went to their beds and took the blessing of slumber.
But when the young Dawn showed again with her rosy fingers,
they went out on their way to the hunt, the dogs and the people,
430　these sons of Autolykos, and with them noble Odysseus
went. They came to the steep mountain, mantled in forest,
Parnassos, and soon they were up in the windy folds. At this time,
the sun had just begun to strike on the plowlands, rising
out of the quiet water and the deep stream of the Ocean.
435　The hunters came to a wooded valley, and on ahead of them
ran the dogs, casting about for the tracks, and behind them
the sons of Autolykos, and with them noble Odysseus
went close behind the hounds, shaking his spear far-shadowing.
Now there, inside that thick of the bush, was the lair of a great boar.
440　Neither could the force of wet-blown winds penetrate here,
nor could the shining sun ever strike through with his rays, nor yet
could the rain pass all the way through it, so close together
it grew, with a fall of leaves drifted in dense profusion.
The thudding made by the feet of men and dogs came to him
445　as they closed on him in the hunt, and against them he from his woodlair
bristled strongly his nape, and with fire from his eyes glaring
stood up to face them close. The first of all was Odysseus,
who swept in, holding high in his heavy hand the long spear,
and furious to stab, but too quick for him the boar drove
450　over the knee, and with his tusk gashed much of the flesh,

tearing sidewise, and did not reach the bone of the man. Now
Odysseus stabbed at him, and hit him in the right shoulder,
and straight on through him passed the point of the shining spearhead.
He screamed and dropped in the dust, and the life spirit flittered from
    him.

455 The dear sons of Autolykos were busy to tend him,
and understandingly they bound up the wound of stately
godlike Odysseus, and singing incantations over it
stayed the black blood, and soon came back to the house of their loving
father. Then Autolykos and the sons of Autolykos,

460 healing him well and giving him shining presents, sent him
speedily back rejoicing to his own beloved country
in Ithaka, and there his father and queenly mother
were glad in his homecoming, and asked about all that had happened,
and how he came by his wound, and he told well his story,

465 how in the hunt the boar with his white tusk had wounded him
as he went up to Parnassos with the sons of Autolykos.
    The old woman, holding him in the palms of her hands, recognized
this scar as she handled it. She let his foot go, so that
his leg, which was in the basin, fell free, and the bronze echoed.

470 The basin tipped over on one side, and the water spilled out
on the floor. Pain and joy seized her at once, and both eyes
filled with tears, and the springing voice was held within her.
She took the beard of Odysseus in her hands and spoke to him:
'Then, dear child, you are really Odysseus. I did not know you

475 before; not until I had touched my lord all over.'
    She spoke, and turned her eyes toward Penelope, wishing
to indicate to her her beloved husband's presence,
but Penelope was not able to look that way, or perceive him,
since Athene turned aside her perception. Odysseus

480 groped for her, and took her by the throat with his right hand,
while with the other he pulled her closer to him, and said to her:
'Nurse, why are you trying to kill me? You yourself suckled me
at your own breast; and now at last after suffering
much, I have come, in the twentieth year, back to my own country.

485 But now that you have learned who I am, and the god put it into
your mind, hush, let nobody else in the palace know of it.
For so I tell you straight out, and it will be a thing accomplished.
If you do, and by my hands the god beats down the arrogant

suitors, nurse of mine though you are, I will not spare you
490 when I kill the rest of the serving maids in my palace.'
     Then in turn circumspect Eurykleia said to him:
'My child, what sort of word escaped your teeth's barrier?
You know what strength is steady in me, and it will not give way
at all, but I shall hold as stubborn as stone or iron.
495 And put away in your heart this other thing that I tell you.
If by your hands the god beats down the arrogant suitors,
then I will give you the list of those women who in your palace
have been mutinous against you, and tell you which are innocent.'
     Then resourceful Odysseus spoke in turn and answered her:
500 'Nurse, why should you tell me of them? There is no need to.
I myself will properly study each and learn of
each. Leave it to the gods and keep the story in silence.'
     So he spoke, and the old woman went back through the hall, to fetch
another basin, for all the water that had been there formerly
505 was spilled. When she had washed him and anointed him with oil,
Odysseus drew his chair closer to the fire, trying
to keep warm, but hid the scar under his ragged clothing.
Circumspect Penelope then began their talking:
'Friend, I will stay here and talk to you, just for a little.
510 To be sure, it will soon be the time for sweet rest,
for one delicious sleep takes hold of, although he may be
sorrowful. The divinity gave me grief beyond measure.
The day times I indulge in lamentation, mourning
as I look to my own tasks and those of my maids in the palace.
515 But after the night comes and sleep has taken all others,
I lie on my bed, and the sharp anxieties swarming
thick and fast on my beating heart torment my sorrowing
self. As when Pandareos' daughter, the greenwood nightingale,
perching in the deep of the forest foliage sings out
520 her lovely song, when springtime has just begun; she, varying
the manifold strains of her voice, pours out the melody, mourning
Itylos, son of the lord Zethos, her own beloved
child, whom she once killed with the bronze when the madness was on
     her;
so my mind is divided and starts one way, then another.
525 Shall I stay here by my son and keep all in order,
my property, my serving maids, and my great high-roofed house,

keep faith with my husband's bed and regard the voice of the people,
or go away at last with the best of all those Achaians
who court me here in the palace, with endless gifts to win me?
530 My son, while he was still a child and thoughtless, would not
let me marry and leave the house of my husband; but now
that he is grown a tall man and come to maturity's measure,
he even prays me to go home out of the palace, fretting
over the property, which the Achaian men are devouring.
535 But come, listen to a dream of mine and interpret it for me.
I have twenty geese here about the house, and they feed on
grains of wheat from the water trough. I love to watch them.
But a great eagle with crooked beak came down from the mountain,
and broke the necks of them all and killed them. So the whole twenty
540 lay dead about the house, but he soared high in the bright air.
Then I began to weep—that was in my dream—and cried out
aloud, and around me gathered the fair-haired Achaian women
as I cried out sorrowing for my geese killed by the eagle.
But he came back again and perched on the jut of the gabled
545 roof. He now had a human voice and spoke aloud to me:
"Do not fear, O daughter of far-famed Ikarios.
This is no dream, but a blessing real as day. You will see it
done. The geese are the suitors, and I, the eagle, have been
a bird of portent, but now I am your own husband, come home,
550 and I shall inflict shameless destruction on all the suitors."
So he spoke; and then the honey-sweet sleep released me,
and I looked about and saw the geese in my palace, feeding
on their grains of wheat from the water trough, just as they had been.'
     Then resourceful Odysseus spoke in turn and answered her:
555 'Lady, it is impossible to read this dream and avoid it
by turning another way, since Odysseus himself has told you
its meaning, how it will end. The suitors' doom is evident
for one and all. Not one will avoid his death and destruction.'
     Circumspect Penelope said to him in answer:
560 'My friend, dreams are things hard to interpret, hopeless to puzzle
out, and people find that not all of them end in anything.
There are two gates through which the insubstantial dreams issue.
One pair of gates is made of horn, and one of ivory.
Those of the dreams which issue through the gate of sawn ivory,
565 these are deceptive dreams, their message is never accomplished.

The contest of the bow is proposed

But those that come into the open through the gates of the polished
horn accomplish the truth for any mortal who sees them.
I do not think that this strange dream that I had came to me
through this gate. My son and I would be glad if it did so.
570 And put away in your heart this other thing that I tell you.
This dawn will be a day of evil name, which will take me
away from the house of Odysseus; for now I will set up a contest:
those axes which, in his palace, he used to set up in order
so that, twelve in all, they stood in a row, like timbers
575 to hold a ship. He would stand far off, and send a shaft through them.
Now I will set these up as a contest before my suitors,
and the one who takes the bow in his hands, strings it with the greatest
ease, and sends an arrow clean through all the twelve axes
shall be the one I will go away with, forsaking this house
580 where I was a bride, a lovely place and full of good living.
I think that even in my dreams I shall never forget it.'
      Then resourceful Odysseus spoke in turn and answered her:
'O respected wife of Odysseus, son of Laertes,
do not put off this contest in your house any longer.
585 Before these people can handle the well-wrought bow, and manage
to hook the string and bend it, and send a shaft through the iron,
Odysseus of the many designs will be back here with you.'
      Circumspect Penelope said to him in answer:
'If, my friend, you were willing to sit by me in my palace
590 and entertain me, no sleep would be drifted over my eyelids.
But it is in no way possible for people forever
to go without sleep; and the immortals have given to mortals
each his own due share all over the grain-giving corn land.
So I shall now go back again to my upper chamber,
595 and lie on my bed, which is made a sorrowful thing now, always
disordered with the tears I have wept, ever since Odysseus
went away to that evil, not-to-be-mentioned Ilion.
There I must lie; but you can sleep here in the house, either
bedding down on the floor, or they can make a bed for you.'
600   So she spoke, and went back up to her shining chamber,
not alone, since others, her women, went to attend her.
She went back to the upper story with her attendant
women, and wept for Odysseus, her beloved husband, until
gray-eyed Athene cast sweet slumber over her eyelids.

BOOK XX

Then the noble Odysseus bedded down in the forecourt,
and spread beneath him the raw hide of an ox, and uppermost
many fleeces of sheep the Achaians had dedicated.
When he had lain down, Eurynome threw a blanket over him.
5   There, devising evils in his heart for the suitors,
Odysseus lay awake; and out of the palace issued
those women who in the past had been going to bed with the suitors,
full of cheerful spirits and greeting each other with laughter.
But the spirit deep in the heart of Odysseus was stirred by this,
10   and much he pondered in the division of mind and spirit,
whether to spring on them and kill each one, or rather
to let them lie this one more time with the insolent suitors,
for the last and latest time; but the heart was growling within him.
And as a bitch, facing an unknown man, stands over
15   her callow puppies, and growls and rages to fight, so Odysseus'
heart was growling inside him as he looked on these wicked actions.
He struck himself on the chest and spoke to his heart and scolded it:
'Bear up, my heart. You have had worse to endure before this
on that day when the irresistible Cyclops ate up
20   my strong companions, but you endured it until intelligence
got you out of the cave, though you expected to perish.'
    So he spoke, addressing his own dear heart within him;
and the heart in great obedience endured and stood it
without complaint, but the man himself was twisting and turning.

25 And as a man with a paunch pudding, that has been filled with
blood and fat, tosses it back and forth over a blazing
fire, and the pudding itself strains hard to be cooked quickly;
so he was twisting and turning back and forth, meditating
how, though he was alone against many, he could lay hands on
30 the shameless suitors. And at this time Athene, descending
from the sky, came close to him, and wore the shape of a lady.
She came and stood above his head, and spoke a word to him:
'Why are you wakeful now, O most wretched of all men?
Here is your house, and here is your wife in the house, and here is
35 your son; and he is the kind of son any man would long for.'
   Then resourceful Odysseus spoke in turn and answered her:
'Yes, O goddess, all you have said was fair and orderly;
yet still, here is something the heart inside me is pondering,
how, when I am alone against many, I can lay hands on
40 the shameless suitors. And they are always here in a body.
And here is a still bigger problem that my heart is pondering.
Even if, by grace of Zeus and yourself, I kill them,
how shall I make my escape? It is what I would have you think on.'
   Then in turn the goddess, gray-eyed Athene, said to him:
45 'Stubborn man! Anyone trusts even a lesser companion
than I, who is mortal, and does not have so many ideas.
But I am a god, and through it all I keep watch over you
in every endeavor of yours. And now I tell you this plainly:
even though there were fifty battalions of mortal people
50 standing around us, furious to kill in the spirit of battle,
even so you could drive away their cattle and fat sheep.
So let sleep take you now. There is annoyance in lying
awake and on guard all night. You will soon be out of your troubles.'
   So she spoke, and scattered slumber over his eyelids,
55 and she, shining among goddesses, went back to Olympos.
But when the sleep had caught him, a relaxing sleep, slipping
the cares from his mind, at that time his virtuous wife wakened
in turn, and cried, sitting up in her soft bed. But after
she had satisfied all her desire with weeping, then she,
60 shining among women, prayed first of all to Artemis:
'Artemis, goddess and queen, daughter of Zeus, how I wish
that with the cast of your arrow you could take the life from inside
my heart, this moment, or that soon the stormwind would snatch me

    away, and be gone, carrying me down misty pathways,
65   and set me down where the recurrent Ocean empties
    his stream; as once the stormwinds carried away the daughters
    of Pandareos. The gods killed their parents, and they were left there
    orphaned in the palace, and radiant Aphrodite
    tended them and fed them with cheese, and sweet honey, and pleasant
70   wine; and Hera granted to them, beyond all women,
    beauty and good sense, and chaste Artemis gave them stature,
    and Athene instructed them in glorious handiwork.
    But when bright Aphrodite had gone up to tall Olympos
    to request for these girls the achievement of blossoming marriage,
75   from Zeus who rejoices in the thunder—and he well knows
    all things, the luck and the lucklessness of mortal people—
    meanwhile the seizing stormwinds carried away these maidens
    and gave them over into the care of the hateful Furies.
    So I wish that they who have their homes on Olympos
80   would make me vanish, or sweet-haired Artemis strike me, so that
    I could meet the Odysseus I long for, even under the hateful
    earth, and not have to please the mind of an inferior
    husband. Yet the evil is endurable, when one
    cries through the days, with heart constantly troubled, yet still
85   is taken by sleep in the nights; for sleep is oblivion of all
    things, both good and evil, when it has shrouded the eyelids.
    But now the god has sent the evil dreams thronging upon me.
    For on this very night there was one who lay by me, like him
    as he was when he went with the army, so that my own heart
90   was happy. I thought it was no dream, but a waking vision.'
      So she spoke, and Dawn of the golden throne came on her.
    Great Odysseus was aware of her voice crying,
    and pondered then, and it seemed to him in his mind that now
    she was standing by his head, and had recognized him already.
95   He rolled together the blanket and fleece, where he had been sleeping,
    and laid them down by the chair in the hall, and taking the oxhide
    out, laid it down, and prayed to Zeus, with his hands lifted:
    'Father Zeus, if willingly you gods led me over
    wet and dry to my land, after giving too much affliction,
100 let one of the waking people send me an omen from inside
    the house; and let Zeus also show me an outside portent.'
      So he spoke in prayer, and Zeus of the counsels heard him.

Good omens in the morning

Immediately he sent his thunder from shining Olympos
high above the clouds, and noble Odysseus was happy.
105 And from the house a mill woman sent him an omen.
She was near by, where the shepherd of the host had set up
his hand mills, and there twelve women in all had been bending
to grind the wheat and the barley flour, men's marrow. The others,
since they had finished grinding their wheat, by now were sleeping,
110 but this one had not ended her work, and she was the weakest.
She stopped the mill and spoke aloud, a sign for her master:
'Father Zeus, you who are lord of the gods and people,
now you have thundered loud from the starry sky, although
there is no cloud. You show this forth, a portent for someone.
115 Grant now also for wretched me this prayer that I make you.
On this day let the suitors take, for the last and latest
time, their desirable feasting in the halls of Odysseus.
For it is they who have broken my knees with heart-sore labor
as I grind the meal for them. Let this be their final feasting.'
120   So she spoke, and great Odysseus welcomed the ominous
speech, and the thunder of Zeus. He thought he would punish the sinners.
    The other serving women in the fine house of Odysseus
had gathered, and were lighting the weariless fire on the fireplace.
Telemachos, a man like a god, rose up from his bed
125 and put on his clothes, and slung a sharp sword over his shoulder.
Underneath his shining feet he bound the fair sandals,
and then caught up a powerful spear, edged with sharp bronze.
He came and stood on the threshold and spoke now to Eurykleia:
'Dear nurse, how have you treated the stranger-guest in our house?
130 With food and a bed? Or has he been left to lie uncared-for?
That is the way my mother is, though she is sensible.
Impulsively she favors the wrong man, the worse one
among mortals, and lets the better man go, unfavored.'
    Then in turn circumspect Eurykleia said to him:
135 'Child, do not find fault with her this time. She is blameless.
For he sat here and drank his wine, as he himself wanted,
but he said he had no more hunger for food. She asked him.
But afterward, when he was thinking of rest and sleep, then
she did tell the serving women to make up his bedding,
140 but it was he, as one forever wretched and without
fortune, who would not sleep in a bed, nor under blankets,

but in the raw hide of an ox and under fleeces
he slept in the forecourt, and we put a blanket over him.'
      So she spoke, and Telemachos went out through the palace,
145 holding his spear, and a pair of light-footed dogs went with him.
He went off to the assembly to join the strong-greaved Achaians.
But Eurykleia, shining among women, the daughter
of Ops, the son of Peisenor, gave orders to the maidservants:
'To work. Some of you keep busy sweeping the palace,
150 and freshen the floor with water, and lay the purple coverlets
over the well-wrought chairs. Some others, wash all the tables
thoroughly clear with sponges, and clean the wine bowls, also
the wrought and double-handled drinking-cups; others, be off
now to the spring to fetch the water, and come back quickly.
155 For the suitors will not long be away from the palace,
but will arrive very early, since this is a public festival.'
      So she spoke, and they listened well to her, and obeyed her,
and twenty of them went on their way to the spring of dark water,
while others, remaining in the house, did their work expertly.
160   Then the haughty menservants came in, and these presently
split the firewood well and expertly, and now the women
came back from the spring, and next after them came in the swineherd
driving in three porkers, which were the best in his keeping.
These he left to graze inside the handsome enclosure,
165 while he himself spoke to Odysseus in words of endearment:
'Friend, have the Achaians been giving you more regard, or
do they slight you still in the halls, as they did earlier?'
      Then resourceful Odysseus spoke in turn and answered him:
'How I wish, Eumaios, the gods would punish the outrage
170 these men do in the violence of their reckless designs, here in
the house of another man. They have no gift of modesty.'
      Now as these two were conversing thus with each other,
Melanthios, who was the herdsman of the goats, approached them,
driving the goats that showed the best in all of his goatflocks
175 to be the suitors' dinner. Two other herdsmen followed him.
Melanthios tethered the goats under the echoing portico,
and he himself now spoke to Odysseus, in terms of revilement:
'Stranger, are you still to be here in the house, to pester
the gentlemen with your begging? Will you not take yourself outside
180 and elsewhere? I think that now you and I can no longer

part, until we have tried our fists. There is nothing orderly
about your begging. And other Achaians are feasting elsewhere.'
    So he spoke. Resourceful Odysseus gave him no answer,
but shook his head in silence, deeply devising evils.
185   The third man to come in was Philoitios, leader of people,
driving in for the suitors a barren cow, and fat goats.
The ferryman had brought these over; they give conveyance
to people generally besides, whoever comes to them.
Philoitios tethered the beasts well under the echoing portico,
190 then went himself and stood close by the swineherd, and asked him:
'Who is this stranger, swineherd, newly arrived to visit
this house of ours? From what people does he claim origin?
Where is his ancestral place and the land of his fathers?
Unlucky man; he is like a king and a lord in appearance.
195 Yet it is true; the homeless men are those whom the gods hold
in despite, when they spin misery even for princes.'
    He spoke, and stood close by Odysseus, and offered his right hand,
and spoke to him aloud and addressed him in winged words, saying:
'Welcome, father and stranger; may prosperous days befall you
200 hereafter; but now you are held in the grip of many misfortunes.
Father Zeus, no god beside is more baleful than you are.
You have no pity on men, once you yourself have created
them; you bring them into misfortune and dismal sufferings.
It has come home to me, when I saw it. My eyes are tearful
205 as I remember Odysseus, since I think he too is wearing
such rags upon him as this, and wandering among peoples
if he is alive at all anywhere, and looks on the sunlight.
But if he is now dead and gone to the house of Hades,
I mourn then for blameless Odysseus, who when I was little
210 set me in charge of his oxen in the Kephallenian country.
Now these cattle are marvelously grown, nor could one
better gather an increase of broad-faced cattle than as
these are bred. But other men tell me to drive them to them
to eat, and they care nothing about the son in the palace,
215 nor tremble before the gods' regard; now they are grown eager
to divide the possessions of the master, who has been absent
long. But here is a problem that the heart deep within me
has long resolved. While the son is here, it would be cowardly
to take my cattle with me and go to another district

Philoitios found to be loyal

220 and alien men; and yet again it grows worse to stay here,
as one set in charge of other men's cattle, and suffer hardships.
And long ago I would have escaped from here, and gone to
some other powerful king, since this is no longer endurable;
yet still I think of that luckless man, how he may come back

225 and all throughout the house may cause the suitors to scatter.'
    Then resourceful Odysseus spoke in turn and answered him:
'Oxherd, since you seem like neither a bad nor a senseless
man—and I myself know what good sense is in you—
so I will tell you this, and swear a great oath upon it.

230 Zeus be my witness, first of the gods, and the table of friendship,
and the hearth of blameless Odysseus, to which I come as a suppliant;
Odysseus will come home again, while you are still here
in the house, and with your own eyes, if you desire to,
you can watch him killing the suitors, who are supreme here.'

235   Then the herdsman of oxen spoke in turn and answered him:
'How I wish, my friend, that the son of Kronos would make good
your saying; then you would see what kind of strength my hands have.'
    So Eumaios also prayed to all the divinities
that they would grant the homecoming of thoughtful Odysseus.

240   Now as these men were conversing thus with each other,
the suitors were compacting their plan of death and destruction
for Telemachos, and a bird flew over them on the left side.
This was a high-flown eagle, and carried a tremulous pigeon.
Now it was Amphinomos who spoke forth and addressed them:

245 'O friends, this plan of ours to murder Telemachos will not
ever be brought to completion; so let us think of our feasting.'
    So Amphinomos spoke, and his word was acceptable to them.
They, when they had entered the house of godlike Odysseus,
laid their mantles down along the chairs and the benches,

250 and set about sacrificing great-sized sheep, and fat goats,
and sacrificing an ox of the herd, and fattened porkers.
They roasted the vitals and distributed them, and they blended
the wine in the mixing bowls, and the swineherd passed the wine cups
about, and Philoitios, leader of men, served them the bread

255 in beautiful baskets, and Melanthios poured the wine for them.
They put forth their hands to the good things that lay ready before them.
    Telemachos, his heart full of guile, seated Odysseus
inside the well-constructed hall, and by the stone threshold,

setting down a poor chair for him, and a little table,
260 and set before him a portion of vitals, and poured wine for him
in a golden drinking cup, and then he spoke a word to him:
'Take your place here and drink your wine in the men's company.
I myself will defend you against the blows and the insults
of all the suitors. This house does not belong to the people,
265 but it belongs to Odysseus; he acquired it; this makes it
mine; and so, you suitors, hold back your spirit for insults
and blows, or else there may be a quarrel and fight between us.'
So he spoke, and all of them bit their lips in amazement
at Telemachos, and the daring way he had spoken to them.
270 Now Antinoös, the son of Eupeithes, said to them:
'We Achaians must accept the word of Telemachos,
though it is hard. Now he threatens us very strongly.
Zeus, son of Kronos, stopped us; otherwise we should before now
have put him down in his halls, though he is a lucid speaker.'
275 So spoke Antinoös, but the other paid no attention.
The heralds came through the town driving the holy hecatomb
of the gods, and the flowing-haired Achaians assembled under
the shady grove of him who strikes from afar, Apollo.
When they had roasted and taken off the spits the outer
280 meats, dividing shares they held their communal high feast.
Then they who were working set down before Odysseus an equal
portion, such as they got themselves, for this was the order
of Telemachos, beloved son of godlike Odysseus.
And yet Athene would not altogether permit the arrogant
285 suitors to keep from heart-hurting outrage, so to make greater
the anguish in the heart of Odysseus, son of Laertes.
There was a man among the suitors versed in villainy;
Ktesippos was his name, and he had his home in Same.
He, in the confidence of his amazing possessions,
290 courted the wife of Odysseus, who had been so long absent.
This man now spoke forth among the insolent suitors:
'Hear me now, you haughty suitors, while I say something.
The stranger has had his share long since, and, as is proper,
an equal one; for it is not well nor just to make light of
295 the guests of Telemachos, who come to him in his palace.
Come, let me too give him a guest gift, so he can give it
as prize to the woman who washes his feet, or to some other

one of the servants in the house of godlike Odysseus.'
    He spoke, and with his heavy hand he caught up an ox hoof
300   that lay by in the basket, and threw it. Odysseus avoided
this by an easy shift of his head. He smiled in his anger
a very sardonic smile. The hoof hit the wall of the well-built
house, and Telemachos spoke now and scolded Ktesippos:
'Ktesippos, it was the better for your heart that it happened
305   so; you missed the stranger, he avoided your missile.
I would have struck you with my sharp spear fair in the middle,
and instead of your marriage your father would have been busy
with your funeral here. Let none display any rudeness
here in my house. I now notice all and know of it, better
310   and worse alike, but before now I was only an infant.
Even so, we have had to look on this and endure it
all, the sheepflocks being slaughtered, the wine drunk up,
and the food, since it is hard for one man to stand off many.
Come then, no longer do me harm in your hostility.
315   But if you are determined to murder me with the sharp bronze,
then that would be my wish also, since it would be far better
than to have to go on watching forever these shameful activities,
guests being battered about, or to see you rudely mishandling
the serving women all about the beautiful palace.'
320   So he spoke, and all of them stayed stricken to silence.
At last Agelaos, son of Damastor, spoke forth among them:
'Dear friends, no man must be angry, nor yet with violent
answers attack what has been spoken in justice. And do not
strike the stranger, as you have done, nor yet any other
325   serving man who is in the house of godlike Odysseus.
But, to Telemachos and his mother, I offer gentle
advice, if this might be pleasing to the hearts of both of them.
As long as the spirits in the hearts of you both were hopeful
that Odysseus of the many designs would have his homecoming,
330   then no one could blame you for waiting for him, and holding
the suitors off in the palace, since that was the better way for you
in case Odysseus did come home and return to his palace.
But now it has become evident that he never will come back.
Come then; sit beside your mother and give her this counsel,
335   to marry the one who is the best man and brings the most numerous
gifts. So you can be happy, control your father's inheritance,

and eat and drink, while she looks after the house of another.'
    Then the thoughtful Telemachos said to him in answer:
'But, by Zeus, Agelaos, I swear, and by the sufferings
340 of my father, who has died or is driven far from Ithaka,
I do not delay my mother's marriage; rather I urge her
to marry the one she wants, and I offer them countless presents.
But I am ashamed to drive her unwilling out of the palace
with a strict word. May this not be the end god makes of it.'
345   So spoke Telemachos. In the suitors Pallas Athene
stirred up uncontrollable laughter, and addled their thinking.
Now they laughed with jaws that were no longer their own.
The meat they ate was a mess of blood, their eyes were bursting
full of tears, and their laughter sounded like lamentation.
350 Godlike Theoklymenos now spoke out among them:
'Poor wretches, what evil has come on you? Your heads and faces
and the knees underneath you are shrouded in night and darkness;
a sound of wailing has broken out, your cheeks are covered
with tears, and the walls bleed, and the fine supporting pillars.
355 All the forecourt is huddled with ghosts, the yard is full of them
as they flock down to the underworld and the darkness. The sun
has perished out of the sky, and a foul mist has come over.'
    So he spoke, and all of them laughed happily at him.
Eurymachos, son of Polybos, began speaking among them:
360 'This stranger newly come from elsewhere has lost his senses.
Come, young men, and give him an escort out of the palace
to get to the marketplace, since everything here is darkness.'
    Then in turn godlike Theoklymenos answered:
'Eurymachos, I do not want you to give me an escort.
365 I have eyes and I have ears, and I have both my feet,
and a mind inside my breast which is not without understanding.
These will take me outside the house, since I see the evil
coming upon you, and not one of the suitors avoiding
this will escape; for in the house of godlike Odysseus
370 you are outrageous to men, and all your designs are reckless.'
    So he spoke, and walked out of the well-settled palace,
and made his way to Peiraios, who hospitably received him.
But the suitors now were glancing one at another, trying
to tease Telemachos about his guests, and laughing over them;
375 and thus would go the word of one of the arrogant young men:

The suitors tease Telemachos

'No one has worse luck with his guests than you, Telemachos.
Here, for one, somebody brought you in this vagabond
who wants his food and his wine, who does not know how to do any
work, who has no strength, but is just a weight on the good land.
380   And now this other one stood up and began to prophesy.
If you would listen to what I say, it would be far better.
Let us put these guests in a vessel with many oarlocks
and take them to the Sicilians. There they would fetch a good price.'
      So spoke the suitors, but Telemachos paid no attention,
385   but looked across at his father silently, always waiting
for the time when he would lay his hands on the shameless suitors.
      The daughter of Ikarios, circumspect Penelope,
had taken her beautiful chair and set it just outside the door,
and listened to every word the men in the hall were saying.
390   For these were laughing aloud as they prepared a dinner
that was sweet and staying, for they had made a very big sacrifice;
but there could not be a meal that was more unpleasant than this one,
such was to be the attack that the powerful man and the goddess
would make on them. For they had first begun the wrongdoing.

BOOK XXI

But now the goddess, gray-eyed Athene, put it in the mind
of the daughter of Ikarios, circumspect Penelope,
to set the bow before the suitors, and the gray iron,
in the house of Odysseus: the contest, the beginning of the slaughter.
5   So she ascended the high staircase of her own house,
and in her solid hand took up the beautiful, brazen
and artfully curved key, with an ivory handle upon it.
With her attendant women she went to the inmost recess
of the chamber. There were stored away the master's possessions.
10   Bronze was there, and gold, and difficulty wrought iron,
and there the backstrung bow was stored away, and the quiver
to hold the arrows. There were many painful shafts inside it.
These were gifts from a friend whom he met in Lakedaimon,
Iphitos, son of Eurytos, one like the immortal
15   gods. These two, in Messene, had encountered each other
in the house of wise Ortilochos, at the time when Odysseus
went there on an errand enjoined by the whole community.
For men of Messene had come in ships with many oarlocks
and lifted three hundred sheep from Ithaka, also the herdsmen
20   with them, so Odysseus traveled far on the embassy
while still a boy, sent by his father and the rest of the elders.
Iphitos was there in search of his horses, twelve mares
he had lost; hard-working mule colts were with them, nursing.
These mares presently were to mean his doom and murder,

25 at the time when he came to the son of Zeus, strong-hearted,
    the man called Herakles, guilty of monstrous actions,
    who killed Iphitos while he was a guest in his household;
    hard man, without shame for the watchful gods, nor the table
    he had set for Iphitos, his guest; and when he had killed him
30 he kept the strong-footed horses for himself in his palace.
    In search of his mares, Iphitos met Odysseus, and gave him
    the bow, which once the great Eurytos had carried, and left it
    afterward to his son when he had died in his high house.
    Odysseus gave him in turn a sharp sword and a strong spear,
35 to begin their considerate friendship, but these two never
    entertained each other; before that, the son of Zeus killed
    Iphitos, son of Eurytos, one like the immortal
    gods, who gave Odysseus the bow. But Odysseus never
    took it with him when he went to war on the black ships,
40 but always it was stored away in his halls, in memory
    of a dear friend; but he carried it at home in his country.
        When she, shining among women, had come to the chamber,
    and had come up to the oaken threshold, which the carpenter
    once had expertly planed and drawn it true to a chalkline,
45 and fitted the door posts to it and joined on the shining door leaves,
    first she quickly set the fastening free of the hook, then
    she inserted the key and knocked the bolt upward, pushing
    the key straight in, and the door bellowed aloud, as a bull
    does, when he feeds in his pasture; such was the noise the splendid
50 doors made, struck with the key, and now they quickly spread open.
    Then she went up to the high platform, where there were standing
    chests, and in these were stored fragrant pieces of clothing.
    From there she reached, and took the bow from its peg, where it hung,
    in its own case, a shining thing that covered it. Thereupon
55 she sat down, and laid the bow on her dear knees, while she
    took her lord's bow out of its case, all the while weeping
    aloud. But when she had sated herself with tears and crying,
    she went on her way to the hall to be with the lordly suitors,
    bearing in her hand the backstrung bow, and the quiver
60 to hold the arrows, with many sorrowful shafts inside it.
    Her serving women carried the box for her, and there lay
    much iron and bronze, prizes that had been won by the master.
    When she, shining among women, came near the suitors,

and promises marriage to the best archer

she stood by the pillar that supported the roof with its joinery,
65 holding her shining veil in front of her face, to shield it,
and a devoted attendant was stationed on either side of her.
Now at once she spoke and addressed a word to the suitors:
'Hear me now, you haughty suitors, who have been using
this house for your incessant eating and drinking, though it
70 belongs to a man who has been gone for a long time; never
have you been able to bring any other saying before me,
but only your desire to make me your wife and marry me.
But come, you suitors, since here is a prize set out before you;
for I shall bring you the great bow of godlike Odysseus.
75 And the one who takes the bow in his hands, strings it with the greatest
ease, and sends an arrow clean through all the twelve axes,
shall be the one I go away with, forsaking this house
where I was a bride, a lovely place and full of good living.
I think that even in my dreams I shall never forget it.'
80   So she spoke, and told the noble swineherd, Eumaios,
to put the bow and the gray iron in front of the suitors.
Eumaios accepted it, in tears, and put them before them,
and the oxherd also wept, when he saw the bow of his master,
but Antinoös scolded the two of them, and spoke out and named them:
85 'You foolish countrymen, who never think of tomorrow,
poor wretches, why are you streaming tears, and troubling the lady
now, and stirring her heart, when she has enough already
of sadness her heart rests on, now she has lost a dear husband.
Go and sit in silence and eat, or else take your crying
90 out of the door and begone, but leave the bow where you put it,
a prize for the suitors to strive for; a terrible one; I do not think
that this well-polished bow can ever be strung easily.
There is no man among the lot of us who is such a one
as Odysseus used to be. I myself have seen him,
95 and I remember well, though I was still young and childish.'
    So he spoke, but the spirit inside his heart was hopeful
that he would be able to string the bow and shoot through the iron;
but he was to be the first to get a taste of the arrow
from the hands of blameless Odysseus, to whom he now paid no attention
100 as he sat in Odysseus' halls and encouraged all his companions.
    Now the hallowed prince, Telemachos, spoke his word to them:
'Ah, how Zeus, the son of Kronos, has made me witless.

My own beloved mother, though she is sensible, tells me
that she will forsake this house and go away with another;
105 and then, in the witlessness of my heart, I laugh and enjoy it.
But come, you suitors, since here is a prize set out before you,
a woman; there is none like her in all the Achaian country,
neither in sacred Pylos nor Argos nor in Mykene,
nor here in Ithaka itself, nor on the dark mainland.
110 You yourselves also know this; then why should I praise my mother?
But come, no longer drag things out with delays, nor turn back
still from the stringing of the bow, so that we may see it.
I myself am also willing to attempt the bow. Then,
if I can put the string on it and shoot through the iron,
115 my queenly mother would not go off with another, and leave me
sorrowing here in the house; since I would still be found here
as one now able to take up his father's glorious prizes.'
    He spoke, and sprang upright, laying aside from his shoulders
the red cloak, and from his shoulders too took off the sharp sword.
120 He began by setting up the axes, digging
one long trench for them all, and drawing it true to a chalkline,
and stamped down the earth around them; wonder seized the onlookers
at how orderly he set them up. He never had seen them
before. He went then and tried the bow, standing on the threshold.
125 Three times he made it vibrate, straining to bend it, and three times
he gave over the effort, yet in his heart was hopeful
of hooking the string to the bow and sending a shaft through the iron.
And now, pulling the bow for the fourth time, he would have strung it,
but Odysseus stopped him, though he was eager, making a signal
130 with his head. The hallowed prince, Telemachos, said to them:
'Shame on me. I must be then a coward and weakling,
or else I am still young, and my hands have yet no confidence
to defend myself against a man who has started a quarrel.
Come then, you who in your strength are greater than I am,
135 make your attempts on the bow, and let us finish the contest.'
    So he spoke, and put the bow from him, leaning it
on the ground, and against the compacted and polished door leaves,
and in the same place leaned the swift shaft against the fine handle,
and went back and sat in the chair from which he had risen.
140 Now Antinoös the son of Eupeithes said to them:
'Take your turns in order from left to right, my companions

all, beginning from the place where the wine is served out.'
   So spoke Antinoös, and his word was pleasing to all of them.
Leodes was the first to arise: the son of Oinops,
145 who was a diviner among them, and sat always in the corner
beside the fine mixing bowl. To him alone their excesses
were hateful, and he disapproved of all of the suitors.
He was the first to take up the bow and the swift arrow
now. He went then and tried the bow, standing on the threshold,
150 and could not string it; before that he ruined his soft, uncalloused
hands, pulling at the string, and now he spoke to the suitors:
'Friends, I cannot string this; let one of the others take it.
Here is a bow such that it will sunder many of the princes
from life and soul, since truly it is far better to die
155 than go on living and fail of that for whose sake we forever
keep on gathering here, all our days in expectation.
Now a man may be hopeful and in his heart desirous
of marrying Penelope, the wife of Odysseus.
But when the bow has been attempted, and all is made plain,
160 then one must court some other fair-robed Achaian woman,
and strive to win her with gifts of courtship; she will then marry
the man she is fated to have and who brings her the greatest presents.'
   So he spoke, and put the bow from him, leaning it
on the ground, and against the compacted and polished door leaves,
165 and in the same place leaned the swift shaft against the fine handle,
and went back and sat in the chair from which he had risen.
But now Antinoös scolded him, and spoke out and named him:
'Leodes, what sort of word escaped your teeth's barrier?
A terrible and shameful word. I am outraged to hear it;
170 if this is to be such a bow that will sunder the princes
from life and soul, because you are unable to string it.
You were not such a one, when the lady your mother bore you,
as ever to be able to manage the bow and the arrows.
But presently the other lordly suitors will string it.'
175   So he spoke, and now urged Melanthios the goatherd:
'Come now, Melanthios, light us a fire inside the palace,
and set beside it a great chair with fleeces upon it,
and bring out from the inside stores a great wheel of tallow,
so that we young men, having heated the bow and rubbed it
180 with fat, can then attempt to bend it, and finish the contest.'

So he spoke, and Melanthios quickly kindled the weariless
fire, and brought out the chair, and laid the fleeces upon it,
and brought out from the inside stores a great wheel of tallow.
The young men heated the bow and tried it, but were not able
185   to string it. They were not nearly strong enough. All this time
Antinoös still held back, as did godlike Eurymachos,
those lords of the suitors, out and away the best men among them.
    Two men, the oxherd and the swineherd of godlike Odysseus,
went out of the house, in company keeping close together,
190   and great Odysseus himself came from the house to join them.
But after they were out of the way of the doors and the courtyard,
Odysseus spoke to the two of them in words of endearment:
'Oxherd, and you too, swineherd, shall I say something to you,
or keep it hidden within? My spirit tells me to speak out.
195   What sort of fight would you put up in defense of Odysseus,
if he were to come suddenly, so, with the god leading him?
Would you fight for the suitors, or would you fight for Odysseus?
Tell me what your heart and spirit would have you answer.'
    Then the herdsman of oxen spoke in turn and answered him:
200   'Father Zeus, if you would achieve this prayer I ask for,
that the man himself would come home with the divinity guiding him,
then you yourself would see what kind of strength my hands have.'
    So Eumaios also prayed to all the divinities
that they would grant the homecoming of thoughtful Odysseus.
205   But when Odysseus had recognized the infallible temper
of these men, then he spoke to them again and answered them:
'I am he. I am here in my house. After many sufferings
I have come home in the twentieth year to the land of my fathers.
And now I see that of all my men it was only you two
210   who wanted me to come; I have not heard one of the others
praying that I should return again and come to my own house.
Therefore I will tell you the truth, and so it shall be;
if by my hand the god overmasters the lordly suitors,
then I shall get wives for you both, and grant you possessions
215   and houses built next to mine, and think of you in the future
always as companions of Telemachos, and his brothers.
But come now, let me show you a proof that shall be manifest,
so that you may know me for sure and trust my identity;
that scar, which once the boar with his white tooth inflicted

220 on me, when I went to Parnassos with the sons of Autolykos.'
   So he spoke, and pushed back the rags that covered his great scar.
 When these two had examined it and recognized everything,
 they burst out weeping and threw their arms around wise Odysseus,
 and made much of him, and kissed him on his head and his shoulders,
225 and so Odysseus also kissed their heads and hands. Now
 the sun would have gone down while they were still thus clamoring,
 had not Odysseus stayed them from it and said a word to them:
 'Now stop your lamentation and wailing, or someone may come out
 from the hall and see us, and tell about it inside. So rather
230 let us go in severally, not all together,
 I first, you after me, but let us have this as a signal
 arranged; for all the others there, who are lordly suitors,
 will not say that you can give me the bow and the quiver;
 but you must carry the bow through the house, noble Eumaios,
235 and put it into my hands, and then you must tell the women
 to bar the tightly fitted doors that close the hall; tell them,
 if any of them hears from inside the crash and the outcry,
 of men who are caught within our toils, that they must not peep in
 from outside, but simply sit still at their work, in silence.
240 Noble Philoitios, your task is to make fast the courtyard
 door with the bolt, and tie the fastening quickly upon it.'
   So he spoke, and went into the established palace,
 and went back and sat in the chair from which he had risen,
 and after him the two thralls of godlike Odysseus entered.
245   Eurymachos by now had taken the bow, and handled it,
 turning it round and round by the blaze of the fire, but even
 so he could not string it, and his proud heart was harrowed.
 Deeply vexed he spoke to his own great-hearted spirit:
 'Oh, my sorrow. Here is a grief beyond all others;
250 it is not so much the marriage I grieve for, for all my chagrin.
 There are many Achaian women besides, some of them close by
 in seagirt Ithaka, and some in the rest of the cities;
 but it is the thought, if this is true, that we come so far short
 of godlike Odysseus in strength, so that we cannot even
255 string his bow. A shame for men unborn to be told of.'
   Then in turn Antinoös, son of Eupeithes, answered:
 'It will not happen that way, Eurymachos. You yourself know this.
 Now there is a holy feast in the community

for the god. Who could string bows then? Put it away now
260   for our good time; but we shall leave all the axes standing
where they are. I do not believe anyone will come in
and steal them away from the halls of Odysseus, son of Laertes.
Come, let the wine steward pour a round of wine in the goblets,
so we can make a libation and put away the curved bow;
265   then at dawn instruct Melanthios, who is the goatherd,
to bring in goats, those far the best in all of his goatflocks,
so that, dedicating the thighs to the glorious archer
Apollo, we can attempt the bow and finish the contest.'
     So spoke Antinoös, and his word was pleasing to all of them.
270   The heralds poured water over their hands to wash with,
and the young men filled the mixing bowls with wine for their drinking,
and passed to all, after they had offered a drink in the goblets.
But when they had poured, and drunk, each as much as he wanted,
resourceful Odysseus spoke to them in crafty intention:
275   'Hear me now, you who are suitors of our glorious queen,
while I speak out what the heart within my breast urges.
Above all I entreat Eurymachos and the godlike
Antinoös, since what he said also was fair and orderly.
Let the bow be for the time, give it over to the divinities,
280   and tomorrow the god will give success to whomever he wishes;
but come now, give me the well-polished bow, so that among you
I may try out my strength and hands, to see if I still have
force in my flexible limbs as there has been in time past,
or whether my wandering and lack of good care have ruined me.'
285   So he spoke, but all of them were wildly indignant,
and feared that he might take the well-polished bow and string it.
Now Antinoös scolded him and spoke out and named him:
'Ah, wretched stranger, you have no sense, not even a little.
Is it not enough that you dine in peace, among us, who are violent
290   men, and are deprived of no fair portion, but listen
to our conversation and what we say? But there is no other
vagabond and newcomer who is allowed to hear us
talk. The honeyed wine has hurt you, as it has distracted
others as well, who gulp it down without drinking in season.
295   It was wine also that drove the Centaur, famous Eurytion,
distracted in the palace of great-hearted Peirithoös
when he visited the Lapiths. His brain went wild with drinking,

and in his fury he did much harm in the house of Peirithoös.
Grief and rage then seized the heroes, they sprang up and dragged him
300   through the forecourt and outside, with the pitiless bronze severing
his ears and nose; and he, having had his brains bewildered,
knew what a disaster his unstable spirit had got him.
Since his time there has been a feud between men and Centaurs,
and he was the first who found his own evil in heavy drinking.
305   So I announce great trouble for you as well, if ever
you string this bow; you will meet no kind of courtesy
in our group, but we shall put you into a black ship
and take you over to King Echetos, one who mutilates
all men; there you will lose everything; sit and be quiet
310   and drink your wine, nor quarrel with men who are younger than you
are.'
    Circumspect Penelope said to him in answer:
'Antinoös, it is neither fair nor just to browbeat
any guest of Telemachos who comes to visit him.
Do you imagine that if this stranger, in the confidence
315   of hands and strength, should string the great bow of Odysseus,
that he would take me home with him and make me his wife? No,
he himself has no such thought in the heart within him.
Let none of you be sorrowful at heart in his feasting
here, for such a reason. There is no likelihood of it.'
320   And now Eurymachos, the son of Polybos, answered:
'Daughter of Ikarios, circumspect Penelope,
we do not think he will take you away. That is not likely.
But we are ashamed to face the talk of the men and the women,
for fear some other Achaian, who is meaner than we are,
325   might say: "Far baser men are courting the wife of a stately
man. They are not even able to string his bow. Then
another, some beggar man, came wandering in from somewhere,
and easily strung the bow, and sent a shaft through the iron."
So they will speak; and that would be a disgrace on all of us.'
330   Circumspect Penelope said to him in answer:
'Eurymachos, there can be no glory among our people
in any case, for those who eat away and dishonor
the house of a great man. Why be concerned over reproaches?
But this stranger is a very big man, and he is built strongly,
335   and also he claims to be the son of a noble father.

Come then, give him the polished bow. Let us see what happens.
For I tell you this straight out, and it will be a thing accomplished.
If he can string the bow, and Apollo gives him that glory,
I will give him fine clothing to wear, a mantle and tunic,
340 and give him a sharp javelin, to keep men and dogs off,
and give him sandals for his feet, a sword with two edges,
and send him wherever his heart and spirit desire to be sent.'
    Then the thoughtful Telemachos said to her in answer:
'My mother, no Achaian man has more authority
345 over this bow than I, to give or withhold, at my pleasure;
not one of those who are lords here in rocky Ithaka,
not one of those in the islands off horse-pasturing Elis;
no one can force me against my will; if I want, I can give it
to the stranger as an outright gift, to take away with him.
350 Go therefore back into the house, and take up your own work,
the loom and the distaff, and see to it that your handmaidens
ply their work also. The men shall have the bow in their keeping,
all men, but I most of all. For mine is the power in this household.'
    Penelope went back inside the house, in amazement,
355 for she laid the serious words of her son deep away in her spirit;
and she went back to the upper story with her attendant
women, and wept for Odysseus, her beloved husband, until
gray-eyed Athene cast sweet slumber over her eyelids.
    Now the noble swineherd took the curved bow and carried it;
360 but all the suitors in the palace cried out against him,
and thus would go the word of one of these arrogant young men:
'Where are you carrying the bow, you sorry and shiftless
swineherd? Those swift dogs that you raised yourself will feed on you
beside your pigs, forsaken by men, if only Apollo
365 and the rest of the immortal gods are propitious toward us.'
    They spoke, and he took the bow and put it back where it had been,
in fear, since many men were shouting at him in the palace,
but from the other side Telemachos spoke and threatened him:
'Keep on with the bow, old fellow. You cannot do what everyone
370 tells you. Take care, or, younger though I am, I might chase you
out to the fields with a shower of stones. I am stronger than you are.
I only wish I were as much stronger, and more of a fighter
with my hands, than all these suitors who are here in my household.
So I could hatefully speed any man of them on his journey

Odysseus easily strings the bow

375   out of our house, where they are contriving evils against us.'
      So he spoke, and all the suitors laughed happily at him,
     and all gave over their bitter rage against Telemachos.
     The swineherd took up the bow and carried it through the palace,
     and stood beside the wise Odysseus, and handed it to him.
380   Then he called aside the nurse Eurykleia, and told her:
     'Circumspect Eurykleia, Telemachos wants you
     to bar the tightly fitted doors that close the house; and then,
     if any of you hear from inside the crash and the outcry
     of men who are caught within our toils, you must not peep in
385   from outside, but simply sit still at your work, in silence.'
      So he spoke, and she had no winged words for an answer.
     Eurykleia barred the doors of the strong-built great hall.
     Philoitios sprang to his feet and went silently outside
     the house, and then he closed the doors of the well-made courtyard.
390   Lying beneath the portico was a fiber cable
     for an oar-driven ship; with that he made fast the doors, and himself
     went in, and sat again on the chair from which he had risen,
     looking toward Odysseus, who by now was handling the bow, turning it
     all up and down, and testing it from one side and another
395   to see if worms had eaten the horn in the master's absence.
     And thus would one of them say as he looked across at the next man:
     'This man is an admirer of bows, or one who steals them.
     Now either he has such things lying back away in his own house,
     or else he is studying to make one, the way he turns it
400   this way and that, our vagabond who is versed in villainies.'
      And thus would speak another one of these arrogant young men:
     'How I wish his share of good fortune were of the same measure
     as is the degree of his power ever to get this bow strung.'
      So the suitors talked, but now resourceful Odysseus,
405   once he had taken up the great bow and looked it all over,
     as when a man, who well understands the lyre and singing,
     easily, holding it on either side, pulls the strongly twisted
     cord of sheep's gut, so as to slip it over a new peg,
     so, without any strain, Odysseus strung the great bow.
410   Then plucking it in his right hand he tested the bowstring,
     and it gave him back an excellent sound like the voice of a swallow.
     A great sorrow fell now upon the suitors, and all their color
     was changed, and Zeus showing forth his portents thundered mightily.

Odysseus shoots through the axes

Hearing this, long-suffering great Odysseus was happy
415   that the son of devious-devising Kronos had sent him a portent.
He chose out a swift arrow that lay beside him uncovered
on the table, but the others were still stored up inside the hollow
quiver, and presently the Achaians must learn their nature.
Taking the string and the head grooves he drew to the middle
420   grip, and from the very chair where he sat, bending the bow
before him, let the arrow fly, nor missed any axes
from the first handle on, but the bronze-weighted arrow passed through
all, and out the other end. He spoke to Telemachos:
'Telemachos, your guest that sits in your halls does not then
425   fail you; I missed no part of the mark, nor have I made much
work of stringing the bow; the strength is still sound within me,
and not as the suitors said in their scorn, making little of me.
Now is the time for their dinner to be served the Achaians
in the daylight, then follow with other entertainment,
430   the dance and the lyre; for these things come at the end of the feasting.'
    He spoke, and nodded to him with his brows, and Telemachos,
dear son of godlike Odysseus, put his sharp sword about him
and closed his own hand over his spear, and took his position
close beside him and next the chair, all armed in bright bronze.

BOOK XXII

Now resourceful Odysseus stripped his rags from him, and sprang
up atop the great threshold, holding his bow and the quiver
filled with arrows, and scattered out the swift shafts before him
on the ground next his feet, and spoke his word to the suitors:
5   'Here is a task that has been achieved, without any deception.
Now I shall shoot at another mark, one that no man yet
has struck, if I can hit it and Apollo grants me the glory.'
      He spoke, and steered a bitter arrow against Antinoös.
He was on the point of lifting up a fine two-handled
10 goblet of gold, and had it in his hands, and was moving it
so as to drink of the wine, and in his heart there was no thought
of death. For who would think that one man, alone in a company
of many men at their feasting, though he were a very strong one,
would ever inflict death upon him and dark doom? But Odysseus,
15 aiming at this man, struck him in the throat with an arrow,
and clean through the soft part of the neck the point was driven.
He slumped away to one side, and out of his stricken hand fell
the goblet, and up and through his nostrils there burst a thick jet
of mortal blood, and with a thrust of his foot he kicked back
20 the table from him, so that all the good food was scattered
on the ground, bread and baked meats together; but all the suitors
clamored about the house when they saw that the man was fallen,
sprang up from their seats and ranged about the room, throwing
their glances every way all along the well-built walls,

25   but there was never a shield there nor any strong spear for them.
But they scolded Odysseus in words full of anger, saying:
'Stranger, it is badly done to hit men. You will never
achieve any more trials. Now your sudden destruction is certain,
for now you have struck down the man who was far the greatest
30   of the youth of Ithaka. For that the vultures shall eat you.'
     Each spoke at random, for they thought he had not intended
to kill the man, poor fools, and they had not yet realized
how over all of them the terms of death were now hanging.
But looking darkly upon them resourceful Odysseus answered:
35   'You dogs, you never thought that I would any more come back
from the land of Troy, and because of that you despoiled my household,
and forcibly took my serving women to sleep beside you,
and sought to win my wife while I was still alive, fearing
neither the immortal gods who hold the wide heaven,
40   nor any resentment sprung from men to be yours in the future.
Now upon all of you the terms of destruction are fastened.'
     So he spoke, and the green fear took hold of all of them,
and each man looked about him for a way to escape sheer death.
Only Eurymachos spoke up and gave him an answer:
45   'If in truth you are Odysseus of Ithaka, come home,
what you have said is fair about all the wickedness done you
by the Achaians, much in your house and much in the country.
But now the man is down who was responsible for all
this, Antinoös. It was he who pushed this action,
50   not so much that he wanted the marriage, or cared for it,
but with other things in mind, which the son of Kronos would not
grant him: to lie in wait for your son and kill him, and then
be king himself in the district of strong-founded Ithaka.
Now he has perished by his own fate. Then spare your own
55   people, and afterward we will make public reparation
for all that has been eaten and drunk in your halls, setting
each upon himself an assessment of twenty oxen.
We will pay it back in bronze and gold to you, until your heart
is softened. Till then, we cannot blame you for being angry.'
60   Then looking darkly at him resourceful Odysseus answered:
'Eurymachos, if you gave me all your father's possessions,
all that you have now, and what you could add from elsewhere,
even so, I would not stay my hands from the slaughter,

until I had taken revenge for all the suitors' transgression.
65   Now the choice has been set before you, either to fight me
or run, if any of you can escape death and its spirits.
But I think not one man will escape from sheer destruction.'
    So he spoke, and the others' knees, and the heart within them,
went slack, but Eurymachos cried a second time, to the suitors:
70   'Dear friends, now this man will not restrain his invincible
hands, but since he has got the polished bow and the quiver,
he will shoot at us from the smooth threshold, until he has killed us
one and all. Then let us all remember our warcraft.
Draw your swords and hold the table before you, to ward off
75   the arrows of sudden death; let us all make a rush against him
together, and try to push him back from the doors and the threshold,
and go through the town. So the hue and cry could be most quickly
raised, and perhaps this man will now have shot for the last time.'
    So he spoke aloud, and drew from his side the sharp sword,
80   brazen, and edged on either side, and made a rush at him,
crying his terrible cry. At the same time, noble Odysseus
shot an arrow, and struck him in the chest, by the nipple,
and the speeding arrow fixed in his liver, and his sword tumbled
out of his hand on the floor, as he, sprawling over the table,
85   doubled and fell, and on the floor the good food was scattered,
and the two-handled goblet. He struck the ground with his forehead
in his paroxysm of pain, and kicking with both feet
rattled the chair, and over his eyes the death mist drifted.
    Amphinomos, springing forward to face glorious Odysseus,
90   made a rush against him, and drew his sharp sword, thinking
he might be forced to give way from the doors; but now Telemachos
was too quick with a cast of the brazen spear from behind him
between the shoulders, and drove it through to the chest beyond it.
He fell, thunderously, and took the earth full on his forehead.
95   Telemachos sprang away, and left behind the far-shadowing
spear where it was in Amphinomos, turning back, for fear
that as he pulled out the far-shadowing spear, some other Achaian
might drive at him in an outrush, or else strike him from close up.
He went on the run, and very soon he reached his dear father,
100   and stood there close beside him and addressed him in winged words:
'Father, now I will go and bring you a shield, and two spears,
and a helmet all of bronze fitting close to your temples.

The battle continues

I too will go and put on armor, and give the swineherd
and oxherd more to wear. It is better for us to be armored.'
105   Then in turn resourceful Odysseus spoke to him in answer:
'Run and fetch them, while I have arrows still to defend me,
or else, while I am alone, they might force me from the doorway.'
    So he spoke, and Telemachos obeyed his dear father,
and went on his way to the inner room, where glorious armor
110 was stored away, and took from inside four shields, and eight spears,
and four helmets plated with bronze and crested with horsehair,
and carried them back, and very soon he reached his dear father.
He was the first of all to put the bronze armor upon him,
and in the same way the two serving men put on their magnificent
115 arms, and stood beside the wise, resourceful Odysseus.
    Odysseus, while he still had arrows left to defend him,
kept aiming at the suitors in his house; and every
time he hit his man, and they dropped one after another.
But when there were no more arrows left for the king's archery,
120 he set the bow so it leaned against a pillar sustaining
the strong-built palace, there by the shining walls, then himself
threw across his shoulders the shield of the fourfold oxhide.
Over his mighty head he set the well-fashioned helmet,
with the horsehair crest, and the plumes nodded terribly above it.
125 Then he caught up two powerful spears edged with the bright bronze.
    There was a side door in the strongly-constructed wall, and also,
next the edge of the threshold into the well-made palace,
a way through the alley, with the door leaves fitting it closely.
Odysseus told the noble swineherd to take a position
130 near this, and watch it. Only one at a time could attack there.
Agelaos cried aloud to all of the suitors:
'Dear friends, could not one man slip away, through the side door,
and tell the people? So the hue and cry could be most quickly
raised, and perhaps this man will now have shot for the last time.'
135   Then in turn Melanthios the goatherd answered him:
'It cannot be, illustrious Agelaos. The fine doors
to the court are terribly close, the mouth of the alley is difficult
to force; one man could hold against all, if he were a fighter.
Come rather, let me bring you arms from inside the chamber
140 to arm you in; for there, I believe, and in no other
place, Odysseus and his glorious son have hidden them.'

Melanthios brings arms to the suitors

So Melanthios the goatherd spoke, and climbed through
to Odysseus' inner chambers by the vents in the great hall.
From there he took out a dozen heavy shields, and as many
145 spears, and as many brazen helmets crested with horsehair,
and went on his way, and quickly handed them to the suitors.
Then the knees of Odysseus went slack, and the heart within him,
as he saw them putting the armor about them, and shaking
the long spears in their hands; he thought it was monstrous
150 treason, and he spoke now in winged words to Telemachos:
'Telemachos, some one of the women here in the palace,
or Melanthios, has made an evil attack upon us.'
      Then the thoughtful Telemachos said to him in answer:
'Father, it was my own mistake, and there is no other
155 to blame. I left the door of the chamber, which can close tightly,
open at an angle. One of these men was a better observer
than I. Go now, noble Eumaios, and close the chamber
door, and see if it is one of the women doing this,
or Melanthios, son of Dolios, which is what I think.'
160   Now as these two were conversing thus with each other,
Melanthios the goatherd went back into the chamber
to bring more splendid armor, but the noble swineherd sighted him.
Quickly he spoke a word to Odysseus standing close by him:
'Son of Laertes and seed of Zeus, resourceful Odysseus,
165 there is that deadly man again, the one we suspected,
on his way into the chamber. Now give me your true instructions,
whether, if I prove stronger than he is, I am to kill him,
or bring him back here to you, so he can pay for the many
transgressions, all that he has devised in your house against you.'
170   Then resourceful Odysseus spoke in turn and answered him:
'Telemachos and I will hold off the haughty suitors,
for all their fury, here inside the palace; you two
twist the feet of Melanthios and his arms behind him,
put him away in the chamber and fasten boards behind him,
175 then make him secure with a braided rope, and hoist him upward
along the high column, till you fetch him up to the roof beams.
Thus, while he still stays alive, he will suffer harsh torment.'
      So he spoke, and they listened well to him and obeyed him.
They went into the chamber. He was there, but he did not see them.
180 Now, he was searching out weapons, deep in the back of the chamber,

and they stood there waiting for him behind the columns, on either
side, until Melanthios the herdsman of goats came over
the sill. In one hand he was holding a splendid helmet,
and in the other the ancient shield, all fouled with mildew,
185   of the hero Laertes, which he had carried when he was a young man.
It had been lying there, and the stitches were gone on the handstraps.
Now they sprang out and seized him, caught hold of his hair and dragged
      him
in, and threw him down on the floor, there in his anguish
of heart, and in the hurtful bond they securely fastened
190   his feet and arms, twisted all the way back, obeying the orders
given by great, enduring Odysseus, the son of Laertes.
Then they made him secure with a braided rope, and hoisted him
high on the column, until they fetched him up to the roof beams.
Then you spoke and jeered at him, O swineherd Eumaios:
195   'Now the whole night long, Melanthios, you shall keep watch
wakefully, laid, as you deserve, to rest on a soft bed,
well aware of the young Dawn throned in gold as she rises
up from the Ocean rivers, at the time when you used to drive in
goats to the palace, so as to make a feast for the suitors.'
200   So they left him there, trussed up in his horrible bindings.
The herdsmen closed the shining door, and put on their armor,
and went and stood beside the wise, resourceful Odysseus.
There both sides stood, breathing valor, the four men holding
the threshold, but inside the house were many and brave men.
205   Now to these men came the daughter of Zeus, Athene,
likening herself in voice and appearance to Mentor.
Odysseus was happy when he saw her, and hailed her, saying:
'Mentor, help me from hurt, and remember me, your companion
and friend, who have done you much good. We two grew up together.'
210   He spoke so, but thought it was Athene, leader of armies.
On the other side in the palace the suitors cried out against her,
and first to threaten was Agelaos, son of Damastor;
'Mentor, never let Odysseus by talking persuade you
to fight against the suitors and defend him. Consider
215   what we propose to do, and I think it will be accomplished.
When we kill these men, the son and the father, you too
shall be killed in their company, for what you are trying
to do here in the palace. You shall pay for it with your own head.

Athene helps Odysseus and his party

But when with the bronze we have taken away the lives of all of you,
220   all the possessions which are yours, both here and elsewhere,
we shall count in with those of Odysseus, nor will we suffer
your sons to go on living here in your halls, nor your daughters
and loving wife to go about in the town of Ithaka.'
    He spoke, and Athene in her heart grew still more angry,
225   and she scolded Odysseus in words full of anger, saying:
'No longer, Odysseus, are the strength and valor still steady
within you, as when, for the sake of white-armed, illustrious
Helen, you fought nine years with the Trojans, ever relentless;
and many men you killed there in the dreaded encounter,
230   and by your counsel the wide-wayed city of Priam was taken.
How is it now, when you have come back to your own possessions
and house, you complain, instead of standing up to the suitors?
Come here, friend, and watch me at work, and standing beside me
see what kind of man is Mentor the son of Alkimos,
235   and how against your enemies he repays your kindness.'
    She spoke, but did not yet altogether turn the victory
their way. She still was putting to proof the strength and courage
alike of Odysseus and his glorious son; and she now,
likening herself to a swallow in their sight, shot up
240   high aloft, and perched on a beam of the smoky palace.
    Now Agelaos, son of Damastor, urged on the suitors,
with Demoptolemos, Amphimedon, and Peisandros
the son of Polyktor, Eurynomos, and the wise Polybos.
For these in warcraft were by far the best of the suitors
245   who still were alive and fighting for their lives; but others
had already fallen before the bow and the showering arrows.
To these Agelaos spoke, directing his words to all of them:
'Dear friends, now this man will have to stay his invincible
hands, since Mentor, after doing some empty boasting,
250   has gone, and these are left alone in the front doorway.
Now, do not all of you throw your long spears at the same time
at him, but let us six throw first with our spears, and it may be
Zeus will grant that we strike Odysseus and win the glory.
We care nothing about the others, once this man has fallen.'
255   So he spoke, and all six aimed their spears, as he told them,
and threw, but Athene made vain all their casts, so that
one man threw his spear against the pillar sustaining

Defeat and death of all the suitors

       the strong-built palace, another into the door, close-fitted.
       One ash spear heavy with bronze was driven into the side wall.
260   But then, after they had avoided the spears of the suitors,
       much-enduring great Odysseus began speaking to them:
       'Dear friends, now I would say it was the time for our turn
       to throw our spears into the midst of the suitors, furious
       as they are to kill us, and add to former evils committed.'
265   So he spoke, and they all aimed their sharp spears and threw them
       straight ahead. Demoptolemos was killed by Odysseus,
       Euryades by Telemachos, Elatos by the swineherd,
       Peisandros by Philoitios, the herdsman of oxen.
       But when all these had fallen, and bit with their teeth the great earth,
270   the suitors drew away into the corner of the palace,
       and the others rushed, and plucked their spears from the fallen bodies.
       Once again the suitors aimed at them with their sharp spears,
       and threw, but Athene made vain most of their casts, so that
       one man threw his spear against the pillar sustaining
275   the strong-built palace, another into the door, close-fitted.
       One ash spear heavy with bronze was driven into the side wall.
       But Amphimedon struck Telemachos on the wrist, with a glancing
       blow, and the bronze ripped the outermost skin; and also
       Ktesippos with his long spear hit Eumaios over
280   the shield, and scratched his shoulder, but the spear flew over, and landed
       void. Then the company of wise, devious-devising
       Odysseus threw their spears into the mass of the suitors.
       This time Odysseus, stormer of cities, struck down Eurydamas;
       Telemachos hit Amphimedon; the swineherd, Polybos.
285   Then Philoitios, herdsman of oxen, struck Ktesippos
       full in the chest, and spoke a word of vaunting over him:
       'O son of Polytherses, lover of mockery, never
       speak loud and all at random in your recklessness. Rather
       leave all speech to the gods, since they are far stronger than you are.
290   Here is your guest gift, in exchange for that hoof you formerly
       gave to godlike Odysseus, as he went about through the palace.'
       So spoke the herdsman of horn-curved oxen; but now Odysseus
       stabbed Agelaos, son of Damastor, from close, with the long spear,
       while Telemachos stabbed Leokritos, son of Euenor,
295   in the midmost belly with the spear, and drove the bronze clean
          through.

End of the battle

He fell then headlong, and took the earth full on his forehead.
And now Athene waved the aegis, that blights humanity,
from high aloft on the roof, and all their wits were bewildered;
and they stampeded about the hall, like a herd of cattle
300 set upon and driven wild by the darting horse fly
in the spring season, at the time when the days grow longer;
but the other men, who were like hook-clawed, beak-bent vultures,
descending from the mountains to pounce upon the lesser birds;
and these on the plain, shrinking away from the clouds, speed off,
305 but the vultures plunge on them and destroy them, nor is there any
defense, nor any escape, and men are glad for the hunting;
so these men, sweeping about the palace, struck down
the suitors, one man after another; the floor was smoking
with blood, and the horrible cries rose up as their heads were broken.
310   Leodes rushed in and caught the knees of Odysseus,
and spoke to him in winged words and in supplication:
'I am at your knees, Odysseus. Respect me, have mercy;
for I claim that never in your halls did I say or do anything
wrong to any one of the women, but always was trying
315 to stop any one of the other suitors who acted in that way.
But they would not listen to me and keep their hands off evil.
So by their own recklessness they have found a shameful
death, but I was their diviner, and I did nothing;
but I must fall, since there is no gratitude for past favors.'
320   Then looking darkly at him spoke resourceful Odysseus:
'If you claim to be the diviner among these people,
many a time you must have prayed in my palace, asking
that the completion of my sweet homecoming be far off
from me, that my dear wife would go off with you, and bear you
325 children. So you cannot escape from sorry destruction.'
So he spoke, and in his heavy hand caught up a sword
that was lying there on the ground where Agelaos had dropped it
when he was killed. With this he cut through the neck at the middle,
and the head of Leodes dropped in the dust while he was still speaking.
330   Phemios the singer, the son of Terpias, still was skulking
away from death. He had been singing among the suitors
under compulsion, and stood with the clear-toned lyre in his hands
by the side door, and his heart was pondering one of two courses:
either to slip out of the hall to the altar of mighty

---

335 Zeus of the court, and crouch at the structure, where once Odysseus
and Laertes had burned up the thighs of many oxen,
or rush up and make entreaty at the knees of Odysseus.
Then in the division of his heart this way seemed best to him,
to seize hold of the knees of Odysseus, son of Laertes.

340 Thereupon he laid the hollowed lyre on the ground,
between the mixing bowl and the chair with its nails of silver,
but he himself rushed in and caught the knees of Odysseus,
and spoke to him in winged words and in supplication:
'I am at your knees, Odysseus. Respect me, have mercy.

345 You will be sorry in time to come if you kill the singer
of songs. I sing to the gods and to human people, and I am
taught by myself, but the god has inspired in me the song-ways
of every kind. I am such a one as can sing before you
as to a god. Then do not be furious to behead me.

350 Telemachos too, your own dear son, would tell you, as I do,
that it was against my will, and with no desire on my part,
that I served the suitors here in your house and sang at their feasting.
They were too many and too strong, and they forced me to do it.'
So he spoke, and the hallowed prince Telemachos heard him.

355 Quickly then he spoke to his father, who stood close by him:
'Hold fast. Do not strike this man with the bronze. He is innocent.
And let us spare Medon our herald, a man who has always
taken care of me when I was a child in your palace;
unless, that is, Philoitios or the swineherd has killed him,

360 or unless he came in your way as you stormed through the palace.'
So he spoke, and Medon, a man of prudent thoughts, heard him;
for he had hidden under a chair, and put on about him
the hide of an ox, freshly skinned, so avoiding black death.
He came out quickly from under the chair, and took off the oxhide,

365 and then rushed in and caught hold of the knees of Telemachos,
and spoke to him in winged words and in supplication:
'Here I am, dear friend. Hold fast, and speak to your father,
before—since he is so strong—he destroys me with the tearing
bronze, in anger over the suitors, who kept ruining

370 his goods in his palace and, like fools, paid you no honor.'
Then resourceful Odysseus smiled upon him and answered:
'Do not fear. Telemachos has saved you and kept you
alive, so you may know in your heart, and say to another,

that good dealing is better by far than evil dealing.

375 But go out now from the palace and sit outside, away from
the slaughter, in the courtyard, you and the versatile singer,
so that I can do in the house the work that I have to.'
So he spoke, and the two went away, outside the palace,
and sat down both together beside the altar of mighty

380 Zeus, looking all about them, still thinking they would be murdered.
Odysseus looked about his own house, to see if any
man still was left alive, escaping the black destruction;
but he saw them, one and all in their numbers, lying fallen
in their blood and in the dust, like fish whom the fishermen

385 have taken in their net with many holes, and dragged out
onto the hollow beach from the gray sea, and all of them
lie piled on the sand, needing the restless salt water;
but Helios, the shining Sun, bakes the life out of them.
Like these, the suitors now were lying piled on each other.

390 Then at last resourceful Odysseus said to Telemachos:
'Telemachos, come now, summon in the nurse, Eurykleia,
so that I can say what is on my mind to say to her.'
So he spoke, and Telemachos obeyed his dear father.
He opened the door and called out to the nurse, Eurykleia:

395 'Rise and come here, aged woman, you who watch over
all that the serving women do here in our palace.
Come here. My father calls you. He has something to tell you.'
So he spoke, and she had no winged words for an answer,
but she opened the doors of the strong-built great hall, and went

400 on inside, but Telemachos went ahead, leading her.
There she found Odysseus among the slaughtered dead men,
spattered over with gore and battle filth, like a lion
who has been feeding on an ox of the fields, and goes off
covered with blood, all his chest and his flanks on either

405 side bloody, a terrible thing to look in the face; so
now Odysseus' feet and the hands above them were spattered.
She, when she saw the dead men and the endless blood, began then
to raise the cry of triumph, having seen it was monstrous
work, but Odysseus checked her and held her, for all her eagerness,

410 and spoke to her and addressed her in winged words, saying:
'Keep your joy in your heart, old dame; stop, do not raise up
the cry. It is not piety to glory so over slain men.

Punishment of the faithless maids

These were destroyed by the doom of the gods and their own hard
    actions,
for these men paid no attention at all to any man on earth
415   who came their way, no matter if he were base or noble.
So by their own recklessness they have found a shameful
death. Now assemble here the women who are in the palace,
both those who have done me no honor, and those who are innocent.'
    Then the beloved nurse Eurykleia said to him in answer:
420   'So, my child, I will tell you the whole truth of the matter.
You have fifty serving women here in your palace,
and these I have taught to work at their own tasks, the carding
of wool, and how to endure their own slavery. Of these
fifty, twelve in all have taken to immorality.
425   They pay no attention to me, or even to Penelope.
Telemachos is but lately come of age, and his mother
would not let him be in charge of the serving women.
But come, let me go up to the shining upper chamber
and tell your wife. Some god has sent down a sleep upon her.'
430   Then resourceful Odysseus spoke in turn and answered her:
'Do not waken her yet, but tell those women who have been
shameful in their devisings to come here to my presence.'
    So he spoke, and the old woman went through the palace,
bringing the message to the women and urging them onward.
435   But Odysseus, calling Telemachos and the oxherd
and swineherd to him, spoke to them in winged words, saying:
'Begin the work of carrying out the bodies, and tell
the women to help, and after that to wash the beautiful
chairs and tables clean, with water and porous sponges.
440   Then, after you have got all the house back in good order,
lead all these maidservants out of the well-built palace
between the round-house and the unfaulted wall of the courtyard,
and hew them with the thin edge of the sword, until you have taken
the lives from all, and they forget Aphrodite, the goddess
445   they had with them when they lay secretly with the suitors.'
    So he spoke, and the women all in a huddle came out,
with terrible cries of sorrow, and the big tears falling.
First they carried away the bodies of all the dead men,
and laid them under the portico of the well-built courtyard,
450   stacking them on each other. Odysseus himself directed them

and hurried them on. They carried the bodies out. They had to.
Then, after they had done this, the women washed the beautiful
chairs and tables clean, with water and porous sponges.
After this Telemachos, the oxherd and the swineherd,
455 scraped out the floor of the strongly constructed house, with shovels,
and the women carried the scrapings way, and piled them outside.
But after they had got all the house back in good order,
leading the maidservants out of the well-built palace,
between the round-house and the unfaulted wall of the courtyard,
460 they penned them in a strait place from which there was no escaping.
Now the thoughtful Telemachos began speaking among them:
'I would not take away the lives of these creatures by any
clean death, for they have showered abuse on the head of my mother,
and on my own head too, and they have slept with the suitors.'
465 So he spoke, and taking the cable of a dark-prowed ship,
fastened it to the tall pillar, and fetched it about the round-house;
and like thrushes, who spread their wings, or pigeons, who have
flown into a snare set up for them in a thicket, trying
to find a resting place, but the sleep given them was hateful;
470 so their heads were all in a line, and each had her neck caught
fast in a noose, so that their death would be most pitiful.
They struggled with their feet for a little, not for very long.
They took Melanthios along the porch and the courtyard.
They cut off, with the pitiless bronze, his nose and his ears,
475 tore off his private parts and gave them to the dogs to feed on
raw, and lopped off his hands and feet, in fury of anger.
Then, after they had washed their own hands and feet clean,
they went into the house of Odysseus. Their work was ended.
But Odysseus said to the beloved nurse, Eurykleia:
480 'Bring me brimstone, old dame, the cure of evils, and bring me
fire, so I can sulphur the hall, and tell Penelope
to come here now, together with her attendant women,
and tell all the serving maids to come here to the palace.'
485 Then the beloved nurse Eurykleia said to him in answer:
'All this you have said, my child, was fair and orderly.
But come now, let me bring you out a mantle and tunic,
and do not stand thus here in the hall, with your broad shoulders
covered over with rags as they are. That would be scandalous.'
490 Then resourceful Odysseus spoke in turn and answered her:

Odysseus cleans the palace

'Before all this, let me have the fire in my palace.'
He spoke, and the dear nurse Eurykleia did not disobey him.
She brought him out the fire and brimstone; and then Odysseus
cleaned his palace, house and courtyard alike, with sulphur.
495   The old woman went off through the fine house of Odysseus,
to take the message to the women and tell them to gather.
They came from the main house, and in their hands held torches,
and all the serving women clung to Odysseus, and greeted him,
and made much of him, and kissed him on his head and his shoulders
500   and hands, admiring him, and sweet longing for lamentation
and tears took hold of him. He recognized all these women.

BOOK XXIII

The old woman, laughing loudly, went to the upper chamber
to tell her mistress that her beloved husband was inside
the house. Her knees moved swiftly, but her feet were tottering.
She stood above Penelope's head and spoke a word to her:
5 'Wake, Penelope, dear child, so that, with your own eyes,
you can see what all your days you have been longing for.
Odysseus is here, he is in the house, though late in his coming;
and he has killed the haughty suitors, who were afflicting
his house, and using force on his son, and eating his property.'
10   Circumspect Penelope said to her in answer:
'Dear nurse, the gods have driven you crazy. They are both able
to change a very sensible person into a senseless
one, and to set the light-wit on the way of discretion.
They have set you awry; before now your thoughts were orderly.
15 Why do you insult me when my heart is heavy with sorrows,
by talking in this wild way, and waking me from a happy
sleep, which had come and covered my eyes, and held them fastened?
For I have not had such a sleep as this one, since the time
when Odysseus went to that evil, not-to-be-mentioned Ilion.
20 But go down now, and take yourself back into the palace.
If any of those other women, who are here with me,
had come with a message like yours, and wakened me from my slumber,
I would have sent her back on her way to the hall in a hateful
fashion for doing it. It shall be your age that saves you.'

Penelope comes down to Odysseus

25   Then the beloved nurse Eurykleia said to her in answer:
'I am not insulting you, dear child. It is all true.
Odysseus is here, he is in the house, just as I tell you.
He is that stranger-guest, whom all in the house were abusing.
Telemachos has known that he was here for a long time,
30   but he was discreet, and did not betray the plans of his father,
so he might punish these overbearing men for their violence.'
    So she spoke, and Penelope in her joy sprang up
from the bed, and embraced the old woman, her eyes streaming
tears, and she spoke to her and addressed her in winged words:
35   'If it could only be true, dear nurse, all that you told me,
if truly he could have come back to the house, as you tell me,
to lay his hands on the shameless suitors, though he was only
one, and they were always lying in wait, in a body!'
    Then the beloved nurse Eurykleia said to her in answer:
40   'I did not see, I was not told, but I heard the outcry
of them being killed; we, hidden away in the strong-built storerooms,
sat there terrified, and the closed doors held us prisoner,
until from inside the great hall your son Telemachos
summoned me, because his father told him to do it.
45   There I found Odysseus standing among the dead men
he had killed, and they covered the hardened earth, lying
piled on each other around him. You would have been cheered to see
        him,
spattered over with gore and battle filth, like a lion.
Now they lie all together, by the doors of the courtyard,
50   while he is burning a great fire, and cleaning the beautiful
house with brimstone. He has sent me on to summon you.
Come with me then, so that both of you can turn your dear hearts
the way of happiness, since you have had so much to suffer,
but now at last what long you prayed for has been accomplished.
55   He has come back and is here at his hearth, alive, and has found you
and his son in the palace, and has taken revenge on the suitors
here in his house, for all the evils that they have done him.'
    Circumspect Penelope said to her in answer:
'Dear nurse, do not yet laugh aloud in triumph. You know
60   how welcome he would be if he appeared in the palace:
to all, but above all to me and the son we gave birth to.
No, but this story is not true as you tell it; rather,

but will not speak to him

some one of the immortals has killed the haughty suitors
in anger over their wicked deeds and heart-hurting violence;
65 for these men paid no attention at all to any man on earth
who came their way, no matter if he were base or noble.
So they suffered for their own recklessness. But Odysseus
has lost his homecoming and lost his life, far from Achaia.'
    Then the beloved nurse Eurykleia said to her in answer:
70 'My child, what sort of word escaped your teeth's barrier?
Though your husband is here beside the hearth, you would never
say he would come home. Your heart was always mistrustful.
But here is another proof that is very clear. I will tell you.
That scar, which once the boar with his white teeth inflicted.
75 I recognized it while I was washing his feet, and I wanted
to tell you about it, but he stopped my mouth with his hands, would not
let me speak, for his mind sought every advantage. Come then,
follow me, and I will hazard my life upon it.
Kill me by the most pitiful death, if I am deceiving you.'
80   Circumspect Penelope said to her in answer:
'Dear nurse, it would be hard for you to baffle the purposes
of the everlasting gods, although you are very clever.
Still, I will go to see my son, so that I can look on
these men who courted me lying dead, and the man who killed them.'
85   She spoke, and came down from the chamber, her heart pondering
much, whether to keep away and question her dear husband,
or to go up to him and kiss his head, taking his hands.
But then, when she came in and stepped over the stone threshold,
she sat across from him in the firelight, facing Odysseus,
90 by the opposite wall, while he was seated by the tall pillar,
looking downward, and waiting to find out if his majestic
wife would have anything to say to him, now that she saw him.
She sat a long time in silence, and her heart was wondering.
Sometimes she would look at him, with her eyes full upon him,
95 and again would fail to know him in the foul clothing he wore.
Telemachos spoke to her and called her by name and scolded her:
'My mother, my harsh mother with the hard heart inside you,
why do you withdraw so from my father, and do not
sit beside him and ask him questions and find out about him?
100 No other woman, with spirit as stubborn as yours, would keep back
as you are doing from her husband who, after much suffering,

Plans to deceive the people

came at last in the twentieth year back to his own country.
But always you have a heart that is harder than stone within you.'
　　Circumspect Penelope said to him in answer:
105 'My child, the spirit that is in me is full of wonderment,
and I cannot find anything to say to him, nor question him,
nor look him straight in the face. But if he is truly Odysseus,
and he has come home, then we shall find other ways, and better,
to recognize each other, for we have signs that we know of
110 between the two of us only, but they are secret from others.'
　　So she spoke, and much-enduring noble Odysseus
smiled, and presently spoke in winged words to Telemachos:
'Telemachos, leave your mother to examine me in the palace
as she will, and presently she will understand better;
115 but now that I am dirty and wear foul clothing upon me,
she dislikes me for that, and says I am not her husband.
But let us make our plans how all will come out best for us.
For when one has killed only one man in a community,
and then there are not many avengers to follow, even
120 so, he flees into exile, leaving kinsmen and country.
But we have killed what held the city together, the finest
young men in Ithaka. It is what I would have you consider.'
　　Then the thoughtful Telemachos said to him in answer:
'You must look to this yourself, dear father; for they say
125 you have the best mind among men for craft, and there is
no other man among mortal men who can contend with you.
We shall follow you eagerly; I think that we shall not
come short in warcraft, in so far as the strength stays with us.'
　　Then resourceful Odysseus spoke in turn and answered him:
130 'So I will tell you the way of it, how it seems best to me.
First, all go and wash, and put your tunics upon you,
and tell the women in the palace to choose out their clothing.
Then let the inspired singer take his clear-sounding lyre,
and give us the lead for festive dance, so that anyone
135 who is outside, some one of the neighbors, or a person going
along the street, who hears us, will think we are having a wedding.
Let no rumor go abroad in the town that the suitors
have been murdered, until such time as we can make our way
out to our estate with its many trees, and once there
140 see what profitable plan the Olympian shows us.'

Odysseus reproaches Penelope

So he spoke, and they listened well to him and obeyed him.
First they went and washed, and put their tunics upon them,
and the women arrayed themselves in their finery, while the inspired
singer took up his hollowed lyre and stirred up within them
145 the impulse for the sweetness of song and the stately dancing.
Now the great house resounded aloud to the thud of their footsteps,
as the men celebrated there, and the fair-girdled women;
and thus would a person speak outside the house who heard them:
'Surely now someone has married our much-sought-after
150 queen; hard-hearted, she had no patience to keep the great house
for her own wedded lord to the end, till he came back to her.'
So would a person speak, but they did not know what had happened.
Now the housekeeper Eurynome bathed great-hearted
Odysseus in his own house, and anointed him with olive oil,
155 and threw a beautiful mantle and a tunic about him;
and over his head Athene suffused great beauty, to make him
taller to behold and thicker, and on his head she arranged
the curling locks that hung down like hyacinthine petals.
And as when a master craftsman overlays gold on silver,
160 and he is one who was taught by Hephaistos and Pallas Athene
in art complete, and grace is on every work he finishes;
so Athene gilded with grace his head and his shoulders.
Then, looking like an immortal, he strode forth from the bath,
and came back then and sat on the chair from which he had risen,
165 opposite his wife, and now he spoke to her, saying:
'You are so strange. The gods, who have their homes on Olympos,
have made your heart more stubborn than for the rest of womankind.
No other woman, with spirit as stubborn as yours, would keep back
as you are doing from her husband who, after much suffering,
170 came at last in the twentieth year back to his own country.
Come then, nurse, make me up a bed, so that I can use it
here; for this woman has a heart of iron within her.'
Circumspect Penelope said to him in answer:
'You are so strange. I am not being proud, nor indifferent,
175 nor puzzled beyond need, but I know very well what you looked like
when you went in the ship with the sweeping oars, from Ithaka.
Come then, Eurykleia, and make up a firm bed for him
outside the well-fashioned chamber: that very bed that he himself
built. Put the firm bed here outside for him, and cover it

180   over with fleeces and blankets, and with shining coverlets.'
       So she spoke to her husband, trying him out, but Odysseus
    spoke in anger to his virtuous-minded lady:
    'What you have said, dear lady, has hurt my heart deeply. What man
    has put my bed in another place? But it would be difficult

185   for even a very expert one, unless a god, coming
    to help in person, were easily to change its position.
    But there is no mortal man alive, no strong man, who lightly
    could move the weight elsewhere. There is one particular feature
    in the bed's construction. I myself, no other man, made it.

190   There was the bole of an olive tree with long leaves growing
    strongly in the courtyard, and it was thick, like a column.
    I laid down my chamber around this, and built it, until I
    finished it, with close-set stones, and roofed it well over,
    and added the compacted doors, fitting closely together.

195   Then I cut away the foliage of the long-leaved olive,
    and trimmed the trunk from the roots up, planing it with a brazen
    adze, well and expertly, and trued it straight to a chalkline,
    making a bed post of it, and bored all holes with an auger.
    I began with this and built my bed, until it was finished,

200   and decorated it with gold and silver and ivory.
    Then I lashed it with thongs of oxhide, dyed bright with purple.
    There is its character, as I tell you; but I do not know now,
    dear lady, whether my bed is still in place, or if some man
    has cut underneath the stump of the olive, and moved it elsewhere.'

205   So he spoke, and her knees and the heart within her went slack
    as she recognized the clear proofs that Odysseus had given;
    but then she burst into tears and ran straight to him, throwing
    her arms around the neck of Odysseus, and kissed his head, saying:
    'Do not be angry with me, Odysseus, since, beyond other men,

210   you have the most understanding. The gods granted us misery,
    in jealousy over the thought that we two, always together,
    should enjoy our youth, and then come to the threshold of old age.
    Then do not now be angry with me nor blame me, because
    I did not greet you, as I do now, at first when I saw you.

215   For always the spirit deep in my very heart was fearful
    that some one of mortal men would come my way and deceive me
    with words. For there are many who scheme for wicked advantage.
    For neither would the daughter born to Zeus, Helen of Argos,

have lain in love with an outlander from another country,
220 if she had known that the warlike sons of the Achaians would bring her
home again to the beloved land of her fathers.
It was a god who stirred her to do the shameful thing she
did, and never before had she had in her heart this terrible
wildness, out of which came suffering to us also.
225 But now, since you have given me accurate proof describing
our bed, which no other mortal man beside has ever seen,
but only you and I, and there is one serving woman,
Aktor's daughter, whom my father gave me when I came here,
who used to guard the doors for us in our well-built chamber;
230 so you persuade my heart, though it has been very stubborn.'
     She spoke, and still more roused in him the passion for weeping.
He wept as he held his lovely wife, whose thoughts were virtuous.
And as when the land appears welcome to men who are swimming,
after Poseidon has smashed their strong-built ship on the open
235 water, pounding it with the weight of wind and the heavy
seas, and only a few escape the gray water landward
by swimming, with a thick scurf of salt coated upon them,
and gladly they set foot on the shore, escaping the evil;
so welcome was her husband to her as she looked upon him,
240 and she could not let him go from the embrace of her white arms.
Now Dawn of the rosy fingers would have dawned on their weeping,
had not the gray-eyed goddess Athene planned it otherwise.
She held the long night back at the outward edge, she detained
Dawn of the golden throne by the Ocean, and would not let her
245 harness her fast-footed horses who bring the daylight to people:
Lampos and Phaethon, the Dawn's horses, who carry her.
Then resourceful Odysseus spoke to his wife, saying:
'Dear wife, we have not yet come to the limit of all our
trials. There is unmeasured labor left for the future,
250 both difficult and great, and all of it I must accomplish.
So the soul of Teiresias prophesied to me, on that day
when I went down inside the house of Hades, seeking
to learn about homecoming, for myself and for my companions.
But come, my wife, let us go to bed, so that at long last
255 we can enjoy the sweetness of slumber, sleeping together.'
     Circumspect Penelope said to him in answer:
'You shall have your going to bed whenever the spirit

desires it, now that the gods have brought about your homecoming
to your own strong-founded house and to the land of your fathers.

260   But since the gods put this into your mind, and you understand it,
tell me what this trial is, since I think I shall hear of it
later; so it will be none the worse if I now hear of it.'
      Then in turn resourceful Odysseus said to her in answer:
'You are so strange. Why do you urge me on and tell me

265   to speak of it? Yet I will tell you, concealing nothing.
Your heart will have no joy in this; and I myself am not
happy, since he told me to go among many cities
of men, taking my well-shaped oar in my hands and bearing it,
until I come where there are men living who know nothing

270   of the sea, and who eat food that is not mixed with salt, who never
have known ships whose cheeks are painted purple, who never
have known well-shaped oars, which act for ships as wings do.
And then he told me a very clear proof. I will not conceal it.
When, as I walk, some other wayfarer happens to meet me,

275   and says I carry a winnow fan on my bright shoulder,
then I must plant my well-shaped oar in the ground, and render
ceremonious sacrifice to the lord Poseidon,
one ram and one bull, and a mounter of sows, a boar pig,
and make my way home again, and render holy hecatombs

280   to the immortal gods who hold the wide heaven, all
of them in order. Death will come to me from the sea, in
some altogether unwarlike way, and it will end me
in the ebbing time of a sleek old age. My people
about me will prosper. All this he told me would be accomplished.'

285   Circumspect Penelope said to him in answer:
'If the gods are accomplishing a more prosperous old age,
then there is hope that you shall have an escape from your troubles.'
      Now as these two were conversing thus with each other,
meanwhile the nurse and Eurynome were making the bed up

290   with soft coverings, under the light of their flaring torches.
Then when they had worked and presently had a firm bed made,
the old woman went away back to bed in her own place,
while Eurynome, as mistress of the chamber, guided them
on their way to the bed, and her hands held the torch for them.

295   When she had brought them to the chamber she went back. They then
gladly went together to bed, and their old ritual.

He tells his story

At this time Telemachos and the oxherd and swineherd
stopped the beat of their feet in the dance, and stopped the women,
and they themselves went to bed in the shadowy palace.
300   When Penelope and Odysseus had enjoyed their lovemaking,
they took their pleasure in talking, each one telling his story.
She, shining among women, told of all she had endured
in the palace, as she watched the suitors, a ravening company,
who on her account were slaughtering many oxen
305   and fat sheep, and much wine was being drawn from the wine jars.
But shining Odysseus told of all the cares he inflicted
on other men, and told too of all that in his misery
he had toiled through. She listened to him with delight, nor did any
sleep fall upon her eyes until he had told her everything.
310   He began with how he had beaten the Kikonians, and then
gone to the rich country of the men who feed on the lotus.
He told all that the Cyclops had done, and how he took vengeance
on him for his strong companions he had eaten, and showed no pity.
How he came to Aiolos, who generously received him
315   and gave him passage, but it was not fated for him to come back
yet to his country, so the stormwinds caught and carried him
out again on the sea where the fish swarm, groaning heavily;
and how he came to Telepylos of the Laistrygones,
and these men had destroyed his ships and strong-greaved companions
320   [all; but Odysseus only got away with his black ship].
He told her of the guile and the many devices of Circe,
and how he had gone into the moldering home of Hades,
there to consult the soul of Theban Teiresias, going
in his ship with many benches, and there saw all his companions,
325   and his mother, who had borne him and nursed him when he was little.
He told how he had heard the song of the echoing Sirens,
and made his way to the Roving Rocks and dreaded Charybdis
and Skylla, whom no men ever yet have escaped without damage.
He told how his companions ate the cattle of Helios,
330   then told how Zeus who thunders on high had struck his fast ship
with the smoky thunderbolt, and all his noble companions
perished alike, only he escaped the evil death spirits;
and how he came to the island Ogygia and the nymph Kalypso
who detained him with her, desiring that he should be her husband,
335   in her hollow caverns, and she took care of him and told him

that she would make him ageless all his days, and immortal,
but never so could she persuade the heart that was in him;
then how, after much suffering, he reached the Phaiakians,
who honored him in their hearts as if he were a god, and sent him
340   back, by ship, to the beloved land of his fathers,
bestowing bronze and gold in abundance on him, and clothing.
And this was the last word he spoke to her, when the sweet sleep
came to relax his limbs and slip the cares from his spirit.
     Then the goddess gray-eyed Athene thought what to do next.
345   As soon as she thought the heart of Odysseus had full contentment
of the pleasure of resting in bed beside his wife, and of sleeping,
immediately she stirred from Ocean the golden-throned early
Dawn, to shine her light upon men, and Odysseus rose up
from his soft bed, and spoke then to his wife, telling her:
350   'Dear wife, we both have had our full share of numerous trials
now; yours have been here as you cried over my much-longed-for
homecoming, while as for me, Zeus and the other gods held me
back from my own country, as I was striving to reach it.
But now that we two have come to our desired bed together,
355   you look after my possessions which are in the palace,
but as for my flocks, which the overbearing suitors have ruined,
many I shall restore by raiding, others the Achaians
shall give me, until they have filled up all of my sheepfolds.
But now I shall go to our estate with its many orchards,
360   to see my noble father who has grieved for me constantly.
But I tell you this, my wife, though you have your own understanding.
Presently, when the sun rises, there will be a rumor
about the men who courted you, whom I killed in our palace.
Then go to the upper chamber with your attendant women,
365   and sit still, looking at no one, and do not ask any questions.'
     He spoke, and put his splendid armor over his shoulders,
and wakened Telemachos and the oxherd and the swineherd,
and told all to take up in their hands their warlike weapons;
nor did they disobey him, but armed themselves in the bronze, then
370   opened the doors and went outside, and Odysseus led them.
By now the light was over the earth, but Athene, hiding
these men in darkness, guided them quickly out of the city.

BOOK XXIV

Hermes of Kyllene summoned the souls of the suitors
to come forth, and in his hands he was holding the beautiful
golden staff, with which he mazes the eyes of those mortals
whose eyes he would maze, or wakes again the sleepers. Herding
5 them on with this, he led them along, and they followed, gibbering.
And as when bats in the depth of an awful cave flitter
and gibber, when one of them has fallen out of his place in
the chain that the bats have formed by holding one on another;
so, gibbering, they went their way together, and Hermes
10 the kindly healer led them along down moldering pathways.
They went along, and passed the Ocean stream, and the White Rock,
and passed the gates of Helios the Sun, and the country
of dreams, and presently arrived in the meadow of asphodel.
This is the dwelling place of souls, images of dead men.
15   There they found the soul of Achilleus, the son of Peleus,
the soul of Patroklos, and the soul of stately Antilochos,
and the soul of Aias, who for beauty and stature was greatest
of all the Danaans, next to the blameless son of Peleus.
So these were gathered around Achilleus, and now came to them
20 the soul of Agamemnon, the son of Atreus, sorrowing,
and around him were gathered the souls of those others, who with him
also died and met their fate in the house of Aigisthos.
First of these two to speak was the soul of the son of Peleus:
'Son of Atreus, we thought that all your days you were favored

25 beyond all other heroes by Zeus who delights in the thunder,
because you were lord over numerous people, and strong ones,
in the land of the Trojans, where we Achaians suffered hardships.
And yet it was to you that the destructive doom spirit
would come too early; but no man who is born escapes her.
30 How I wish that, enjoying that high place of your power,
you could have met death and destiny in the land of the Trojans.
So all the Achaians would have made a mound to cover you,
and you would have won great glory for your son hereafter.
In truth you were ordained to die by a death most pitiful.'
35   The soul of Agamemnon, son of Atreus, answered:
'O happy son of Peleus, Achilleus, like the immortals,
who died in Troy, far away from Argos, and around you others
were killed, Trojans and the best men among the Achaians,
as they fought over you; and you in the turning dust lay
40 mightily in your might, your horsemanship all forgotten.
We fought on for the whole day long, nor would we ever
have stopped fighting, if Zeus had not stopped us with a whirlstorm.
But when we had carried you to the ships, away from the fighting,
we laid you out on a litter, and anointed your handsome body
45 with warm water and with unguents, and by you the Danaans
shed many hot tears, and cut their hair short for you; and also
your mother, hearing the news, came out of the sea, with immortal
sea girls beside her. Immortal crying arose and spread over
the great sea, and trembling seized hold of all the Achaians.
50 And now they would have started away, and gone on the hollow
ships, had not a man of much ancient wisdom halted them,
Nestor, whose advice had also shown best before this.
He in kind intention toward all spoke forth and addressed them:
"Hold fast, Argives; do not run away, O young Achaians.
55 It is his mother coming out of the sea with immortal
sea girls beside her, to be with her son, who has perished."
    'So he spoke, and the great-hearted Achaians stayed from
their panic. Around you stood the daughters of the Sea's Ancient,
mourning piteously, with immortal clothing upon them.
60 And all the nine Muses in sweet antiphonal singing
mourned you, nor would you then have seen any one of the Argives
not in tears, so much did the singing Muse stir them.
For ten and seven days, alike in the day and the night time,

we wailed for you, both mortal people and the immortals.
65 On the eighteenth day we gave you to the fire, and around you
slaughtered a great number of fat sheep and horn-curved cattle.
You were burned in the clothing of the gods, and abundant
ointment and sweet honey, while many Achaian heroes
moved in armor about the pyre where you were burning,
70 with horses and on foot, and a great clamoring rose up.
But after the flame of Hephaistos had consumed you utterly,
then at dawn we gathered your white bones, Achilleus,
together with unmixed wine and unguents. Your mother gave you
a golden jar with handles. She said that it was a present
75 from Dionysos, and was the work of renowned Hephaistos.
In this your white bones are laid away, O shining Achilleus,
mixed with the bones of the dead Patroklos, son of Menoitios,
and apart from those of Antilochos, whom you prized above all
the rest of your companions after the death of Patroklos.
80 Around them then, we, the chosen host of the Argive
spearmen, piled up a grave mound that was both great and perfect,
on a jutting promontory there by the wide Hellespont,
so that it can be seen afar from out on the water
by men now alive and those to be born in the future.
85 Then your mother, asking the gods for the gift of beautiful
prizes, set them in the field for the best of the Achaians.
I in my time have attended the funerals of many
heroes, at those times when, because a king has perished,
the young men gird themselves for sport and set up the prizes;
90 but these your heart would have admired beyond any others,
such beautiful prizes as were set up by the goddess, silver-footed
Thetis, for your sake. You were very dear to the gods. So,
even now you have died, you have not lost your name, but always
in the sight of all mankind your fame shall be great, Achilleus;
95 but what pleasure was there for me when I had wound up the fighting?
In my homecoming Zeus devised my dismal destruction,
to be killed by the hands of my cursed wife, and Aigisthos.'
    Now as the spirits were conversing thus with each other,
there came approaching them the courier Argeïphontes,
100 leading down the souls of the suitors killed by Odysseus.
These two in wonderment went up to them as they saw them,
and the soul of Agamemnon, son of Atreus, recognized

glorious Amphimedon, the dear son of Melaneus,
who, in his home in Ithaka, had once been his guest-friend.
105 First of the two to speak was the soul of Agamemnon:
'Amphimedon, what befell you that you came under the dark earth,
all of you choice young men, of the same age, nor could one, gathering
the best men out of all a city have chosen otherwise.
Was it with the ships, and did Poseidon, rousing a stormblast
110 of battering winds and waves towering prove your undoing?
Or was it on the dry land, did men embattled destroy you
as you tried to cut out cattle and fleecy sheep from their holdings,
or fighting against them, for the sake of their city and women?
Tell me what I ask. I claim that I am your guest-friend.
115 Or do you not remember when I came into your house there,
together with godlike Menelaos, to rouse up Odysseus
so he would go to Ilion on the well-benched vessels
with us? And we were a whole month crossing over the wide sea,
having hardly persuaded Odysseus, sacker of cities.'
120   Then in turn the soul of Amphimedon answered him, saying:
'Son of Atreus, most lordly and king of man, Agamemnon,
I remember it all, illustrious, as you tell it.
I will tell you well and truthfully the entire story
of how our wretched end came in death, how it was accomplished.
125 We were courting the wife of Odysseus, who had been long gone.
She would not refuse the hateful marriage, nor would she bring it
about, but she was planning our death and black destruction
with this other stratagem of her heart's devising.
She set up a great loom in her palace, and set to weaving
130 a web of threads long and fine. Then she said to us:
"Young men, my suitors now that the great Odysseus has perished,
wait, though you are eager to marry me, until I finish
this web, so that my weaving will not be useless and wasted.
This is a shroud for the hero Laertes, for when the destructive
135 doom of death, which lays men low, shall take him, lest any
Achaian woman in this neighborhood hold it against me
that a man of many conquests lies with no sheet to wind him."
So she spoke, and the proud heart in us was persuaded.
Thereafter in the daytime she would weave at her great loom,
140 but in the night she would have torches set by, and undo it.
So for three years she was secret in her design, convincing

the Achaians, but when the fourth year came, with the seasons returning,
and the months waned, and many days had been brought to completion,
one of her women, who knew the whole of the story, told us,
145 and we found her in the act of undoing her glorious weaving.
So, against her will and by force, she had to finish it.
Then she displayed the great piece of weaving that she had woven.
She had washed it, and it shone like the sun or the moon. At that time
an evil spirit, coming from somewhere, brought back Odysseus
150 to the remote part of his estate, where his swineherd was living.
At that time the dear son of godlike Odysseus came over
from sandy Pylos, voyaging in his black ship. These two,
after compacting their plot of a foul death for the suitors,
made their way to the glorious town. In fact Odysseus
155 came afterwards; Telemachos led the way, and the swineherd
brought in Odysseus, wearing sorry clothing upon him,
in the likeness of a wretched vagabond, an old man
leaning on a stick, and poor was the clothing he had upon him.
Not one of us, even of the older ones, was able
160 to recognize who he was when he appeared so suddenly,
but we treated him rudely with evil words and with blows. Odysseus,
nevertheless, endured for the time with steadfast spirit
to be pelted with missiles and harshly spoken to in his own palace;
but then, when the purpose of aegis-bearing Zeus had stirred him,
165 he, with Telemachos, took away the glorious armor,
and stowed it away in the chamber, closing the doors upon it.
Then, in the craftiness of his mind, he urged his lady
to set the bow and the gray iron in front of the suitors,
the contest for us ill-fated men, the start of our slaughter.
170 Not one of us was able to hook the string on the powerful
bow, but all of us were found far too weak for it;
but when the great bow was given into the hands of Odysseus,
then all of us spoke out and threatened the man, telling him
not to give the bow, however much he might argue.
175 Only Telemachos urged him on and told him to give it.
Then much-enduring Odysseus, in his hand accepting it,
easily strung the bow, and sent a shaft through the iron.
He stood on the threshold, and scattered out the swift shafts before him,
glaring terribly, and struck down the king Antinoös.
180 Then he shot his baneful arrows into the others,

aiming straight at them, and they dropped one after another.
It could be seen then that some one of the gods was helping him,
for these men, chasing us through the house in their strength and fury,
killed us, one man after another; the floor was smoking
185 with blood, and the horrible cries rose up as our heads were broken.
So, Agamemnon, we were destroyed, and still at this moment
our bodies are lying uncared-for in the halls of Odysseus;
for our people in the house of each man know nothing of this,
they who would have washed away from our wounds the black blood,
190 and laid us out and mourned us; for this is the right of the perished.'
     The soul of Agamemnon, son of Atreus, answered him:
'O fortunate son of Laertes, Odysseus of many devices,
surely you won yourself a wife endowed with great virtue.
How good was proved the heart that is in blameless Penelope,
195 Ikarios' daughter, and how well she remembered Odysseus,
her wedded husband. Thereby the fame of her virtue shall never
die away, but the immortals will make for the people
of earth a thing of grace in the song for prudent Penelope.
Not so did the daughter of Tyndareos fashion her evil
200 deeds, when she killed her wedded lord, and a song of loathing
will be hers among men, to make evil the reputation
of womankind, even for one whose acts are virtuous.'
     So these two were conversing each with the other, standing
in the gates of Hades, underneath the earth's secret places.
205   The others went from the city, and presently came to the country
place of Laertes, handsomely cultivated. Laertes
himself had reclaimed it, after he spent much labor upon it.
There was his house, and all around the house ran a shelter,
in which the slaves, who worked at his pleasure under compulsion,
210 would take their meals, and sit, and pass the night. There was also
an old Sicilian woman there, who duly looked after
the old man out on the estate, far away from the city.
There Odysseus spoke a word to his son and his servants:
'Go now, all of you, inside the strong-fashioned building,
215 and sacrifice the best of all the pigs for our dinner
presently; but I myself will make trial of my father,
to see whether he will know me and his eyes recognize me,
or fail to know me, with all this time that has grown upon me.'
     So he spoke, and gave his thralls their weapons of warfare,

220 and they went quickly on their way to the house; but Odysseus
went closer to the abundant orchard, searching. He did not
find either Dolios, as he came into the great orchard,
nor any of his thralls, nor his sons, for all these had gone off
to gather stones and make them into a wall retaining
225 the orchard, and the old man had guided them on their errand;
but he did find his father alone in the well-worked orchard,
spading out a plant, and he had a squalid tunic upon him,
patched together and ugly, and on his legs he had oxhide
gaiters fastened and patched together, to prevent scratching,
230 and gloves on his hands because of the bushes, and he was wearing
a cap of goatskin on his head, to increase his misery.
Now when much-enduring great Odysseus observed him,
with great misery in his heart, and oppressed by old age,
he stood underneath a towering pear tree and shed tears for him,
235 and deliberated then in his heart and his spirit
whether to embrace his father and kiss him and tell him
everything, how he was come again to his own dear country,
or question him first about everything, and make trial of him.
In the division of his heart this way seemed best to him,
240 first to make trial of him and speak in words of mockery.
With this in mind, noble Odysseus came straight up to him.
He was digging around a plant with his head held downward,
and now his glorious son stood near, and spoke to him, saying:
'Old sir, there is in you no lack of expertness in tending
245 your orchard; everything is well cared for, and there is never
a plant, neither fig tree nor yet grapevine nor olive
nor pear tree nor leek bed uncared for in your garden.
But I will also tell you this; do not take it as cause for
anger. You yourself are ill cared for; together with dismal
250 old age, which is yours, you are squalid and wear foul clothing upon you.
It is not for your laziness that your lord does not take care of you,
nor is your stature and beauty, as I see it, such as
ought to belong to a slave. You look like a man who is royal,
and such a one as who, after he has bathed and eaten,
255 should sleep on a soft bed; for such is the right of the elders.
But come now, tell me this and give me an accurate answer.
What man's thrall are you? Whose orchard are you laboring?
And tell me this and tell me truly, so that I may know

whether this is really Ithaka I have come to, as that man
260   told me just now as I encountered him on my way here:
not a very sensible man, for he had no patience
to tell me all or listen to what I said, when I asked him
about my friend from abroad, whether he still lives and is somewhere
here, or is dead now and down in the house of Hades.
265   And I tell you this; listen to me and understand me.
Once I entertained a friend in my own dear country,
when he came to our house, nor has any man been dearer
to me, among all those who have come from afar to my palace.
He announced that he was by birth a man of Ithaka,
270   and said that his father was Laertes, son of Arkeisios.
I took him into my own house and well entertained him
with proper hospitality, since there was abundance
in the house, and gave him presents of friendship, as was becoming.
I gave him seven talents of well-wrought gold, and I gave him
275   a mixing bowl made all of silver, with flowers wrought on it,
and twelve mantles to be worn single, as many blankets,
as many handsome cloaks, also the same number of tunics,
and aside from these four comely women, whose skill in handiwork
was without fault; and he could choose the ones that he wanted.'
280   Then his father, shedding tears, said to him in answer:
'Friend, this land that you have reached is the one you were seeking;
but violent and reckless men are in control of it,
and the grace of those countless gifts you gave is all gone for nothing.
If you had found him yet alive in the land of Ithaka,
285   he would have sent you along with gifts in return, and given
good entertainment, as is right for him who has given.
But come now, tell me this and give me an accurate answer.
How many years is it since you entertained that unhappy
guest of yours, my son—did he ever live?—an ill-starred
290   man, one whom, far from his country and his own people,
the fish have eaten in the great sea, or else on the dry land
he has been spoil for wild beasts and for birds; and his mother
and father, whose child he was, did not give him his rites nor mourn him,
nor yet did his bountiful wife, circumspect Penelope,
295   wail for her husband on his bier, as would have been fitting,
nor close his eyes; for that is the right of those who have perished.
But tell me this too, tell me truly, so that I may know it.

by Laertes his father

What man are you and whence? Where is your city? Your parents?
Where is your swift ship standing now, that brought you to this place,
and your godlike companions? Or did you come as a passenger
in someone else's ship, and they let you off, and went on?'
    Then resourceful Odysseus spoke in turn and answered him:
'See, I will accurately answer all that you ask me.
I am from Alybas, where I live in a famous dwelling,
and am the son of Apheidas, son of the lord Polypemon.
My own name is Eperitos; now the divinity
drove me here on my way against my will, from Sikania.
And my ship stands nearby, off the country, away from the city.
But as for Odysseus, this is by now the fifth year since
he went from there, and took his departure out of my country.
Unhappy man. Indeed, the bird signs were good at his going.
They were on his right; and I too rejoiced as I sent him
off, and he rejoiced as he went. My heart was still hopeful
that we would meet in friendship and give glorious presents.'
    He spoke, and the black cloud of sorrow closed on Laertes.
In both hands he caught up the grimy dust and poured it
over his face and grizzled head, groaning incessantly.
The spirit rose up in Odysseus, and now in his nostrils
there was a shock of bitter force as he looked on his father.
He sprang to him and embraced and kissed and then said to him:
'Father, I am he, the man whom you ask about. I am
here, come back in the twentieth year to the land of my father.
But stay now from your weeping, shedding of tears, and outcry,
for I tell you this straight out; the need for haste is upon us.
I have killed the suitors who were in our palace, avenging
all their heart-hurting outrage and their evil devisings.'
    Then in turn Laertes answered him and said to him:
'If in truth you are Odysseus, my son, who have come back
here, give me some unmistakable sign, so that I can believe you.'
    Then resourceful Odysseus spoke in turn and answered him:
'First, then, look with your eyes upon this scar and know it.
The wild boar inflicted it with his white tusk, on Parnassos,
when I went there; for you and my queenly mother had sent me
to Autolykos, my mother's dear father, so I could be given
those gifts, which he promised me and consented to when he came to us.
Or come then, let me tell you of the trees in the well-worked

300

305

310

315

320

325

330

335

orchard, which you gave me once. I asked you of each one,
when I was a child, following you through the garden. We went
among the trees, and you named them all and told me what each one
340 was, and you gave me thirteen pear trees, and ten apple trees,
and forty fig trees; and so also you named the fifty
vines you would give. Each of them bore regularly, for there were
grapes at every stage upon them, whenever the seasons
of Zeus came down from the sky upon them, to make them heavy.'
345 He spoke, and Laertes' knees and the heart within him went slack,
as he recognized the clear proofs that Odysseus had given.
He threw his arms around his dear son, and much-enduring
great Odysseus held him close, for his spirit was fainting.
But when he had got his breath back again, and the spirit gathered
350 into his heart, once more he said to him, answering:
'Father Zeus, there are gods indeed upon tall Olympos,
if truly the suitors have had to pay for their reckless violence.
But now I am terribly afraid in my heart that speedily
the men of Ithaka may come against us here, and send out
355 messages everywhere to the Kephallenian cities.'
Then resourceful Odysseus spoke in turn and answered him:
'Never fear, let these concerns not trouble your thinking;
but let us go to the house which lies here next to the orchard,
for there I sent Telemachos on ahead, with the oxherd
360 and the swineherd, so that they could most quickly prepare our dinner.'
So he spoke, and the two went into the handsome dwelling;
and when they had come into the well-established dwelling place,
there they found Telemachos, and the oxherd and swineherd,
cutting up a great deal of meat, and mixing the bright wine.
365 Meanwhile the Sicilian serving maid bathed great-hearted
Laertes in his house, and anointed him with olive oil,
then threw a handsome mantle about him. Also, Athene,
standing by the shepherd of the people, filled his limbs out,
and made him taller and thicker to behold than he had been.
370 He stepped forth from the bath, and his son looked on in amazement
as he saw him looking like one of the immortal gods to encounter.
So he spoke to him and addressed him in winged words, saying:
'Father, surely some one of the gods who are everlasting
has made you better to look upon for beauty and stature.'
375 Then in turn the thoughtful Laertes said to him in answer:

'O father Zeus, Athene and Apollo, if only
as I was when, lord of the Kephallenians, I took
Nerikos, the strong-founded citadel on the mainland
cape; if only I could have been such yesterday in the palace,
380 with armor upon my shoulders, to stand beside you and fight off
the suitors' attack; so I would have unstrung the knees of many
there in the hall, and your heart within you would have been gladdened.'
  Now these two were thus conversing one with the other.
And all, when they had finished their work and made ready their dinner,
385 took their places in order on chairs and along the benches.
Then they were putting their hands to the dinner, and now there drew
   near
the aged Dolios, and the old man's sons were with him,
coming from their toilsome work, for their mother had called them.
This was the old Sicilian woman, who had raised them, and carefully
390 looked after the old man, now that great age had seized him.
These, when they saw Odysseus and recognized his identity,
stood still in the hall in astonishment; but Odysseus
had words of conciliation for them, and so he addressed them:
'Sit to dinner with us, old man, and let be your wonder;
395 for a long time now we have been eager to put our hands to
food, but we waited for you in the halls, ever expecting you.'
  So he spoke, and Dolios, opening his arms wide, ran straight
to him, and took Odysseus' hand at the wrist, and kissed it,
and spoke aloud to him and addressed him in winged words, saying:
400 'Dear master, since you have come back to us, who wanted you
but expected you no more—but the very gods have brought you
back—we heartily welcome you; may the gods give you blessings.
And tell me this and tell me truly, so that I may know it.
Does circumspect Penelope know all the truth of this
405 and that you have come back, or shall we send her a messenger?'
  Then in turn resourceful Odysseus said to him in answer:
'She already knows, old man. Why should you trouble to do this?'
  He spoke, and Dolios sat down again on the polished
chair; so too, around great Odysseus, the sons of Dolios
410 came to speak to him in welcome, and shake hands with him,
and then went back in order to sit by their father, Dolios.
  So these were busy in the hall preparing their dinner;
but Rumor, a messenger, went swiftly through all the city,

crying aloud the terrible death and doom of the suitors;
415 and the people as they heard it came, from their several places,
to gather, with groaning and outcry, before the house of Odysseus.
They carried the corpses out of the house, and each one buried
his own, and sent back all who had come from the other cities,
giving them in charge of fishermen to take in their fast ships.
420 They themselves, sorrowful at heart, gathered in assembly.
But when they were all assembled and in one place together,
Eupeithes stood up and addressed them, since unforgettable
sorrow was stored away in his heart for the sake of Antinoös,
his son, who was the first to be killed by noble Odysseus.
425 For his sake weeping tears he now stood forth and addressed them:
'Friends, this man's will worked great evil upon the Achaians.
First he took many excellent men away in the vessels
with him, and lost the hollow ships, and lost all the people,
and then returning killed the best men of the Kephallenians.
430 Come then, before he can make his way quickly over to Pylos,
or else to shining Elis, where the Epeians are lords, let us
go, or else we shall then be shamed forever; all this
shall be a disgrace, even for the men hereafter to hear of,
if we do not take revenge on the murderers of our brothers
435 and sons; for there would be no pleasure in my heart to go on
living, but I would wish to die and be with the perished.
So let us go, before they cross the sea, and escape us.'
    He spoke, weeping, and pity took hold of all the Achaians.
But now Medon arrived, and with him the inspired singer,
440 from the palace of Odysseus, since now the sleep had left them;
they stood in their midst, and amazement seized upon each man of them.
Then Medon, full of prudent thoughts, spoke forth and addressed them:
'Hear me now, you men of Ithaka; for Odysseus
devised what he did, not without the consent of immortal
445 gods. I myself saw an immortal god who was standing
beside Odysseus. In every way it resembled Mentor.
An immortal god was seen, at one time in front of Odysseus
urging him on, and then next time he would rout the suitors,
and dash about the hall, while they fell one after another.'
450 So he spoke, and the green fear took hold of all of them.
Now Halitherses, Mastor's son, an aged warrior,
spoke to them. He alone saw what was before and behind him.

Now in kind intention toward all he spoke forth and addressed them:
'Hear me now, you men of Ithaka; hear what I tell you.
455 It is by your own weakness, dear friends, that these things have happened.
You would not listen to me, nor to Mentor, shepherd of the people,
when we told you to make your sons give over their senseless
mood; for they, in their evil recklessness, did a great wrong
in showing no respect to the wife, despoiling the possessions,
460 of a lordly man. They thought that he never would be coming
home. Now let it be thus. Hear me, and do as I tell you.
Let us not go there. He who does might incur some evil.'
So he spoke, but more than half who were there sprang up
with a great cry—though others stayed where they were assembled—
465 since Halitherses' speech did not please their hearts, but they listened
to Eupeithes, and now suddenly they ran for their armor.
Now they, when in the shining bronze they had shrouded their bodies,
assembled all in a body in front of the spacious city.
Eupeithes was their leader in their foolishness. He thought
470 he would avenge the slaughter of his son, but he was not
ever to come back, but must himself encounter his death there.
Now Athene spoke a word to Zeus, son of Kronos:
'Son of Kronos, our father, O lordliest of the mighty,
tell me what I ask. What does your mind have hidden within it?
475 Will you first inflict evil fighting upon them, and terrible
strife, or will you establish friendship between the two factions?'
Then Zeus the gatherer of the clouds said to her in answer:
'My child, why do you ask and question me in these matters?
For was not this your own intention, as you have counseled it,
480 how Odysseus should make his way back, and punish those others?
Do as you will; but I will tell you how it is proper.
Now that noble Odysseus has punished the suitors, let them
make their oaths of faith and friendship, and let him be king
always; and let us make them forget the death of their brothers
485 and sons, and let them be friends with each other, as in the time past,
and let them have prosperity and peace in abundance.'
So he spoke, and stirred on Athene, who was eager before this,
and she went in a flash of speed down the pinnacles of Olympos.
When the men had put away their desire for delicious feasting,
490 much-enduring great Odysseus began speaking among them:
'Let someone go out now and see if they are approaching.'

He spoke, and Dolios' son went out, as Odysseus told him.
He went and stood on the threshold and saw them all drawing closer.
Now presently he spoke in winged words to Odysseus:
495 'Here they are, coming close to us, so let us arm quickly.'
So he spoke, and they sprang up and put on their armor,
Odysseus with his three, and the six sons of Dolios;
and with them Dolios and Laertes put on their armor,
gray though they were, but they were fighters perforce. And now,
500 when all of them in shining bronze had shrouded their bodies,
they opened the doors, and went outside, and Odysseus led them.
But now came their way the daughter of Zeus, Athene,
likening herself in appearance and voice to Mentor.
Seeing her, much-enduring great Odysseus was happy,
505 and presently he spoke to his dear son, Telemachos:
'Telemachos, now yourself being present, where men do battle,
and the bravest are singled out from the rest, you must be certain
not to shame the blood of your fathers, for we in time past
all across the world have surpassed in manhood and valor.'
510 Then the thoughtful Telemachos said to him in answer:
'You will see, dear father, if you wish, that as far as my will goes,
I will not shame my blood that comes from you, which you speak of.'
So he spoke, and Laertes also rejoiced, and said to them:
'What day is this for me, dear gods? I am very happy.
515 My son and my son's son are contending over their courage.'
Then standing close beside him gray-eyed Athene said to him:
'Son of Arkeisios, far dearest of all my companions,
make your prayer to the gray-eyed girl and to Zeus her father,
then quickly balance your far-shadowing spear, and throw it.'
520 So Pallas Athene spoke, and breathed into him enormous
strength, and, making his prayer then to the daughter of great Zeus,
he quickly balanced his far-shadowing spear, and threw it,
and struck Eupeithes on the brazen side of his helmet,
nor could the helm hold off the spear, but the bronze smashed clean
    through.
525 He fell, thunderously, and his armor clattered upon him.
Odysseus and his glorious son fell upon their front fighters,
and began to strike with swords and stab with spears leaf-headed.
And now they would have killed them all, and given none of them
homecoming, had not Athene, daughter of Zeus of the aegis,

Reconciliation by Athene

530   cried out in a great voice and held back all the company:
      'Hold back, men of Ithaka, from the wearisome fighting,
      so that most soon, and without blood, you can settle everything.'
        So spoke Athene, and the green fear took hold of them,
      and in their terror they let fall from their hands their weapons,
535   which fell all on the ground at the cry of the goddess speaking.
      Striving to save their lives, they turned in flight toward the city.
      With a terrible cry, much-enduring Odysseus, gathering
      himself together, made a swoop, like a high-flown eagle.
      But the son of Kronos then threw down a smoky thunderbolt,
540   which fell in front of the gray-eyed daughter of the great father.
      Then the gray-eyed goddess Athene said to Odysseus:
      'Son of Laertes and seed of Zeus, resourceful Odysseus,
      hold hard, stop this quarrel in closing combat, for fear
      Zeus of the wide brows, son of Kronos, may be angry with you.'
545   So spoke Athene, and with happy heart he obeyed her.
      And pledges for the days to come, sworn to by both sides,
      were settled by Pallas Athene, daughter of Zeus of the aegis,
      who had likened herself in appearance and voice to Mentor.

GLOSSARY

NOTE. In the spelling of names, I have followed the same practice as in my translation of the *Iliad*. Mostly, I have simply transliterated the Greek, as for instance *Agelaos*, not *Agelaus*. In some cases, however, I have made exceptions and followed familiar usage; and sometimes I have simply translated (*Dawn, Graces*). The exceptions to my normal practice are: Achaians, Apollo, Argives, Athens, Circe, Crete, Cyclopes, Cyprus, Danaans, Dawn, Dorians, Egypt, Elysian Field, Graces, Hades, Helen, Hermes, Jason, Lotus-Eaters, Ocean, Penelope, Phoenicia and Phoenicians, Priam, Roving Rocks, Sicilians, Sirens, Thrace, Trojans, Troy.

This glossary is not an index, but gives at least one reference for each name. References are to book and line.

Achai'ans: The most general term for "Greeks," including the people of Ithaka, i.90; ii.7, etc.

A'cheron: River in the land of the dead, x.514.

Achil'leus: The great hero of the *Iliad*, whose ghost talked to Odysseus, xi.467, etc.

Adres'te: Handmaid of Helen, iv.122.

Agamem'non: Leader of the expedition against Troy, murdered by Aigisthos, i.30; iii.143, etc.

Agela'os: Son of Damastor, a suitor, xx.321, etc.; killed by Odysseus, xxii.293.

Aiai'a: Circe's island, x.135.

Ai'akos: Father of Peleus, grandfather of Achilleus, xi.471, 538.

Ai'as: (1) Son of Telamon, who quarreled with Odysseus over the armor of Achilleus, xi.469, etc.; (2) son of Oïleus, drowned by Poseidon, iv.499–510.

Aie'tes: Brother of Circe, x.137; xii.70.

Ai'gai: City in Achaia, favored by Poseidon, v.381.

Aigis'thos: Son of Thyestes, lover of Klytaimestra and murderer of Agamemnon, killed by Orestes, i.29; iii.194, etc.

Aigyp'tios: Elder of Ithaka, father of Eurynomos, ii.15.

GLOSSARY

Aigy'ptos: The river of Egypt, the Nile, xiv.257.

Aio'lia: The island of Aiolos (1), x.1.

Ai'olos: (1) Mortal king in charge of the winds, x.1; (2) father of Kretheus, xi.237.

Ai'son: Son of Tyro and Kretheus, xi.259.

Aithio'pians: The Ethiopians, a distant people visited by Poseidon, i.22; v.282, etc.

Ai'thon: Name assumed by Odysseus in conversation with Penelope, xix.183.

Aito'lia: Country in central Greece, xiv.379.

Akas'tos: A king in western Greece, xiv.336.

Akro'neos: A Phaiakian, viii.111.

Ak'toris: Maid of Penelope, xxiii.228.

Alek'tor: A Spartan, whose daughter married Megapenthes, iv.10.

Alkan'dre: Lady of Thebes in Egypt, wife of Polybos (2), iv.126.

Al'kimos: Father of Mentor, xxii.234.

Alki'noös: King of the Phaiakians, vi.12; vii.185, etc.

Alkip'pe: Handmaid of Helen, iv.124.

Alkmai'on: Son of Amphiaraos, xv.248.

Alkme'ne: Mother of Herakles, ii.120; xi.266.

Alo'eus: Husband of Iphimedeia, putative father of Otos and Ephialtes, xi.305.

Alphei'os: River in the western Peloponnese, iii.489.

A'lybas: City of unknown location from which Odysseus pretended to have come, xxiv.304.

Amni'sos: A place in Crete, xix.188.

Amphi'alos: A Phaiakian, winner in jumping, viii.114; 128.

Amphiara'os: Son of Oïkles and grandfather of Theoklymenos. He was one of the seven against Thebes, xv.244–247.

Amphi'lochos: Son of Amphiaraos, xv.248.

Amphi'medon: One of the suitors, xxii.242; killed by Telemachos, xxii,284; his ghost told the ghost of Agamemnon about the slaughter of the suitors, xxiv.103.

Amphi'nomos: One of the suitors, xvi.351; son of Nisos, from Doulichion, best of the suitors and best liked by Penelope, xvi.394; befriended Odysseus and was warned by him, xviii. 119–150; killed by Telemachos, xxii.89–94.

Amphi'on: (1) Son of Antiope, and builder, with his brother Zethos, of Thebes, xi.262; (2) lord of Minyan Orchomenos, xi.283.

Amphi'thea: Grandmother of Odysseus, xix.416.

Amphitri'te: Queen of the sea, iii.91, etc.

Amphi'tryon: Husband of Alkmene, putative father of Herakles, xi.266.

Amytha'on: Son of Kretheus and Tyro, xi.259.

Anabasi'neos: A Phaiakian, viii.113.

Anchi'alos: (1) Father of Mentes, i.180; (2) a Phaiakian, viii.112.

Andrai'mon: Father of Thoas, xiv.499.

Antiklei'a: Mother of Odysseus, xi.85.

Anti'klos: One of the Achaians in the Wooden Horse, iv.286.

Anti'lochos: Son of Nestor, killed at Troy by Memnon, iii.112; iv.187, etc.

Anti'noös: Son of Eupeithes, one of the two leading suitors, i.383; ii.84, etc.;

struck Odysseus with footstool, xvii.462; first to be killed, by Odysseus, xxii.8.

Anti'ope: Daughter of Asopos, mother of Amphion and Zethos, xi.260.

Anti'phates: (1) King of the Laistrygones, x.107; (2) father of Oïkles, xv.242.

An'tiphos: (1) Companion of Odysseus, killed by the Cyclops, ii.17; (2) an elder of Ithaka, xvii.68.

Apeir'e: The home of Eurymedousa, vii.8.

Aphei'das: Pretended name of Odysseus' father in his conversation with Laertes, xxiv.305.

Aphrodi'te: Daughter of Zeus, goddess of love and beauty, iv.14, etc. In the *Odyssey* (though not in the *Iliad*) she is the wife of Hephaistos, viii.267, etc.

Apol'lo: Or Phoibos Apollo, son of Zeus and Leto, iii.279, etc. He plays no major part in the *Odyssey*, but the day when the suitors are killed is a festival day for him, xx.278. His arrows, like those of Artemis, bring sudden and painless death, iii.280, etc.

Ar'es: Son of Zeus, god of war, lover of Aphrodite, viii.267, etc.

Are'te: Wife of Alkinoös, queen of the Phaiakians, vii.54, etc.

Arethou'sa: A spring on Ithaka, xiii.408.

Arkei'sios: Father of Laertes, xvi.118, etc.

Are'tos: Son of Nestor, iii.414.

Argeïphon'tes: "The slayer of Argos," an epithet of Hermes, i.38; v.43, etc.

Ar'gives: The Greeks who went to Troy, i.61, etc.; also, the people of Mykene or Sparta, iii.309, etc.

Ar'go: The ship of the Argonauts, xii.69.

Ar'gos: The dog of Odysseus, xvii.292.

Ar'gos: City or district in the northeast Peloponnese, or simply "Greece," i.344, iii.251, etc.

Ariad'ne: Daughter of Minos, killed by Artemis. Her ghost was seen by Odysseus in the land of the dead, xi.321.

Arkei'sios: Father of Laertes, xvi.118, etc.

Arnai'os: The true name of Iros, xviii.5.

Arta'kie: A spring on Lamos, x.108.

Ar'temis: Daughter of Zeus and Leto, sister of Apollo, vi.102, etc. Her arrows, like those of Apollo, bring sudden and painless death, xv.410, etc.

Aso'pos: A river and river god in Boiotia, father of Antiope, xi.260

A'rybas: A lord of Sidon, father of Eumaios' nurse, xv.426.

Asphal'ion: Henchman of Menelaos, iv.216.

As'teris: A little island off Ithaka, iv.846.

Athe'ne: Or Pallas Athene, goddess, daughter of Zeus, i.44, etc.

Ath'ens: The famous city in east-central Greece, iii.278.

At'las: Titan, father of Kalypso, i.52.

At'reus: Father of Agamemnon and Menelaos, i.35, etc.

Atryto'ne: Epithet of Athene, iv.762.

Auto'lykos: Father of Antikleia, so grandfather of Odysseus, xi.85; xix.394, etc.

Auto'noë: Handmaid of Penelope, xviii.182.

GLOSSARY

Bo'ëthoös: Father of Eteoneus, iv.31.

Boö'tes: The constellation of that name, v.272.

Chal'kis: A place on the west coast of Greece, opposite Ithaka, xv.295.

Charyb'dis: A monster of the coast in the form of a great whirlpool, xii.104, etc.

Chi'os: A large island off the coast of Asia Minor, iii.170.

Chlo'ris: Wife of Neleus and mother of Nestor, whose ghost Odysseus saw in the land of the dead, xi.281.

Chro'mios: Son of Neleus and Chloris, brother of Nestor, xi.286.

Cir'ce: The goddess and enchantress of Aiaia, Book x throughout, also viii.448; ix.31, etc.

Crete: Large island, domain of Idomeneus, iii.191, etc. Pretended home of Odysseus in various lying stories, xiii.256; xiv.199; xix.172.

Cyclo'pes: A monstrous people encountered by Odysseus and his men, ix.106, etc. In the singular, the Cyclops means Polyphemos, i.69; ii.19, etc.

Cy'prus: Large island in the easternmost Mediterranean, iv.83, etc.

Damas'tor: Father of Agelaos, xx.321.

Dan'aans: The Greeks who went to Troy, i.350, etc.

Dawn: Properly Eos, the goddess whose rising brings the day, ii.1; v.1, etc. Wife of Tithonos, v.1; mother of the killer of Antilochos (presumably Memnon), iv.188; in love with Orion, v.121; carried off Kleitos, xv.250.

Deï'phobos: Son of Priam, husband of Helen at the time of the fall of Troy, iv.276; viii.518.

De'los: Island in the Aigaian Sea, sacred to Apollo, vi.162.

Deme'ter: Sister of Zeus, who loved Iasion, v.125.

Demo'dokos: The blind singer of the Phaiakians, viii.44, etc.

Demopto'lemos: Suitor killed by Odysseus, xxii.242; 266.

Deuka'lion: King in Crete, father of Idomeneus, xix.180.

Di'a: An island in the Aigaian, xi.325.

Dio'kles: Lord of Pherai, iii.488; xv.186.

Diome'des: Son of Tydeus, a great hero of the *Iliad*, iii.180.

Diony'sos: God of wine, xxiv.75; accuser of Ariadne, xi.325.

Dme'tor: Son of Iasos (2), king of Cyprus, xvii.443.

Dodo'na: Site of an oracle of Zeus in northwestern Greece, xiv.327; xix.296.

Do'lios: An old servant, specially attached to Penelope, iv.735; works on the estate with Laertes, xxiv.222; father of Melanthios, xvii.212; of Melantho, xviii.322.

Dor'ians: Presumably, the "conquerors," located by Odysseus in Crete, xix.177.

Douli'chion: A large, but not positively identified, island in the domain of Odysseus, i.246, etc. (In the *Iliad*, it is in the domain of Meges.)

Dy'mas: A Phaiakian, father of Nausikaa's best friend, vi.22.

Echene'os: Aged Phaiakian counselor, vii.155; xi.342.

Eche'phron: A son of Nestor, iii.413.

E'chetos: A cruel king somewhere in western Greece, xviii.85; xxi.308.

E'gypt: The country, iii.300; iv.351, etc.

GLOSSARY

Eido'thea: Sea nymph, daughter of Proteus, iv.365.

Eileithyi'a: The goddess of childbirth, xix.188.

E'latos: A suitor, killed by Eumaios, xxii.267.

Elat'reus: A Phaiakian, viii.111.

E'lis: City and district of the western Peloponnese, opposite Ithaka, iv.635, etc.

Elpe'nor: Companion of Odysseus, killed by accidentally falling from the roof, x.552; Odysseus talked with his ghost, xi.51.

Ely'sian Field: The far fortunate place where Menelaos is ultimately to find his home, iv.563.

E'nipeus: A river in Thessaly, loved by Tyro, xi.238.

Epei'ans: People of Elis, xiii.275, etc.

Epei'os: The builder of the Wooden Horse, viii.493; xi.524.

Eper'itos: Name assumed by Odysseus when he talked with Laertes, xxiv.306.

Ephial'tes: Son of Poseidon and Iphimedeia, brother of Otos, gigantic child killed by Apollo, xi.308.

E'phyre: Place of unknown location, apparently in Western Greece, i.259; ii.328.

Epikas'te: More familiarly known as Iokaste, the wife and mother of Oidipodes, xi.271.

E'rebos: The dark place of the dead, x.528.

Erech'theus: Hero of Athens, vii.81.

Erem'boi: An unidentified people visited by Menelaos during his wanderings, iv.84.

Eret'meus: A Phaiakian, viii.112.

Eriphy'le: Wife of Amphiaraos, who caused his death, xi.326.

Eryman'thos: A mountain in the northwest Peloponnese, vi.104.

Eri'nys: Fury, or a goddess of curses, xv.234.

Eteo'neus: Henchman of Menelaos, iv.22.

Eteokre'tans: A people of Crete, thought to mean "True-Cretans," xix.176.

Euan'thes: Father of Maron, ix.197.

Euboi'a: A large island east of central Greece, iii.175; vii.321.

Eue'nor: Father of Leokritos, ii.242, etc.

Eumai'os: The noble swineherd of Odysseus, xiv.55, etc.

Eume'los: Lord of Pherai, husband of Iphthime, thus brother-in-law of Penelope, iv.798.

Eupei'thes: Father of Antinoös, i.383, etc.; killed by Laertes in the final battle, xxiv.523.

Eury'ades: Suitor, killed by Telemachos, xxii.267.

Eury'alos: A young Phaiakian, rude to Odysseus, viii.158, etc.

Eury'bates: The herald of Odysseus, xix.247.

Eury'damas: A suitor, xviii.297; killed by Odysseus, xxii.283.

Eury'dike: Daughter of Klymenos, wife of Nestor, iii.451.

Euryklei'a: The old nurse of Odysseus and of Telemachos, i.428, etc.

Eury'lochos: Second in command of Odysseus' fleet, x.205, etc.; a relative of Odysseus, though sometimes at odds with him, x.441.

Eury'machos: Son of Polybos (1). One of the two leading suitors, i.399; ii.177, etc.; attacked Odysseus, xviii.394; killed by Odysseus, xxii.79.

Eury'medon: King of the giants, father of Periboia, vii.58.

GLOSSARY

Eurymedou'sa: Nurse of Nausikaa, vii.8.

Eu'rymos: Father of Telemos, ix.509.

Eury'nome: Housekeeper and nurse of Penelope, xvii.495, etc.

Eury'nomos: Suitor, son of Aigyptios, ii.21; xxii.242.

Eury'pylos: Leader of the Keteians, killed at Troy by Neoptolemos, xi.520.

Eury'tion: A drunken centaur, xxi.295.

Eu'rytos: Father of Iphitos, archer, king of Oichalia, killed by Apollo, viii.224, etc.

Gai'a: Mother of Tityos, vii.324.

Gerais'tos: Promontory on the island of Euboia, iii.178.

Gere'nian: Epithet of Nestor, iii.68, etc.

Gor'gon: A staring monster, xi.635.

Gor'tys: A place in Crete, iii.294.

Gra'ces: Properly, the Charites, goddesses of beauty, vi.18, etc.

Gy'rai: A rocky island in the Aigaian Sea, iv.501.

Ha'des: Properly Aïdes, lord of the dead, iv.834; xi.47, etc.

Ha'lios: A son of Alkinoös, viii.119.

Halither'ses: An Ithakan, gifted in prophecy, favorable to Odysseus, ii.157; xxiv.-451, etc.

He'be: Daughter of Zeus and Hera, bride of Herakles after his immortalization, xi.604.

He'len: Wife of Menelaos, the cause of the war, iv.12, etc.

He'lios: The sun god, i.8, etc. Odysseus' men slaughtered some of his cattle, xii.260–390.

Hel'las: A name for the country of Achilleus (as in the *Iliad*) xi.496; more widely, apparently as "Greece" generally, i.344, etc.

Hel'lespont: The strait (Dardanelles) by Troy, xxiv.82.

Hephais'tos: The immortal artificer, iv.617, etc.; in the *Odyssey* (not in the *Iliad*) married to Aphrodite, who played him false with Ares (according to the song of Demodokos), viii.266–366.

He'ra: Wife of Zeus, queen of the gods, iv.513.

Her'akles: Or Hercules, son of Alkmene and Zeus, xi.268; a great archer, xiii.224; killer of Iphitos, xxi.26; immortalized and married to Hebe, xi.601–604.

Her'mes: Often called Argeïphontes, son of Zeus and Maia, messenger of Zeus, i.38, etc.

Hermi'one: Daughter of Menelaos and Helen, iv.14.

Hippodamei'a: Handmaid of Penelope, xviii.182.

Hip'potas: Father of Aiolos (1), x.2.

Hy'lakos: Father of Kastor (2), xiv.204.

Hyperei'a: Former home of the Phaiakians, near the Cyclopes, vi.4.

Hypere'sia: City in Achaia, home of Polypheides, xv.254.

Hyperi'on: (1) Epithet of Helios, i.24, etc.; (2) father of Helios, xii.176.

Iar'danos: River in Crete, iii.292.

Ias'ion: Hero beloved by Demeter, v.126.

GLOSSARY

I'asos: (1) Father of Amphion (2), xi.283; (2) father of Dmetor, xvii.443.

Ido'meneus: Lord of Crete, a great hero of the *Iliad*, iii.191; xiii.259, etc.

Ika'rios: The father of Penelope, i.328, etc.

Ikma'lios: Artificer, who made Penelope's chair, xix.57.

I'lion: The city of Troy, ii.18, etc.

I'los: Son of Mermeros, apparently king of Ephyra, i.259.

I'no: Also called Leukothea, daughter of Kadmos, once mortal, now a sea goddess, v.333; 461.

Iol'kos: Place in Thessaly, home of Pelias, xi.257.

I'phikles: Lord of Phylake, captor of Melampous, xi.290.

Imphimedei'a: Mother of Otos and Ephialtes, xi.305.

I'phitos: Son of Eurytos, friend of the young Odysseus, foully murdered by Herakles, giver of the great bow to Odysseus, xxi.11–41.

Iphthi'me: Wife of Eumelos and sister of Penelope, to whom she appeared in a dream, iv.797.

I'ros: The name Arnaios commonly went by; the beggar who fought with Odysseus, xviii.1–107; so named after the goddess Iris, who otherwise does not appear in the *Odyssey*, xviii.6.

Is'maros: Thracian home of the Kikonians, ix.40.

I'thaka: Island off the west coast of Greece, i.18, etc., home of Odysseus; its position described, ix.21–26.

I'thakos: Builder of a well on Ithaka, xvii.207.

I'tylos: Son of Zethos (2) and "the nightingale," daughter of Pandareos (presumably Prokne), killed by his mother, xix.523.

Ja'son: Master of the ship Argo, xii.72.

Kadmei'ans: The people of Thebes (2), xi.276.

Kad'mos: Founder of Thebes (2), father of Ino, v.333.

Kalyp'so: Goddess-nymph, daughter of Atlas, i.14; 52; befriended and lived with Odysseus, v.14–268, etc.

Kassan'dra: Daughter of Priam, captive mistress of Agamemnon, murdered with him, xi.422.

Kas'tor: (1) Son of Leda and Tyndareos, brother of Polydeukes, semi-immortalized by Zeus, xi.298–304; (2) son of Hylakos, pretended father of Odysseus in his story as told to Eumaios, xiv.204.

Kauko'nes: A people, presumably near Pylos. Athene, disguised as Mentor, announces that she will visit them, iii.366. Apparently, therefore, they are not the same as the people in the *Iliad* mentioned at *Iliad* X.429 and XX.329.

Kephallen'ians: People of Kephallenia or, especially in Book xxiv, of the whole community of islands, xx.210; xxiv.355; 377; 429.

Ketei'ans: The people of Eurypylos, xi.520.

Kiko'nians: The Thracians of Ismaros, raided by Odysseus, ix.39–61.

Kimmer'ians: A people near the land of the dead, xi.14. In historical times, the name applies to a non-Greek people of the Black Sea who raided Asia Minor in the seventh century B.C.

GLOSSARY

Klei′tos: Son of Mantios, snatched away by the Dawn, xv.250.

Kly′mene: Heroine seen by Odysseus in the land of the dead, xi.326.

Kly′menos: Father of Eurydike, iii.452.

Klytaimes′tra: Agamemnon's wife, who took Aigisthos as a lover, iii.265–272; accomplice in Agamemnon's murder, and murdered Kassandra, xi.421–434.

Kly′tios: Father of Peiraios, xv.540.

Klytone′os: A son of Alkinoös, viii.119.

Knos′sos: A city in Crete, xix.178.

Koky′tos: A river in the land of the dead, x.513.

Kratai′is: Mother of Skylla, xii.124.

Krei′on: Father of Megara, xi.269.

Kre′theus: Son of Aiolos (2), husband of Tyro, father of Aison, Pheres, and Amythaon, xi.258, etc.

Kro′nos: Father of Zeus, i.386, etc.

Kro′unoi: A place on the western coast of Greece, opposite Ithaka, xv.295.

Kte′sios: Father of Eumaios, xv.414.

Ktesip′pos: A violent suitor, who threw a cow's hoof at Odysseus, xx.288–303; killed by Philoitios, xxii.285.

Kti′mene: The sister of Odysseus, xv.363.

Kydo′nians: A people of Crete, iii.292; xix.176.

Kylle′ne: Mountain in Arkadia, the home of Hermes, xxiv.1.

Kythe′ra: Island off the southern tip of Greece, ix.81.

Kytherei′a: Aphrodite, the lady of Kythera, viii.288; xviii.193.

Laer′kes: Goldsmith in Pylos, iii.425.

Laer′tes: Son of Arkeisios, father of Odysseus, i.189, etc. Rejuvenated by Athene, fights in the last battle, xxiv. 513–525.

Laistry′gones: A giant cannibal people encountered by Odysseus and his men, x.80–132.

Lakedai′mon: The country of Sparta, domain of Menelaos, iii.326, etc.

La′mos: The city of the Laistrygones, x.81.

Lampe′tia: Nymph, daughter of Helios and Neaira, who tended her father's cattle, xii.132; 374.

Lam′pos: One of the Dawn's horses, xxiii.246.

Lao′damas: Favorite son of Alkinoös, vii. 170; viii.117, etc.

La′pithai: The people of Peirithoös, xxi.297.

Le′da: Wife of Tyndareos, mother of Kastor and Polydeukes, xi.298.

Lem′nos: Island in the northern Aigaian, favored by Hephaistos, viii.283, etc.

Leo′des: A weak and well-meaning suitor, with prophetic skill, xxi.144, etc.; killed by Odysseus while begging for mercy, xxii. 310–329.

Leo′kritos: A suitor, ii.242; killed by Telemachos, xxii.294.

Les′bos: Island off Asia Minor, where Odysseus wrestled with Philomeleides, iv.342, etc.

Le′to: Mother (by Zeus) of Artemis and Apollo, vi.106, etc.; Tityos tormented after death for assaulting her, xi.580.

Leuko′thea: Ino's name as a divinity, v.333.

GLOSSARY

Lib'ya: The Greek name for Africa, iv.85; xiv,295.

Lotus-Eaters: Mysterious people visited by Odysseus and his men, ix.82–104.

Mai'a: Mother of Hermes, xiv.436, etc.

Mai'ra: Heroine seen by Odysseus in the land of the dead, xi.326.

Malei'a: Southeastern cape on the mainland of Greece, iii.288, etc.

Man'tios: Son of Melampous, grandfather of Theoklymenos, xv.242.

Ma'rathon: District near Athens, favored by Athene (also, site of the subsequent battle), vii.80.

Ma'ron: Priest of Apollo at Ismaros, ix.197.

Mas'tor: Father of Halitherses, ii.157; xxiv.451.

Me'don: Herald of Odysseus in Ithaka, loyal to Penelope and Telemachos, iv.677, etc.; spared by Odysseus after the slaughter, xxii.361.

Megapen'thes: Son of Menelaos and a slave girl, iv.11; xv.100, etc.

Me'gara: Daughter of Kreion, wife of Herakles, xi.269.

Melam'pous: A famous soothsayer, xi.291; xv.256.

Mel'aneus: Father of Amphimedon, xxiv.103.

Melan'thios: Son of Dolios, goatherd who sided with the suitors and insulted and kicked Odysseus, xvii.212, etc.; aided the suitors in their battle, xxii.135; mutilated by Telemachos and the herdsmen, xxii.474.

Melan'tho: Daughter of Dolios, favored but treacherous maid of Penelope, xviii.321; xix.65.

Mem'non: Son of the Dawn, see iii.112 (where, however, he is not named); handsomest of men, xi.522.

Menela'os: Husband of Helen, great hero of the *Iliad*, iv.2, etc.

Menoi'tios: Father of Patroklos, xxiv.77.

Men'tes: Name assumed by Athene on her first visit to Telemachos, i.105, etc.

Men'tor: Ithakan friend of Odysseus, to whom he entrusted his household when he went to Troy, ii.225, etc.; frequently impersonated by Athene, ii.268; xxii.206; xxiv.548, etc.

Mer'meros: Father of Ilos, i.259.

Mesaul'ios: Thrall of Eumaios, xiv.449.

Messe'ne: Territory in southwestern Greece, xxi.15.

Mi'mas: A mountainous promontory of Asia Minor, opposite Chios, iii.172.

Mi'nos: Son of Zeus and king of Crete, xix.178; judge in the land of the dead, xi.568; father of Ariadne, xi.322.

Min'yan: Name applied to Orchomenos, xi.284.

Mou'lios: Doulichian herald attached to Amphinomos, xviii.423.

Myke'ne: (1) a fabulous heroine of the past, ii.120; (2) the city of Agamemnon, iii.304.

Myr'midons: The people of Achilleus and Neoptolemos, iii.188, etc.

Nau'bolos: Father of Euryalos, viii.115.

Nausi'kaa: Daughter of Alkinoös and Arete, who befriended Odysseus, vi.17, etc.

Nausi'thoös: Founder of the Phaiakian settlement on Scheria, vi.7; son of Poseidon and father of Rhexenor and Alkinoös, vii. 56–63.

GLOSSARY

Nau'teus: A Phaiakian, viii.112.

Neai'ra: Wife of Helios, mother of Phaethousa and Lampetia, xii.133.

Ne'leus: Father of Nestor, former king in Pylos, iii.409, etc.

Neopto'lemos: Son of Achilleus, xi.506.

Ne'rikos: Place (on Leukas) once taken by Laertes, xxiv.378.

Ne'ritos: (1) Mountain of Ithaka, xiii.351; (2) builder of a well on Ithaka, xvii.207.

Nes'tor: The old hero of the *Iliad,* king in Pylos, i.284; iii.17, etc.

Ni'sos: King in Doulichion, father of Amphinomos, xviii.127, etc.

Noë'mon: Ithakan friend of Telemachos, who lent him his ship, ii.386; iv.630.

Ocean: Or Oke'anos, the waters surrounding the world and the god of those waters, iv.567; x.139; xi.639, etc.

Odys'seus: The hero, first mentioned by name, i.21; son of Laertes, iv.555, etc.; and of Antikleia, xi.85.

Ogy'gia: Kalypso's island, i.85, etc.

Oidi'podes: Or Oedipus, hero of Thebes (1), xi.271 (in Homer, strictly, Oidipodes).

Oï'kles: Father of Amphiaraos, xv.243.

Oi'nops: Father of Leodes, xxi.144.

Oky'alos: A Phaiakian, viii.111.

Olym'pos: The home of the gods, i.102, etc.; described, vi.42.

One'tor: Father of Phrontis, iii.282.

Ops: Father of Eurykleia, i.429.

Orcho'menos: Minyan city in Boiotia, xi.284.

Ores'tes: The son of Agamemnon, who avenged him, i.30; 298; iii.306, etc.

Ori'on: A hero loved by the Dawn, killed by Artemis, v.121; his ghost seen by Odysseus in the land of the dead, xi.572; as a constellation, v.274.

Or'menos: Father of Ktesios, xv.414.

Orsi'lochos: Son of Idomeneus, in a story told by Odysseus, xiii.260.

Orti'lochos: Father of Diokles, iii.489; host to Odysseus in Messene, xxi.16.

Orty'gia: A place of uncertain location, where Artemis killed Orion, v.123; a place (the same?) "where the sun makes his turnings," near the Homeric Syria, xv.404.

Os'sa: A mountain in Thessaly, xi.315.

O'tos: Son of Poseidon and Iphimedeia, brother of Ephialtes, gigantic child killed by Apollo, xi.308.

Paië'on: The god of medicine, iv.232.

Pal'las: Epithet of Athene, i.125, etc.

Pandar'eos: Father of "the nightingale," xix.518; his daughters carried away by the stormwinds, xx.66.

Pan'opeus: A city in Phokis, xi.581.

Paph'os: A place on Cyprus, favored by Aphrodite, viii.362.

Parnas'sos: A great mountain in central Greece, xix.394, etc.

Patrok'los: Companion of Achilleus, a great hero of the *Iliad,* iii.110, etc.

GLOSSARY

Peirai'os: Man of Ithaka, friend and companion of Telemachos, xv.540, etc.

Peiri'thoös: Hero of former times, friend of Theseus, xi.631; king of the Lapiths, who punished Eurytion, xxi.296.

Peisan'dros: Son of Polyktor, a suitor, xviii.299; killed by Philoitios, xxii.268.

Peise'nor: (1) Herald in Ithaka, ii.37; (2) father of Ops, grandfather of Eurykleia, i.429, etc.

Peisis'tratos: Son of Nestor, greets Telemachos and Athene, iii.36; accompanies Telemachos to Sparta, iii.482, etc.

Pelas'gians: A mysterious people, variously located in the *Iliad*; in the *Odyssey*, they are found in Crete, xix.177.

Pe'leus: Father of Achilleus, v.310, etc.

Pe'lias: Son of Tyro and Poseidon, king in Iolkos, xi.256.

Pe'lion: A mountain in Thessaly, xi.316.

Pene'lope: Daughter of Ikarios, wife of Odysseus, i.223, etc.

Periboi'a: Daughter of Eurymedon, mother, by Poseidon, of Nausithoös, vii.57.

Perikly'menos: Son of Neleus and Chloris, brother of Nestor, xi.286.

Perime'des: A companion of Odysseus, xi.23; etc.

Pe'ro: Daughter of Neleus and Chloris, a great beauty, xi.287.

Per'se: Nymph, daughter of Ocean, x.139.

Perse'phone: Goddess, wife of Hades, queen over the dead, x.491, xi.47, etc.

Per'seus: Son of Nestor, iii.414 (not to be confused with the gorgon slayer).

Pha'ethon: One of the Dawn's horses, xxiii.246.

Phaethou'sa: Nymph, daughter of Helios and Neaira, who tended her father's cattle, xii.132.

Phaia'kians: The people of Alkinoös, v.35, etc.

Phai'dimos: King of the Sidonians, friend of Menelaos, iv.617.

Phaid'ra: Heroine seen by Odysseus in the land of the dead, xi.321.

Phais'tos: City in Crete, iii.296.

Pha'ros: Island off Egypt where Menelaos captured Proteus, iv.355.

Phe'ai: A place on the mainland opposite Ithaka, xv.297.

Phei'don: King of Thesprotia, xiv.316.

Phe'mios: Son of Terpias, the singer who sang for the suitors, i.154, etc.; his life spared by Odysseus, xxii.331.

Phe'rai: (1) A place in Thessaly, the home of Eumelos, iv. 798; (2) a place between Pylos and Sparta, the home of Diokles, iii.488.

Phe'res: Son of Kretheus and Tyro, xi.259.

Philoi'tios: The oxherd who remained loyal to Odysseus, xx.185, etc.

Philokte'tes: A great hero and master bowman of the Trojan War, iii.190; viii.219.

Philomele'ïdes: A wrestler of Lesbos, thrown by Odysseus, iv.343.

Phoeni'cia, Phoeni'cians: A nation and its people, noted as seafarers, traders, and slave traders, living on the Syrian coast, iv.83; xiv.288, etc.

Phoi'bos: Epithet of Apollo, iii.279, etc.

Phor'kys: An old man of the sea, xiii.345; father of Thoö'sa, i.72.

Phron'ios: Father of Noëmon, ii.386, etc.

Phron'tis: Son of Onetor, the steersman of Menelaos, iii.282.

Phthi'a: The home of Achilleus, xi.496.

GLOSSARY

Phy'lake: The home of Iphikles, xi. 290; xv.236.

Phy'lakos: A hero, possibly the same person as Iphikles, who imprisoned Melampous, xv.231.

Phy'lo: Handmaid of Helen, iv.125.

Pie'ria: Mountainous district near Mount Olympos, v.50.

Plei'ades: The constellation, v.272.

Poi'as: Father of Philoktetes, iii.190.

Poli'tes: A companion of Odysseus, x.224.

Pol'ybos: (1) Father of Eurymachos, i.399; (2) man of Egyptian Thebes, visited by Menelaos and Helen, iv.126; (3) craftsman, who made a ball used by the Phaiakians, viii.373; (4) suitor, xxii.243; killed by Eumaios, xxii.284.

Polydam'na: Egyptian lady, wife of Thon, who gave Helen a tranquilizing drug, iv.228.

Polydeu'kes: Son of Leda and Tyndareos, brother of Kastor (1), semi-immortalized by Zeus, xi.298–304.

Polykas'te: Youngest daughter of Nestor, who gave Telemachos a bath, iii.464.

Polyk'tor: (1) Builder of a well on Ithaka, xvii.207; (2) father of Peisandros, xviii.299.

Polyne'os: Father of Amphialos, viii.114.

Polype'mon: Father of Apheidas, xxiv.305.

Polyphei'des: Son of Mantios, a prophet, father of Theoklymenos, xv.249–256.

Polyphe'mos: Greatest of the Cyclopes, son of Poseidon, blinded by Odysseus, i.70; ix.403, etc.

Polyther'ses: Father of Ktesippos, xxii.287.

Pon'teus: A Phaiakian, viii.113.

Ponto'noös: Herald of Alkinoös, vii.182, etc.

Posei'don: Brother of Zeus, lord of the sea, enemy of Odysseus, i.20, etc.; father of Polyphemos, i.68–73, etc.

Pramnei'an wine: A wine used medicinally, origin unknown, x.235.

Pri'am: King of Troy, iii.107, etc.

Prok'ris: Heroine seen by Odysseus in the land of the dead, xi.321.

Pro'reus: A Phaiakian, viii.113.

Pro'teus: The old man of the sea, iv.365–570.

Prym'neus: A Phaiakian, i.112.

Psy'rios: Island off Chios, iii.171.

Py'los: The city of Nestor on the southwest coast of Greece, i.93, etc.

Pyriphle'gethon: A river in the land of the dead, x.513.

Py'tho: Apollo's sanctuary on the slopes of Mount Parnassos, viii.80; xi.581.

Rhadaman'thys: Presumably king in the Elysian Field, iv.564.

Rhei'thron: Harbor on Ithaka, i.186.

Rhexe'nor: Son of Nausithoös, father of Arete, vii.63.

Roving Rocks: Located near the Sirens, xii.61; xxiii.327.

Salmo'neus: Father of Tyro, xi.236.

Sam'e or Samos: Large island (later Kephallenia), next to Ithaka and in the domain of Odysseus, i.246, etc.

GLOSSARY

Sche'ria: The land of the Phaiakians, v.34, etc.

Sicilian: Used of a people referred to as dealing in slaves, xx.383; provenence of Laertes' slave woman, xxiv.211, etc. (actually, the word is Si'kelos, which in Greek elsewhere refers to a native people in Sicily, or Sike'lia).

Si'don, Sidon'ia: City of the Phoenicians, xiii.286, etc.

Sika'nia: A place referred to by Odysseus, perhaps to be identified with Sicily, xxiv.307.

Sin'tians: Friends of Hephaistos in Lemnos, who spoke an uncouth language, viii.294.

Si'rens: Singing, dangerous creatures of the sea, xii.39, etc.

Sis'yphos: Hero tormented in the land of the dead, condemned to roll a stone forever uphill, xi.593.

Skyl'la: A man-eating monster who preyed on Odysseus' men, xii.85; 245, etc.

Sky'ros: Island from which Odysseus brought Neoptolemos to Troy, xi.509.

So'lymoi: A people visited by Poseidon, v.283.

Sou'nion: A sea cape of Attika, near Athens, iii.278.

Spar'ta: The city of Menelaos, i.93, etc.

Stra'tios: A son of Nestor, iii.413.

Styx: The river or waterfall by which the gods swear, v.185; located in the land of the dead, x.514.

Sy'ria: An island of uncertain location, the original home of Eumaios, xv.403.

Tan'talos: Hero tormented in the land of the dead, xi.582.

Taph'ians: A people, not certainly located, on or near the western coast of Greece, i.105; xiv.452.

Taÿ'getos: A mountain range in Lakedaimon, vi.103.

Teire'sias: Theban seer, who retained his powers even in the land of the dead, x.492, etc.; consulted by Odysseus and foretells his future, xi.90–137.

Tek'ton: Father of Polyneos, viii.114.

Te'lamon: The father of Aias (1), xi.553.

Tele'machos: The thoughtful son of Odysseus and Penelope, i.113, etc.

Te'lemos: Prophet of the Cyclopes, ix.509.

Te'lephos: Father of Eurypylos, xi.519.

Tele'pylos: City of the Laistrygones, x.82.

Te'mese: Place alleged to be her destination by Athene disguised as Mentes, i.184.

Te'nedos: Island off Asia Minor, near Troy, iii.159.

Ter'pias: Father of Phemios, xxii.330 (but the form of his name is uncertain).

Thebes: (1) City of Egypt, iv.127; (2) city of the Kadmeians in Boiotia, xv.247, etc.

The'mis: Goddess of what is right and proper, who supervises the assemblies of men, ii.68.

Theokly'menos: A man of prophetic family, fugitive from Argos, befriended by Telemachos, xv.223, etc. (first named, xv.256).

The'seus: Great hero of Athens, who carried Ariadne away from Crete, xi.322, etc.

Thespro'tians: A people of the northwest mainland, xiv.315, etc.

GLOSSARY

The'tis: Nereid, married to Peleus, mother of Achilleus, xxiv.91.

Tho'as: Son of Andraimon, hero at Troy, xiv.499.

Thon: Egyptian, husband of Polydamna, iv.228.

Tho'ön: A Phaiakian, viii.113.

Thoö'sa: A nymph, daughter of Phorkys, mother of Polyphemos, i.71.

Thrace: Territory north of Greece, favored home of Ares, viii.361.

Thrasyme'des: Son of Nestor, iii.39, etc.

Thrina'kia: The island of Helios, where his sacred cattle were pastured, xi.107; xii.127, etc.

Thyes'tes: Father of Aigisthos, iv.517.

Titho'nos: The husband of the Dawn, v.1.

Ti'tyos: A hero tormented in the land of the dead, xi.576; mentioned, vii.324.

Tritogenei'a: A name for Athene, iii, 378.

Tro'jans: The people of Troy, i.237, etc.

Troy: The domain of Priam, whose city was Ilion, i.2, etc.

Ty'deus: Father of Diomedes, iii.167, etc.

Tynda'reos: Father of Kastor and Polydeukes, xi.298; of Klytaimestra, xxiv.199.

Ty'ro: A fabulous queen, ii.120; her ghost talked with Odysseus in the land of the dead, xi.235.

Zakyn'thos: Large island, part of the domain of Odysseus, i.246, etc.

Ze'thos: (1) Son of Antiope, and builder, with his brother Amphion, of Thebes, xi.262; (2) father of Itylos, xix.523.

Zeus: Son of Kronos, most powerful of the gods, i.10, etc.